This copy of

PADDLES!

Belongs to

Pauma Valley Coutry Club Library

Paddles!

Paddles!

The Foibles and Finesse of One World War Two Landing Signal Officer

John A. Harper
Captain, USNR (Ret.)

Schiffer Military History
Atglen, PA

ACKNOWLEDGMENTS

In efforts to recount events of fifty years earlier, accuracy and substance are enhanced through the resources and memory of many persons. I shall cite a few:

– Air Group 24 reunions, organized by Ralph "Tuffy" Chase and held on even years, provided the genesis for *Paddles*.

– The National Museum of Naval Aviation's Symposium '94 on "The Marianas Turkey Shoot" and "American Aces" fanned the flame and introduced me to the Naval Aviation literary world.

– Michael Walker and John Hodges of the Naval Historical Center Operations Archives Branch for their patience and persistence in my behalf.

– Steve Millikin and Carl Snow at the HOOK magazine – Steve for encouraging me by printing some of my works, and Carl for generously opening the HOOK library to me and assisting in my research.

– RADM Roger Box, USN (Ret.), former Sixth Fleet Battle Group Commander, for introducing me to archival sources in and around San Diego and refining some ship's ceremonies for me.

– Ray Wagner, librarian, at the San Diego Air & Space Museum.

– Col. Tommy Tilley, USAF (Ret.), one of the first to fly a P-40 off *Ranger* to Africa in 1942 as a member of the Fifty-Seventh Fighter Group, for adding critical detail to my account of transporting P-40s to Africa.

– Bill Willert of VT-30 for CVLG-30 rosters, "My First Combat Mission", a history of VT-30, and the identity of pilots in "Darkest Day" and "Fog."

– Jack Barbour, CVLG-24 Air Intelligence Officer for an insightful critique.

– CDR Hugh McLinden, USN (Ret.), for coaching me on events involving SBD pilots of VC-24.

– Warren Omark, with Navy Cross for sinking a Japanese carrier, for introducing me to the National Museum of Naval Aviation's Symposium '94.

– Collin Oveland, VF-24 fighter ace for his recollection of fighter operations.

– CAPT Ben Tate, USN (Ret.), with Navy Cross for sinking a Japanese carrier, for helping me get it right in "Night Lights."

Book Design by Robert Biondi.

Printed in the United States of America.
ISBN: 0-7643-0077-6

We are interested in hearing from authors with book ideas on related topics.

Published by Schiffer Publishing Ltd.
77 Lower Valley Road
Atglen, PA 19310
Phone: (610) 593-1777
FAX: (610) 593-2002
Please write for a free catalog.
This book may be purchased from the publisher.
Please include $2.95 postage.
Try your bookstore first.

Contents

Foreword

The great air admirals – Mitscher, Radford, Jocko Clark – led the Fast Carriers across the Pacific to victory in World War II. Myriads of brilliant pilots flew the *Hellcats, Avengers, Dauntlesses, Helldivers*, and *Corsairs* that bludgeoned the Imperial Japanese Navy and island targets. And tireless ships' crews kept the mighty flattops afloat and in fighting trim over the monumental counteroffensive of 1943-45.

Many books have been written by and about all these important players in the high drama of that oceanic struggle. But not until now has the story been told from the standpoint of the one critical figure upon whom the operations of each fast carrier *absolutely* depended – the landing signal officer.

With his outstretched paddles, the LSO waved each plane aboard or "off" dozens of times a day, days and weeks or even months on end. If he made the wrong call just once, the very survival of the ship was at risk. The LSO *had* to be the best there was in his job – infallibility was his creed! It was not for nothing that pilots sometimes teasingly nicknamed him "Crash."

In *Paddles*, John Harper has finally told the story of the LSO from his own hair-raising experiences aboard the light carrier *Belleau Wood*. Combining vivid memory with colorful prose, he has caught the flavor of life at sea as a combat LSO. For this literary achievement, added to his own part in the Pacific victory, he has earned from us all a hearty "Well Done!"

Clark G. Reynolds

Clark G. Reynolds is the author of *The Fast Carriers: The Forging of an Air Navy,* and *The Fighting Lady: The New Yorktown in the Pacific War.*

1

CONVERSION

The orders signalled the end of those delightful days as an instructor in Lieutenant Commander "Jumpin' Joe" Clifton's Fighter Gunnery department at Naval Air Station Miami, that compact little double-mat airfield at Opa Locka, Florida. I would miss those months training boot fighter pilots in the subtle arts of air-to-air gunnery, attack tactics, individual air combat, and even dive bombing; flying the stubby little single-seat Grumman F3F biplane fighter with its fuselage mounted main battery of two machine guns – one .30 and one .50 caliber, and a landing gear that retracted snugly into either side of the forward fuselage. The meat of the orders, dated October 6, 1942, was this copy of a Naval Air Training Command dispatch:

ENS. JAMES R ENGLISH JR A V (N) USNR JOHN
A HARPER A V (N) USNR SHAILER R CUMMINGS
A V (N) USNR EUGENE R HARDIN JR A V (N) USNR
HEREBY DETACHED PROCEED JACKSONVILLE FLO
REPORT CHIEF AIR OPERATIONAL TRA AIR OPERA-
TIONAL TRA COMMAND NAS DUTY INVOLVING FLY-
ING UNDER INSTRUCTION AS LANDING SIGNAL
OFFICERS.

Paddles!

The orders authorized, " . . . travel via privately owned 1941 black Ford sedan, Fla. license number 1D-62045" – MY CAR.

"DAMN! I wanted orders to a fleet fighter squadron. Son-of-a-bitch! This is going to keep me out of combat for at least a year, maybe longer." I mused as Shailer Cummings and I sipped gin and tonic on the patio of our cozy three bedroom Miami Shores bungalow. You see, NAS Miami's skipper, Captain Rule, had certified that there were no quarters available for us on the station.

"Might keep us alive a little longer," Shailer offered.

Cummings was a compact little guy about five-foot-nine, his small, angular, face framed by a shock of wavy black hair. His brown black eyes were confrontational.

Ensign Edward M. "Red" Volz burst through the screen door with his characteristic rolling gait announcing: "Hey, you guys; I understand you both got orders to be Landing Signal Officers. So did I." Red showed his supercilious humor with the quizzical look in his light brown, perpetually bloodshot eyes, which matched his carrot hair. His long frame with the round shoulders seemed to sway as he talked. "I'm going to JAX, how about you?" Red's orders were identical to ours except for the names.

Cummings: "Yeah, we're going to JAX too. Christ! We've got five days to cover the three hundred plus miles to Jacksonville so we ought to be able to find some parties around here before we head north. What do you think?"

"A masterful thought, Shailer", I agreed. "Hell, we'll need a day or two to get packed up, anyway. Hey, what the hell are we going to do about the house. We can't just leave Leo here all by himself."

"Yeah we can," Red assured us. "It'll be easy for him to find a couple of guys to move into this mansion . . . it says here. Hell, Ray'll be delighted to help . . . Heh heh."

Ray Eden was our landlord and sometime benefactor, and a piece of work he was; short and slight of stature, he sported a white pith helmet, military style white shorts and shirt – with epaulets, knee high white sox, and white buck shoes, the better to broadcast his unabashed arrogance. To complement this outrageous image, Ray effected a British accent and spoke in terse half sentences laced with expletives and mild obscenities accented with generous arm gestures, usually ranting about one or the other of his tenants, most of whom were instructors at NAS Miami and therefore well known to us.

"Hey you're right," I agreed. "Ray'll give Leo a ration of shit about letting us get out of town but, as usual, he'll reach into his bag of tricks and produce two or three new boys who just checked in as instructors – or students – we are getting some officer students now, y'know . . . Hell, he might even find a girl or two. D'you think Leo could handle it?," I leered.

Once we took care of our responsibilities and covered all the local farewell parties, Shailer, Red, and I each covered the three hundred, fifty miles to JAX in our own way. It was important to travel by day as the top hemisphere of all automobile headlights were blacked out due to the ever present German U-Boat threat to coastal shipping. Driving my 1941 black Ford sedan and wearing my uniform, I was mistaken more than once for a Florida highway patrolman, and, cruising well over the speed limit of thirty-five miles per hour, I collected a few hostile stares as I zipped by the locals.

> WESTERN UNION
> ZA 1143 15=WINTERHAVEN FLO 8 1111A   1942 OCT 8 PM 12 11
> PEGGY GREEN
> KAPPA ALPHA THETA HOUSE EAST LANSING MICH
> HAPPY BIRTHDAY DARLING EXPECT A GIFT WHEN I AM
> SETTLED IN JAX
> ALL MY LOVE
> JOHNNY

I had met Peggy Green during her first month at Michigan State. She was sixteen then and had a magnetism I couldn't shake. I wrote to her a lot, so she wouldn't forget me. I didn't know if it was working 'cause I didn't get much back. *Well, this is the second year I've been away for Peg's birthday, and I guess there'll be more. The war's heating up and I'll probably be out there pretty soon. Maybe I'll get some leave, or at least travel time, when I get through with this training.* I lamented.

We all checked in at NAS JAX under the wire on 11 October and, SUR-PRISE! We were issued new orders, dated October 12, 1942, which directed us to proceed back to NAS Miami, again for "DUTY INVOLVING FLYING UNDER INSTRUCTION AS LANDING SIGNAL OFFICERS."

Well, here's another delay for Peggy's birthday present. Guess I'd better wire her what's goin' on. Here we go again – back to Miami – one-by-one in our own cars. This time we agreed to hire a room at a plush Miami Beach hotel for the last two nights of our travel allowance and carouse the Miami night life before reporting back to NAS Miami for duty – And we would contact good old Ray Eden to arrange new housing for the three of us.

Mary Roe was a comely girl whom I had met when I was stationed in Jacksonville as a Seaman 2nd V-5, Aviation Cadet in waiting, a year and a half earlier. She was my classmate John Halstead's girl and we double dated a few times, but John washed out of flight training and was now at some far away station being a navigator, weather guesser, or something. Mary had written me a couple of notes suggesting that we ought to get better acquainted. Hmmmm?

Mary was a typical southern belle – five foot one, eyes of brown, and one size above "tiny." She had a fragile sort of beauty, with fine brown hair brushed back in a casual coif, and a nice, but not generous, figure. She had that southern belle wistfulness over any relationship with a "bowey." A couple of days in Jacksonville gave us time to get better acquainted.

As the war raged abroad and German U-Boats threatened ships off the Florida coast within sight of the Ponte Vedra Country Club, the club welcomed naval officers and their young ladies – as their contribution to the war effort I suppose. Dancing to "Jersey Bounce", "Moonlight Cocktail", "Amapola", and other current hits, filled our night together and we found the Ponte Vedra beach ideal for sun, surf, and a little smooching the next day. We got acquainted.

Red, Shailer, and I rendezvoused in Miami Beach, as agreed, two days before we were to report in to NAS Miami, and checked into the Tatum Hotel, right on Miami Beach. After the second night making the rounds of the Miami Beach night spots, and closing the last one, I decided to do a little body surfing in the Atlantic while Red and Shailer retired for the night.

After slipping through the barbed wire barricade protecting Miami Beach from an improbable enemy invasion by sea I found the sand surprisingly clean and still warm from the previous day's sun. The full moon hung in the southern sky bathing surf and beach in its soft glow and doubtless helping the German U-Boats offshore find their targets. Right on cue, there was an oil tanker burning on the horizon, torpedoed by a U-Boat, but the night was otherwise calm and the water so-o-o refreshing, especially since the oil slick from the sinking oiler had not yet found the beach.

Chapter 1: Conversion

"HALT! WHO GOES THERE?" was the greeting from the beach as I emerged, blissfully, from the surf. The dark form of a man stood about ten yards from the slap of the surf, his rifle aimed purposefully at my midsection.

The effects of our night on the town had not completely left me so I still felt a little silly. Trying to subdue the urge to make some kind of smart ass remark, I responded shakily: "Ensign John A. Harper, U.S. NAVY, 106365," and scrambled clumsily to attention with both hands reaching for the stars, my swimming trunks dripping sea water. I almost laughed out loud when I visualized this unlikely beach scene. "I was just taking a dip in the ocean – refreshing." Was all I could think to say.

"ADVANCE AND BE RECOGNIZED," commanded the human form who, by now, was recognizable as a soldier, U.S. Army, I could hope. I tried to shake off the effects of our night of bar hopping and slogged deliberately through the surf and up onto the beach, hands still raised in supplication, to within about ten feet of the soldier. "HALT! Stop right there and toss me your identification."

Oh! Oh! All I've got on me is my trunks. Christ, I even took my dog tags off to go surfing. I reflected. "All my identification is in my hotel room right there in the Tatum Hotel, room 622," I sputtered. "I am on official travel to report to my new duty station, NAS Miami, tomorrow. I can take you to my room and show you my identification."

"I ain't buyin' that. You're part of an enemy espionage mission. You stay here while I call up reinforcements." The soldier kept his rifle trained on my naked belly button.

"CORPORAL OF THE GUARD, POST 25!," called the soldier, as loud as he could. Then, "Corporal of the Guard, Post 25" could be heard from the next sentry to the south and then, very faintly, another "Corporal of the guard, Post 25" from farther south. If there were more calls relaying my captor's request they were far enough away to be drowned out by the roar of the surf.

"Just call my fellow naval officers in room 622 there in the Tatum Hotel." I felt an urgency. "We're travelling together and they can confirm what I told you."

"We ain't gonna do nothin' 'til the corporal gets here. Anyway, I don't have a phone. Now, march ahead of me up to my guard shack – See it right up there?" He signalled with the muzzle of his rifle." And we'll wait for the corporal there." At the guard shack the soldier ordered, "Sit down in the sand, cross your legs, and clasp your hands behind your head – be quiet 'til the corporal gets here!" He was smart enough to stay at least six feet away from me with his rifle steadily pointed at my chest.

My new found friend really didn't know what to make of me. He was afraid to believe that I really was an American naval officer. The soldier was a tall gangly lad with a proud young germanic face and closely cropped brown hair. This freshly drafted farm boy was more scared than I was as he kept scanning the surf for "my comrades", fearing that he could be badly outnumbered any second if his suspicions were true. "Where's the rest of your force?," he demanded, fearfully.

"Would you please point that rifle in some other direction, soldier, or be damned sure the safety's on. I won't go anywhere, honest."

"You are suspected of being an enemy agent. Stay where you are and be quiet until the corporal gets here. He'll decide what we do with you."

"Where're you from soldier?," I ventured.

"Nebraska . . . er . . . Don't ask me questions. You're the prisoner. I ask the questions! Now, how did you get here, in a submarine?"

"I told you, I am Ensign Harper, U.S. NAVY, I am staying right there in the Tatum Hotel, and I was just going for a swim . . . How long have you been in the army?"

"There's 'NO TRESPASSING' signs posted all along the beach just below the hotels, and you couldn't have gotten through the barbed wire." He tried to look menacing. "Never mind how long I've been in the army – Are you a German spy?"

"It was easy to get through the barbed wire – right over there – it must have been cut – and, no, I am not a German spy, I am an American Naval Aviator!" *Oh well, I guess we'd better just wait for the corporal.* "You're doing a very good job here, soldier. What's your name?"

"Don't flatter me," he frowned. "You're under arrest! Just be quiet and wait!"

The corporal finally stomped up with three of his men. "What's your problem, Miller? What's the big emergency?"

My soldier jumped to attention and shifted the rifle to his left hand so he could salute. "Sir, this here guy came up out of the ocean about an hour ago and claims to be an ensign in the Navy but he ain't got any identification. If he's an infiltrator he's alone cause I ain't seen nobody since he came ashore. Says he's staying there in the Tatum Hotel with his friends."

"All we have to do is go up to room 622 and . . .", I started.

"SHUT UP! We'll get around to you soon enough," boomed the corporal. "Does he have a weapon or any equipment, Miller?

Chapter 1: Conversion

"No sir. Just them funky trunks – no I.D. and no identifyin' marks."

"We'll get to the bottom of this," snapped the corporal. "Kranz, Morgan," he commanded. "Stand the prisoner up and keep him under control – Shahan, keep him covered!"

"O.K. Mister Mermaid," he growled at me. "Let's hear your story – first, identify yourself."

"I am Ensign John A. Harper, U.S. Navy, file number 106365 – just getting some R and R during my official travel from NAS Jacksonville to NAS Miami, my next duty station. I was just taking a dip in the ocean after an evening tour of Miami Beach and I left my I.D. in my hotel room." By this time I was completely sober, and shivering a little in the cool night air. "As I told Private Miller, my travelling companions, two other Navy ensigns, are up in room six twenty-two in the Tatum Hotel there. They will identify me."

"I suppose you didn't see any of the NO TRESPASSING signs along the beach and you just strolled through the barbed wire barricade. That wouldn't be easy." The corporal drew his service piece for effect. "Now tell me where you really came from and when the rest of your force is going to land."

"I've told you the whole truth, Corporal, and I might suggest that your watch sergeant won't be happy if you roust him out of bed at three AM to confirm the identity of an errant naval officer when you could've done it yourself." I strung him along. "Think of how proud he'll be when you make your full report of the capture, detention, and identification of a misbehaving swabby fly boy through your excellent powers of deduction." Ahah! He's weakening. I thought. "Why don't we just ease up to room six two two, let my shipmates identify me, and we can all go our way, you having solved the mystery of the soggy swabby. Hey! Corporal, I'm gettin' cold standin' out here."

"God damn if he don't talk like a Navy creep." The corporal slapped his leg. "Okay, fly boy, if that's who you are, lead on – and no funny moves – this Colt .45'll be pointed at your back the whole way – Wait! Shahan, Kranz, Morgan, spread out along the beach and search for other intruders – Shahan, you're in charge – Miller, resume your patrol." The corporal was at his drill sergeant best. "O.K. let's go – Let 'im go men, I got 'im covered." The corporal jabbed me forcefully in the back with his .45 as I started off toward the hotel, but he stayed a safe distance behind me the rest of the way.

At room 622 the corporal ordered me to stand aside and he kept me covered while he knocked on the door. Bang! Bang! Bang! "OPEN UP!" The corporal made enough noise to wake the whole hotel and in a moment doors began to open and sleepy faces began complaining about the noise waking them up, but nothing was stirring in 622. "Okay. If there's nobody in there you won't like what the sergeant and I will do to you back at the command post."

"Hey Red, Shailer, it's me, Harpo," I hollered. "Fer Chrissake answer the door, I'm under arrest by the Army! – Knock again Corporal . . . Pleeeease?"

Bang! Bang! Bang! He bashed the door harder.

"Hey you guys, wake up! come out and identify me!," I wailed at the door.

By now the hallway was full of hotel guests complaining about the noise we were making and threatening to call the house dick.

"Go back to bed people!," the corporal commanded. "I'm trying to identify this suspected enemy spy."

With that the irate guests retreated to their rooms with fearful whispers and suspicious looks at the two of us.

The door opened. It was Red, his sad, soft brown eyes even blearier than usual and his perpetually pink, hairless chest glowing above his white Navy skivvies.

"Do you know this guy?," demanded the corporal.

Red surveyed the situation with an officious air, carefully noting the corporal's .45 pointed at my bare, shivering chest, and, with that mischievous twinkle in his eye, indignantly pronounced: "I never saw the son-of-a-bitch before in my life." and slammed the door.

"That's it, Buddy! Now we're going to see my sergeant." The corporal emphasized his point with a sharp jab with his .45. "Get back to the elevator . . . SPY!"

"Hey Red, COME BACK! This guy's serious. He thinks I'm a spy. You've got to identify me! HELP!" . . . Silence.

"Shut up and get back to the elevator – ON THE DOUBLE! The corporal barked. "DAMN IT! I almost believed you were an American . . . Push the button for the elevator – NOW! We're goin' to show you what Army interrogation IS!"

The seconds ticked by and the floor indicator showed that the elevator was almost here. I shuddered at the thought of interrogation.

"ATTENTION ON DECK! Corporal, unhand that sorry Naval officer and secure your side arm." It was Red, fully dressed in his rumpled white uniform and officer's cap, showing all the gold braid that an ensign could show plus one measly campaign ribbon under his wings, storming down the hotel corridor to my rescue

Chapter 1: Conversion

. . only he forgot his shoes. "This is Ensign Harper of the United States Navy. Release him – NOW!

"But Sir, this man . . ."

"ENSIGN HARPER, Corporal, not 'this man!'," Red raged. "Come to attention, Corporal, and salute your superior officers!"

"Yes sir." The corporal saluted reluctantly. "But Ensign Harper apparently ignored the Off Limits signs and the barbed wire on the beach to swim in the ocean, sir. We thought he was a German spy or part of an espionage party delivered by a German U-boat, sir."

"Well, he'sh not a shpy." Red was slurring his words now, and the corporal and I could both smell the booze with every word. "Give him to me. I'll she that he'sh propply reprobated . . . er, repreminded . . . er somethin'."

"You got him sir." The corporal suppressed a laugh as he slipped his pistol into its holster. "I hope you both make it to your duty station in one piece tomorrow." He saluted and was gone.

Whew! I'm free! – from him and his Army – but not from Red and Shailer and their inevitable needling.

2

BOUNCE

0900, 17 October 1942. Lieut. Stu Stephens stood at the front of the ready room to which we had been ordered to report. "Welcome back to Miami. Say! It's really nice to see so many familiar faces." All six of us had been instructors at NAS Miami until we got our orders to Air Operational Training Command ten days earlier, so Mr. Stephens knew us all. "This will be your introduction to 'Landing Signals'."

Red, Shailer, and I had encountered Mr. Stephens as an instructor in Lieut. "Bags" Bagdanovich's tactics department during our first training activity as cadets at Miami, about a year earlier. Stu had that rugged handsomeness of NAVY men who have spent years at sea, his tanned and weathered face giving him the appearance of a man older than he was. I guessed he was about forty. He had flown torpedo bombers in the fleet – Douglas TBD *Devastators* – and had two years of LSO duty before coming to Opa Locka as an instructor back in 1941. When NAS Miami was directed to establish primary training for Landing Signal Officers Stu got the job. There was no branch, no section, just Stu. We listened very carefully as he continued his briefing.

"As you will recognize more and more, Landing Signals is a lonesome job. As a member of ship's company you are not part of the carrier's air group but you must become an integral part of the air group society. For the most part the pilots will look up to you but, to be effective, you must gain the absolute confidence of every aviator in the air group." Stu emphasized *absolute*. "But when that airplane comes up the groove, you are the sole authority as to whether a safe landing can be made. You'll make mistakes, and airplanes will crash as a result, but you must not admit mistakes lest you lose the confidence of the pilots. That's the painful part of the job." He continued without interruption. "We'll start out with Field Carrier Landing Practice – FCLP – otherwise known as 'Bounce Drill', in SNJ advanced trainers, the same aircraft you'll qualify aboard ship in when you get to Carrier Qualification Training Unit – CQTU – Norfolk."

Stu knew that none of us were carrier qualified. We had all come directly out of instructing, our first job as Naval Aviators. So we had a lot of learning to absorb before going to the fleet, where pilots would depend on us to bring them aboard safely under all conditions. "After you've figured out what a carrier approach should look like and what all the LSO signals mean, you'll take turns on the ground watching me bring 'em in, and then trading off to wave your classmates in, while I watch and kibitz. That'll give you some excitement." He chuckled. "That phase'll take about a week." Stu paused for a drink of his coke. "We'll use the rest of your time here refining your carrier approaches and LSO skills, using your classmates as victims." Stu grinned. "I'll ring in an occasional instructor to give you the feel of the real thing and they'll give me some feedback on how you guys are doing. They'll be pilots with carrier experience flying some of our old fleet aircraft – F3F fighters, SBC *Helldivers*, and maybe some Northrop BT-1 bombers." Stu was obviously pleased with the prospect.

"In a few weeks you'll be ready to go up to CQTU Norfolk to qualify in carrier landings and begin LSO training aboard ship in preparation for LSO duty at sea. The fleet's gettin' lots o' new carriers and you guys are needed to man those new Landing Signals platforms as soon as you get trained, so we're goin' to move fast. Any questions?," Stu asked.

"Sir, how long will we be here before we go to Norfolk?," Hardin asked. "I need to know to make arrangements for housing."

"I can't give you an exact date, but your LSO training is scheduled for six weeks so you can figure you'll be detached early in December, give or take a few days." Stu showed a little impatience. "Is that good enough?"

"Yes sir, I guess. We don't get quarters aboard the station, you know, so we'll just get something on a monthly basis," Hardin groused.

"I had a feeling most of you'd need to make some arrangements for quarters, so you're all dismissed 'til muster tomorrow at oh seven hundred . . . in this room." He pointed at the deck. "See you then."

Red, Shailer, and I found Ray Eden in his office in North Miami, feet on desk, along with his pith helmet, puffing a long Pall Mall cigarette at the end of a six inch ebony holder, the better to punctuate his eccentric manner. "Hi-ya pals!" – Ray's standard greeting – "Gawd almighty, that was a short cruise – just long enough for me to find Leo some mates for your old diggings – so that's out." He sat up to his desk and opened a well worn notebook. "But I've just the thing for you three characters, an authentic log cabin – two bedrooms, full bath, and a fully equipped kitchen. Come on, blokes! I'll show it to you."

A mile south on Dixie Highway, there it was, an honest to God log cabin, made out of real logs, stained a rustic red, making it glow with a warm reflection of the afternoon sun. Two swaying palm trees graced the front lawn and the classic front porch swing creaked gently in the afternoon breeze, inviting young lovers to sit and spoon. Inside, the living room was to the right, dining room and kitchen to the left, and two small bedrooms and a bath were straight back. The whole place was clean and cozy with furnishings straight out of the 1800s.

"Wow! This is just like the beach cottage up in the thumb of Michigan where my family vacationed one summer, furniture and all," I marvelled. "Look at the old rocking chair with the needle point cushion, and the hooked rug. Takes me back to my childhood."

"Yeah! Think of the parties we can have – eerie! Every party is Halloween! The girls'll love it," Shailer enthused. "What do ya say? Let's take it." His eyebrows rose in a sign of discovery. "I'll take the double bed room and you guys can have the twin beds . . . er . . . it's closer to the bathroom." As if that made any difference in a house this small.

"Christ's sake Shailer, the bedrooms are smaller than the rooms at the B.O.Q.," Red complained. "So you put dibs on the biggest one. Why don't we flip."

"Okay, Okay." Ray took charge. "You gents can settle your bunking arrangements later, and even schedule your bath and toilet." He laughed at his own humor. "Do you want it or don't you? If you do, let's get back to my office and bless the lease. You give me two months rent, and I'm on my way to dinner."

"Hold it, Ray," I put in. "Before we get all signed, sealed, and delivered, you've got to get us a housekeeper who will cook too. I'm tired of cookin' breakfast for these ingrates all the time and I'd like to have this place neater than that last mess we were in."

"Ingrates, he says." Shailer feigned inner distress. "Maybe we ought to change your nickname to 'Neato'."

"Nah," Red snickered. "That army corporal he charmed last night already gave him a new nickname – 'Mister Mermaid'."

Chapter 2: Bounce

"Anyway, I think Harpo's right," Shailer agreed. "Can you find us someone like that, Ray?"

"I've got just the lady for you, lads," Ray announced. "Mrs. MacGregor – she and her husband live alone and he works at the grocery. She'll just love you boys – and she'll mother you to death. I'll send 'er over tomorrow first thing."

"Can't do that," Red countered. "We've all got muster at oh seven hundred and we don't know when we'll be free. One of us'll call you around noon to set up an interview, Okay?"

"Aye lads, that's splendid." Ray was in his element – Command.

Red and I met with Mrs. MacGregor at our log cabin while Shailer was off getting his first taste of Landing Signals. Ray was right. She was an absolutely delightful person, with her grandmotherly presence and her mild Scottish brogue. She made me think of my dear Swedish mother, with her lovable femininity, sweetness of spirit, and self assured manner.

"Good Afternoon Misses MacGregor, I'm John and this is Ed." I slapped Red on the back. "The other one's Shailer. We're delighted that you are willing to keep house for us."

"Mr. Eden told me 'bout what ye'll be needin' so I'll tell y' what's to do, lads." Mrs. MacGregor took charge. "I'll come in early to cook breakfast for ye and I'll stay to straighten up the place, then I can come back to cook ye'r dinner." Mrs. MacGregor was very specific about the scope of her duties.

"That's perfect." Red approved – and so did I. "But how do we get the food in for breakfast and snacks? Can you do that?"

"If ye give me ten dollars now I'll get the food in and when I run out o' money I'll let ye know." Then she mellowed. "Ye seem to be nice boys. I'm sure we'll get along just foin. Now ye won't be needin' me the rest of the day, will ye?"

We gave her the ten bucks and one week's pay in advance and she happily bid us good-day.

"Well, even after drawin' straws with Shailer we still got the twin room with one dresser." Red was unpacking and we were arguing over which drawers each would get in the only dresser. "Hey! I'm taller'n you are so I ought to have the top two drawers."

"Oh no you don't," I challenged. "We'll alternate. You can have the top drawer 'cause you're a whole inch taller than I am, but then we alternate. I get two and four!"

Paddles!

"Okay, you win – Big deal – Hey, who's that lovely?" Red nodded toward the framed portrait I had just placed, carefully, on my side of the dresser.

"Peggy Green." I polished the frame. "She's the gal I went with in college, at Michigan State." I thought about the last time I saw Peggy, on a date, dancing at Coral Gables, just outside East Lansing. I savored the memory of having her in my arms. "I spotted her one night in the dorm when I got back from a date with another dorm dweller. You know me – not very sentimental – but that was one of those 'across the crowded room' things. One word comes to mind when I think of her: CUTE." *But she was much more than that. With her little pug nose and arched eyebrows she was the "Pug Nosed Dream" among the "polka dots and moonbeams" we were all singing about that year – the face framed by her dark brown bangs. She had a compact little figure just my size and when her magnetic hazel eyes met my steely blues I experienced a sensation I hadn't felt before. Love? I didn't know. But I knew I had to meet her.* "Hell, she wouldn't go out with me for a month 'cause I'd dated her roommate." I shook my head. "She must've gotten an 'A' in her mom's 'Hard to Get One-Oh-One' class."

"She must be stuck on you or she wouldn't send you a FRAMED portrait," Red needled. "She doesn't want you to forget her."

"Are you kiddin'?," I fumed. "I'll tell you how I got that 'framed portrait'." I snatched Peggy off the dresser. "I'd been buggin' her for a picture ever since I left State. The last time she wrote back and said she couldn't afford one 'cause it cost ten dollars for a set of five. So I sent her ten bucks and, guess what? She sent me the whole friggin' set, including a wallet size bonus print – had this one framed myself." I complained. "What the hell she thought I was goin' to do with the rest of the pictures, I don't know." I looked at the ceiling. "Maybe she thought I'd send 'em to her other boyfriends." I sat back on the bed and grabbed my head with both hands. "Christ! I can't tell whether she really likes me and is playing hard to get or is just humoring me 'cause o' the war. She's sure got me hooked."

"Yeah, you must think she's pretty special," Red scolded. "Hell! That's the only girl's picture you've got. Fer Christ's sake, Harp, if you're so damned stuck on her, why don't you marry her?"

"I've asked her." My shoulders sagged. "But I guess she wants to play the field some more. 'Specially with me gone all the time," I wheezed. "She probably thinks I'll be dead pretty soon anyway," I groaned. "Hell, she's got another boyfriend who's a fresh caught Army shavetail with orders to the First Army – The Big Red One! Talk about high risk!" I put Peggy's portrait back on the dresser. "Oh well, someday maybe."

Chapter 2: Bounce

"Good morning, gentlemen," Stu began. "Today you'll get your first taste of the carrier landing approach and learn the signals we use to bring airplanes aboard ship." He was addressing our LSO class gathered in a small knot on the taxiway of the outlying field at Bell's Farm, our SNJ advanced trainers parked nearby. He had a log yeoman with him to record his remarks on our approaches. "This is the landing pattern we will use for FCLP. It's pretty close to the one you'll use aboard ship." Stu held a small chalk board showing an elongated pattern with straight lines for the upwind and downwind legs and one hundred eighty degree arcs denoting the turns at each end. "You'll take off – here where you see the deck painted on the runway – climb out straight ahead to about a hundred feet above runway elevation. Set up an interval of thirty or forty seconds from the plane ahead of you. Turn downwind, maintaining your hundred feet, and adjust your distance abeam the deck – here – so your wing tip appears right over the center of the runway. Lower your landing gear and flaps and reduce your airspeed to eighty knots, and when your wing tip appears at the LSO position, begin your turn to the deck." Stu pointed to the point where the downwind leg met the downwind arc. "Make this a constant radius turn, let down to about twenty feet and reduce airspeed to seventy knots, for a nice three-point attitude. This is sometimes called the 'cross-leg' or the 'ninety' but there is no straight leg here, just a continuous turn into the groove."

Putting down the chalk board, Stu used his hands to illustrate the turn into the "groove." "I'll pick you up where you have about forty-five degrees to turn to the deck. Your continuous left turn will make it easy to see us around the nose of your aircraft. I'll give you signals to adjust your altitude and airspeed so I can give you a 'CUT' when you get to the 'ramp' – er – the end of the painted deck."

"Here are all the signals you may expect to see coming up the groove," Stu announced as he held the paddles straight out as in a semaphore 'R'. "A 'ROGER' means your approach is just right. A 'HIGH'." He held the paddles high, forming a 'U'. "Means you're high. And when I hold the paddles at knee level, like this, you are too low. A 'Fast' looks like a semaphore 'F', left arm out straight and right arm down at my side; and a 'SLOW' signal, or 'COME-ON' is a sweeping motion, like swimming the breast stroke." Stu talked as he demonstrated, describing each signal and specifying the actions required to comply. "You slant your arms one way or the other to get the pilot to increase or decrease his bank angle to line up with the deck center line.

"As you might expect, a LOW or COME-ON is a clue that you're getting into trouble. Your first response must be to add throttle. If it's a LOW, ease the nose up a little, maintain your airspeed, and climb until you get a ROGER, then level off. If it's a COME-ON, ease your nose down as you gain airspeed to resume a three-point attitude for a ROGER, then adjust your throttle setting to maintain airspeed and altitude. Never forget that CUT." He drew the paddle across his throat. "And WAVE-OFF, crossing and uncrossing the paddles over my head, sometimes frantically, are absolutely mandatory signals, for very good reasons."

"When you get the CUT, chop the throttle, drop your nose, and bank toward the deck center line. Then pull your nose up and make a tail first landing, as though you are trying to catch a wire on the ship." He demonstrated with his hands, as though with stick and throttle. "Here on the field, you immediately add throttle, raise your flaps, take off, retract your gear, and rejoin the traffic pattern. If you get a WAVE-OFF, add full throttle, retract your gear, and make a well controlled jog to the left, and pass me to port." He made a smooth left sweep with his right hand. "When you've regained airspeed, raise your flaps, rejoin the pattern, and try again."

"Well, here comes my demonstration team." Apparently on cue, four F3Fs zoomed in over the FCLP runway in tight right echelon, broke smartly, and began making carrier approaches, with Stu waving corrective signals.

"Now watch this F3F as he makes his turn from the downwind leg." Stu had his signal paddles ready and was describing the approach as I stood very close behind him so as not to confuse the approaching pilot while Stu waved his signals. The rest of the class stood about twenty feet to our right, each waiting his turn to stand behind Stu for the best view of the approaches.

Stu was a kind of fatherly figure to most of us youngsters – I was the youngest at twenty-one – and his demeanor was one of a coach, not a teacher. He acted as though we already had the skills of an LSO and all he had to do was refine them, so working with him was a very pleasant learning experience.

"This turn from downwind leg into the groove should be continuous at the same turn rate – bank angle – as he comes down to about fifteen feet over the deck, in a three point attitude, right up to the CUT position, lined up with the center of the deck." Stu raised his paddles to a ROGER. "I pick him up right here, where he has about forty-five degrees to turn to the deck – he's a little high so I show him a HIGH signal." Stu raised his arms to hold his paddles steady as high as was comfortable.

"Notice he eases off a little throttle, drops his nose a little and, as I come to a ROGER, he pulls up his nose and adds a little throttle to maintain altitude and airspeed." Stu held his paddles level with his shoulders. "Now he's perfect as he approaches the CUT position." At the CUT, the pilot cut his engine, made a perfect, tail first landing right in the middle of the "deck" painted on the runway, and immediately added full throttle to take off again and reenter the FCLP pattern.

"That was easy – just a HIGH, a ROGER, and a CUT – he responded perfectly," Stu enthused.

"No wonder they call it 'bounce drill'," I commented. "Oh! Here comes another one up the groove."

"Yeah. This guy's turn rate isn't enough to line him up in the groove so I give him a left bank signal." Stu slanted both arms to port, signalling more left bank." He looked like a drunken aviator demonstrating how he made his turn into the carrier. "Uh-huh, that's good. Now he's a little fast. See how he's not in a three-point attitude but a little nose down? So I give him a FAST." We heard the power come off a little and, as the plane slowed, the pilot eased the nose up to a three-point attitude and added throttle back to hold that speed and altitude. "Perfect." Stu purred as he came to a ROGER, then a CUT, and another landing within the painted deck followed. After the four F3Fs had made six approaches each and we had all had an opportunity to stand behind Stu for the real LSO vantage point, the little biplane fighters rendezvoused, buzzed the field in a tight fingertip formation, and disappeared to the southeast.

"Okay men, now that you know what a carrier approach looks like you should all make perfect passes." Stu grinned wickedly. "Man your aircraft, take off, and form the FCLP pattern. I'll give you twelve bounces each and call you down to critique your performance." He sent us off for our first "bounce drill."

"Well, I must say you all did pretty well for your first bounce drill." We sat on the taxiway drinking in Stu's critique of our first field carrier landings. He read from his LSO's log, kept by the log yeoman, citing the good and bad points of each pilot's approaches, giving us all a comprehensive lesson in the variety of errors possible in making a carrier approach. "Now get in your airplanes for another dozen approaches, think about the errors you made the last time and try to make approaches that require no correction from me." Stu eyed each of us in turn. "Work toward a ROGER all the way." He made a ROGER with his paddles. "When you're through I'll give you the 'return to base' signal and I'll brief you on your last sequence in the ready room when I get back."

Back in the ready room Stu finished his debriefing, then announced: "Air Operational Training Command wants me to get all you budding flag wavers checked out in the J2F." Stu was talking about the Grumman J2F *Duck*, the single-engine biplane utility amphibian that looked like an F3F with a big pontoon welded on its belly. The landing gear retracted visibly into the sides of the huge float just like the gear retracts in to the F3F's forward fuselage. "Cummings! Harper!"

Shailer and I leapt to our feet, "Aye aye, Sir."

"I've got you two scheduled for Monday morning. Meet me here at oh seven hundred."

Saturday morning was to be a relaxing one for Red and me. We both had the morning off so we just relaxed after breakfast and got acquainted with our temporary home.

"Hey, Harp!," Red screamed, with a tinge of fear in his voice. "Look what I found." He pointed to a moving mass that looked like termites eating something.

"What the hell is that?," I recoiled from the sight.

"Damned if it isn't a whole brood of baby scorpions munchin' on the carcass of a big one." Red stirred the swarm with a small stick. "I just knocked them down out of a niche in the logs over the front door." He pointed with the stick. "We'd better get 'em the hell out of here." He dashed off to the kitchen to get the broom.

BANG BANG! "Someone's at the door, Red," I called. "I'll get it."

Red was just getting back with the broom and dust pan when I opened the door to see Ray Eden grinning in at me.

"Hi-ya, pals," he crowed as he yanked open the screen door and lurched into the house. "How's the old slut treatin' ya."

"Hey! Wait a minute," I scolded. "I resent you referring to Mrs. MacGregor that way, Ray."

"Yeah! Me too," Red chimed in. "Our Mrs. MacGregor is a charming and sensitive woman. So . . . knock it off, damn it!

"I'm sorry if I offended your sensibilities, gentlemen," Ray sniffed. "I was just asking after your well being."

"Well. Our well being, as you put it," Red pronounced, haughtily, "is being diminished by this swarm of scorpions here."

"Oh!," Ray recoiled from the sight. "Those are nasty little buggers . . . You'd better check your shoes in the morning – They love to sleep in shoes."

"Yeah?," Red challenged. "How the hell are we goin' to get rid of 'em?"

"You cahn't, pals." Ray waved his arm for effect. "I'd guess you'll just have to christen this place 'The Scorpion's Den'."

We did.

3

STARLIGHT

"Hey Harpo, I hear they got that band from the Outrigger to play for the dance at the O'Club tonight." Red was struggling into a freshly starched white uniform, de rigueur for such functions. "Ugh! This choke collar is tight . . . It's the band that Carmen sings for . . . You remember Carmen." He gave a lecherous grin.

"Damned right I do," I crowed, sitting down to put on my spotless white buck shoes. "That ought to make for a romantic evening." Carmen was the Latin bombshell whom Red had brought out to the O'Club pool to entertain George Searle and me on a pass from the dispensary where we were interned for a week – George for face wounds suffered when he ran his Buick convertible into a palm tree and I for catarrhal drip. Her favorite song was "Tangerine" and she gave it a sensuous treatment, complete with suggestive body moves. "Who're you draggin' t'night?" I asked.

"Joan Holly. You remember her. That crazy wild babe from down in Coral Gables." Red rolled his eyes. "She's a bucket of fun, but I sure wouldn't want to be married to her. What a circus that would be."

Joan was a plump little bundle of energy about five foot two at about a hundred and twenty-five pounds. Mischief oozed out of every pore. She's the one who'd jump into your lap and, when you looked a little quizzical, she'd say: "What's the matter, ya nervous, Mervis?" Everyone was "Mervis" to her when she was wooing in her bombastic style. What a wildcat!

"Crazy wild, huh?" I finished tying my shoes. "Sex pot I'd call her . . . Jeez, Red, you'll have to drive all the way to Coral Gables to pick 'er up. Hell, that's half way to Key West. Then you'll have to take her home again." I cautioned. "You may not make it back before dawn."

"Maybe not, but that's okay. I've got the morning off tomorrow . . . Uh – who're you takin'."

"Peggy Rogers. Remember? She's the gal I took to that goin' away party just before we started on our round trip to JAX."

"Oh yeah. The statuesque brunette," Red nodded. "Isn't she some relation of Jim Stewart's?"

Lieut. Stewart was a flight instructor whose wife, Carol, was a very attractive brunette. They had a baby daughter named Katie. I had gotten to know the family pretty well on my visits to their house to see Peggy.

"Yeah, she's Carol's baby sister. I sighed as I savored the image of her youthful charm. "Came out in August for a visit and she's been here ever since. Carol likes having her here to take care of Katie . . . I like it too," I grinned. "She's from Redondo Beach, near L.A." Peggy wasn't exactly what you'd expect from L.A. She was more sophisticated than most nineteen year old girls I'd known but she was surprisingly modest and unassuming. "We've been out together a lot in just a month. I think she likes me. I'm sure glad we got ordered back here for our LSO training instead of stayin' in JAX."

"Well, I gotta get out of here. Joan's expectin' me at eighteen thirty so we can get to the Club in time for the dance." Red slammed the screen door behind him and roared off in his black 1939 Ford.

"Hi, John," Carol Stewart greeted me at her front door. "Peg isn't quite ready. Come on in and sit down."

"Thanks, Carol," I said, as I walked into their small, but comfortable, living room.

"Hi John." Jim got up and shook hands. "Care for a drink while you're waitin' for Peg?

"No thanks, sir. I'm sure I'll get plenty to drink at the Club. Peg's usually pretty prompt."

"How's Stu treatin' you guys in LSO school?," Jim asked as he sank into his easy chair. "From what I hear that's a real whirlwind course."

"Yeah, six weeks from scratch and we're supposed to be ready to go to Nor-

Chapter 3: Starlight

folk for CARQUAL . . . er – carrier qualification." I marvelled as I took a seat. "Stu's really great – acts like we already know how to do it and all he's doin' is refinin' our skills. After a week it seems to be workin'. Now he says he's going to check us out in the J2F," I enthused. "Says LSOs are supposed to be checked out in all the ship's aircraft, including the utility airplanes, 'cause we have to double as utility pilots. Have you flown the J2F?"

"Yeah. You'll enjoy flying the *Duck* off the water. It's a whole new experience." Then Jim turned serious. "Y'know, bein' an LSO's a tough job. You're out there on the fan-tail, all by yourself, with responsibility way beyond your rank and experience. I don't envy you." Then he turned to gaze out the window in a kind of reverie. "I knew Stu on the old *Yorktown* when we were in Torpedo Five and he got tapped to be the LSO. I'd already transferred back here before one of the fighters bounced his landing, missed all the wires, hit the island, and burned. Stu's a different guy now." He turned to look up the staircase with a smile. "Oh! Here comes Peg."

Wow! I breathed to myself, leaping to my feet. Peggy seemed to float down the stairs, her pale aqua marquisette off-the-shoulder gown projecting an alluring aura around her modest figure. *Oops! my "wow" must have leaked out cause Jim and Carol looked at me with knowing smiles.* "Hi, Peggy," I managed.

"Sorry to keep you waiting." She wasn't. "I hope you warriors had enough time to fight a battle or two." Peggy was needling us.

"We were talking about John's new job as a Landing Signal Officer, a very tough, thankless job, but good for the career." Jim was being very serious.

"Johnny can handle it. He's a tough guy." Peggy couldn't hold back a little giggle. "Okay, honey, I'm ready. Lets go."

"Thanks for the encouragement, sir." I bowed just a little. "See you later."

"Don't be too late." Carol gave us her mother act. "But we won't stay up for you."

"They're playing 'Tangerine.' Shall we dance?," I invited.

We finished our drinks and moved easily to the dance floor. Suddenly she was in my arms, her left hand caressing the back of my neck and her warm body pressed against mine, eagerly it seemed. Peggy's figure seemed fuller in this circumstance, and she seemed taller, partly because of her upswept black hair and partly because of her spike heels. I could look directly into her deep brown eyes and almost tell what she was thinking. Then her cheek was soft against mine and her bare shoulder invited a kiss.

Paddles!

"Now they're playing 'In The Mood', kind of jumpy, don't you think?," I suggested. "Let's get another drink and go out by the pool . . . Rum and coke for you, right?"

"O.K. Johnny, but remember what 'mother' Carol said," Peggy chided.

"Hey, honey, Carol was talking about TIME, not place," I countered.

It was a dark, moonless night, and we sat very close together in an easy embrace on a patio lounge chair talking softly about us. As our eyes became adapted, billions of stars became visible, casting an eerie, melancholy glow. "You're on your way, aren't you, Johnny?," Peggy probed, finally.

"What do you mean?," I flinched a little.

"I mean you're on your way to sea duty pretty soon, aren't you. Jim warned me that you would be," She wheedled. "When do you leave?"

"I'm supposed to get orders to carrier qualification in Norfolk around the first of December, that is if I make it through this course." I ventured. "I don't know what happens after that. Don't worry, we'll keep in touch and we'll be able to see each other when I get some leave."

"You WANT to go, don't you?," Peggy was pouting. "Jim told me you wanted to get out of instructing and into combat at sea."

Jeez, I'm already getting hen pecked, and this is supposed to be a romantic moment. "Well, he's right. That's what I got in the NAVY for. But bein' an LSO isn't combat so I'll try to transfer to a fighter squadron. But let's just enjoy tonight." I hugged her and kissed her on the cheek.

She turned and gave me a long kiss, full on the mouth, while caressing the back of my neck. *Ooh! There's that mysterious tingle.*

"I love you Johnny," Peggy whimpered. "I don't want you to get killed."

Oh oh! What do I say now? This is gettin' out o' hand. Christ, I really love Peggy Green, back in East Lansing, but I like this Peggy a lot, and we have a lot of fun together. How do I change this conversation to "lets have fun"? "Hey, darlin', I don't want to die either." I drew her close and we kissed for a long minute to the distant strains of "Poinsiana." "But I don't want to talk about it on a nice night like this." I stood up and offered my hand. "Hey, there's some smooth music. Let's dance!"

"Hey Harpo." Red came at us dragging Joan on his right arm. "Everybody's goin' over to the 'Snake Ranch' for a party. Lets go." The "Snake Ranch" was a palatial five bedroom, five bath, modern ranch which was home to five NAS Mi-

30

ami flight instructors. It was a "U" shaped building with an Olympic size pool between the wings. A real plush layout.

"D'you want to go, Peg?," I asked. "It only takes ten or fifteen minutes to get over there. It'll be a lot of fun."

"I'd love to," She brightened. "But I probably ought to get home by two or two-thirty."

"We can do that, honey." I gave her hand a squeeze. "Y'ever been over there, Ed?"

"No. You lead, I'll follow."

BANG! "What was that?," Peggy shrieked, somewhat in panic. Red had rammed our rear bumper.

"Jeez!," what's that for. We're already going fifteen miles over the speed limit." I sped up a little. Fortunately the road was on a section line, straight as a string.

CRUNCH! "Christ's sake, he did it again, and we're comin' up on a dead end, ninety degree left turn." I carefully came to a stop at the STOP sign, with Red's bumper still pushing on mine.

I hopped out and went back to confront Red. "What the hell do you think you're doing, Ed?," I raged. "We were goin' sixty-five back there and you were still pushin'. Keep that up and we'll either get killed or arrested. Now knock it off!"

"I'm sorry Harp," Red wheezed. "I can't help it. Joan keeps pushin' on my accelerator foot."

"Well, put her in the back seat, before we have a disaster," I commanded. "Better yet, put her in the trunk, and lock it." I was mad as hell and gave Joan the hardest look I could muster.

Suddenly there was a car pulling up right behind Red's. "It's the cops," I warned.

"What seems to be the trouble here, sir?" The "sir" was probably in deference to my uniform. "Do you need help?"

"No problem, Officer. I was just giving my friend directions on where we're going," I assured the officer, as soberly as possible.

"Are you going to another party?," The officer probed, sensing we'd been to one already.

"Yes sir," I affirmed.

"You, sir, in the car. Get out of the car, please," The officer ordered, courteously. "I'd like to see if you can stand up straight too."

Red got out and stood, more or less at attention. "Yes sir, officer, I'm fine." He only swayed a little.

"You gentlemen seem to be okay. Now just drive carefully and don't drink any more this morning. I don't want to have to inquire as to your health later today. Good morning." The officer got in his car, turned around and drove off.

When I told Peggy what was going on she could hardly believe it. "What a witch. But what are we going to do now?" She was scared, and I didn't blame her.

"I think the cop got her settled down, and Red's a pretty mean character. He'll handle her." I tried to act calm. "Now, I'm going to drive very deliberately, at the speed limit, and if they do it again I'm going to stop and really raise hell."

"Well, where the Hell have you guys been," was Tim Gile's greeting to the "Snake Ranch." "The party's already into the second phase, free-style swimming and diving, uniform optional."

"Yeah, I can see," Red ventured. "My God! There're guys in there with whole uniforms on and some with nothin', 'cept maybe their scivvies. NOBODY'S got a swimmin' suit on."

"The girls all have their undies on cause I can see their bra straps above the water," Peggy giggled.

"The bar's right over there. Get yourselves a drink, take off your clothes and jump in," Tim invited. "Water's fine and the company's better."

SPLASH! Just back at the pool with our drinks, Peggy, Red, and I were inundated with a giant geyser, erupting just below the high diving board. "Oh God! I'm soaked," Peggy gurgled. "What was that?"

As the waves calmed down, a tousled head of hair appeared above the water. "For Christ's sake!," Red hollered. "It's Joan, and she must've done a cannonball off the high board. Ha! Lost her bra in the process." A lecherous grin curled his mouth. "See 'er strugglin' to put it back on? God! I'd better be careful where I take that female."

"You know I'm never one to say 'I told you so', Ed," I chided. And to Peggy: "Hey, honey, I'll get us a drink and then we can get comfortable and take a dip." I was unbuttoning my white uniform.

"Can't," Peggy pouted.

"Why not?"

"Never mind," She said with a shrug. "Just can't."

Chapter 3: Starlight

"You Okay?," I asked as I swam up to Peggy where she sat on the edge of the pool, bare feet in the water, tearing methodically at her beautiful marquisette dress.

"Yes, I'm fine, and I'm enjoying the party!" She was still pouting. "Would you get me another drink, please."

"Yeah, but knock it off with the dress destruction," I scolded as I climbed out of the pool, my scivvies dripping water. "Keep it up and you won't be able to wear it again."

I don't care," Peggy sulked.

Out on the highway again: "Boy! It's a relief not having Red and Joan behind us." I commented as I drove very carefully back to Opa Locka with Peggy snuggled close, under my right arm . . . No answer. She was sound asleep, and I could feel her easy, rhythmic breathing. I just kept driving.

"Peggy! You're home. Wake up!," I whispered as I shook her gently. "C'mon honey. You gotta get up to your room." I shook her a little harder . . . Nothing!

Oh oh! She's really asleep, or passed out. Now how am I going to get her upstairs to her room? Jeez, I hope the Stewarts left the door open for her. I got out and tiptoed up to the door. *YES. Unlocked. That's a relief.* I opened the passenger side door and shook Peggy again, harder . . . Nothing. *Oh well, I ought to be able to do this.* I reached in the car and slid Peggy's inert form part way out of the car, facing me. As gently as possible, I lifted her left arm over my shoulder and reached my right arm around her back while I lifted her legs with my left.

Okay, J.A., very quietly up the steps to the porch. I staggered just a bit and, reaching the front door, quietly opened it. *Now to slip upstairs without disturbing Jim and Carol.* BONK! Peggy's head hit the newel post. *Christ! If she wasn't unconscious already, she is now.* Peggy didn't even whimper.

Step by step I eased up the stairs. *Oh oh! I hope these stairs don't creak. Just a few more steps now . . . Hmm. I wonder which room is Peggy's . . . Ah! Must be this one. Door's open and it's kind of frilly . . . Okay. Just lay her down on the bed – easy now – good.* There she lay, limp as a rag, looking angelic. I checked her head for a newel post wound. *Good. Just a bump. Now what do I do? She wouldn't want to be in bed all night with her shoes on.* The shoes came off and went into the shoe rack in the closet. *Those stockings have to come off too.* The hose peeled off easily after I unsnapped the garters. *Where to put 'em? On top o' the dresser's okay . . . There! Hmm. She looks awfully uncomfortable in that dress. Probably ought to take it off. I wonder if she'd mind. Probably be glad in the morning.* I reached

33

under Peggy's back and lifted her up so I could unzip her dress. She sighed, or groaned, I didn't know which . . . "D'you want me to take your dress off so you'll be more comfortable?" . . . Another sigh. I proceeded to unzip her dress. I rolled her back and forth to get the hem of her dress up above her hips and pulled it over her head. Her slip came right with it. The rumpled dress and slip went on hangers in the closet. Next, the garter belt was unhooked and joined the stockings on the dresser.

Standing back, I couldn't suppress a quiet gasp. I had seen her lots of times in two piece bathing suits but this was different. Her bra was so sheer as to reveal each enchanting contour of her firm breasts while her flimsy panties accentuated the beautiful curve of her hips. *Ahah! I see why she wouldn't go in the pool . . . Hmmm – Learn something every day.*

I wonder if her bra is uncomfortable to sleep in . . . Nah, I'd better not – Not with her unable to object.

I stood, hypnotized by her radiant beauty, for what seemed like a long while. Then I kissed her gently on the lips and whispered, "Good night Peggy . . . darling", and stole silently down the stairs and out into the starlit night, locking the front door behind me.

"Hi, Katie," I called, as I leapt out of my forty-one Ford. "Is Peggy around?" It was ten A.M., Sunday, and Katie was playing with the garden hose in the front yard of the Stewarts' home. She wore a flower print two piece bathing suit – a little presumptuous for a two-year-old. Her blond shoulder length hair framed a round cherubic face.

"Hi, mister." Katie gazed up at me with her big, inquisitive blue eyes. "Aunt Peg's still in her room. Want me t' get 'er for ya?"

"Would you please."

Katie skipped up the front steps in typical girlish fashion and disappeared into the house.

Minutes later: "You don't want to see me right now, Johnny." Peggy purred while peeking around the front door jam. "I just got up, and I'm a mess."

She's right. She looks terrible – hair all messed up, dark circles under her eyes, and no makeup. "You look great honey. I just dropped by to see how you're feelin'. You were in pretty bad shape last night," I ventured.

"Can you wait a few minutes? Maybe I can get presentable," Peggy cooed.

"Yeah, but I've got to fly at thirteen hundred so I don't have much time," I cautioned.

Chapter 3: Starlight

"I'll make it quick." I could hear Peggy running up the stairs to her bedroom. *Hmm. Her bedroom. I know it well.*

"Hi," Katie chirped, running up to the concrete bench where I taken up a waiting pose. "You're Johnny, aren't you."

"Yes, Katie." I patted her tousled head. "Do you remember sitting in my car with Aunt Peggy and me? That was about a month ago."

"Yes, I 'member, Johnny," she giggled. Then she chattered on about her toys and friends. She was asking questions about Peggy and me when Peggy came down the front steps.

"Thanks Katie, for entertaining Johnny while I got presentable." Peggy looked better but the dark circles still showed under her eyes. "Now go and play so we can talk." Then, after Katie had gone back to the hose: "Thanks for the fun night last night, Johnny, but what happened? She gave me an anxious gaze. "I don't remember getting home."

"We got home okay, but you were sound asleep, out like a light." I looked over at Katie, playing with the hose. "I had to carry you up to your room."

She flushed a little. "Well, I must have been awake enough to get undressed." It was almost a question.

"I undressed you." I said, softly, avoiding her eyes. "I thought you'd be more comfortable."

"Oh." Peggy blushed all the way to her hair line. Then, changing the subject: "Where've you been?"

"Just got a hop in an F2A so I could tap in on that oxygen." The Brewster F2A *Buffalo* was the only modern fighter we had at Miami and the only aircraft on the station with breathing oxygen. "I like to fly the F2A after a night like last night. The oxygen does a job on a hangover."

"You were flying already this morning?" Peggy seemed incredulous. "After what we drank last night?"

"Sure. It's easier for me than it is for you," I said, trying to comfort her. "That Rum and Coke is bad stuff – Hard on your head – I stick to scotch."

After a few more minutes of conversation I announced, "I'd better get going or I'll be late for bounce drill. Mr. Stephens is going to let us try our flag waving on some instructors this afternoon." I stood up and took her hand. "I've got the duty tonight." I kissed her lightly on the cheek. "I'll call you tomorrow."

"Careful." Peggy blew me a kiss as I climbed into my car.

4

DUCKS

"Good morning, gentlemen," Stu Stephens greeted Shailer and me in the LSO ready room. "As you know, the Grumman J2F *Duck* is a utility amphibian designed to operate off airfields and aircraft carriers as a land plane and in and out of water bases as a seaplane. The landing gear operates just like on an F3F." He extended his arms downward and then drew his hands up to either side of his chest. "Just like the F3F, the *Duck* doesn't have any flaps. On land or off the carrier she handles kind of like a sluggish F3F, but water operation is something else."

"The main thing to watch out for in water operation is 'porpoising' – pitching up and down. Porpoising happens when the lift on the wings fights the water forces on the hull." He made an up and down motion with his right hand. "Porpoising can cause a nasty crash if not properly controlled." Stu drew a rough graph on the blackboard showing angle of attack on the vertical scale and air speed on the horizontal. "You'll notice that both curves show a very high angle of attack at very low air speed, like at the beginning of your takeoff run or at the end of your landing run-out." He used a pointer to accent the low speed end of the curves. "At increased airspeed both curves show decreasing angle-of-attack for safe operation." He swept the pointer to the high speed end of the curves. "You want to keep the angle of attack between these two lines. Porpoising will occur above the top curve, while there is a tendency to dive if angle of attack is below the lower line. Understand?"

Chapter 4: Ducks

"But how do we know what our angle of attack is?," I puzzled.

"You don't need to know the actual angle of attack. You just need to have a feel for where you are on this curve." He slapped the blackboard with his pointer. "As you'll see when we go out and fly, there are easy rules for both takeoff and landing. Let's go."

"All three of us?," Shailer wondered.

"Yeah. No problem," Stu assured us. "One of you can sit in the bilges. There's a crew seat down there and a headset jack. You can take turns flying."

"First, we've got to pick out a good clear stretch of water to operate on," Stu instructed, keying the hand held mike as we circled over Biscayne Bay at about fifteen hundred feet. "This little cove over here is okay, and it's clear of boats. Next we have to figure out which way the wind is blowing – no wind socks out here, you know." "See the wind streaks on the water?" Stu dipped a wing so we could all see. "That's the 'wind line', but now we've got to figure out the wind DIRECTION. The waves will appear to be moving down wind."

"Okay. Cummings. Get on the controls lightly and just feel what I do." I could hear Stu on the intercom from my seat in the bilges. "Gettin' down to the right final approach altitude is kind o' like landing at night. You want to keep your eyes focused on the horizon so you can sense when the water flattens out below you. Then you slow down to about carrier approach airspeed descending slowly until you hit the water."

CRASH! *Wow! He really meant "HIT" the water, didn't he. Sounded like the float was coming off of the airplane. I was thinking* when Stu cheered: "Yeah, that was a pretty smooth landing."

"Yes sir?" Shailer wasn't quite sure. "It sure makes a hell of a noise when you touch down."

"I'll second that," I hollered into the hand held mike. "It's REALLY noisy down here."

"Notice that I ease the nose up as we slow down until I have the stick full back against the stop when the airplane stops planing and sinks noticeably to its normal floating depth," Stu coached as he went.

"Now, I'll just taxi back to about the spot where we touched down," Stu announced as he added power. "Don't be bashful about adding enough power to get control out of the rudder. It takes quite a bit to get the airplane turned out of the wind – she wants to weathercock – and you have to keep your speed up taxiing downwind for the same reason." I could see out the side window that we were surfing along at a pretty good clip. "Turning back upwind is easy. I just kick the rudder the way I want to turn and chop the throttle." I felt the airplane lurch to the left and wallow nearly to a stop, into the wind.

"Okay, Cummings, get back on the controls and follow me thorough this take-off." The airplane shuddered as Stu added full throttle and then began to bounce up and down on the small waves in Biscayne Bay. "Holding takeoff power – I've got the stick full back with full right rudder. You can feel when she gets up on the step – same feeling as when a speed boat begins to plane. Notice I'm holding the nose too high and we're porpoising a little, so I let the nose drop just a little and the porpoising stops. Holding the nose at about the same attitude as for a land takeoff I don't have to do anything. The airplane just lifts off the water when it gets to takeoff airspeed." Things suddenly got quiet in the bilges as we staggered into the air.

"Okay, Cummings, trade places with Harper so he can get some stick time," Stu yelled over the sputter of the idling engine as we bobbed up and down on the water after Shailer's fourth landing.

"Did you learn anything while Cummings was checkin' out?," Stu shouted as I climbed up out of the bilges.

"Yes sir," I shouted back to him as I fastened my safety belt and shoulder straps and plugged in my helmet ear phones.

"Enough to try a takeoff on your own?," I heard through the intercom.

"Yes sir, I think so. Main thing is to keep the nose high 'til we get up on the step and then drop it to a normal takeoff angle of attack," I said into the microphone, with as much confidence as I could muster.

"You've got the keys. Now see if you can execute." He caught my eye in the mirror mounted in the trailing edge of the upper wing. "Make a turn to port after you are comfortably airborne."

Okay, J.A., this is easy, just hold the stick in your gut and pour on full throttle. Whoa! Water flyin' everywhere. Near zero forward visibility. The airplane feels like it's standing on its tail, bouncing up and down on the waves. Oops! Turnin' left a little. God! It takes full right rudder to keep her straight.

"You're doin' fine, Harper," Came Stu's calm assurance. "Just keep the nose up 'til she slides up on the step." Then came the lurch, forward and upward, that signalled that the airplane was on the step.

Chapter 4: Ducks

Oops! She's porpoising. Get the nose down!

"Okay. That was good. Just hold that attitude and she'll fly right off the water. You don't have to pull 'er off," Stu coached calmly.

Airborne. Hmm, that was easy. Only problem was I didn't get the nose down quite soon enough. Now, ease into a left turn.

I saw Stu in the mirror, signalling left turn with his thumb. "Good. Now turn downwind and make an approach to land about where we started our takeoff run. Are you reading the wind streaks?"

"Yes sir, I see 'em, and I think the wind's about fifteen knots."

"Yeah, that's about right," Stu agreed. "You heard what I told Cummings – nose full up after touch down."

Okay, constant descent – keep 'er lined up with the wind streaks – air speed down to about sixty-five knots – HOLD THAT – keep scanning the horizon – slow the descent a little now. CRASH! *Hmm, not as noisy up here. Throttle to idle – ease the stick back as she slows down – keep 'er straight.* SWOOSH. Suddenly, the airplane sank to its floating depth and seemed to stop, dead.

"Good," Stu cheered into my ear phones. "You just need to ease the nose down a little smoother during takeoff. You were a little fast at touchdown but the landing came off just fine. Let's try two or three more of those until you feel comfortable. Are you okay down there Cummings?"

"Yes sir, but it sure is a rough and noisy ride down here."

"Now you guys'll know how your crewman feels when you go someplace in this machine." Stu chided.

"All right gentlemen, I want you to take charge of these approaches." Stu was preparing Jim English and me for this FCLP session as we awaited the first group. "I'll just stand behind you and comment." He shaded his eyes with his hand and searched to the southeast. "You'll be going to the Carrier Qualification Unit – CQTU they call it – up in Norfolk before long so I'll expect steady performances. Aha! here they are now." Four stubby little F3Fs buzzed the runway at three hundred feet, broke up, and entered the downwind leg.

Fortunately these pilots had done this a lot and could be expected to make pretty good approaches without any assistance from me. But with Stu talking in my ear, I was able to relax and feel confident.

After bouncing another division of F3Fs and a group of six SBCs – Curtiss *Helldivers* – with Jim and me taking turns at the paddles and Stu coaching all the time, we strolled over to our transportation, an old N3N-3 primary trainer and an NE-1 Piper Cub.

"Both you guys did pretty well with these approaches, but you need to anticipate a little better. Know when a guy comin' up the groove is accelerating or decelerating so you can correct early, before it becomes an overcorrection." Stu was briefing Jim and me, using the LSO's log we had kept for him during this bounce session. "Besides just looking at the airplane's attitude, concentrate on the engine and airplane sounds, to get a feel for what's going to happen next. It'll take a little time out here but if you concentrate on it you'll get the feel pretty quickly."

As Jim climbed into the NE-1 Stu hollered, "You may secure when you get back to base, English. I'll see you at morning muster."

"Aye aye, sir." Jim waved as he taxied to the end of the runway.

We watched as the little Cub putted down the runway, jumped into the air, and turned to the southeast.

The N3N-3 biplane trainer was appropriately dubbed "Yellow Peril" because it was painted yellow – for trainer – and because students were usually at the controls – a recognized peril. *Yeah. The old N3N; the first airplane I ever soloed, just a year and a half ago at Elimination Base, NAS Grosse Ile – and my primary trainer at Pensacola.*

"Now we're gonna do a little duck huntin'," Stu announced.

"How're you gonna do that, out o' this 'Peril'?"

"Hell, it's just like shootin' enemy fighters out of the gunner's seat in a scout bomber. I'll show you. You take the front seat and fly us out to duck country." Stu climbed in the rear seat and unlimbered his 12 Gauge Winchester. "Just take off and head west toward the Everglades. I'll tell you what to do next. There're some dikes with roads on them out there where we can land if we have to."

"There they are!," Stu yelled into the slipstream – we had no "Gosports" – face pieces with a speaking tube running between the cockpits. "A flock o' Mallards!" I could see him pointing down and to the left in the wing mounted mirror just above me. "Now, ease on down there and join up in a loose right echelon, and I'll get a shot or two. Can you hear me?"

"Yeah," I yelled. "But how're we goin' to retrieve 'em?"

"I'll show you." Stu grinned into the mirror. "Don't worry. It's easy."

I assumed from his manner that he could, indeed, shoot down one of the ducks so I turned toward the flock and eased off on the throttle to slow down to duck speed – about sixty knots – and let down to the formations's altitude – about seventy-five feet – to assume a right echelon position. I gingerly closed to about fifty yards from the last duck and held that position. The ducks acted like we weren't even there.

"Hey! Move up a little forward of this one and close in a little so I have a good shot at him and his leader," Stu yelled.

"Okay!" I gave him a thumbs up in the mirror and added a little throttle to ease forward so the last two ducks were just abaft our port beam at a range of about thirty yards. The ducks just kept on flapping. BLAM! . . . BLAM! Feathers flew and both ducks folded their wings and fell toward the Everglades seventy feet below. "You got 'em," I hollered.

"You like that, huh?" Stu grinned into the mirror. And then: "I got it!" I felt the stick shake violently, the signal that Stu was taking control.

Keeping his eyes glued on the spot where the two ducks splashed, Stu banked sharply, picked the dyke closest to the ducks, made a turning, carrier type approach, lined up with the dyke road, cut the throttle, and planted the N3N right in the middle of the dyke, as if the road had arresting gear.

"Hold the brakes." Leaving the engine idling, Stu leapt to the ground and raced to the water's edge. "Here's one right here. The other one is floatin' right out there. Hold on." SPLASH SPLASH SPLASH. Stu was wading out to retrieve the other duck. "I got 'em both – hold it – I'll be right there." With that, he ran up, tossed the two dead mallards in my lap, and clambered back into the rear seat, soggy flight suit and all.

"Okay, I got it," Stu hollered, shaking the stick as he snapped on his safety belt. Then he lined the N3N up with the dyke, added full throttle while holding the brakes, let the brakes go, and took off.

"Now you take over." The stick shook. "Get us back to NAS while I get out of this wet flight suit and into some khakis." He grinned into the mirror. "See what you can do when you're a carrier pilot?"

"Yeah! That was really something. D'you do that often?"

"Only during duck season."

"Hey, Harpo, Mary's here again," came Red's voice over the phone in the LSO ready room. Mary Roe had driven down from Jacksonville to surprise me and she didn't want to go home without a date. "Listen to this." Red described the scene: "I'm sittin' in the rockin' chair readin' the paper. Mary kneels down next to me and whimpers, 'Ayed, do you think Johnny LUUVES me?'." Red aped her southern accent. "I told her 'HELL NO!' as forcefully as I could, but she still wants to see you."

"Where the Hell is she now?," I demanded.

"How the hell would I know," Red countered. "Shoppin' I suppose. Isn't that where girls go? . . . But don't worry JOHNNY, she'll be back," Ed teased.

"Thanks a hell of a lot. Damn it! I told her not to come down here. For Christ's sake. The last time she came down I took her to Kitty Davis' for dinner, took in a couple o' clubs, and when we got home she wanted my bed and told me I could sleep on the couch, such as it is, that old wicker thing," I groused. "Said she'd had a bad riding accident so her romance was limited to kissing. I'm not makin' that mistake again." I was searching for an escape. "If she comes back, tell 'er I'll be along about eighteen thirty." *Then what?*

"Whaddya mean, 'IF'," Red chortled. "She'll be back all right – and hurry up." Ed's impatience was showing. "I don't want to have to entertain 'er any more."

"Okay, okay! I'll get there as soon as I can." I was trying to think what to do with Mary. *Better get her a Motel – hamburgers for dinner – and send her home tomorrow. Yeah, that'll work – I hope.* I dreaded the process.

"Navy Key West, this is Navy Seven seven zero, request water landing instructions." I was circling just north of NAS Key West with Stu Stephens' brother Frank in the back seat of the J2F *Duck*. Chief Aviation Machinist's Mate Smith was secured in the bilges against the possibility of a mechanical problem. Stu had asked me to take his brother, a civilian, to Key West, without the slightest hint as to his mission, which was apparently official.

"Navy Seven seven zero, this is Navy Key West. Wind northwest, fifteen knots, moderate chop, ebb tide. Sea way is clear. You're cleared to land."

The Air Station lay on a spit of land at the east end of Stock Island with the seaplane recovery ramps sloping northward into the sheltered cove that served as their seaplane operating area.

Switching to intercom I announced, "Prepare to land. Mr. Stephens, snug up your shoulder harness. Smith, secure all loose gear."

"All secure aye, sir," Chief Smith acknowledged.

"All snug," Frank reported.

The loud rush of water against the hull told us we were down and skipping along the "moderate chop", then, SPLOOSH. The *Duck* did its sinking act, stopping dead in the water. I added power and, with considerable difficulty, turned the *Duck* downwind to taxi toward the seaplane ramps. The "moderate chop" threw water up into the propeller and the quartering wind blew it back on us. By the time we got close to the ramp we were soaked to the bone.

Now, Stu said to head for the ramp at moderate water taxiing speed and lower the gear in time to roll up on the ramp. Then give it enough power to climb up the ramp and onto the parking apron – simple.

While holding the landing gear crank handle with my right hand I released the up lock and let gravity extend the gear while holding the crank handle to prevent it running away. *Hmm. The water really reduces the runaway tendency. It's not hard to hold at all.* This was the first time I had lowered the gear in the water.

Whoa! A second ago I was lined up with the ramp. Now I'm off to the right, going farther right, and the quartering wind's blowing me onto the breakwater – too close now – time to get out o' here! I remembered to chop the throttle and kick full right rudder as I cranked the gear up, and the *Duck* lurched around into the quartering wind. I poured the coal on to get back out into deep water.

Whew! I made it. But what the hell happened? What pushed us off to the right of the ramp? Not the wind. It was from our starboard quarter. Hmm. "Ebb tide" the tower said. Let's see. The tide must go out toward the Gulf of Mexico, west-ward. Yeah, that would be flowing left to right when I'm approaching the ramp. I know. I'll start my approach lined up to the left and let the current carry me into the center of the ramp. Well, here goes.

I lined up about fifty feet left of the ramp and got her stabilized on a crabbing course toward the center of the ramp and lowered the gear.

Whoa! Here we go again. With gear down the *Duck* slowed down so much that the current took over and we were again headed for the rocks west of the ramp with the wind blowing us on shore. *Cut power! Full right rudder! Gear up! Lets get the hell out o' here!*

Jeez, what do I do now? Gotta get Frank on the Air Station or my ass is a grape. Hmm . . . Y'know, if I leave the gear up 'til I'm just short of the ramp I can probably keep my speed up and maintain a crabbing course to the ramp . . . Okay. That's it. Last try.

This time I lined up about seventy-five feet left and made my target the left edge of the ramp. *Ooh, lookin' good. Trouble is I don't know how steep the ramp slopes into the water. Gettin' close. Okay. Gear down . . . NOW!* I unlocked the gear handle and cranked frantically. CRUNCH! We came to a grinding stop with the float about half out of the water. *Oh oh! I didn't get the gear down in time. Now what to we do?*

A swarm of sailors slogged out into the water and pushed us out, away from the ramp, and one of them hollered: "GEAR DOWN NOW!"

Christ! we're drifting! I thought, as I frantically cranked the gear down all the way. "Gear down and locked!," I shouted.

The whole crew half waded, half swam, around to the tail of the *Duck* and pushed us up onto the ramp and into a nearby parking spot.

Chief Smith leapt to the concrete and reported glumly, "She's leakin' sea water out of a hole just for'rd o' the step, sir. You must've run aground." There wasn't even the hint of derision, though I thought there should have been.

As I hopped down off the float a full lieutenant stomped up, eyes blazing. "Why the hell didn't you SAIL her in, MISTER?" Talk about derision. It was hung all over the "MISTER."

"Sail her in? How do you do that, sir?," I asked, lamely. "This's the first time I ever tried it, sir, and . . ."

"You God damned carrier pilots are all alike. You think you can do anything without any training. How'd you like to try to land on a carrier without any FCLP?" My shiny, month old Lieut.(jg) bars were a sharp contrast to the salty railroad tracks worn by my critic.

"Sir, when I got checked out, I . . ."

"By some other dumb ass carrier pilot I'll bet." He was venting his obvious animosity toward carrier pilots and, I guessed, his disappointment at being stuck in P-Boats.

"Yes Sir, one of our senior instructors at NAS Miami. Would you tell me how I should have done it, sir?" I bowed just a little. "My name's Harper, sir." I extended my hand.

The lieutenant ignored my hand, "Well, your senior instructor ought to get busted."

Frank Stephens had climbed off the other side of the airplane and was striding purposefully toward the operations building. "Okay, Lieutenant (Junior grade) Harper, I'm Lieutenant George Proctor, Operations Officer, VP-17, stationed here at NAS Key West." He was cooling off a little now. "Didn't anyone ever tell you about sailing a seaplane?"

"No Sir."

"Well, look," Proctor began, warming to his subject. "When the wind is blowing onto the ramp, as it is today, it will blow the airplane onto the ramp with no help from the airplane's engines."

"Yes Sir, I sure found that out."

"Yeah, I noticed," he scolded. "Now, think of how to make the wind help you, eh? Just hold the airplane into the wind." He demonstrated with his right hand. "Let her idle, and drift backward, toward the ramp, at the wind's pace." Proctor was in his element. "If you need to correct your course, just turn to present one side of the airplane to the wind so it acts like a sail. The airplane will skid in the direction you turned the nose. If you need more correction to get to the course line you need, just add power. That'll also slow your progress toward the ramp. Do you understand?"

"Aye sir. I used to race sailboats on Lake Michigan so I think I understand the principle." I fawned a little. "Thanks a lot for the lesson." Shifting to my other problem I sighed. "I wish I could try it out but we seem to have a leak in the hull. D'you suppose we could get that fixed this morning, sir."

"I'll take you to the maintenance officer," Proctor offered. "And I'll give you some advice, Mister." He poked his right index finger at my chest. "Stay out of situations you don't know how to handle."

"Aye Aye, Sir," I almost saluted. "Hey Chief, come on, we're going over to maintenance to see if we can get this boat patched up. You know what we need don't you?"

"Yes sir." The chief kneeled down to take a closer look at the damage. "A little tin bender work ought to do it."

Two hours later and no sign of a metalsmith. "Didn't they say they'd send somebody out within an hour?," Chief Smith mused.

"Yeah," I agreed. "I don't think these P-Boat characters like having us carrier weenies around. You'd think they'd fix us up so we could get out of their hair."

"It's not much of a leak, Sir," Smitty ventured. "We could probably get off before we took on more than a gallon or two, especially with this wind, fresh onto the ramp, so you wouldn't even have to taxi."

Hmm. All I need is to sink one of our two Ducks. Talk about embarrassed. I'd probably get busted back to Ensign, or maybe Warrant Officer or something. Chief's right though. Wind's perfect. I can taxi off the ramp, crank the gear up, pour the coal on, and pull her off the water.

I started the engine, Smitty pulled the chocks and climbed into the bilges with the biggest rag he could find, and we taxied toward the ramp. In a moment, we were surrounded by the seaplane ramp crew waving us back. "Okay. Here we go," I yelled back to Smitty, waving the crew aside. "This is your idea, Chief. If I get busted will you give me a job?"

In the water now. We gotta be leakin'. "Hey Chief," I yelled down into the hull. "How does it look?"

"Just gettin' the rag wet now, sir," I heard from below. "We'll make it okay, just get 'er goin'."

Ahh. We're floatin' now. Crank the gear. No, dummy, ya gotta unlock it. There. CRANK! Crank fast! Ugh. Hurry . . . There, gear's up, locked – Stick back – FULL THROTTLE! "How's it look now, Chief?," I yelled as loud as I could because I didn't have a hand to hold the mike.

"Comin' in kind of fast now, Sir." I barely heard him over the engine noise. "Better get us off the water." Smitty's voice was calm, but urgent.

Son-of-a-bitch! This is takin' longer than I thought it would, with this wind.

"Get 'er up sir. We're leakin' pretty bad now," Smitty hollered.

Yeah! That's why it's takin' so long. That gash in the hull's givin' extra drag, and the water in the bilges isn't helpin' any, either. Damn! Got the nose too high. Get it down and plane! Yeah, that's better. The *Duck* slipped up onto the step.

"That's worse, Sir," Smitty hollered, with a touch of panic. "Comin' in by the bucketful now."

The *Duck* lurched into the air and everything seemed to get quiet, even with the characteristic ear piercing propeller whine. *Whew! We're up.*

"Hurray! We made it," Smitty hollered, with a tone of deep relief.

"Hey, Chief, you okay down there?," I managed, into the intercom mike.

"Yes Sir. Now I am. The water was up to my knees. I was gettin' worried, but it's drainin' out now . . . Request permission to move up to the aft cockpit, sir."

"Yeah, Chief. Come on up here. You might dry out before we get back to NAS." I said with a thankful shudder as we climbed to cruising altitude.

5

CARQUAL AND BUBBLES

"NEO flight, this is NEO-1. There she is. Right echelon and close up tight." Jim English's voice came into our ear phones. We guessed that the "NEO" radio call stood for Neophyte. Being the senior, Jim led our group of four SNJ-3Cs. The "C" designation meant the trainers were fitted with a tail hook and structural modifications necessary for carrier landings. USS *Charger*, an escort, or "Jeep", carrier relegated to pilot carrier qualification duty, was steaming in the Chesapeake Bay to avoid the German U-Boats lurking in the Atlantic just outside Hampton Roads. Shailer flew Jim's wing while I led the second section with "Junior" Hardin on my wing. "Junior" and I slid over into the right echelon. My stomach turned over at the thought of my first carrier landing.

"FLYTRAP, this is NEO one. Four chickens, bearing one nine zero, three miles, standing by for CARQUAL. All need eight. Over."

"NEO one, this is FLYTRAP. You're cleared to enter FLYTRAP pattern. Over."

"This is NEO one, Wilco, cleared to pattern."

"Flight, check hooks down. FLYTRAP'S turnin' into the wind, FOX flag's at the dip." Jim led us down to masthead level, past *Charger*'s starboard side, lining up with the wind streaks. "Stand by for the break." Seconds later he patted his head, pointed to Shailer, and banked smartly left to enter the downwind leg as we had been taught. Shailer did the same, and I was next.

Okay. Easy turn to downwind leg. I coached myself. *Whoa! Look at the size of that deck. Whoever called it a "postage stamp" was right . . . Hah! FOX two blocked. Jim's lookin' good comin' up the groove . . . Yeah! He's aboard okay. Caught an early wire, looks like . . . Abeam the Island – turn now. Constant rate turn. Yeah! Shailer's started his deck run for launch. Great timing. The LSO seems closer than in FCLP.*

HIGH. Signalled the LSO. *Ease throttle a little. Nose down a bit. Feel the sink. . . .* Now ROGER! *Nose up – eeeasy – add throttle.* Now a SLANT LEFT! *Okay. Drop the left wing a little.* ROGER now . . . *Comin' up on the ramp.* CUT! *Jam throttle off – Drop nose – Bank to deck center line – Stick full back to get the tailhook down!* CRASH! WHEEEE! – the shrill sound of the arresting wire running out. *On deck! Wow! My first carrier landing – No time to think about it now.*

The deck officer waved both hands, palms forward, toward the stern signalling me to release the brakes and roll backward with the wind. Then he clenched both hands, commanding: BRAKES! As soon as the crewman had released my tailhook from the arresting wire I got the HOOK UP signal and raised my tailhook. Next, the whirling two fingers, the signal for full throttle – Then, when he approved the sound of my engine, the deck officer pointed dramatically forward, thrusting his whole body toward the bow of the ship. Brakes off, my airplane lurched forward and accelerated smoothly. I got the tail up passing the island and eased her into the air yards short of the forward end of the flight deck. Then a smart right turn to clear my slipstream from the deck and a turn back to parallel the ship's course.

Whew! One landing out of the way. Seven to go. Oh oh! There's Junior, sliding in behind me. Must've gotten a WAVE-OFF – Too close, I guess – Deck probably wasn't clear . . . Start the turn to down wind now . . . Looks like the right interval . . . Crosswind now – Shailer runnin' down the deck for launch . . . Hmm. I was high last time – Ease 'er down – Nose up – Three point attitude. Steady. LOW! says Paddles. *Nose up – add a little throttle.* COME-ON! *Oh oh! I'm sinking – more throttle.* HIGH! *Damn! I over controlled.* WAVE-OFF! *Full throttle – bank left – climb past the LSO platform and parallel the ship's course. There's a lesson; I'd rather be a little high than low and slow.*

"NEO flight, This is NEO one. Rendezvous FLYTRAP angels one after you get eight." I heard Jim as I made my last approach. CUT! CRUNCH. Wheeee. *Ahhh! The sweet sound of success.* I had my eight carrier landings.

"Hi! Mr. Harper. What brings you here to the asshole of the universe?," Jim Anderson greeted me as I strolled into the Breezy Point Officers' Club, in search of Shailer's wife, Dot. Jim was the cadet at Miami who had a spectacular midair collision during one of our "Attack Tactics" flights and got out of it with a broken arm and some bruises. We got to know his unbridled humor well during our soirées from hospital confinement – Jim with his right arm in that grotesque cast propped up to shoulder level – Tim Gile soothing his ulcer with Scotch and milk – George Searle with his fat lip – and I with my post nasal drip. The girls loved the humor of it.

Jim was a little guy with a slight build, sandy hair, and a smiling freckled face. He actually looked like Spankey of the "Our Gang" comedy series. His Ensign's bars showed a little salt and his Khaki shirt was just rumpled enough to give that "fleet" look.

"Hey, Jim. Great to see you. Call me John, or Harpo, your choice." We shook hands. "Bein' an LSO trainee at the Carrier Qualification Training Unit . . . uh – CQTU to you – brings me here," I shrugged. "A bunch of us Miami instructors got tapped for LSO training and got our heads shaped by Stu Stephens, the Opa Locka LSO guru. You probably remember English, Cummings, and Volz from Miami. They're here too. I'm the only one from "Jumpin' Joe" Clifton's department. Guess they wanted to spread the pain. Not much trainin' left though. I got orders to *Ranger*. So what're you doin' here?"

"I'm in Commander Blackburn's FIGHTING Seventeen," Jim bragged, with emphasis on FIGHTING. We both knew "Tommy" Blackburn from Clifton's gunnery department. "I guess he asked for me. We're gettin' *Corsairs*, uh, F4Us. A real Cadillac of an airplane. I just got checked out last week." Jim's chest puffed just a little. "C'mon, let's have a drink."

"Can't right now. I'm meetin' Cummings' wife here and I wouldn't want to make her look for me." I scanned the area. "We're goin' to pick up Shailer at the hangar and all go to dinner downtown. He's out on the *Charger* now, wavin' CARQUALS." The idea light came on. "Hey! You're goin' on *Bunker Hill*, aren't you. Cummings is your LSO. D'you want to join us?"

"Oh! Hi Dot." I walked over and took her hand. Jim followed. "Hey, this is Jim Anderson, a friend of ours from Miami. Jim, this is Dot Cummings, Shailer's wife."

Dot was quite tall, with a lean angular figure and an attractive face, framed by her wavy, jet black, shoulder length hair. She wore a casual beige herringbone skirt and a green cardigan sweater over an embroidered white cotton blouse, giving her the type of confident beauty I associated with Vassar girls.

"Glad to meet you, Mrs. Cummings. Harpo was telling me about your plans and asked me to join you." Jim turned on the charm. "Would you mind?"

"Sounds like fun to me," Dot invited. "But please call me 'Dot'. Shailer tells me you're lots of fun. Now you can prove it."

"You're too kind," Jim fawned. "But I do have a few new stories I might try after we've had a couple of drinks."

"Well, I see he's not back yet," I concluded as I brought Shailer's nineteen forty-one maroon Chevy convertible to a skidding stop in front of the hangar. "I'll get a report on his ETA from OPS. Be right back." I tossed over my shoulder to Dot and Jim as I jumped out of the car and took the ladder two rungs at a time, up to CQTU Operations.

"Sorry Sir," Skopinski, the duty yeoman, answered. "We sent an extra CARQUAL group out just fifteen minutes ago. Mr. Cummings won't be in for another hour and a half or so."

"Can you get him on the radio for me?"

"I can try, Sir." "Ski" keyed his radio microphone. "FLYTRAP, this is NEO base, over."

"I hear you, NEO. What d'you need, over," came the reply, squawking in from *Charger.*

"Can you put Lieutenant Cummings on? Over."

"Stand by, NEO. I'll find 'im."

A couple of minutes later, "Hello NEO, Cummings here."

I grabbed the mike, "Hey, Shailer. Harpo here. I've got Dot here, and I ran into Jim Anderson at the club, so he's joinin' us. What's your ETA? Over."

"Great, but we just got another swarm o' qualifiers. That'll take about another hour. I already had a snack in the wardroom. Why don't you three go ahead and have dinner and pick me up about twenty hundred."

"Wilco. Twenty hundred here at CQTU OPS."

"Roger. See you then. Out."

"Thanks, 'Ski'. I guess we'll do what he says. See you later."

"G'night, Sir."

"Table for three, please." Nantucket was the best sea food restaurant in Norfolk, never mind that a New England special was a rarity on their menu. But they made up for it with superb local fare, like Chesapeake and Lynnhaven oysters and crabs, Little Neck and Cherrystone clams, and bluefish from the outer banks. While the outside looked like any other building in downtown Norfolk, the interior decor was strictly "old wharf" with rotted pilings, fish nets, and ships' wheels serving as booth dividers. The window table where the hostess seated us overlooked the main street, not any body of water.

"Good evening." The tuxedoed waiter bowed just a little. "Would you care for something to drink?"

"I got an idea. Champagne for the reunion!," Jim announced, gleefully.

"O.K. with me," I said, cautiously. "How about you, Dot?"

"I'll just have a little, thanks," Dot demurred. "I don't want to be tipsy when we meet Shailer."

Jim perused the wine list with a cosmopolitan air and paused for effect. "The Cordon Rouge Brut, please." He made his selection with a flair seemingly beyond his tender years. "Three glasses."

The waiter delivered the champagne in an elegant silver ice bucket and opened it with a ceremonial POP. Jim swirled the few drops the waiter had poured into his glass and examined it in the light. With a sniff at the lip of the glass he pronounced, "Hmm, nice nose." Then, after tasting it dramatically: "Magnificent, very dry with just a hint of fruit. You may pour." He granted with an elegant wave of the hand. Then, raising his glass in a toast, he announced solemnly, "To our missing naval hero, Lieutenant Jay-Gee Cummings." We had to drink to that.

Half way through the meal I summoned the waiter. "Another of the same, please. This one's dead."

The silver bucket came back with a fresh bottle of Cordon Rouge, which the waiter promptly opened. This time I tasted it, but I couldn't match Jim's ceremony. "Tastes okay to me."

Dinner and champagne exhausted, Jim and I split the bill, tipped the waiter, and helped Dot out of her chair.

"Oh oh!," Dot chirped as she floated through the Nantucket's foyer, barely escaping entrapment by one of the big fish nets. "I can't walk straight. Shailer'll know I've been drinking."

"Yeah! Here he comes now," I announced as we sat in Shailer's convertible on the parking apron watching Shailer taxi his SNJ up beside us and cut the engine, the line crewman chocking the wheels. Dot hopped out to greet him as he hopped down off the wing.

Paddles!

"God, Honey, what've you been drinkin'," Shailer demanded after he had given Dot a long, welcoming kiss. "You even look a little flushed."

"Champagne, Sir," Jim announced proudly from the back seat of Shailer's car. "A little celebration."

"Celebration? For what?" Shailer was a little put out, I guessed. "And stop calling me 'sir'."

"Yes sir – I mean okay, Catwalk," Jim stammered. "We thought . . ."

"We thought we'd celebrate the reunion," I finished for Jim.

"What reunion, fer Christ's sake?," Shailer challenged, still steaming.

"Well . . . er – there's you and Dot – and Jim and me – and. . .", I planned and rationalized as I went along. "I know, we can get some more Champagne and invite Shirley Volz over to your house. Red's out on shakedown."

"Yeah. We could invite the McConnells next door, too." Shailer was warming to the idea. "He's goin' to be my assistant on *Bunker Hill.*"

"I'll call Brad Ripley, you remember him from Miami. He'll think of some other Opa Locka refugees." Jim polished the idea.

"Okay, let's go. Where's the nearest liquor store?," Shailer hollered as he squealed tires past the corner of the hangar.

"Let's just get some more champagne," I proposed, as we stomped into the liquor store. "How many d'you think?"

"Couple o' bottles ought to be enough," Shailer ventured.

"Hell, Catwalk, two bottles isn't enough, just for us," I scolded. "We just polished off two bottles, the three of us."

"Yeah, I could tell," Shailer frowned. "Okay, let's get four."

At that Jim chimed in, "Hey! With all the people you're inviting, you better get eight."

"What do you mean 'all the people I'm invitin'," Shailer bristled. And then: "Well, Okay. What the Hell, if we don't drink it all, we'll keep it for another party . . . Wait a minute." Shailer halted us as we staggered out of the liquor store laden with shopping bags full of champagne. "Hell, we couldn't get eight bottles of champagne in our ice box if it was empty. Now we gotta get some ice." He dashed back into the store to ask directions to the nearest ice house.

"Here's a nice piece," Jim crowed as he herded a humongous block of ice along the sheet metal chute in the ice house, slipping and sliding and finally flopping flat on his face while a hundred pounds of ice slid menacingly toward us at ever increasing speed. CRASH! As Shailer and I jumped aside the block of ice smashed through the door into the ice house office, lodging against the side of the counter.

"Hey! Yer s'pose t' use the tongs, sir," the wide-eyed clerk yelled through the door.

"Fer Christ's sake, Jim, that chunk o' ice won't even fit in our house, much less in our sink," Shailer bitched, as we helped Jim to his feet.

"We need it, sir! . er . I mean CATWALK, we gotta cool those bottles off fast," Jim blurted out, feigning urgency. "Hell, I'm gettin' thirsty already. How much for the ice, my man," Jim demanded, arrogantly.

"A quarter."

The next morning, airborne out of NAS Norfolk: *Oh my God! That takeoff was shaky – Ouch! My head – I've never had a headache like this one . . . Eight bottles of Champagne for five people smacks of suicide . . . Hmm – maybe it's a Migraine. God damn! We gave a party and nobody came – except Shirley Volz, and she didn't drink much.*

I was bound for Creed's Field where I would get acquainted with Lieutenant Charlie Iarrobino, *Ranger*'s assistant LSO, and start working with Air Group Four. Commander Vossler, the CQTU skipper, had told me my orders to *Ranger* were on the way and that I would go aboard as second assistant LSO.

After a real ragged landing at Creed's I headed straight for the scuttlebutt for a drink of water. Hell! I was still drunk from the Champagne and my head hurt, bad. After ingesting about a quart of nice cool water I began to sober up, but my head still hurt and there was no Aspirin in sight. A temperature of ninety-five and humidity at ninety percent didn't help matters.

I found Iarrobino in the ready room talking to a group of pilots. "Hi Harpo." We had met before, at the O' Club. "Hey, you guys. This is John Harper – Harpo to you. He's comin' aboard for this cruise to work with us at landing signals." Charlie started the introductions. "This is 'Pete' Peterson, commanding the Torpedo Four detachment that's going with us to Africa – Geoffrey 'Hail' O'Mary there – Phil Collins, we call him 'Tom' – George 'The Hat' Hatfield – and Russ 'Shakin'' Aiken." There were handshakes all around. "You'll meet the others as we go along."

The placards on their flight suits told me that "Pete", was a full lieutenant, "Hail", "Tom", and "The Hat" were jay-gees and "Shakin'" was an ensign. "Pete", about six feet tall with weathered features, showed his Scandinavian heritage with his blond crew cut and piercing blue eyes. O'Mary was a short quiet guy with the black kinky hair and impenetrable black eyes of a black irishman. *Jesus! How can this little guy handle that big Avenger. He can't be over five-foot-six.* I thought to myself. "The Hat", quite handsome under his tousled red hair, showed the marks of an Ivy League B.M.O.C. in his hand tailored uniform shirt and confident manner. Aiken was a lean six-foot-two with corn silk hair and an angular, English looking, face – very young.

"Jesus Christ, Harpo, What the hell happened to you," Charlie chided. "You're pale as a ghost, bleedin' from both eyes, and those look like valpacs under your eyes." Think you're goin' to live?"

"I'm fine, sir," I lied. "But I could use an Aspirin."

"Hell! I can fix that," Shakin' offered, unzipping the little pocket on the left sleeve of his flight suit. "Shit! I keep these with me all the time. Big nights make for the big head in the morning." He handed me the Aspirin bottle, proudly.

"God damn, its hot out here," Charlie shouted over the noise of the five TBF *Avengers* taking off for bounce drill. "How're you feelin' Harpo?"

"Much better, Sir," I exaggerated, but the Aspirin was having some beneficial effect. "Jeez! Those TBFs are big airplanes."

"Biggest single engine airplane in the world," Charlie bragged. "Wait'll you see one comin' up the groove."

I didn't have to wait long. "I'll be a son-of-a-bitch! The long belly on that TBF really shows up in a three point attitude. What a monster!" I shouted in amazement as I peeked over Charlie's shoulder watching him bring the first *Avenger* to the CUT position. ROGER all the way.

WHOOSH! "Wow! That was a smooth approach. And the touchdown seemed quieter than an SNJ." I marvelled, as Charlie turned to pick up the next TBF coming up the groove.

"Yeah, that was Pete. He's a smooth son-of-a-bitch. Been flyin' *Avengers* off *Ranger* since Grumman invented 'em. Got a couple o' hundred carrier landings. He's the squadron exec." Charlie stopped abruptly. "Oh oh! Here comes Shakin'. Now you'll see a contrast." Iarrobino showed Aiken a HIGH.

"Awful high isn't he?," I suggested.

"'Bout out o' range, but we'll work on 'im." Charlie shook his HIGH signal and we heard a drastic power change. The *Avenger* began settling dangerously.

"DAMMIT!," Charlie cursed as he shifted to a frantic COME-ON. "Come on with the power, Aikin, you idiot!" We heard the sudden surge of power. "Yeah!" Charlie cheered. "Now stabilize, You dumb shit! A little lower now." He signalled HIGH-DIP.

Aiken pulled the power off again and began settling. "I give up. Fer Christ's sake, he doesn't even know what a HIGH-DIP is," Charlie cursed as he flashed a frantic WAVE-OFF. "Aiken just came over from CQTU. Don't they teach 'em anything over there?"

"Listen up, men!" Back in the ready room, Iarrobino was addressing the pilots who had just completed bounce drill. "Pete: You made six nearly identical approaches. Every one smooth but just a little fast. That's okay if you don't mind seeing the ramp when you get your CUT."

"O'Mary: Your speed and altitude control is pretty good, but you consistently angle into the deck. You're making your turn from the downwind leg too sharp, leaving yourself no choice. Make that a constant rate turn all the way into the groove."

"I can't see over the nose unless I angle, sir," O'Mary pled.

"Get another cushion then," Charlie ordered. "You won't get aboard with that angling approach."

"Hatfield: You're having trouble with airspeed control because you're too fast on the downwind leg. Get stabilized at five or ten knots above the approach speed before you start your cross leg turn. Then concentrate on managing your own speed and make your corrections with as little throttle adjustment as possible."

"Collins: Nice approaches, but you're lining up on the starboard side of the deck. Just move the LSO a little toward the center of your windshield."

"Aiken: Do you know what a HIGH DIP is? I had to give you one almost every approach and you kept over controlling. Tell me. How do you respond to a HIGH DIP?"

"Means just a little high, doesn't it, Sir?," Aiken ventured.

"Yeah," Iarrobino coaxed. "Go on. What else?"

"Well, I guess I should lose some altitude, huh?"

"That's right. How?," Charlie was reeling him in.

"Pull off some power, and . . ."

"JESUS CHRIST!," Charlie exploded. "Where in God's name did you ever learn that?"

"CQTU I guess, Sir." Shakin' was shakin' in his boots.

Paddles!

"Well, you're goin to UN-learn it fast, son, before you kill yourself and we lose an airplane." Iarrobino was very serious. "You'll muster here tomorrow at oh-six hundred for a briefing on signals and responses. Then you'll get your final exam with the oh-seven hundred FCLP. I mean FINAL."

"Any questions men?" Charlie resumed his calm demeanor. "Otherwise you're dismissed. Muster oh-seven hundred tomorrow for FCLP." He started to leave, then turned abruptly to face Aiken. "And stay off the booze tonight!"

After the pilots had jostled each other out of the ready room door, Charlie sighed, "Where the hell do they find these kids anyway?"

6

INTO AFRICA

"Langley Tower, this is NAVY 7851, one SNJ over Buckroe, request landing clearance." Lieutenant Commander Stuart's voice came through my ear phones in the back seat of the SNJ advanced trainer we used for transportation. Bill Stuart was *Ranger*'s Landing Signal Officer – my boss.

"NAVY 7851, have you in sight," came the tower's response. "You're cleared to enter the pattern for runway two six. Wind two eight zero, fifteen to eighteen knots. Check two P-40s on down wind leg. You're number three to land. Over."

"Roger, Langley Tower. I'm cleared number three to land, runway two six," Stuart responded, banking left to enter the downwind. "Have two P-40s in sight, downwind."

"See all those P-40s lined up on the west end of the ramp down there, Harper?," Stuart prompted over the intercom.

I scanned neatly parked Curtiss *War Hawks* on the parking apron as it passed under our left wing. "Yes sir."

"Well, we're goin' to take the whole batch of 'em to Africa next week to reinforce the desert campaign against Field Marshal Erwin Rommel, Germany's "Desert Fox" – Classified info, mind you."

"Wow – All of 'em sir?," I gawked. "On *Ranger*? Where the hell are we goin' to put 'em – not to mention where we'll put our Air Group?"

"I'll give you the plan later, son," Stuart assured me just before touching down about fifty feet beyond the runway threshold, tail wheel first. Then he taxied smartly to park among the P-40s.

Paddles!

Stuart jumped down from the wing of our SNJ and strode toward the Army major who greeted us. "Hi, Billy. How many do I get today?" His grin wrinkled his weathered face from forehead to Adam's apple and lit up his blue-green eyes. Major Billy Bloodworth was the operations officer for the Three Twenty-Fifth Fighter Group, the guys with the P-40s.

Stuart was a Cock-of-the-Walk kind of guy – about five foot seven and a hundred and forty pounds. Doffing his helmet, he revealed a freckled bald head rimmed by well trimmed rust-red hair matched by his shaggy carrot eyebrows. His swagger was exaggerated by his noticeably bowed legs.

"Colonel George wants to try a full group launch today," Bloodworth reported, "D'you think we're ready?"

"Great idea," Stuart responded. "With only three days left before we shove off, we need a couple of dress rehearsals to get everybody ready."

"Here they come, Harper," Stuart noted as we watched the P-40s taxi out to the end of the runway, Lieutenant Colonel George in the lead. "You'll be my log yeoman today – got it?" He handed me the small green covered journal. "Log each aircraft's tail number and I'll give you comments on each launch." He pointed down the runway. "That soldier down there is stationed where the runway is marked to simulate the forward end of the flight deck. He'll signal whether each aircraft gets off before reaching the deck-edge mark. Log that too."

"Aye aye, Sir," I acknowledged. You must've been trainin' these guys for a while if they're ready for a group launch, sir."

"Only a week," Stuart shuddered. "But we're goin' to hoist their aircraft aboard next Monday and they've got to be ready to fly off the ship."

Colonel George taxied up, canopy open, goggles down, and white scarf billowing in the slipstream. "Hold it right there!," Stuart commanded to no one in particular as he held his clenched fists high.

The P-40 came to a full stop and held it as the P-40 pilots had been briefed to do. Stuart's "Rev" signal – two fingers of the right hand rotated above his head – brought forth the sharp whine of the big three bladed propeller driven by the twelve cylinder Allison V1710 engine at three thousand RPM. Only after Stuart's ear told him the engine was delivering full power and Colonel George signalled a thumbs-up did Stuart, with studied flourish, bring his right arm down and point dramatically toward the soldier down the runway.

The P-40 accelerated rapidly, but drifted to the left until George got enough right rudder control to overcome the propeller torque and barely hold the airplane on the runway, raising his tail abruptly and maintaining that attitude until he yanked the *War Hawk* off the runway and staggered into the air – but only after knocking out a runway boundary light.

"How's it goin' Stuart?," Colonel George shouted, as he jumped from his jeep. He had landed, parked his airplane, and roared out to watch the last of his chickens launch. George was the living image of an Army pursuit pilot – tall and lean, with a handsome, weathered face and wavy gray hair. He wore Army cavalry breeches and boots, topped by the obligatory leather flying jacket decorated with silver leaves on the shoulder epaulets and a leather name placard showing silver wings with star and wreath. His uniform cap showed the typical Air Corps slouch.

"Only fair, Colonel," Stuart reported. "Most of 'em have the same problem you had – not enough right rudder."

"Yeah. That's something we'll have to get used to," George mused.

"Exactly right," Stuart urged. "Unless you want some of your aircraft in the port catwalk – or worse – over the side. Well, here comes another of your troops." Bill raised his clenched fists and waited for the P-40 to come to a full stop.

At the two-finger signal the P-40 came to life with its characteristic propeller whine and held it until Bill gave him the go signal. "Whoa!," Bill yelled into the slipstream. "Right rudder! For Christ's sake, RIGHT RUDDER!" All to no avail as the P-40 turned abruptly left and tore off between the runway lights and across the open area between runways. The power came off suddenly, just before the aircraft struck a ditch, shearing off the landing gear and sliding to an abrupt stop. Instantly, the pilot was out and running clumsily toward us with parachute flopping behind.

"God damn these fuckin' junior birdmen," George cursed, in the direction of the approaching pilot. "I've got more than my share of these simpering high school kids. Shit! I'll be lucky to get half of these birds to Africa. We'll never get that one fixed in time. I'll have to see if I can steal one from some other squadron. Fat chance."

"Okay, Colonel," Bill tried to calm George down. "Let's get back to the ready room and give 'em a de-briefing, emphasizing RIGHT RUDDER."

"I'll get their attention first," George bristled. "Maybe the idiots will listen this time."

"Sir, You know you almost did the same thing," Stuart chided, then shifted to encouragement: "Don't worry. You and your guys are goin' to make it just fine. And I'll bet you find a replacement airplane."

At the top of *Ranger*'s brow at the Norfolk Naval Operating Base pier I turned to salute up and aft, toward the approximate location of the stars and stripes, then a salute to the officer of the day with: "Request permission to come aboard, sir."

"Permission granted," came the perfunctory response.

"I'm John Harper, the new assistant LSO," I began, not sure I should offer my hand. "This is my first time aboard." That was probably obvious but up to this time I had only come aboard a carrier by air.

"Glad to meet you," The Lieutenant (j.g.) in blues, with ceremonial sword, offered his hand. "Larry Adler here. Glad to have you aboard. You'll be working with Commander Stuart and Charlie Iarrobino, I guess."

Adler stood an inch taller than I and seemed slightly over weight. He had a round face with a prominent nose, beady black eyes, and close cropped black hair showing below his well starched white officer's cap. He sported the American Campaign ribbon signifying at least one sea cruise.

"How do I find my quarters?," I asked.

"Do you have an assigned stateroom?," Adler inquired.

"Yeah, three twelve."

Adler turned to the marine on duty with him. "Private, show Lieutenant Harper to his stateroom, three twelve." And to me: "This is Private Donner. He'll show you the way.

"Aye aye, sir," Donner acknowledged with a smart salute. "Come this way, sir."

"Your first time aboard a carrier, sir?," Donner inquired as we picked our way forward through the airplanes.

"I've been on and off *Charger* and *Card* for carrier landing qualification, but I never got below decks, except to the ready room and wardroom." Soon I realized that the hangar deck was absolutely packed with P-40s, to the extent that two of them were suspended from the overhead.

"You can probably guess this is the hangar deck, sir, also designated the first deck, and it is the armored deck." Donner shouted over his shoulder as we continued forward through a water tight door and into a narrow passageway. "Now we're in officers' country." A few steps farther and Donner pointed down through a hatch in the deck, directing: "Take this ladder down two decks, sir. You'll find your stateroom on the port side aft o' the ladder."

"Thank you," I said, starting down the ladder.

"S'cuse me, sir, but considering where your quarters are, you need to know about General Quarters," Donner began. "When G.Q. is sounded, you get two minutes to get up through this water tight hatch before the crew closes it and dogs it shut. They secure the one we just came through the same way." He pointed back at the bulkhead hatch, then to the ladder going up. "From here you can continue up this ladder to the oh three deck. The ready rooms are up for'rd and you can get to the flight deck by one of the athwartships passageways. Good luck, sir," Donner saluted.

"Thanks again." I returned Donner's salute and turned to descend the ladder.

Whew! I sure don't like the idea of living below the armored deck. This sounds like an indoctrination for new boy reserve aviators. The sight of my two pieces of aviator's green luggage was a welcome relief, delivered as advertised.

Hmm. Cozy little cabin – about half the size of a room in the BOQ – double bunks – a tiny desk and a small closet. All I need, I guess. No sign of a room mate. That would make it a little crowded. I'll just hope.

"Mr. Harper?"

I turned to discover a sailor peering in at me. "Yes, I'm Harper," I affirmed.

"Commander Anderson would like to see you in his office, sir," he announced.

"Yeah? When," I countered.

"Now, sir. I'll show you the way," the sailor offered.

Commander William Donald Anderson was *Ranger*'s air officer and therefore the senior man in my chain of command. All I knew about him was that he was one of the early naval aviators and seemed highly respected.

"Lieutenant (j.g.) Harper reporting, sir," I announced from just outside the air office.

"Come on in, Harper – Sit down, THERE," Commander Anderson ordered, gesturing toward the designated chair. He was seated in a comfortable leather swivel chair behind a desk that looked very large in the small shipboard office. He was a large man, somewhat out of shape I gathered by the bulges in the khaki shirt whose collar sported two silver oak leaves. His wavy, graying blond hair, curled mous-tache, and florid cheeks gave him the look of an English squire.

"Welcome aboard *Ranger*, Harper. I understand you've been training with Stuart and Iarrobino," said Anderson, drawing on his well worn Meerschaum pipe.

"Yes sir. FCLP with the VT-4 detachment and a little work with the Army over at Langley Field, sir."

Paddles!

"Good. Then you know we're going to Africa to deliver those P-40s," Anderson began in his fatherly manner. "It'll be a pretty dull trip for a few days since we can't fly our TBFs until we get rid of the Army. You're just temporary here, but I understand you'll be ordered to another carrier as soon as we get back. This lull in flight operations is your opportunity to learn something about how an aircraft carrier operates." He tapped the Meerschaum in the desk ash tray. "You know a little about aircraft recovery operations but you'll learn a lot more when we start flying the TBFs on ASW patrol. Get to know the flight deck officer, Lieutenant Commander Ottinger, and the arresting gear officer, Lieutenant (j.g.) Tyler." He poured a new charge of tobacco into the handsome pipe and tamped it down. "Ottinger was the 'Exec' of VB-4 until we transferred him to ship's company to run flight deck operations. 'Tip' Tyler is a reserve officer with a mechanical engineering degree from MIT, fresh out of the arresting gear school at the Philadelphia Navy yard. What he doesn't know about arresting gear nobody needs to know." Anderson's pride showed. "Learn as much as you can from these gentlemen." He flashed his Zippo lighter and drew fiercely on the Meerschaum to light it and then leaned back in his chair, exhaling a cloud of smoke.

"Aye, Aye, sir. I appreciate the opportunity," I started. "I already learned that I've got to move fast when I hear General Quarters since I bunk below the armored deck."

"Oh yes, General Quarters." The commander leaned forward and took the pipe in his right hand. "You don't have a General Quarters station unless we are recovering aircraft. I want you to stick with Stuart and Iarrobino and learn. We could encounter German U-Boats at any time, so I suggest you drill yourself on how to make it topside before they dog the hatches. Your flight quarters station is topside on the flight deck – assisting Mr. Ottinger during launch in any way he may specify – and Stuart and Iarrobino at Landing Signals during recovery."

"Now, go and get yourself squared away." The commander seemed irritated. "And get rid of that preppy black knit tie." He poked the stem of his pipe at my tie. "You're in the NAVY now, not in your FRAT house!" There was derision all over the "FRAT."

I think it looks pretty classy, myself, sir. I thought. But I didn't say it.

"I'm sure you have a uniform tie, like this one." He flipped his black tie for emphasis.

"Yes sir, I have one."

Chapter 6: Into Africa

"Then WEAR it, and BURN that knit monstrosity," He shouted, with a scowl, blowing a large cloud of tobacco smoke at me. "Until then, MISTER, you're out of uniform."

Oh oh. I already goofed. It's obvious that Commander Anderson doesn't cotton to preppy reserve officers and insists on strict adherence to the uniform regulations.

Back at my stateroom I started unpacking my bags.

"Hi Lieutenant Harper." It was Grogan, the Army pilot who had run his P-40 off the runway and into a ditch. He peered in at me through the parted curtains at my door. He was a scrawny kid, only about five-foot-six, with a heavily pock marked face, greyish eyes, and unkempt dishwater blond hair. "Looks like we're neighbors." He took a couple of steps into my stateroom. "I think all of the 325th is billeted on this deck and the one above, except for Colonel George and the squadron commanders. They're up on the oh two deck with the Navy. What're you doin' down here?"

I took him to be a warrant officer by the rank insignia on his collar, a blue bar rimmed in gold. "Oh – hi Grogan." I wasn't thrilled with the neighborhood. "What do I call you? I'm not familiar with your rank insignia."

"We're 'flight officers'. The Army ran out of its ration of second lieutenant slots so they made almost our whole class Flight Officers – a non-rank," Grogan groaned. "Christ, about a third of the group is flight officers."

"I wasn't in on your last two launch drills at Langley," I began. "How'd you guys do? D'you think you're ready to launch off *Ranger*?"

"Pretty well, I guess," Grogan squirmed. "'Least nobody ran off the runway. But I ain't lookin' forward to tryin' to get my P-40 airborne off this boat."

Hmm. "My P-40" he says. "I gather Colonel George got a replacement for that airplane you busted," I ventured.

"Yeah." Grogan flushed a little. "Scrounged one from some squadron that's not scheduled to go until April – Pretty good airplane, too – Better'n the one I had."

"Don't forget; FULL right rudder when you crank up, and hold it until you start turning right on your take-off run, then straighten out," I coached. "You'll make it just fine.

"Thank you, sir," Grogan backed out through the curtains. "See you later."

Paddles!

CLANG! CLANG! CLANG! TOO-WEEEE! The boatswain's pipe sounded over the P.A system. "ALL HANDS, MAN YOUR BATTLE STATIONS – ALL HANDS, MAN YOUR BATTLE STATIONS!"

God Damn! I woke with a start. *General Quarters. What the Hell time is it, anyway? Where's the damned light switch? There – light on – DAMN! Now I can't see a thing.* I thought, squinting in the bright light. *Off with the friggin' light . . . Christ! It's two-thirty.* I could barely read the radium dial on my watch. *You dumb shit! You probably already used up a whole minute screwin' around with the light. And you got blinded in the process.* I was cussin' myself for not planning and drilling my G.Q. escape procedures. *C'm on. Shirt on! Pants on! Socks – T'hell with the socks. – Shoes! Never mind the laces! GO!*

My eyesight was returning in the dimly lit passageway as I ran . . . CRUNCH! "OWW! My head," I groaned as I picked myself up off the deck. *Son-of-a-bitch! That ladder slopes down just right to catch a guy in the head – Damn! It's bleedin' – Never mind. HURRY! Double steps up one ladder – around to the next – Double steps up.* CLONK! "OW!" *Shit! Hit my head on the water tight hatch . . . CLOSED!* I could hear the crew dogging the hatch down. BANG BANG. I beat on the hatch. "Open up. I gotta get to my battle station," I lied, as loud as I could yell . . . No answer.

Shit! I'm stuck below decks. Just what I didn't want to happen. I could hear the rush of personnel on the first deck en-route to their battle stations.

"Hey! What the hell's goin' on?" I recognized Grogan's voice. "What're you waitin' for."

"'Fraid we're stuck, Grogan." I was embarrassed. "Hatch's already secured – dogged from the top side."

"What do we do now?," he demanded.

"Might as well go back to our bunks and relax . . . and hope we don't get torpedoed." I resolved to make a timed escape plan and drill myself before the next call to battle stations.

"Morning Harpo," Charlie Iarrobino greeted from the base of the island, his hair and clothes flapping in the fresh Atlantic breeze.

"Hi, Charlie." I gave a casual salute. "I see they've got our four TBFs lined up, starboard side, for'rd o' the island."

"Yeah," Charlie shrugged. "That leaves the aft flight deck for parking P-40s for their daily engine run up – can't fly 'em anyway, long as the Army's aboard.

Chapter 6: Into Africa

"How's it goin' anyway? Y'gettin' acquainted with the ship okay?"

"Okay, so far, I guess," I ventured. "Only I'm billeted on the third deck, down in the bilges. Hard to sleep with all that paint chippin' goin' on." I rubbed a little sleep out of my eye. "Do they do that all day and all night?"

"Emergency – three shifts," Iarrobino groaned. "NAVY's been goin' for years just paintin' over the old paint. When *Wasp* was sunk the NAVY realized that all those layers of paint just fueled the fires aboard ship." He grimaced. "She went up like a torch – so we're chippin' off all the old paint. New fleet order says only one coat o' paint from now on."

"Wow!," I exclaimed. "That's scary." Then: "I don't have a room mate but I'm surrounded by Army fly boys – and last night I got stuck below decks during General Quarters. What the hell happened to require G.Q. . . . . U-Boat scare?"

"Naw," Charlie snickered. "Cap'n Durgin always calls a G.Q. drill the first night out to be sure everyone knows where their battle stations are – and how to get there!" With that, he laughed out loud – at me, obviously. "What the hell happened to your head? Looks serious."

"Oh, nothin'. Just bonked it on the ladder trying to get topside in the dark last night."

"Oww, that smarts," Charlie sympathized.

"Yeah, sure did. Doesn't hurt much any more though," I lied.

"That's not all," I confessed further. "I got chewed out by Commander Anderson yesterday for wearing my black knit tie. 'Preppy' he called it – bad start."

"Don't worry," Charlie soothed. "The air boss always hazes reserve officers when they come aboard. I can vouch for it." He grimaced. Then, shifting to business: "He told me to be sure you get a complete familiarization with flight deck operations, from launching to landing, and the intricate art of spotting aircraft on deck, too." He started aft and waved at me to follow. "C'mon. George Ottinger is back aft, tending his flock of *War Hawks*."

"I see we've got company," I commented, looking off across the sea as we strolled aft.

"Yeah." Charlie pointed toward the largest of the accompanying ships. "That's *Tuscaloosa*, an old heavy cruiser, there's our oiler, *Chicopee*, to keep the force in fuel oil, and those destroyers out there form a screen to stop the U-Boats – we hope. These waters are infested with the buggers."

As we approached the flight deck officer, the P-40s spotted aft began coming to life, their engines first sputtering, then assuming their characteristic purr.

Paddles!

"Hey, George, this is John Harper, our third LSO – Harpo to you," Charlie began. "Harpo, meet George Ottinger."

As we shook hands Charlie continued: "The air boss told me to be sure he gets acquainted with all aspects of flight deck operations, so we're starting with you."

"Yeah, Andy said I could use him while you're not recovering aircraft – like from now 'til we lose these P-40s." Ottinger was warm, though official. "Hell, I can always use an extra hand."

"How often do they run up the P-40s, Mr. Ottinger?," I queried.

"Call me George, for Christ's sake. We're not runnin' a parade up here," Ottinger shot back. He was a chunky guy almost six feet tall, apparently in excellent physical shape at about 185 pounds. His ruddy face featured steel blue eyes, a small, straight, nose and high cheek bones, revealing his German heritage. His yellow cotton helmet and yellow T-shirt identified him as a airplane director. Hell, he was the BOSS plane director.

"How often we run up the P-40s was a big bone of contention with Colonel George." Ottinger waved his arms at the mass of whirling propellers. "For God's sake! He wanted to run 'em up every day. I mean EVERY FUCKIN' ONE every day. I got him down to every other day, with Andy's help." He was proud of that. "But that means we gotta re-spot BOTH the flight deck and the hangar deck, EVERY DAY – SEVENTY-FIVE God damned airplanes. We sure as hell can't run up thirty airplanes on the hangar deck." He threw his hands up in a sign of resignation. "Oh, what the hell, it's good exercise for the crew – keeps 'em out o' trouble since we can't operate anyway."

"What do you do with the ones hangin' in the overhead?," I asked.

"Hah! I told the Colonel." Ottinger stood a little taller. "Whoever flies those birds off'll just have to pray a lot. Was he pissed!" Ottinger threw his head back and laughed out loud. "'Best I can do.' I told him."

CLANG! CLANG! CLANG! TOO-WEEEE! "ALL HANDS, MAN YOUR BATTLE STATIONS . . . ALL HANDS, MAN YOUR BATTLE STATIONS!" *Whoa! G.Q. again. Hmm. Oh three forty-eight – probably not a drill – okay – escape plan: No light! Shirt – pants – socks – shoes.* Out the door I went. *Whoa! Idiot – forgot your life jacket – okay – got it. GO! Good – makin' good time – Now, miss the friggin' ladder! – Whew! Up two ladders and out through the open hatch . . . Made it!*

Chapter 6: Into Africa

As I returned the salutes from the dogging crew I thought: *Well, we detached from our support ships last evening with just two destroyers – "cans" in NAVY lingo – Ellyson and Rodman, for our two hundred mile run in to launch the Army for Safi, on the coast of Morocco. We heard there could be U-Boats in the area.*

Up on the moonlit flight deck I found Iarrobino among the crowd of curious "airdales" and Army pilots. "What's happenin', Charlie?"

"U-Boat contact, I understand," he yelled, excitedly. "Cap'n's maneuverin' to avoid a torpedo."

Yeah. Feel the starboard list – turning port – HARD!

"Stand clear the starboard side," came Captain Durgin's urgent voice over the bull horn. "Torpedo close aboard!"

Ignoring the warning, I was drawn, with half of the flight deck crowd, to the forward starboard catwalk – where the action was.

"There it is!" Someone was pointing straight down at the sea surface. "TOR-PEDO!"

I watched, spellbound, as the torpedo traced a dim line of bubbles only feet from our hull. Then the ship heeled hard into a turn to starboard to clear the ship's starboard quarter from the torpedo's path. *Whew! There it was, all right. And there we were, hangin' over the rail like a bunch o' cat birds. Jesus Christ, if the damn thing had exploded under us we'd all be DEAD MEAT. DUMB – DUMB. Well, I'm learnin' – fast enough to keep alive – I hope.*

Up on the flight deck there was a fresh breeze from the north northeast, fifteen knots I guessed, and a clear sky with just a few high cirrus. Today, we would launch the seventy-five *War Hawks* of the Three Twenty-Fifth Army Fighter Group. Commander Anderson had issued a number of instructions to the P-40 pilots, the last of which closed with: "Do not take this sheet or anything written with you that has *RANGER* on it. Refrain from any mention of *RANGER* or NAVY. Remember, we still have to get back."

I had stood by while Ottinger launched our four TBFs without incident. Then Captain Durgin had turned *Ranger* back to its easterly course to close the distance to the coast of Morocco while the TBFs established their sector antisubmarine patrols.

"C'm on over here, Harpo." Ottinger led me over to the starboard side, by one of the retracted barrier stanchions. "I usually launch aircraft from this tub, but Bill trained these Army fly boys, so he gets to launch 'em."

Paddles!

Bill Stuart was leaning against the wing of the first P-40 in line, giving Colonel George some last minute encouragement. *Don't worry about the colonel Bill, talk to some of those flight officers – They're scared shitless – Oh well – We gave 'em a final briefing – Too late now for any more help – They're on their own.*

Ranger heeled to starboard in her turn back into the wind, and the stacks belched black smoke as she accelerated to flank speed to give the Army as much wind across the deck as possible.

"Hey. This is only half of the P-40s, George," I yelled, into the freshening wind. "Are we only launchin' this many?"

"Naw," Ottinger drawled. "Colonel George's goin to have to join up the first thirty-nine and wait for us to bring up the hangar queens and launch 'em before he can head for the beach." He grinned. "You should o' heard 'im bitch about that. But Andy told 'im those were the facts of carrier life, and he shut up."

"STAND BY TO START ENGINES," roared Commander Anderson's voice on the bull horn. "STAND CLEAR OF PROPELLERS." The FOX signal flag flew at the dip, signifying imminent flight operations. Bill Stuart stepped back to starboard, clear of George's airplane. "START ENGINES."

Colonel George's starter sounded its grinding wail and his engine sputtered, then came to life with its twelve cylinder purr. The forty odd *War Hawks* followed suit, bringing a cacophony of engine and propeller noise along with the vibrant tonal beat generated by the difference in propeller RPM. One by one the pilots gave the thumbs up, after the customary engine check.

"LAUNCH AIRCRAFT," commanded the bull horn and FOX was two-blocked.

Stuart gave George the "Rev." signal with his small checkered flag. The *War Hawk's* engine roared to its three thousand RPM military power rating and I could see that George was holding full right rudder. His white scarf streamed from his neck and his chin jutted forward in a defiant sign of confidence as he put his goggles down and jabbed his right fist out of the cockpit, giving the THUMBS UP.

With the customary dramatic flourish, Stuart thrust his whole body toward *Ranger's* bow to point the checkered flag at the horizon, his khaki uniform flapping violently in the 35 Knot wind.

Yeah! Straight down the deck just like we taught him – tail up – very smooth – now, perfect lift-off – right at the deck edge in a three point attitude – easy right jog – Perfect! After his perfect launch, Colonel George climbed to 1,500 feet to wait for his chickens to rendezvous. *He's goin' to have a long wait.* I thought.

Chapter 6: Into Africa

The yellow shirted plane director brought the next P-40 out of its deck spot to the deck center stripe and gave him two clenched fists. It was one of the flight officers whose name I didn't know. His goggles were already down and the stoop of his shoulders telegraphed tension. As Stuart gave him the rev. signal the pilot's face was frozen in a mask of fear. *Like I said – Scared shitless.* At Bill's launch signal he released the brakes and hunched forward in fearful reaction to the short deck run ahead. To stop his drift to port he jammed on full right rudder and swung back to starboard. The tail came up abruptly – too high – he S-turned down the deck. The *War Hawk* went off the bow in a nose down attitude and disappeared from view.

"Christ in the foothills, George! I think we lost one," I screamed.

"Naw," Ottinger yelled back, unconcerned. You'll see 'im in a second.

And so we did, as he climbed out to join Colonel George.

With the first deck load launched, Ottinger had ordered his flight deck crew to bring the rest of the P-40s up from the hangar deck using both forward and after elevators. "God Damn, George, that was quick," I marvelled. "Less that fifteen minutes, I figure."

"Shit! We do a hell of a lot better'n that with our NAVY airplanes," Ottinger bragged. "These things take up too much room . . . not too bad so far, though." He grinned. "Damn near lost one in the drink, but he made it okay. I hope that one that clipped the port catwalk doesn't have a flat tire. That'd make for a hairy landing on the beach."

"Hi, Major," I waved to Major Jacobs, 45th squadron commander, as he hustled to his airplane, the first in line. "Good luck, and flame a couple of Messerschmitts for us."

"Thanks, Harpo, I'll do it." Jacobs waved back. "And you guys have a safe cruise back to Norfolk – and thanks for the ride."

"Now there's a smooth one," I confided to Ottinger. "This guy ought to be a carrier pilot, for Christ's sake. Watch this."

"Lookin' good!," Ottinger exclaimed, as Jacobs started down the deck, straight as a string, tail up, then down to float smoothly off the deck in a gentle right turn. "You're right about this guy. Best o' the bunch so far."

"Oh oh." I flinched a little as the next *War Hawk* taxied up to Stuart. "Here comes Grogan."

"Yeah? What the hell does that mean?," Ottinger asked, with a frown.

Paddles!

"Grogan's the guy who ran off the runway during launch drill at Langley and folded the gear in a ditch," I explained. "Good place for 'im – on Jacobs' wing. He'll learn fast or die young."

We were interrupted by the whine of Grogan's propeller at military power. *Uh huh – full right rudder like I told 'im – holdin' the center line, so far. Shit! I told him to let up on the right rudder when the airplane starts turning right but he's not straightening out.* "Get off the right rudder, Grogan, you idiot," I yelled, in vain, into the wind.

The airplane lurched to port just before the wheel would have gone into the starboard catwalk. *I'll be damned. He actually picked his right wheel up with his ailerons.* The tail came down abruptly, actually placing the tail wheel in the water-way before the *War Hawk* staggered into the air and skidded off to starboard. *Whew! How he did that I don't know.* Grogan raised his gear and regained control of the airplane to climb out, trailing Major Jacobs.

"There they go, all seventy-five of 'em," Bill Stuart crowed as we stood on the flight deck watching the 325th buzz by at mast head level in a neat formation of three squadrons in fingertip fours, Colonel George and his two wingmen out front. "A bit hairy, but they all made it."

"Pretty sharp bunch, huh?," I ventured.

"Taught 'em all they know," Stuart grinned. Then, in a serious tone: "I wonder how many of those guys'll be alive a month from now. That P-40's no match for the ME-109 the Krauts are sending to Rommel."

7

CHALLENGES

The dispatch orders, delivered over the signature of Captain Calvin T. Durgin, Commanding Officer, U.S.S. *Ranger*, read as follows:

WHEN DIRECTED BY CO ABOUT FEB 15 LT(JG) JOHN
A HARPER A VN USNR DETACHED PROCEED NEW YORK NY
REPORT COM THREE FOR FIRST AVAILABLE TRANSPORTA-
TION PORT SCORON 24 MAY BE ARRIVAL REPORT CO
SCORON 24 TEMPORARY DUTY INVOLVING FLYING X
UPON COMMISSIONING BELLEAU WOOD DETACHED PRO-
CEED REPORT BELLEAU WOOD DUTY INVOLVING FLYING
AS LANDING SIGNALOF XX

"Hey! Charlie." I found Iarrobino in the VT-4 ready room. "Help me with this, will ya? What's a 'SCORON'? And what in Hell is a 'BELLEAU WOOD'? A ship, I presume, but what kind, and what do they need ME for?"

"Whoa! Harpo." Charlie held up both hands, palms toward me. "I gather you got your orders. Lemme see."

"Here. I hope you can decipher this dispatch jargon."

"Hmm," he mused. "Means you're goin' to VS-24, a scouting squadron that's trainin' up to deploy aboard *Belleau Wood*." Charlie smiled at my naïvete. "'A' *Belleau Wood*, as you say, is one of the new class of small fast carriers being built

71

on light cruiser hulls – about ten or twelve thousand tons displacement. Smaller than *Ranger*, but a lot faster."

"I wonder who the boss LSO is," I thought aloud.

"I'll bet you're IT." Charlie clapped me on the back. "What the hell, the trainin' we gave you here qualifies you to be the number one. Besides, they're punchin' out carriers so fast CQTU can't keep up with the demand for LSOs. When're you leavin'?"

"Right away," I grinned. "Already checked out and got all my gear in my car. Might as well drop in and see my sister before I have to report. She lives on Long Island." Then: "I want to thank you and Mr. Stuart, and Mr. Ottinger and his crew for a great cruise." I extended my hand. "It was a hell of a learning experience."

As we shook hands Charlie said, "Good luck, Harpo. You'll need it. The Japs are sinkin' our carriers right and left out there."

"The CAG's been lookin' for you, Mr. Harper." The Yeoman offered from behind his grey steel desk at NAS Floyd Bennett as I took a seat on the overstuffed brown leather couch of the type found in all senior officers' offices. "We formed up last December and we're just about up to complement – but without an LSO." The plaque on his desk announced "Y2 C. A. Jansen."

BZZZZZ! "Yes Sir," Jansen answered his phone. "Yes sir, he's here – Aye Aye, sir." Then, to me: "You can go in now, sir."

"Thanks," I tossed back as I opened the door marked: "Lieut. Comdr. F. MASSEY, CAG-24."

"Lieutenant (j.g.) Harper reporting, sir," I announced, as I saluted the man behind the desk.

Massey sat, slumped at his desk, showing a deep weariness borne, no doubt, of the massive task of preparing an air group for deployment aboard a carrier. He rose and eased around his desk to extend his hand. "Welcome aboard, Harper," he offered, with some enthusiasm showing through his subdued manner. Massey was a slight man with a thin face, a prominent, beak-shaped nose, high forehead, and sparse, graying brown hair. His deep set sad eyes betrayed the same weariness, and a kind of foreboding, but no fear, per se.

"Sit down," Massey ordered, as he returned to his desk chair. "You're late! . . . But that's not your fault. CQTU can't keep up with carrier launchings. But it means you've got a lot of work to do and not much time to do it . . . and you'll be alone until we get another LSO to help."

Chapter 7: Challenges

"Yes sir. I think I know what to do and how to do it." I exaggerated my confidence to give him confidence – but he had his own thoughts.

"We're flying three different aircraft types with only four or five pilots who have ever been on a carrier before and we're scheduled to go to sea in May." He frowned, showing the strain in his twitching jaw muscles. "And I haven't yet gotten approval from the air station to fly bounce drill here." The frustration showed as he continued, "Your first job, Harper, is to find a way to conduct FCLP on Floyd Bennett – you'll have to negotiate with the station operations officer, Lieutenant Commander Greene, or find another field." He pressed his challenge.

Whoa! Little old jay-gee John is going to negotiate with a lieutenant commander – good luck. This job's gettin' bigger by the minute. "I should think training your air group would be top priority for the station command." I was incredulous.

"You'd think so, wouldn't you," Massey retorted. "But these guys don't know a war is going on, and don't want to know. Add to that the fact that we have to do enough night FCLP to be ready to night qualify aboard ship during our shake down cruise in May. . . Oh! By the way. I understand you were a gunnery and bombing instructor at Miami," Massey ventured.

"Yes sir. I worked for Commander Clifton down there," I bragged. "We used mostly F3Fs for our fixed gunnery; and dive bombing in an F3F is quite a thrill – no dive flaps you know."

"As I said before, we've only got four or five pilots who have ever been to sea," he continued. "I'm one of them and the bomber and fighter squadron commanders are two others. Then we have two fighter pilots who've been in the fleet and know what gunnery and bombing are about. The other senior pilots are career instructors. Beyond that, we've got a flock of ensigns barely out of training." Massey leaned forward, elbows on his desk, "Harper, I want you to teach my bombing squadron how to dive bomb with their SBDs and my torpedo squadron how to do fixed gunnery with that pea shooter we have in the nose of our TBFs." He leaned back again and watched me with an air of anticipation.

Whew! These shoes are getting bigger by the minute. First I'm supposed to put the arm on a reluctant station ops officer and now I'm supposed to teach whole squadrons how to bomb and shoot. "Sir, I know how to do it, but I'm so junior, and . . ."

"Never mind," Massey interrupted. "The squadron commanders are all for it. The main thing is to get the techniques across to the division leaders. That'll only take three or four flights and then you can check squadron proficiency before we go to sea." He was pleading, almost as though I had a choice. I knew I didn't.

What a job! All of a sudden I'm the authority, not only on carrier landing, but on weapon employment. Only four months ago I was still a lowly ensign. I sat taller in my chair as the tingle of pride washed over me. "I'll do the best I can, sir."

"Just so we understand each other," Massey summarized. "You have three main tasks: First, you will make the air group ready for flight operations at sea – BOTH DAY AND NIGHT – which includes your second task of arranging for FCLP on Floyd Bennett – and third, you will bring my bombing and torpedo squadrons up to minimal proficiency in dive bombing and gunnery."

"Yes sir. I understand," I acknowledged. "The first is what I'm trained for and the third was my job at Miami so I'm confident I can do those. Negotiating with a station ops officer two ranks senior to me is stretching it. I'll need your backing, sir." I pled.

"You'll have it, of course," Massey smiled. "But I want you to develop the options and work to find common ground with Greene." Continuing, Massey announced, "Captain Pride says he wants to see you as soon as you report. Take the SNJ to Mustin this afternoon. When you get there, just request transportation to the New York Shipyard over in Camden. You'll find the captain in his office aboard *Belleau Wood*, still under construction in the yard. He'll be expecting you – and get rid of that knit tie, MISTER," Massey suddenly erupted. "You're out of uniform, and, if I know Captain Pride, he won't be as patient as I've been up to now. You're dismissed!" He stood to accent the point.

"Aye aye, sir. Right away." *Hmm. And I thought Commander Anderson would be the only stickler about my knit tie. Must be a fetish with these canoe school guys. Well, I think that's the last chance for my knit tie, and it looks so stylish with the green uniform. Guess I better trash the handsome thing.* I thought as I retreated out of Massey's office.

As I watched the snow covered Pennsylvania countryside pass under the wing of the SNJ, I anticipated meeting Captain Pride with some trepidation. *Hmm. Captain Alfred M. Pride. Known to his peers as "Mel." I hear he's one of the early Naval Aviators and that he pioneered some of the arresting gear designs used in the fleet today. I guess it's good to have a skipper who knows a lot about the critical ship's gear. Gee, I've never spoken directly to a captain. Commander Gerald Bogan pinned on my wings and Commander Anderson chewed me out for being out of uniform but I've never been that close to a CAPTAIN. Oh oh. Here's Mustin Field.*

"NAVY Mustin, this is NAVY Oh Seven Six, one SNJ three miles northeast, request landing instructions."

"NAVY Oh Seven Six. This is NAVY Mustin. You're cleared to enter landing pattern for runway five, wind north, variable to northeast, ten knots. No other traffic at this time. Report downwind – over."

"She's right over there, sir," my driver announced as we drew to a stop near a dry dock in the New York shipyard in Camden. He got out, stepped around and opened my door, and I got out.

"Thanks," I shouted over the din of the ship construction.

"You're welcome, sir," the driver replied, without saluting. Then: "Request permission to visit ships service while you're in there, sir."

I thought for a minute. "I'm not sure how long this will take. Probably about an hour, but it could be longer. I'm meeting my skipper for the first time. Let's see." I consulted my watch. "It's now fifteen forty-five. Be back here at sixteen forty-five."

"Aye aye, sir," the driver acknowledged with a salute, and climbed back into the car.

As the NAVY car disappeared around the corner I scanned the lines of the dark form looming before me in the dry dock. *Hmm. Very narrow hull and sharp bow lines. She doesn't look at all like Ranger. Built for speed, looks like. Yeah, Charlie said she was a fast carrier . . . Uh huh – Stacks jutting out of the starboard side, around the flight deck – Island's only about a quarter the size of Ranger's – Must not be finished yet – Flight deck doesn't extend all the way to the bow – Maybe that's not finished, either.* There was the continuous clatter of rivet guns and the intermittent shower of sparks marking welding activity. It was clear that the urgency of war was driving this shipyard crew. The banner on the side of the brow announced "USS BELLEAU WOOD" in bold letters.

A marine private first class greeted me with a salute as I stepped off the brow onto the hangar deck. "Please state your business, sir."

"Lieutenant (jg) Harper reporting aboard for duty," I responded, as I fumbled for my orders. "Captain Pride is expecting me."

"Just a second, sir." The marine scanned my orders. "Hey, Sarge. This officer's reportin' for duty." He handed my orders to his sergeant, seated behind a beat-up grey steel desk with absolutely nothing on it. "Says he's s'posed to see the cap'n."

"Well, take 'im up there, then," the sergeant ordered. "And get back here – ON THE DOUBLE."

"Welcome aboard *Belleau Wood*," Captain Pride grinned broadly, returning my salute. "I'm certainly glad to see you, son. I've been waiting for an LSO for months." He exulted, as he stepped smartly around his desk to shake my hand, his sparkling blue eyes signalling his great pleasure.

"Glad to be aboard, sir." The regulation reply seemed inadequate to the occasion as I was fairly overwhelmed by the genuine warmth of the captain's welcome.

"Come and sit down over here," the captain invited as he made himself comfortable in the NAVY issue brown leather couch. I joined him.

Captain Pride was a round man about five foot nine with a full florid face marked by severe burn scars and a very high forehead fringed with sparse strawberry blond hair. *Hmm. I noticed a definite limp as he stepped over to the couch. Must have been in a serious airplane crash.*

"Tell me about your first meeting with Massey." The Captain leaned toward me in anticipation. "What are your priorities?"

I outlined my three major tasks as agreed with Massey.

The captain's eyes widened as I spoke, "Are you telling me that the NAS Ops officer won't allow bounce drill on the station?"

"That's what Commander Massey told me, sir," I ventured. "As I said, sir, that's my . . ."

"Your first priority. Right!" Pride's face flushed to a bright pink. "God DAMN complacent, do-nothing, beach bound NAVY. Don't they know a war is going on?"

"Commander Massey said they didn't, sir," I injected, cautiously. "He says they don't want to know."

"Yeah? Well I'll see that they find out," the captain fumed. "You get over and see that ops officer – uh, what's his name?"

"Lieutenant Commander Greene, sir."

"Well then." Pride's eyes hardened. "You get over and see Greene first thing tomorrow morning, remind him that there's a war going on, and tell him we've got to have FCLP on Floyd Bennett! Understand?"

"Yes, sir." I felt I was trapped. "But, being just a Jay Gee I have a little trouble . . ."

Chapter 7: Challenges

"Trouble, Hell," Pride shouted. "Tell 'im I said so." Then, angrily: "Greene's going to have a lot of trouble if we can't complete our training."

"Okay." He calmed down and his face returned to its normal mottled pink. "Now, about this gunnery instruction. Do you think you'll have time for that and still get enough bounce drill in to be ready for sea by May?"

"I think so, sir," I ventured cautiously. I really wanted the gunnery job. "When we're able to get on Floyd Bennett for FCLP I'm sure our hours will be limited. As you know, sir, the squadrons have hardly any pilots who know how to bomb and shoot. Sounds important to me." I prayed he wouldn't object.

"Okay," the captain sighed. "But don't forget your primary task – getting the air group ready for operations aboard this ship – DAY AND NIGHT!"

"Now." Pride leapt up out of the couch. "Let's take a little stroll on the flight deck and you can tell me what you learned on your *Ranger* cruise." He limped out of the office at a brisk pace with me in close pursuit. "We'll be back in twenty minutes." He tossed to his yeoman.

Marching down the flight deck at his rolling gait, he invited: "Now. Tell me about the *Ranger* experience."

"Well, sir." I wasn't quite sure what he wanted to know. "We couldn't operate our TBFs until after we got rid of the P-40s off Safi. Commander Anderson, the air officer . . ."

"Yes, 'Andy' Anderson," Pride perked up. "Fine officer. I know him well."

"Well," I continued, knowing we were on common ground. "Commander Anderson told me to get acquainted with every facet of flight deck operations by working with Lieutenant Commander Ottinger, his flight deck officer. Mister Ottinger taught me all the ropes, from deck spotting to arresting gear." *God! This old guy is in great shape, in spite of his obvious crash injuries.* The captain's pace was making me just a little breathless.

"Great. That's what I'd hoped for. Andy did his duty." The Captain grinned broadly, eyes sparkling. "I think I'm getting Benny Freedman as flight deck officer and you'll be number two on the flight deck, in addition to your landing signals duties." He stopped at the aft end of the flight deck to watch some work being done on the fantail.

Jesus. I'm gettin' more new jobs. Now I'll be working during both launch and recovery. I thought as I felt that pride welling up again.

"What do you think of this flight deck, Harper?," the skipper asked, as he started back up the deck..

"Narrower than *Ranger*. I think."

"A lot narrower, you'll find," he pronounced. "Just seventy-two feet, water-way to waterway. These CVLs have the narrowest flight decks in the fleet. It was as wide as they could get on these light cruiser hulls. This was to be U.S.S. *New Haven*, CL-76, when the keel was laid." Then: "Well, what happened after the Army left?"

"Semi disaster, sir," I frowned. "We started with four TBFs and six pilots from Torpedo Four for ASW duty and ended up with only two flyable TBFs and one less pilot."

"God! What happened?"

"One TBF pilot lost control on launch and veered off the port side into the water." I winced. "The depth bombs went off when they got to their fuzed depth. Arming wires were probably knocked off by the force of the crash, the "gunny" said. The plane guard destroyer picked up the two crewmen but the pilot was lost. The other TBF was high and fast at the cut. He went through the barrier and crashed the island – no fire and no one injured."

"Would I know the lost pilot?," Pride asked with obvious concern.

"I doubt it, sir. It was Lieut.(jg) Geoffrey O'Mary – know 'im?"

"Guess not . . . Were you waving that barrier crash?" He grimaced as we started down the ladder to his office.

"No sir," I continued. "But that brings me to the other half of the disaster. I didn't wave any airplanes aboard during the whole Africa cruise."

Pride stopped dead in his tracks. "That means you have had no LSO experience at sea. Now, there's a sad state of affairs." The disappointment showed.

"Really not so sad, sir," I ventured. "I waved a lot during our week long training cruise in the Chesapeake – F4Fs, TBFs, and SBDs."

"Well, that's a little better," Pride mused as he slumped back in his couch. "But you certainly have a lot of training to do in a short period of time."

Well, that Red Bank, New Jersey excursion didn't get us anywhere. Hell, I didn't even like going in there in an SNJ. I mused as I cruised east along the south coast of Long Island in the big *Avenger*, still in search of an outlying field where we could conduct bounce drill.

I had gotten Commander Greene to agree that if I couldn't find a satisfactory outlying field, he would consider FCLP on Floyd Bennett during light traffic hours. Mitchell Army Air Field turned me down flat, as did Republic Aviation. Grumman was at least sympathetic, but they said the unscheduled nature of their operation precluded any scheduled activity like ours and besides, I found that their obstructions would be a real problem. So I was down to scouting little private airports.

The Red Bank Airport was a little grass field with obstructions all around. The fixed base operator was aghast at my description of FCLP. I knew if the field were a little wet we would fill it with muddy ruts and probably get an airplane stuck for the duration.

Maybe Suffolk County Airport will offer some promise. Looked pretty good on the chart. Ahh, there it is now . . . Hmm. Two runways look about 3,500 to 4,000 feet long. Not bad. But they're grass too. Oh well. It's a dry day so I might as well try it. "Suffolk tower, this is NAVY 6374, an *Avenger*, circling at two thousand feet, request landing instructions."

"NAVY 6374, Suffolk tower, runway one-three, wind southeast twelve to fifteen, enter traffic downwind at one thousand feet. Traffic is a Piper on base leg. Report turning base."

"Suffolk, this is NAVY, turnin' base, gear comin' down. What's the field condition? Dry, I hope."

"Yeah, NAVY. Dry and firm. You're cleared to land."

Good. Pretty clear approach to this runway. No obstructions to a fifty foot cross leg if we pick the right deck location.

CRUNCH, RUMBLE RUMBLE. *Hmm – Runway pretty firm with a little roughness typical of grass fields – Not bad – wonder what happens when it rains.*

I was able to stop the big *Avenger* about half way down the runway at the center taxiway. As I turned in to the ramp it looked pretty crowded with Piper Cubs and the like so I folded my wings. *Wow! Look at all those eyes bugging out.* The crowd that had collected when I showed up overhead looked on in stunned astonishment.

"Welcome to Suffolk County." A young man in an old Army flight jacket was there to shake my hand as I stepped off the last foot hold in the side of the TBF. "I'm Wayne Frandsen, Airport Manager. Come on. I'll buy you a cup o' coffee."

"Glad to meet you." I really was. "I'm Lieutenant (jg) Harper, Landing Signal Officer for Carrier Air Group twenty-four training at Floyd Bennett. I need to talk to you about access to your airport. We can do that over your coffee, thanks."

As we settled in a booth in the tiny coffee shop I described the kind of air space and time we needed.

"I'd really like to accommodate you, sir," Frandsen responded, straining to be helpful. "I could close the airport between dawn and eight o'clock and after six in the evening." He was trying. "As you see, our ramp is pretty crowded. I don't know where I'd park your airplanes."

"We wouldn't need parking except for one SNJ that I would fly over in," I offered. "The others would just touch down and take off and return directly to Floyd Bennett at the end of each session."

"I have to tell you that we can't even operate Pipers for a couple o' days after a rain," Frandsen cautioned. "You'd probably have to wait a week with those big airplanes."

"How about night operations?," I ventured.

"Sorry, no runway lights," he shrugged. "Jeez, I'd really like to help, Lieutenant, but I don't think we can give you enough to meet your training needs."

"You're right, unfortunately." I closed the conversation. *Not really "unfortunately." Hell! Now I've got the ammo I need to get some concessions out of Greene.* "I really appreciate your effort, Wayne. Thanks for the cooperation – and the coffee. Now I'll see if I can get out of here without blowing away a Piper Cub or two."

"Hi, honey," I greeted Jeanne Hoyt, NAVY nurse lieutenant, in the lobby of the Commodore Hotel. "Right on time, I see by the Commodore clock." The twenty foot high clock in the Commodore Hotel lobby was a favorite meeting place.

"The NAVY imbues admirable traits," she chided, with a toss of her shoulder length blond tresses. "NAVY trained you too, I see."

"Naw. You were the draw." I smoothed it on. "I wouldn't miss a minute of your charm."

"Whoa." Jeanne flinched. "Gettin' syrupy here." She tossed back with a mischievous grin.

Jeanne was a handsome woman, a couple of years older than I and senior to me by virtue of her nurse's appointment. She was about my height even with her low uniform heels. Her regulation coiffure framed a comely face with its light complexion, soft blue eyes, and typically Anglo-Saxon features. A lovely figure struggled to be recognized through her tailored blue uniform. I had enjoyed her free spirit during our previous dates.

"I thought maybe we'd slip over to the Lincoln Hotel for a couple of drinks and dinner," I ventured. "Artie Shaw is playing over there. Great dancing! What do you think?"

"Sounds good to me," she assented, eagerly. "I enjoy your dancing."

Chapter 7: Challenges

"My car's parked on top of Grand Central Station," I bragged. "We'll just catch a cab."

"That was great, Johnny," Jeanne purred as we stepped out on Pennsylvania Avenue in front of the Lincoln Hotel. "Artie Shaw sure is easy to dance to." Her eyes sparkled in the bright New York lights.

"Don't I get any credit?," I pouted a little, for effect.

"Ooooh!" Jeanne eyed me. "No conceit in your family. You took it all with you."

"Ouch," I flinched. "Ya got me . . . Hey darlin', it's such a nice night. Why don't we walk back. It's not far."

"Charmed," Jeanne warbled as she took my arm for the stroll.

After a block or two, "Can you come up to my room for a drink and a little conversation?," I dared.

"Your room?," came Jeanne's startled reaction. "At the Floyd Bennett B.O.Q.? I don't think we could do that."

"No, no, honey," I cooed. "My room at the Madison Hotel."

"Your room at the Madison?" She was incredulous. "How long have you had that?"

"Since seventeen hundred today." *Boy! I hope she buys it.*

"Why?" Her eyes were still wide, eyebrows raised.

"Just for us, honey." I gave her arm a squeeze. *I can dream can't I?*

"Sounds like a nice finish for a wonderful evening," she mused. "Let's."

"Nice drinks – mmm – nice music – mmm," Jeanne murmured between our sensuous kisses. "You're – mmm – pretty ingenious, mmm – Lieutenant."

We lay together on the single bed listening to soft music wafting from the radio. I had gotten her blouse off and the feeling of her bare skin aroused my desire.

"Just a minute," she whispered as she slipped out of her skirt.

"You're pretty clever – mmm – yourself – Lieutenant," I sighed as I slipped out of my trousers.

Our legs intertwined. "Shall – mmm – I?," I said, softly, as I worked on the hooks on her brassiere.

No answer – mmm – bra unhooked. Jeanne pulled away and drew her arms through the straps and tossed her bra on the floor. *Oooh! What beautiful breasts.*

Paddles!

That nurse's uniform hides a lot. I pulled her to me in a full embrace, feeling her firm breasts against my bare chest. "You're – mmm – wonderful." I could feel my sexuality spreading throughout my body.

RRRRRINGGG. *God damn! My morning wake up call.* I went limp and reached for the phone. "Yeah – five o'clock – thanks." I slammed the phone down. It was 0500. I had to get going!

"What was that?," Jeanne demanded, with a hoarseness that betrayed her sexual desire.

"My wake up call, damn it!," I cursed. "Gotta go, honey. Bounce drill at 0600, the only time old Greeney would let us do it," I groused as I slipped into my pants.

"Well, what about me?," she demanded as she shielded her breasts with folded arms.

"Stay here as long as you like – bill's paid," I tried to reassure her as I knotted my tie. "Here's five bucks in case you need a cab."

"Well, thanks a hell of a lot," Jeanne scolded. "What do you think I am, a 'B' girl or something?"

Hmm. The first time I've heard her swear. "No, no, honey. I think you're real class. I owe you the transportation." Then sheepishly: "May I call you again?"

"Don't bother."

8

BRIDGES AND BOMBS

"Hey, 'Tab'. Thanks for comin' out to keep the log for me," I greeted Ensign Rodney C. "Tab" Tabler who had buzzed out in the jeep after bouncing with the first group this morning. What time've you got?"

Tab was tall and lean and just a little bit awkward, as though his body had not quite matured. His handsome baby face was topped by a tousle of sandy hair and his soft blue eyes betrayed the innocence of youth. Hell! He looked like a high school basketball player.

"Oh seven fifteen," Tab answered, checking his watch. "This 'bounce drill' at oh-six-hundred really cuts into our partying." Then, regarding my ashen pallor and the bags under my eyes, he ventured: "You look like you had your share last night. How much sleep did *you* get?"

"Don't ask," I grimaced. "I had this live one goin' just when I got the wake up call to come out here an bounce you guys. No sleep . . . No more girl friend either . . . Oops! Here comes number one . . . Hey, Tab, d'you know who these guys are?"

"I think it's Bob Ross's division," Tab started. "You know, 'Nosmo' King, 'Stink' Innis, and 'Hoot' Gibson. Then we've got 'Dirty Eddy' March and 'Arky' Snowden to make it six.

"Okay, a little high," I thought out loud as I signalled the approaching Wildcat. "Nice adjustment – yeah, this is Ross alright – smooooth." I showed ROGER – then CUT. "OWW." I cried. CRUNCH – the touch down – then the engine roar as Ross raised his tail for take-off.

Paddles!

"What the hell was the 'OWW' for," Tab inquired.

"I hit myself in the mouth givin' the CUT, damn it." I fingered my lip. "I'm tryin' to develop a distinctive CUT motion where I twirl the paddle on my right index finger just under my chin." I demonstrated. "I missed that time." *What price vanity!*

"Yeah. You missed alright. Your lip's bleedin'," Tab snickered. "Pretty distinctive cut though – I'm impressed."

I had just graduated from the old paddle design featuring a circular frame of aluminum tubing twelve inches in diameter with a small integral handle and a disc of red or yellow canvas laced into the frame. The new design had an oblong frame 10 by twelve inches, integral handle, and four strips of bright fluorescent cloth suspended from longitudinal wires in the frame, giving a brilliant fluttering action in the wind and enhancing my theatrical CUT signal.

"By the way, you and Collin looked pretty steady this morning," I commented. "About ready for night bounce, you think?"

"Yeah, I guess," Tab ventured. "But not on *this* runway!"

"Ahh, here's 'Dirty Eddie'," I announced as I picked up the approaching Wildcat. "You can sure tell he's been on and off a carrier a few times. He's always a little rough, but you can tell he knows exactly what he's doin'." I hollered over my shoulder as I signalled HIGH. "That means he gets a lot of signals, but his responses are always perfect." CUT – CRUNCH – ROAR.

What the hell is this?," I demanded, as the duty jeep came roaring up the taxiway. "Oops! Here comes 'Arky'. C'mon, Arky, we're over here." I shouted as I gave a frantic left bank signal. "Okay, now slow down." I coaxed with an emphasized FAST signal. "Oh, to hell with it." WAVE-OFF.

"Tab," I called. "Notes on 'Arky': Late turn into groove – L.T.I.G. – a big capital 'F' for fast – and a 'WO'. Then: "What the hell's this all about?"

"It's the station J.O.D., Harpo," Tab wheezed. "Says the operations officer wants to see you in his office – now."

"I'll be in in about fifteen minutes," I yelled, as I picked up Ross's Wildcat with a firm "Roger." "Soon as I finish with this flock."

"You don't understand, sir," the little ensign quivered. "Commander Greene ORDERS you to call your aircraft down – NOW – sir! A – a – and report immediately to his office – uh – SIR." He backed up a couple of steps.

"Okay, Okay. Wait 'til I call 'em down." *Jesus Christ. What the hell is Greene's problem NOW?*

Chapter 8: Bridges and Bombs

"God Dammit, Harper." Greene stood behind his desk full of papers and books, face red, eyes bulging, shaking a piece of paper in his right hand. "I go out on a limb and let you conduct carrier landing practice during off hours and a week later you've got 'em flying under bridges." He was shaking all over. "Ever since I cleared your FCLP I've had irate citizens complaining about being rudely awakened by low flying aircraft. Now I get panic calls about airplanes flying under the Rockaway bridge – and the sheriff just got here, raisin' hell about your guys flyin' low all over the county . . . and now the 'severe hazard to bridge traffic', I'm quoting." He took a deep breath. "What the HELL is going on, Harper?"

"Yes sir, Commander – er – good morning, Sheriff," I managed, meekly, as my mind raced to find the right words to satisfy both of them. "I'm Lieutenant (jg) Harper." I purred, extending my hand.

"I'm Sheriff Carbo." His hand remained on his Colt .45. "And I'll tell you somethin', Mister," he scowled, as he fingered his side arm. "We won't tolerate that kind of willful disdain for the public safety by you Navy fly boys." He puffed up his chest and growled: "NOT IN THIS COUNTY!!"

"There must be some reasonable explanation for such blatant disregard for the residents around here," Greene challenged in language meant to placate the sheriff. "Is there?" Greene's eyes were pleading for an answer that would satisfy the sheriff, if not himself.

Well! I think Greene's on my side, at least until the sheriff leaves. Diplomacy, God damn it, Harpo! Forget your disdain for civilian functionaries. Do not – repeat – DO NOT remind the sheriff that there is a war going on. Nice and polite now.

"Well sir." I bowed, ever so slightly, as my mind raced to develop the story. "We have orders from the U.S. NAVY to get this air group ready for continuous operations off the light aircraft carrier *Belleau Wood* under combat conditions beginning in May – JUST TWO MONTHS FROM NOW!"

"Maybe so." The sheriff was still fuming. "But that doesn't give you guys a license to fly under bridges and generally terrorize our citizens with frivolous low flying."

"Here's the problem, Sheriff," I continued calmly, ignoring the insult. "A carrier pilot must arrive at the carrier at about fifteen feet above the deck at an air speed about ten knots above stalling," I demonstrated, using my right hand as the airplane and my left as the deck. "To reach that position in stabilized flight, the pilot must avoid any drastic flight path or airspeed variations, especially during his cross leg – uh – the turn from down wind into the groove, or final approach." I watched the sheriff's eyes widen. "When we practice it at an airfield we try to keep the downwind leg at a hundred and fifty feet above the terrain but we must drop down to about fifty feet in the cross-leg in order to stabilize our approach and, on runway three zero, that means flying under the bridge." Then, drawing on the sheriff's exposure to para-military training, I concluded: "You wouldn't want your deputies to go against the bad guys without realistic training, would you?"

"No, but . . .," the sheriff stammered.

"Then you can understand why we need this realistic training to make us ready to face OUR bad guys, the Japs and the Germans." *Whew. See how that works.*

"Well . . . okay, Commander." The sheriff tried to ignore me and turned to Greene, choosing his words carefully. "I guess I understand your problem, and I hope you can understand mine." His tone had moderated considerably.

"Oh! Yes, Sheriff." Greene sensed the softening and jumped right in. "I can certainly understand your problem. As you know, I get quite a few complaints directly." Greene gave it the sympathetic touch. "In peace time we did all our fleet operational training at remote fields but this is war time and we can't find any usable remote fields around here." *Yeah, Carbo. Don't you know a war is going on? Greene said it.* "Mister Harper tried very hard to find one."

You bet I did, Commander, with Massey breathing down my neck and you refusing any FCLP on Floyd Bennett.

"Tell you what I'm goin to do Sheriff," Greene fawned. "We'll close runway three zero to carrier landing practice. That'll take care of the bridge problem." He wisely avoided asking the sheriff's approval. He just let it sit there in the middle of the room.

The prolonged silence gave witness to the sheriff's dilemma. "Well, that's good, sir," he offered, slowly. "But it'd sure help if you could keep 'em from flyin' low over the housing." Now he was being cooperative.

"What do you think, Harper?" Greene eyed me suspiciously.

"We can live with closing three zero, I guess," I conceded, showing reluctant concern. "Some of the guys are bitchin' about flyin' under the bridge anyway." Then, referring to the aerial photo of the station on Greene's wall I tried to save what I could. "Runway three is the only other one that requires low flying over housing, but – er – if we can use just the north half of it, sir . . . " I gave Greene and inquisitive glance. "We solve that problem." I watched Carbo's eyes. "We'd probably have to fly over the edge of the parking apron, but that's in your jurisdiction, anyway, Commander." I gloated a little.

"Does that sound okay to you, Sheriff?," Green ventured.

"We-e-ell . . . I don't know." Carbo wanted to be sure he had all the concessions he could squeeze out of Greene.

"Notice that Harper's plan keeps his pilots from flying west of Flatbush Avenue, AT ALL, on carrier landing practice." Greene kept trying. "That should help a lot."

"Yeah, I guess it does," Carbo conceded, grudgingly. "Well then, Commander." Carbo was ready with his demand. "You will assure me that those planes will NEVER fly low over our housing or under Rockaway Bridge. CORRECT?"

Greene looked at me for some kind of a signal.

I just shrugged as if to say, "You got it boss."

"Yes, I will assure you that our planes won't fly under Rockaway Bridge – er – and they won't bother your housing areas." Greene appeared to be swearing on a bible as he still held up the paper in his right hand and had his left hand on some book.

There were hand shakes all around and the sheriff turned, opened the door, and left. The door closed.

"God Damn you Harper!" Greene's face reddened. "You better make all that come true."

Morning, gentlemen," I began. "I guess you'd call this Bombing 202. Your credits will depend on how many ships you sink when we get out to the fleet." I was in the SBD squadron ready room with Lieutenant Lamb, and Ensigns Dobbs, McLinden, Birchfiel, and Candioto.

"Freddy" Lamb was a TBF pilot whom Massey had pressed into service temporarily to command the SBD part of VC-24. Freddy was tall – about six-foot-two, medium build, with a lumbering kind of a swagger, à la Gary Cooper. A heavy shock of brown hair fell over his long forehead, topping his sharp features. Freddy's sparkling eyes betrayed a jolly, if mischievous disposition.

"Duffy" Dobbs' grey complexion was accented by soft, grey eyes and topped with a rumpled shock of brown hair, projecting a perpetually dour image. He wore a thin moustache the color of his hair.

Hugh "Mac" McLinden could have been out of a Hollywood casting office for the part of "Boston Irishman", which he was, with his jet black hair, dark brown eyes, and irreverent manner. "Mac" was a big, handsome, guy at about five-foot-eleven and a hundred and eighty five pounds.

Bob Birchfiel, known as "Benny the Birch", towered over the rest of us at about six-foot-six, and very lean. His fine English features and blue eyes were topped by neatly combed blond hair.

F. "Candy" Candioto (Hell. Only his mother knew his first name) was a round little Italian, only about five foot seven, with straight black hair falling over his round face with its jolly smile and sparkling brown eyes. A Santa costume would have suited him better than the flight coveralls he wore.

"You all did pretty well on your Bombing 101, out on Fire Island yesterday," I started. "But the big wind we had showed that some of you didn't quite handle the wind problem." I drew a target circle and a wind line on the blackboard. "Two things to remember about wind: First; make all aiming corrections by banking to the aim line and banking back to your basic heading." I demonstrated with my right hand aimed at the target image on the blackboard. "DO NOT SKID your corrections with the rudder; and second; you have to estimate wind direction and velocity by the way your sight drifts off the target and aim up the wind line an appropriate distance at the point of bomb release." I drew a sight reticule at the edge of the target, up the wind line.

"How d' hell do I do dat, Harpo?," "Candy" moaned. "I feel like I'm goin' sideways by d' time I get to d' release point."

"That's because you ARE, 'Candy'," I countered. "I could tell by where your bombs went – wa-a-ay down wind of the target. Today, keep the ball centered and *always* use ailerons to turn to a new sight line, unless it's a pure pitch correction . . . think about it."

"Okay." I held up my hands to stop the free-lance conversations. "Here's what were going to do today." I moved to the chart on the bulkhead. "I talked this PT skipper into towing a target sled for us in the gunnery area south of Fire Island – here – along the south shore of Long Island." I pointed to the area and recalled that Lieutenant "Chip" Chambers had welcomed the opportunity for his gun crew to track a simulated air attack. "We're going to make a coordinated attack on the sled by executing a breakup as we would for landing, to get some separation, and then rolling in to our dives simultaneously. Any questions? . . . Okay, lets go."

"Sugar flight, this is Sugar One," I announced to my flight of six SBD *Dauntlesses*. "Target eleven o'clock, course zero-nine-zero, speed about fifteen knots. Stand by for the break."

Switching channels, I called, "MT-87, this is Sugar One – flight of six – three miles northwest – angels twelve. Have you and target in sight. Stand by for coordinated attack on target."

The sled kicked up a white wake a thousand yards aft of the PT boat, making it stand out among the scattered whitecaps on the blue-green Atlantic, streaked by a twenty knot surface wind from the southwest.

"Roger, Sugar One – have you in sight – proceed with exercise." I could tell it was the "Chip" Chambers himself. I gathered that PT Boat skippers operated their boats much as airplane pilots operate their aircraft.

With the target at nine o'clock and the flight in right echelon, I patted my head, pointed to "Mac" on my right wing, and broke left forty-five degrees. As I continued a gentle turn I craned my neck to watch as each SBD broke at a little greater angle to provide our tactical spacing.

"Stand by to dive, 'guns'," I shouted back to my rear seat gunner as I split the dive flaps, rolled the *Dauntless* into a seventy degree dive on the target, and found myself hanging on the shoulder straps. Looking to my left, I could see four other SBDs in a dive parallel to mine, spaced about two hundred yards apart. *Where the hell is the other one?* I wondered as I held the sled in my sight, dropped my practice bomb, and pulled out, wrenching the airplane to the left so I could see the other bombs bracket the target.

"Sugar, this is sugar one, who the hell didn't dive?," I snarled into the microphone.

"Sugar three didn't dive, sir," Came the confession. "Got a sick gunner – returnin' to base." It was Dobbs.

I was afraid he wasn't up to this.

"Sugar three – this is four – you'll be sicker than your gunner if you do that!" I heard "F for Freddy" growl. "Keep us in sight, rendezvous on Harpo's wing, and complete the bombing exercise – and remember, I'm right behind you.

Looking left, I could see Dobbs sliding into position on my left wing. *Well, he flies formation pretty well, anyway.*

"MT-87, you got scores?," I called on the other channel.

"Yeah, Sugar," Came "Chip's" voice. "One, six o'clock, ten yards; Two, eight o'clock fifteen yards; Three, direct hit; Four, ten o'clock, forty yards; Five, no drop. We only got five, no six."

"Thanks MT-87. How'd your gunners do?"

Paddles!

"Christ, Sugar, I hope the Germans don't do that to us," Chambers groused. "We could only track two of you guys the way you were spaced. We'd be dead meat."

Back to our tactical channel: "Hey Sugar Four, you don't need any more lessons. You got a direct hit." I could see Freddy Lamb smiling as we rendezvoused. "Candy – I think you've got it – y'only missed fifteen yards – crosswind at that. Sugar Five; you tossed your bomb – must've released during your pullout. Sugar Six; no drop – check your switches. Our tactical spread worked well – scared the hell out of that PT boat skipper." Then: "Okay, 'Duffy', stick with us. Your gunner'll live through it."

"Hi, Art," I greeted Art Taylor in the lobby of the B.O.Q. "That was some exciting stuff you exposed me to last night at the Magic Castle, downtown. Thanks a lot." Lieutenant (jg) Art Taylor was a big man at about six feet tall and, I'd guess, about two hundred ten pounds. He was actually "Talos the Magician" in civilian life, and apparently a pretty good one, judging from the way all the magicians and prestidigitators at the Magic Castle greeted him. He seemed to work his magic about once a week to get an airplane to fly up here from Norfolk where his squadron, VB-16 operated Curtiss SB2C *Helldivers.*

Art's long shiny black hair was hardly regulation but no doubt enhanced his magic act. His bottomless light blue eyes were set deeply into his flushed face. The side pockets of his green uniform blouse bulged with pipes and a variety of pipe tobacco and paraphernalia. He was ever in the process of cleaning, charging, lighting, smoking, or knocking tobacco residue out of a pipe on the heel of his shoe, exuding a scent which combined the pungent aromas of the various tobaccos, smoke, ash, and the fragrant briars he smoked.

"Well, you're welcome," Taylor drawled in his Nebraska farm boy accent, a far cry from the soft Slavic accent he invoked at the Magic Castle. "Any time . . . only you're not to reveal any of our secrets."

"Did you see this announcement about a dance at the Knights of Columbus Hall tonight?" I referred to a notice on the bulletin board. "Says Naval Aviators are specifically invited – says there'll be lots o' girls." I scratched my temple. "What's Knights of Columbus, anyway?"

"The Knights of Columbus is a Catholic church based community service organization – er – kind o' like Rotary, only religious," Taylor advised, patiently. "In that setting I wouldn't expect an orgy."

Chapter 8: Bridges and Bombs

"Well, I think I'll go down anyway and see what kind of girls they have in Brooklyn. It's only a fifteen minute drive. D'you want to go?"

"Okay," Taylor grumbled. "Sounds like a cotillion to me. I'll be your chaperone," He snickered. "You'll probably need one." Art was ragging me about the disparity in our ages – he was nearing thirty.

"Maybe you can hook up with one of *their* chaperones," I needled.

"Like I said, Harpo, cotillion," Taylor groaned, surveying the attendance at the dance. "Not a one of these babes is over twenty – jail bait."

"Don't despair, Art," I chided. "There's your charmer, over there." I nodded discreetly toward an older woman – obviously a chaperone.

"God!," Art recoiled. "Not that! "I thought they'd have teachers for chaperones. "She's somebody's GRANDmother, fer Christ's sake."

"Okay. Don't say I didn't try," I chuckled. "See that brunette with the slinky black dress out there?"

"Hold it." Art grabbed my arm. "Don't you see that big guy she's dancing with? Maybe you need a body guard instead of a chaperone."

"No sweat," I shot back as I picked my way through the dancers. "May I cut in?," I inquired politely, as I tapped the big guy on the left shoulder. *Yeah, he's big alright – about six foot two, two ten. Probably a football player.*

"Get lost," snarled the big guy as he turned his back on me and danced away.

As I caught up to them I tapped the big guy on the shoulder again. "Excuse me. May I cut in." I instinctively ducked a little.

"I told you to get lost, fly boy." Big guy gave me an elbow.

"C'mon, Greg," the girl injected. "We invited these Navy flyers from Floyd Bennett and I'd like to dance with this one." She swept her hand in a shooing gesture. "I'll see you later."

"Okay, 'Mike'." Greg released her. "But don't forget you're going home with me tonight."

"If you're nice," the girl scolded as she eased over and wrapped her left arm around my neck. "Hi, handsome. Now that you're my prisoner, I need your name, rank, and serial number."

"You're a demanding captor," I laughed. Then, squaring my shoulders: "Lieutenant (junior grade) John A. Harper, United States Navy, at your service, Ma'am. My serial number's a military secret." I announced with an official air.

Whoa! She's more beautiful than I had thought from a distance – a face of

Paddles!

parchment white skin punctuated by a pair of full, pouting lips, and deep, inquiring brown eyes, crowned by a cascade of shimmering black hair in a wave that covered the right half of her forehead and . . . whew – the plunging neck line of her simple black dress barely restrains her full breasts.

The band was playing "That Old Black Magic" and Mike snuggled into my arms. "Mike's a funny name for a girl," I whispered into her ear. "Is that really your name?"

My real name is Margaret – Margaret Ann Markham – my close friends call me 'Mike'. She drew me close to her and whispered: "Call me 'Mike', Johnny."

Oooh! There's that feeling again. I thought as her warm body pressed against mine, causing that warm tingle I had felt when I got close to Peggy Rogers . . *Yeah . . . and Peggy Green too . . . Margaret Ann Green . . . hmm – same name as Mike's.*

"Oh oh," Mike warned. "Here comes Greg." The band was signalling the end of "That Old Black Magic" and the big guy was storming out to claim Mike for the next dance.

"Okay, Fly boy, that's enough," Greg announced with a threatening glance as he reached out to retrieve Mike.

"No!," Mike countered, with conviction. "We're going to dance the rest of this set." She put her arm around my neck and we danced away to "Rum and Coca Cola" while she gave an excellent imitation of a Rhumba.

Suddenly, I felt a powerful hand on my left shoulder turning me to face the big guy. "That's enough, I said," he yelled right into my face.

"Are you having trouble with this brute, Harpo?" The voice was calm and assertive. It was Taylor, freezing Greg with his practiced "Dracula" glare and his soft Slavic accent, and appearing magically to swell in bulk.

"Who is this guy?," Greg whined, more or less at Mike.

"I am 'Talos' of Slovenia," Taylor announced with a menacing stare at Greg. "Harpo, here, is within my protective web." He waved his hand as though he held a wand.

Greg shrank a little and replied quietly, "Your friend is trying to steal my girl."

"I am NOT 'YOUR GIRL'," Mike asserted, angrily.

By now a circle of dancers had surrounded us in anticipation of some action. Talos gave Greg another of his "Evil Eye" stares but said nothing. Instead, he reached in one of his bulging pockets, drew out a deck of cards, and fanned them expertly. "Take a card – any card!" He continued to stare into Greg's eyes, hypnotically. Reflexively, Greg reached out and drew a card. "Okay. Now what?"

"Memorize your card," Taylor ordered, as though to a hypnotized subject. Then after a few moments. "Is it memorized?"

As though in a trance, Greg replied, hesitantly, "Yes." I think he almost added "Master."

"Now put it back in the deck," Taylor ordered. "If I identify your card you leave the girl and my friend alone until THEY invite your company."

Greg carefully returned the card and Taylor shuffled the deck with ceremonial flair. "Is this your card?" He demanded, still staring into Greg's eyes and holding up the three of clubs.

With that, Taylor took Greg gently by the arm and steered him through the crowd to a hail of applause, whispering something in his ear as they went. The MASTER and his subject.

"Hey, Mike. Who was that girl my friend Taylor was dancing with as we left the hall?," I asked, as I drove to Mike's house, under her direction, my right arm drawing her gently to me.

Mike glanced up, registering surprise. "That's no 'girl', Johnny. That's Miss Crawford, the diocesan secretary," She snickered. "She was one of our chaperones"

"Not bad lookin' for her age," I ventured. "About right for old Talos."

"They did seem to be enjoying themselves." Mike agreed. Then: "That was a wonderful evening, Johnny." Mike sighed and snuggled closer as we drew to a stop in front of her house. "You're a wonderful dancer."

House? Hmmm. Looks more like a mansion to me. "Gee, Mike," I wrapped her up in both arms. "Anyone can be a great dancer with you as a partner."

"Oh no you don't," Mike scolded as she pulled away from my kiss. "I've got to go in."

"Whoa," I cautioned as she opened the car door. Then, leaping out of the car, I took her hand. "Let's do this right." I whispered as we started up the stairs to the front door where I took her in my arms again.

"No no NO!," "Mike" whispered musically, as I tried again for a kiss. "Not tonight Johnny." Call me, I'd like to know you better."

I tingled all over as I drove back to pick up Talos, my savior.

9

GUNS AND GRUMMAN

"Hello Jack, this is Harpo – a flight of six TBFs entering west end of gunnery area, angels seven for fixed gunnery practice. Say your position, over." Looking right I could see four TBF *Avengers*; "Feets" Tate was on my right wing, "Jay" Smith led the second section with "Tuffy" Chase and George Agar as his wingmen. Looking left I saw "Rover" Omark grinning up from his open cockpit.

"Have you in sight, Harpo," Jack replied. "I'm orbiting, angels five, about five miles east of you." Ensign Robert "Jack" Thelan had drawn the tow duty and was circling in one of VF-24's *Wildcats* at five thousand feet in the west end of the gunnery area south of Fire Island, with the target sleeve streaming five-hundred feet aft.

"I got ya, Jack," I crowed. "I'll bring my flight south of you and take up a heading of zero nine zero. When we pass you, turn to heading zero nine zero and hold angels five – Flight, this is Harpo – Echelon right!" I called as we cruised two thousand feet above, ahead, and to the right of Jack's *Wildcat*, in position for high side fixed gunnery runs.

"Hey, you guys," Jack wailed. "Remember! Keep your angle high and stop shooting if you get in a tail chase. This armor plate is kind o' thin.

"Don't worry, Jack. These are small bullets," I laughed, referring to the single .30 caliber gun in the nose of the TBF. Then: "Flight. This is Harpo. Jack's got the essence. Now, commence gunnery runs." Then to my crew on intercom, "Stand by

94

for maneuvering." MY crew? *Hmm. They're Massey's crew and he insisted they go with me on this flight.*

I rolled the big *Avenger* left to begin a firing run. *Son of a bitch! This takes a lot more effort than I thought. Aileron forces are HUGE. Sure doesn't act like a fighter! Okay, like I briefed the TBF pilots, turn into the target early, set the pipper about a hundred feet up the tow line, let the target come into your sight, and pull in to hold your lead. Aaaargh! God damn! Takes all my strength to hold my lead – FIRE . . . Uh-huh. Tracers look like they're goin' into the mouth of the target sleeve . . . Whoa! What a shudder . . . I guess we're close to the stall – Cease firing!* The *Avenger* kind of wallowed into level flight below and behind the target and I poured the coal on to gain some altitude and slip over above and to the left of the target – in a position to watch Feets' run.

"Delaney here, sir. I think I'm goin' to be sick." It was my radioman-torpedoman down in the bilges with only a tiny window to see out of.

"Peters here, sir. Me too." Peters was the gunner up in the ball turret, looking aft.

"Sorry about that, fellas. You'll just have to get used to it," I sympathized.

"Flight! This is Harpo." I began my critique. "You all had the same problem I had, to varying degrees." (Sympathy). "This big bird is hard to man handle and you big guys have the advantage over us little guys. A couple of you got sucked into a tail chase because you didn't start your aim point far enough up the tow line," I coached. "Do that, and then hold your lead for a hundred and fifty knot target, and watch your tracers fly right into the mouth of the sleeve."

"Jeez! Harpo. I almost spun in," Tate croaked.

"So did I, 'Feets'. We're all learnin' this drill together," I empathized. "Okay, everybody ready? Follow me."

As the six torpedo pilots gathered around the target sleeve spread out on the hangar floor some of them crawled along the sleeve counting their color coded bullet holes. The ordnance crew had dipped the bullets into slow drying paint before loading the airplanes: Red, plain, in lieu of white, blue, black, green and yellow, for airplanes numbers one through six, in that order.

"Jesus, Hawpo, ah didn't think you could do THAT with a TBF," Feets drawled. "Feets" was Ensign Benjamin Colonna Tate, a big burly farm boy from the Virginia hill country who looked like he should still be wearing his bib overalls or a high school football uniform with the number seventy-two on the jersey. His bushy

Paddles!

eyebrows and deep set blue eyes dominated his round face.

"Yeah, this TBF's pretty versatile," Agar injected. "You can even DIVE BOMB with the damned thing." Ensign George Agar towered above the rest of us at about six foot three and, big boned as he was, he must have weighed about two thirty. He had a long face with a long, prominent nose to match. He obviously had the muscle to man handle the *Avenger.*

"GLIDE bombing, thirty or forty degrees, yeah," Smith cautioned. "But no more. She's designed primarily for torpedo delivery and shallow glide bombing." Tall and very lean, Lieut.(jg) J. H. "Jay" Smith had been active in the Naval Air Reserve while pursuing a law degree at Columbia Law School and went on to run one of Pan American's major operations. Jay seemed older than his thirty-two years with his noticeably lined face and almost white hair and he definitely had the edge when it came to aviation knowledge. "This type of gunnery is just about the safe limit for the TBF."

"One thing's for sure," Rover added in his Brooklyn brogue as he stood up from the target. "I can't pull hard enough to hurt that machine. Apparently I didn't hurt the sleeve either." Ensign Warren Omark, who was dubbed "Rover" as a tribute to his performance in the presence of young women, and whose handsome baby face made him look like a high school kid, was just about the ninety-five percentile example airplane engineers design for; five foot ten, a hundred and fifty or sixty pounds. His reddish hair and blue-green eyes testified to his Scandinavian heritage.

"Hot damn!," Chase yelled from his kneeling position on the sleeve. "I found six blue holes. I HIT IT!

"I hate to tell you 'Tuffy'," I injected as I scanned the color list. "The blue ones are Rover's. Yours are green."

I never knew why they called Ensign Ralph Chase "Tuffy" because he had such a mild manner, with his Kentucky twang and a kind of a rocking gait. His tousled head seemed small for his tall lean frame and his inquiring blue eyes gave him a shy look.

The argument over the *Avenger's* maneuverability and design limits raged on as we finished counting the hits on the sleeve.

"Here we go, Sonny," my brother-in-law exulted. "I'm going to show you how to get across Manhattan with the minimum of stops." We were on our way over to pick up my aunt Eleanor at her elegant three bedroom apartment on West

96

Chapter 9: Guns and Grumman

End Avenue at Eighty-Fourth street.

Ray Rhonheimer had married my sister when she was a show girl in the Ziegfield Follies and he played piano in the pit. Now, Ray managed the Astoria Theater, one of his father's string of movie theaters, and he and my sister lived in a luxurious penthouse over the theater. Ray was a round little man about five foot five with full cheeks, a pencil moustache, and a receding hairline topped by slicked back black hair parted in the middle. He had a penchant for things British, like the Rolls Royce Bently he deftly wove through the Queensborough Bridge traffic. He wore a Harris tweed cap and fingerless pigskin driving gloves and drew on a Player's cigarette through a long silver cigarette holder.

"That was quite a number you brought over last night. It was Irma wasn't it?," Ray ventured as he slipped down the right lane and turned right to blend smoothly with north bound Second Avenue traffic. "This is the first step; whenever you come to a red light, turn right! . . . Have you known Irma long?"

"About a month, I guess – all double dating." I was building an excuse. "She went with this buddy of mine who just got killed last Friday. I thought we could cheer her up."

"You didn't tell us about that," Ray chided as he went through the yellow light and squealed tires into Sixty-Sixth Street westbound. "Well, we did pretty well for a while, until the booze got to her."

"Yeah, I'm sorry about the mess." I was mortified. "I really appreciate you and Mary Louise being so nice to her."

"Well, it can happen to anyone," Ray philosophized as he screeched around the corner to join Madison Avenue north bound. "Did you notice we haven't stopped yet and we're half way across Manhattan. How'd your buddy get killed?"

"He and three other pilots of our fighter squadron were bringing some airplanes back from Quonset Point," I winced. "Three of 'em flew into the beach on Fire Island at cruising speed – that's all. One of 'em was a friend of mine from high school."

The Bently squealed to a stop behind an old DeSoto stopped in the left turn lane at Seventy-Ninth Street. "Well!" Ray eyed me with a strange curiosity. "You certainly seem relaxed, considering you just lost three of your friends." With that, Ray jammed the Bently into first and followed the DeSoto into Seventy-Ninth Street only inches behind his rear bumper, then passed him on the right with an acceleration that snapped my head back. "Seems so callous, Sonny, not like you."

"You've got to get used to it," I tossed back easily as we whizzed through

Central Park, an apt setting for our conversation. "Hell, I've lost quite a few friends since I've been in the NAVY."

"That's pretty scary," Ray breathed, as he turned north on West End Avenue and parked snugly at the curb in front of the canopy that protected the entrance to my aunt's apartment building. "How the NAVY can convert a sensitive kid – you were, you know – into a hard headed war fighter in two years, I don't know. I wouldn't have believed it if I hadn't seen it."

Jesus, Ray, I'm not that tough. I thought. "It'll get worse before it gets better, Ray," I sighed. "Hell, we're not even in the war zone yet."

"Fifth floor, Willy," Ray instructed the elevator operator.

"Yassah, Mistah Ray," Willy grinned as he turned the control handle smoothly to the right. "Gwine t' see Miz Gordon, ah knows."

The elevator accelerated upward.

God damn! Stuck in Norfolk again. I had come down from Floyd Bennett the day before at Commander Vossler's request to help out with TBF CARQUALs on U.S.S *Card*, another jeep carrier steaming in the Chesapeake Bay. I had brought an SBD down for some modifications at the Overhaul and Repair facility – O&R – and the airplane wasn't going to be ready for a couple of days.

"Hey Ski," I called to the CQTU yeoman, "Is Commander Vossler around? I've got to get some transport back to Floyd Bennett."

Ski looked up from his typewriter. "No sir. He went down to Creeds for the rest of the day. Sorry," he shrugged. "'Sides, that SNJ's the only one we've got, and we need it." His eyes brightened. "Why don't you check with O&R. They're always needin' pilots to deliver airplanes – somewhere."

"Thanks for the idea." I started out the door. "Maybe I'll try it."

I've got it! Talos ought to be just about ripe for a trip to New York. The back seat of an S-B-Deucey is better 'n stayin' here all night. I made a bee line for VB-16 ready room in the next hangar, Taylor's squadron.

The ready room was empty except for one pilot in his stained and rumpled flight suit smoking a cigarette and drinking a Coke. The squadron duty officer I guessed. His brow furrowed as he drew hard on his cigarette. "Sorry buddy. Art bought it a couple of weeks ago."

Son-of-a-bitch! No wonder I haven't seen him lately. "What the hell happened?"

"Mid-air collision on a bombing run," the duty officer cringed. "Made a big hole in the ground not far from the target. The other pilot and gunner got out okay."

He shook his head. "Nothin' left of Art to send home." Then: How'd you know 'im?"

"Occasional night life in the big city." *God damn! What a loss. He was a real talent.* "Well, I got to get movin' – unless you've got an airplane I can take to Floyd Bennett." I said with a hopeful glance.

"No such luck partner," he grinned. "We need all the birds we can get – every day!

I burst into the dispatch office of O&R like I owned the place. "You've got an airplane that needs to go to Floyd Bennett. Right?," I announced. "Well, I'm your man." *Come on, man. ANY kind of airplane. PLEEZE!*

The duty officer looked up from his pocket novel, wearily. "Nope . . . Sorry," he said, flatly, and my heart sank. "But we do have an SNB that we're tryin' to deliver to Quonset. Can you fly a twin Beech?"

Hot damn! Here's my chance – But, shit, I've never flown an SNB, or any other twin, for that matter – But he said "CAN you fly an SNB" – Hell yes, I can fly ANYTHING! – This is my opportunity. make it smoooooth, J.A. "Yes sir. Tell you what. I've GOT TO get back to Floyd Bennett tonight but I'll see to it that your twin Beech gets to Quonset tomorrow . . . okay?"

He looked relieved. "Sounds good to me," he said, reaching in the desk drawer for the logs and transfer papers. "Here, sign this receipt for the airplane, right here . . . good. Now, sign the aircraft log book, here . . . Okay, that'll do it. Here's the whole package: Log book, maintenance records, pilot's handbook, and certificate of origination. You got it. Good luck."

"Thanks," I called over my shoulder as I went for the door.

"Hold it," called the duty officer. *Oh oh. The jig is up, damn it.* "You've got to have a co-pilot y' know."

Whew! Is that all. "No sweat." I shot back with false nonchalance as my mind raced to think of someone I could take with me. *Don't fuck it up now, dummy.* "Er . . a couple of guys from our air group also need transport back. We can handle it."

"Good."

Whew! Well, I guess he was happy to get rid of the airplane.

Mac McLinden and I sat in the cockpit of the twin Beech scanning the pilot's handbook for clues on how to fly the damned thing. "Hey, Mac, it's a good thing the weather's good. We're goin' to get out of here VFR direct. That takes a little hate out of the game."

99

Paddles!

Grinning his evil grin, Mac announced, "I've got the book, Harpo. You fly – I'll coach. . . heh heh."

"How do you like that, Mac. We're multi-engine qualified," I gloated as we cruised just off the coast of Maryland's Eastern Shore at 7,000 feet.

"Yeah, that was a pretty smooth takeoff for a student." A typical McLinden left handed compliment. "I hope your landing's that good."

Hah! There's that evil grin again. "Good thing you've got that handbook," I revelled. "Shit! We even got the autopilot workin'. Damned if those multi-engine weenies don't have it cushy."

"Pure luxury, Harpo." Mac flashed a lecherous grin. "All we need is a couple o' dollies up here and we've got it made."

"Grumman tower, this is NAVY One One Oh, an FM-1 *Wildcat,* three miles southwest, request landing instructions," I called as the field at Beth Page came into view. General Motors had taken over *Wildcat* production when Grumman got saturated with the new F6F *Hellcat,* hence the FM-1 designation.

"NAVY One One Oh, this is Grumman tower – have your special clearance – You're cleared to land, runway two one – wind southwest, ten; traffic is an F6F entering downwind leg."

"Roger, Grumman tower, have the F6F in sight." I turned to follow the *Hellcat.* "Entering downwind behind the F6F." *Wow! The new fleet fighter. Maybe I'll get to see one close up while I'm here. . . . .* "Grumman tower – One One Oh turnin' base – gear comin' down."

"One One Oh's cleared to land – Taxi to the big hangar – someone'll meet you there."

Taxiing in after landing I spotted a ground crewman signalling me toward a parking space on the parking apron jammed with new F6Fs. A small man in a business suit stood a few feet away, hands in pockets.

"Welcome to Grumman, Mister Harper," I heard as I hopped down off the *Wildcat's* wing. "I'm Gordon Israel," the man announced as he extended his hand. "I hear you've got a little problem with your Brand X *Wildcats.*" Mr. Israel stood about five foot eight and was stockily built at about a hundred and seventy-five pounds. His pudgy, weathered face bore the confident smile of someone with long experience with such "little problems", and his piercing blue eyes made me believe he knew how to solve them.

Chapter 9: Guns and Grumman

"Thank you, Mister Israel." I shook his hand. "Name's John, sir."

"Okay, John. Call me Gordon." Israel strolled toward the hangar. "The NAVY Bureau of Aeronautics Rep couldn't make it but he sends his regards."

"I guess that makes my visit legal," I commented, with a knowing grin.

"We'll go up to my office – I've got a couple of engineers waiting – and figure out what your problem is. I presume this is one of the offending machines." Israel looked back at the FM-1 as four crewmen began pushing it into the hangar.

"Yes sir. We've got five of 'em so far and we'll never get 'em aboard at night with the approach lights the way they are." The approach light on a carrier airplane was a small, box like fixture mounted in the leading edge of the left wing and fitted with a three piece lens – green on top and red on the bottom separated by a very narrow amber band. The light fixture was adjustable over a narrow range so that the LSO would see red if the aircraft were slow, green if too fast, or amber if the airplane were in the ideal approach attitude.

"Hi, fellas. Thanks for comin' over," Israel greeted the two engineers as we entered his office. "Meet Lieut.(jg) John Harper, Landing Signal Officer for Air Group Twenty Four, forming up at Floyd Bennett . . . This is Ed Beckhardt, one of our structural engineers, and that's Phil Birdsong, head of our "mod" shop." We all shook hands and sat down around the small conference table adjacent to Israel's desk.

Whew! Pretty big office. About twenty by thirty, I'd guess. All kinds of exotic airplane models and framed pictures all around the office. This guy must be IM-PORTANT. The small name plaque on Israel's desk announced: "CHIEF DESIGN ENGINEER." *Yeah! That's important all right. What's the Chief Design Engineer doin' payin' attention to me, a lowly jay-gee.*

"Okay, let's get started." Israel sank into his leather swivel chair. "Whoa, just a minute. Anybody want coffee?" He pointed at each of us as we nodded. "How d'you like yours, John?"

"Sugar please."

"Janet?," he called, as he held down the intercom button. "Four coffees please – sugar for the NAVY type." Then, to me, "Okay, John. Tell us about your problem."

"Well, the fighters had their first night bounce drill last Friday night and we had a hell of a time with the FM-1s," I began. "The first couple were F4F-4s, and they were just fine. But the next one scared the hell out of me. He showed constant RED all the way up the groove while I was giving him a frantic COME-ON." I waved my hands, imitating a COME-ON signal. "When he got to the ramp he was goin' like a scalded dog – floated half way down the runway after the CUT." I demonstrated with my hand. "All the FM-1s had the same problem. The F4Fs were all Okay."

"Naturally," Beckhardt smiled wickedly. "Do you know those lights are adjustable?"

"Yeah," I smiled. "I found that out readin' the maintenance manual. Then I got a screwdriver from maintenance, went out to one of the FM-1s and adjusted its approach light, down about ten degrees. Then, after adjusting all the FM-1s and describin' the problem to four of our best fighter pilots, I sent 'em out for night bounce, urging 'em to watch their airspeed carefully. Result? They were still too fast – and showin' red all the way – but not as bad as before."

"How did it boresight, after you reset it?," Birdsong asked.

"What do you mean, boresight?," I gaped.

"Y' know," Birdsong drawled. "The approach light is in the wing leading edge at about eye level, and the airplane sets in the approach attitude." He explained, patiently. "Just stand out about a hundred feet in front of the airplane and have a mechanic adjust the light so you see the amber."

"Hey." My eyes lit up. "Thanks for the clue. I'll use it once I get these lights to work right." I nodded to Birdsong. "But that's not the end of my story. After that last night bounce drill, I tried to adjust the lights down some more, but I couldn't. They were bottomed out on the structure." I shrugged. "That's why I asked you for help."

"Sounds like G.M. didn't mount them as our drawings specify," Beckhardt frowned.

"Tell you what we'll do," Israel began, directing his remarks to Beckhardt and Birdsong. "Harper's FM-1 is in the hangar. I want you guys to figure out what the problem is and prepare a specification for modification at the line maintenance level. John's got to get back this evening so you'll have to make it quick. Understand?"

"Yeah," Beckhardt answered thoughtfully. "Let's see – inspection – design – Spec. rough draft – Final." He was counting the minutes and hours. "How about three this afternoon?" He offered as he got out of his chair.

"Sounds okay to me," Israel nodded. "Okay with you, John?"

"Perfect." I meant it. "While I'm here I sure would like to see an F6F close up. We're supposed to get *Hellcats* pretty soon."

Chapter 9: Guns and Grumman

"Yeah. We can handle that. right, Phil? Take Harper with you and get some-one to give him a tour of the F6F production line," Israel ordered. "We reconvene here at three PM.

"Thanks Gordon," I called over my shoulder as we went out the door.

At 1500 I poked my head into Israel's office, "Are you ready for me, Gordon?"

"Come on in and sit down, John." Israel waved his hand at an easy chair near his desk. "You're right on time. Ed and Phil should be along any minute." He leaned over and took a sip of coffee. "How about a cup o' coffee?"

"I'd like one, thanks, Gordon." I was about saturated, but I thought I'd join the crowd. "I have to thank you for the wonderful treatment I have enjoyed here today."

"Janet – coffee for the NAVY type," he called into the intercom box. Then, to me, "Did you get a good tour?"

"Sure did – thanks to you. I'll be damned if Phil didn't call the pilots' office and arranged to have one of your test pilots give me the tour. Next thing I know, here comes this good lookin' blonde. 'I'm Suzanne Fornier. Are you Lieutenant Harper?,' she says, reachin' for a handshake. She's a test pilot, for Christ's sake." I shook my head in amazement.

"Yeah," Israel laughed. We've got a bunch of 'em since most of the male aviators are off fightin' the war."

"Well, she sure knew what the hell she was talkin' about," I continued, still amazed. "Knew all about the F6F – of course, she flies 'em – gave me a full briefing on the differences between *Wildcat* and *Hellcat*. And I got to sit in a *Hellcat* and FEEL the controls." My enthusiasm showed. "She even gave me a pilot's handbook so I can be ready to fly at the first opportunity."

"I think we've got it, chief," Ed announced as he and Phil burst into the office and plopped a sheaf of papers on the conference table. Janet followed Ed and Phil in with three coffees.

"That's great that you've got it, Ed," Israel challenged. "But, tell me, Phil, will a run o' the mill swabby mechanic be able to figure it out?"

"Yeah, I think so." Phil squirmed a little. "Harpo knows the drill, so he can coach 'em." He glanced at me with a sympathetic grin. "Or do it himself."

"We'll have to refine it a bit before we send it over to the BuAer Rep," Ed cautioned. "Anyway, it's a good thing they show SLOW. At least nobody'll spin in."

10

SHAKEDOWN

The movement of *Belleau Wood* and her air group toward a rendezvous for her shakedown cruise began one day in May 1943. The ship eased out of her slip at Philadelphia NAVY Yard, en-route to the Naval Operating Base, Norfolk, while Hi Massey led his air group from NAS Floyd Bennett to their new, temporary home – Creeds Field, southeast of Norfolk. Meanwhile, I took the air group SNJ, picked up our flight deck officer, Lieut. Comdr. Benny Freedman at NAS Mustin Field at the Philadelphia Navy Yard, and continued on to NAS Norfolk.

First thing the next morning, Benny and I borrowed a carrier suitable SNJ-3C from CQTU to fly down to Creeds and brief the air group on procedures for the initial training exercises aboard *Belleau Wood*, cruising in the Chesapeake Bay with a single destroyer escort as plane guard, safe from the Nazi U-Boats lurking in the Atlantic.

"Gentlemen . . . GENTLEMEN!," I called out to quiet the ready room filled to standing room only with all the pilots of Air Group 24. "This is Lieutenant Commander Benny Freedman, *Belleau Wood*'s Flight Deck Officer." I waved to Benny, standing beside me and bowed slightly. "Mister Freedman's in charge of all operations on the flight deck – launching AND recovery – I report to him when we get to sea." There were nods and subdued greetings from the assembled pilots.

Freedman stood about five foot eleven and weighed, probably, about a hundred and seventy-five pounds. His kinky blond hair combed back from his generous forehead and his bulging light green eyes hinted at a Jewish heritage and his prominent, sunburned nose and full lips confirmed it. "I'm glad to meet all you gentlemen – finally," he began. "We came down here to give you a feel for what to expect during these exercises – a learning experience for all of us. While you are adapting your carrier experience to this narrowest of flight decks – it's over ten feet narrower than the narrowest escort carrier – my crew will be developing our airplane handling and spotting methods. I'd like ten airplanes on the first flight – three each TBF and SBD, and four F4Fs so we can work on spotting you for'rd with a manageable group the first time." He looked over at me and I nodded. *Don't ask me, Benny. You're runnin' the flight deck.* "You'll probably notice some confusion and hesitancy on the part of our plane directors so be patient with them." He made a calming gesture with his hands. "Then, while we re-spot the deck for launch, Harpo will debrief you on your landings." He looked at me. "Right?"

"Right, sir," I affirmed. I had been looking around the room greeting each pilot with eye contact, a nod, and a smile. "Hey!," I yelped. "Where's Candy?" I meant Candioto, of course.

"Lost him around Cape May on the way down from Floyd Bennett," Freddy Lamb sighed. "Along with Bill Bowers."

"What the hell happened to 'em, anyway?," I demanded.

Anderson spoke up: "I had the second section – Webber on my left wing and Bowers on my right, with Candy in his back seat." He used his hands to show a formation. "Freddy and I had the CAG's TBFs bracketed about five hundred feet above 'em when we ran into a big thunderbumber we couldn't get around – or under."

"Yeah. The clouds were right down to the water," Massey interjected. "Johnny Curtis called to say he had his fighters on top – in the clear at fifteen thousand feet. So I decided the safest thing to do would be to climb up through the clouds and get on top."

"Just after we went into the clouds," Andy continued. "We hit the damndest slipstream I've ever been in." He flailed his hands around to demonstrate a stall-spin. "We must've slid in behind the TBFs – is all I can say – Tossed me on my back and I had a hell of a time recovering on instruments."

"Yeah! Me too," Webber chimed in. "I broke out of the clouds in a forty-five degree glide." He wiped his forehead. "Barely pulled out before I hit the water."

"We were lucky to get under the clouds – VFR – and landed at NAS Cape May," Freddy sighed. "My section stayed together and Andy and Webber followed us in . . . But no Bowers – or Candy. I understand the Coast Guard never found a trace of 'em." Then with a sad smile, "We really miss Candy – He was such a happy guy."

"Yeah," I murmured. "Just when he found out how to get a bomb on target." I looked back to Benny. "Oh – Were you finished?"

"No – er – we won't use the catapult until we get the deck run down pat." He toyed with his little black and white checkered launch flag. "Looks like we'll have thirty or thirty-five knots across the deck so we'll have plenty of deck space to deck run everybody. I'd like to start tightening up the launch interval so start your right turn as soon as you feel comfortable off the bow. Any questions?"

"Yeah," Massey spoke up. "What order are you going to launch us in?"

"Oh, yeah." Benny scratched his forehead. "TBFs will go off first, then the SBDs, followed by the fighters.

The ready room buzzed with muted conversation.

"Okay – OKAY," Benny shouted over the din. "I'd like you to send the rest of your airplanes out just one hour after the first flight – uh – That would be twenty more, right?"

"That's right," Massey agreed. "But how are you going to handle all of us at once?"

"We'll launch the first ten before we bring the second flight aboard." Benny took a deep breath. "The second flight'll give us some experience spotting the for'rd flight deck full and striking some of you below on the for'rd elevator to the hangar deck." He gazed up at the overhead in thought. "Uh . . . If I think we're ready for it we may bring the first flight back aboard for a total air group deck spot . . . If not, we'll send the first flight back to the beach."

More mumbling from the pilots.

"Yeah. We're all learnin' at once." Benny turned to me, "Okay, Harpo. Tell 'em about landing."

"I guess the only thing different will be the *really* narrow deck Benny mentioned. You'll have to put the LSO closer to the center of your windshield comin' up the groove – and let's start right now working on a good landing interval – thirty seconds." I used my hands to demonstrate an approach pattern. "Put yourself at the ninety degree position when the guy ahead of you is getting a cut." I moved my hands around. "Backing it up, you want to start your turn off the downwind when the plane ahead of you is at the ninety." I spread my arms in an inviting gesture. "Any questions?"

Chapter 10: Shakedown

"Yeah." McLinden raised his hand. "How the hell are you guys goin' to get aboard – without an LSO?

The room erupted in mocking laughter.

"Worry not, gentlemen." I held up my hand in a confident gesture. "My new assistant is on board and we've got an SNJ with a Tailhook."

My new assistant, Lieut.(jg) Walter Wujcik, greeted Benny and me as we hopped off the wing of the SNJ just before the deck crew struck the airplane below on the after elevator. "Welcome aboard, Commander." He saluted Benny, shouting over the elevator warning horn, "Commander Dahl would like to see all three of us on the bridge."

Wujcik had joined us at Floyd Bennett only days before we migrated south to Norfolk to board the ship for this shakedown cruise. "Weej", as we called him, was tall and well built at about six foot two and a hundred and eighty-five pounds. His handsome Polish features were complemented by a shock of wavy blond hair and light blue eyes which, along with his quiet manner, signalled a natural shyness.

Up on the bridge, Dahl returned our salutes. Then: "Just one thing, men." Dahl frowned. "Remember that this is just an exercise – just like carrier qualification – No urgency required. Understand?"

A chorus of "Yes sir" responded.

"Harpo." Dahl poked his finger at the button on my shirt. "Don't hesitate to wave 'em off if they aren't just right – and I want you to handle all of 'em today – Wujcik can work some after we get some success under our belts."

"Yes sir! I'll take 'em all today."

"And, Benny – I want you to be damned sure the engines are just right before you launch 'em." He swung his hand in a cutting motion. NO WATER LANDINGS!"

"Yes sir, Ted," Benny nodded. "Extra cautious."

"Okay, men." Dahl patted each of us on the back in his fatherly manner. "They'll be here in fifteen minutes – Make it good!"

Why should I say anything about working on a good interval. Benny didn't. I led the way down the ladder to the flight deck.

As Wujcik and I stepped off the ladder on the port side of the island for our stroll back to Landing Signals the gray-green Chesapeake showed only an occasional whitecap under the cloudless summer sky indicating a ten knot surface wind from the southwest – ideal conditions for our first flight operations. The FOX flag

Paddles!

flew at the dip from the signal yard arm, signifying imminent flight operations, and the little red flag fluttered at Fly Control.

"I'm sure glad you joined us when you did, 'Weej'," I crowed, happily. "For a while I thought I was goin' to make this cruise alone."

"You're not as glad as I am, Harpo. Christ! I had orders to *Gambier Bay.*" He wiped his forehead. "Those 'Jeeps' have paper thin hulls and max out at about fifteen knots – sittin' ducks. I found out you needed an assistant and talked Commander Vossler into changing my orders. Whew! That was close."

"Hi Davy," I called across the deck to Lieut.(jg) Dave Kolb, the arresting gear officer. "Little Davy" as he was known, was a rugged little spark plug of a guy, about five foot eight and a hundred and eighty pounds – all muscle and nerves. His jutting jaw signalled his determination, and the directness of his sharp brown eyes confirmed it.

"We'll be ready." Little Davy threw us a "thumbs up" as the barriers came up behind him, punctuating the commitment, and we stepped gingerly over the three quarter inch arresting cables which had been raised on their "fiddlebridges" with the pull of a lever by one of Kolb's crew.

"Aasch! God damn!," Wujcik coughed. "This damn smoke'll kill us before we get to the platform. Aarschh." Is this normal, for Christ's sake?"

"I guess," I sighed. "Oww! Comes with little cinders too, I see."

With the wind off our starboard bow we were being peppered with pea sized cinders and the diesel smoke that issued from the stacks arrayed along the starboard side, amidships. "I remember gettin' smoked out a couple of times on *Ranger* – but no cinders. Happens when they're crankin' up to full engine power, I guess."

"Well." I looked up as the ship heeled to port. "Skipper's turnin' us into the wind. That'll stop the smoke attack."

"There they are." Wujcik pointed at the three *Avengers* and three SBDs bunched together in two tight sections, circling a mile astern, the four fighters trailing above and behind.

"Hi Monahan," I called down into the catwalk as we stepped onto the Landing Signals platform. "How's everything comin'."

"Communications with Fly Control established, sir." He tapped the sound powered phones covering his ears. "Here's your paddles."

Boatswain's Mate Third Class Edward J. Monahan was my talker, spotter, and all around keeper of the Landing Signals station. Talker was a apt job for Monahan, with his booming voice, New York Irish brogue, and a commanding tone beyond his third class rating – and his age – hell, he was only twenty. Because of his boyhood interest in airplanes he was good enough to be pressed into service as the gunnery department's aircraft spotter on the old heavy cruiser *Brooklyn* during operation "Torch", the Allied invasion of French North Africa in October 1942, where she sank five French warships. That confused the hell out of Monahan 'cause he thought the Frogs were our friends. Now he was the Air Department's Master-at-Arms and my aircraft spotter. We had just met Monahan the day before when Benny and I went aboard at NOB Norfolk. I wanted to get our signals straight so I called for a meeting at the Landing Signals station.

"Who's this?" I pointed to the other sailor in the catwalk with Monahan.

"This here is Seaman Callagee, sir." Monahan grabbed the other man's arm. "I got him assigned to help – er – like checkin' the deck and barrier condition – er – and he'll stand by to drop the windscreen if it's necessary. Y' said y' needed a man to do that, sir."

"You're right, Monahan. We need 'im." Then: "Glad to have you aboard – er – Callagee?" I wasn't sure.

"Yes sir." The young sailor faced me and stood proudly at attention. "That's me, Seaman First Class Robert Callagee. Glad to be wit ya, sir."

"Okay, Monahan." I stooped down to hand him the green canvas bound ledger I had drawn from ship's stores the day before. "I want you to keep the Landing Signals log."

"Yes sir." Monahan took the 5"x7" notebook. "What do I log?"

"Log the date and time at the beginning of each recovery operation. Then note the type and number of each aircraft . . . and Mister Wujcik or I – who's ever waving – will give you comments on each approach." I handed him a pencil. "Log all our comments – understand?"

"Thanks, sir." Monahan pulled a pen out of his shirt pocket. "I've got a pen . . . er – what kind of comments, sir?

"A critique of each approach – goods and bads – with specifics – for use in debriefing the pilots." I could tell he was a bit baffled. "We'll use LSO shorthand . . . That book will be our permanent record of all recovery operations."

"Hey! Here comes Massey with his torpeckers," Wujcik yelled as we were buffeted by the swirling wind. "Right up the wind streaks."

The CAG would make the first arrested landing on *Belleau Wood* – barring any glitches.

DOO-DEE-DOO-DEE. The yodel sounded, the FOX signal flag was two blocked, and the white flag replaced the red one at Fly Control. "RECOVER AIR-CRAFT," Commander Dahl roared over the bull horn. The ship held a steady course, putting the wind five or so degrees off the port bow and generating about 35 knots relative wind.

"Barriers and wires up, sir," Monahan yelled. "Fly Control says take 'em when you can get 'em." Then: "Gear, flaps, hook; all down, sir."

With all that wind across the deck, compared to FCLP, the big *Avenger* seemed to hang in the groove, showing its long belly and the tailhook hanging straight down from the very tip of the tail cone.

"A little slow now," I commented as I swam an easy COME-ON. "Good . . . Hold that altitude . . . Over here a little." I showed a SLANT PORT. "Hold it Forsythe." I snickered, holding a ROGER . . . then CUT. The *Avenger* seemed to float down to the deck. CRUNCH . . . WHEEE. The sound of the arresting wire running out. "Good – second wire – log this: 'O.K. – S.S.' for slow start – 'L.U.R.' for lined up right side – and circle a two – indicating second wire."

"Well. Massey got the first landing," I called to Wujcik.

"Yeah. And all the torpeckers and SBDs looked pretty good," Wujcik commented. "Except they're all havin' some trouble findin' the center of this narrow deck." He pointed aft. "Here come the fighters. This ought to be a little more exciting."

"Yeah. This is Johnny Curtis and his division." I pointed as the four little *Wildcats* buzzed by the starboard side. Lieutenant Commander Curtis, the fighter skipper, was an experienced carrier pilot and had shown it in FCLP.

"Gear, flaps, hook, all down, sir," Monahan yelled.

The little *Wildcat* looked like a toy hanging by a string, with its baby carriage landing gear, and the little tailhook dangling from its tail. "A little fast." I chanted, as I flashed the FAST signal. More left bank now – got to get to the center of this narrow deck." I tilted the paddles to port. "Okay . . steady." CUT . . . CRUNCH . . . WHEEEEE. "PERFECT! Right on the number three wire." I crowed, as Kolb gave Curtis the PUSH BACK signal, then BRAKES until his crewman released the wire from the hook, then a vigorous wave on up the deck. "F.S. – fast start – small l.u.r. – O.K. – circle three"

I turned to pick up "Nosmo" King, starting his approach, as Curtis gave a burst of throttle and sped up the deck, barriers popping up behind him as he passed.

"Deck clear, barriers. . . NOW!," Callagee yelled.

Chapter 10: Shakedown

"Hey, for bein' such a wild-ass bastard ashore "Nosmo" sure is a smooth son-of-a-bitch in the groove." I tossed over my shoulder to Wujcik as I flipped King a HIGH DIP . . . ROGER . . . CUT . . CRUNCH . . WHEEEE.

"Yeah!," Wujcik crowed. "First wire."

Hmm – He must've been sinkin' a little at the CUT after the HIGH DIP." I commented. Then: "Monahan – V.G. for very good, and S.A.R. – settled at the ramp – circle a one . . . "Y' know, Weej, we're learnin' technique with every landing."

"Gear, flaps, hook – all down, sir."

We were three days out of Norfolk bound for nobody knew where – except the skipper and the navigator – zig zagging and cruising at high speed to reduce the risk of a U-Boat encounter and constantly drilling on some aspect of combat or emergency ship operation.

I slumped into my desk chair back in my stateroom after an early breakfast, and let off some steam. "God Damn, Leo!," I groused to Captain Leo Dulacki, U.S. Marine Corps, with whom I shared stateroom 215. "The Exec is sure running a tight ship. How long is this stuff supposed to last?" I waved my arm at the bulkhead. "For Christ's sake, we're havin' General Quarters every day, gunnery drills, abandon ship drills, man overboard drills, and when we start flight operations I have to show up for every Flight Quarters, launchin' or recoverin' – makes no difference. I turned to look out the port hole at the destroyer six thousand yards to starboard. "When does it end?"

"When does it end? Hah!," Dulacki snapped. "I'll tell you when it ends. When this green crew is ready for continuous operation IN COMBAT." He banged his fist on the little desk. "God damn it Harpo. That's what a shakedown cruise is for," he raged. "No matter how experienced the crew is, the skipper's got to get 'em workin' as a team. And this is far from an experienced crew." He shook his head. "Drill – drill – and drill some more, that's the only way to build a fighting crew, and we'll be in the thick of the fight sooner than you think."

Leo was the commander of the Marine detachment aboard *Belleau Wood* and had considerable experience forming up combat teams in the Marines. He was a hard little guy, about five-foot-nine and a compact 160 pounds. His dispassionate face was accented by expressionless grey eyes that could look at you without acknowledging you were even there. He was the perfect stateroom mate – quiet, neat, and well disciplined. His Polish heritage matched well with the crew, which was fifty percent polish, drawn from the Camden, New Jersey area where *Belleau Wood* was built.

Is that why you keep a gun in our room all the time?" I nodded at the .30 cal. machine gun standing in the corner.

"God damned right." Dulacki grabbed the gun and began field stripping it. "I've got to know these guns better than any of my men – with the possible exception of my gunnery sergeant." He winked. "You'll notice I operate the gun director and work in the loading crew on our 40MM mount during gunnery drills." His chest swelled a little as he dropped the last piece of the machine gun on his desk. "There."

The bugle blared "Charge" over the ship's sound system, then: TOOWEEE – the Boatswain's pipe and – "ALL HANDS. MAN YOUR FLIGHT QUARTERS STATIONS FOR LAUNCHING AIRCRAFT."

"Got to go, Leo. I hope you get that thing back together," I chided, as I slipped on my yellow woolen knit sweater with the big Chenille letters on the back shouting "HARPO" – like in the movies. Another ego touch. Yellow was the color worn by anyone whose job was to direct aircraft. Plane pushers wore blue, the gas crew red, and arresting gear and catapult gangs green. All wore matching cotton helmets, except me; another bow to the altar of individuality.

"Hi, Benny," I hailed Freedman at the aft end of the island structure. "How're these guys doin, launchin' off this narrow deck?," I shouted over the roar of aircraft engines on the flight deck aft, as the ship heeled to port turning into the southwest breeze.

Benny turned to greet me. "No sweat Harpo." We braced against the freshening wind as we strode aft. "We'll have plenty of wind and plenty of deck so a deck run shouldn't be any challenge." He turned to look up the deck to where the catapult was. "I'll try some catapult launches after they get used to this." We stopped abeam the first TBF. "Stick with me while I launch 'em so you hear the same engine sounds I do. You're my backup you know."

Benny's hunched posture and long arms brought to mind an ape, coincidentally, since the plane pushers who worked for him were traditionally dubbed "deck apes." He wore a yellow dyed scivvy shirt with "FLY 1" stenciled front and back over his uniform khaki shirt. *No pretenses here,* I thought as I looked down at my hand knit yellow sweater, a little embarrassed.

At the sound of the yodel the signalman two-blocked FOX, the white flag came out at Fly Control, and Commander Dahl's voice blared "LAUNCH AIR-CRAFT" over the bull horn.

"Hey, Harpo – Weej! The squadrons are goin' to finish their group grope with a coordinated attack on the target sled, right about now," Jack Barbour announced as he rushed through the ready room on his way to the flight deck. "Come on – It'll be a real show."

We were cruising in the relative safety of the Gulf of Paria, between Venezuela and the island of Trinidad, our destroyer escort standing well clear of the target sled.

Lieutenant Barbour was the group Air Combat Intelligence Officer – ACIO – so Massey always brought him into preflight briefings since he would be instrumental in strike planning and coordination with other air groups in the combat zone. A graduate of Stanford University, Jack had been a stock broker in civilian life before he entered the Quonset Point Officer Candidate School – OCS – where he was selected for intelligence duty upon his graduation.

We all streamed out of the ready room and up the catwalk ladder to the flight deck and began our easy stroll aft where we would have an unobstructed view of the target sled – a thousand yards aft – and the coordinated attack. "God damn! Now I know why they call Omark "Rover," I exclaimed. "Did you catch him charmin' the pants off those señoritas last night?" We had sampled a few of the bars in Port of Spain, our temporary port city in Trinidad, where every other song was "Drinkin' Rum and Coca Cola", alternately in English and Spanish.

"Yeah, but did you see "Nosmo", over in the corner with that one honey at the 'Bahia'?" Wujcik rolled his eyes. "Never saw him after that – wonder if he got back to the ship okay." Ensign W. R. King's nickname, "Nosmo", derived from the ubiquitous "NO SMOKING" (NOSMO KING) signs. He was tall, lean, handsome, and irreverent, shunning the usual courtesies and protocol of NAVY life. Girls were attracted to his laid back manner and off-the-wall humor.

"Must've," Barbour interjected. "He was in the prelaunch briefing this morning." He shook his head. "Just as sassy as ever."

"You were pretty quiet last night, Harpo." Wujcik gave me a sly glance. "You seemed stiff – never even unbuttoned your blouse."

I blushed a little. "Uh – didn't want to make a fool of myself." *Yeah, you dumb shit. Takin' along that Luger was the dumbest thing you've done in a long time – against Captain's orders so I had to keep it hidden – couldn't relax all evening. How the hell could I have used the damned thing anyway, for Christ's sake – and WHY?* I cursed myself. *God damned egomaniac, that's what you are. Grow up, will ya, dimwit.* I had bought the 7.65MM Luger at Stoger Arms in New York on one of my forays into the city with Art Taylor, and one of the ship's boatswain's mates had fashioned a handsome canvas shoulder holster, of which I was very proud.

"Hey! There they are." Wujcik pointed to the sky on our port bow. "Lookin' good." The group was still in cruising configuration, with Massey's *Avengers* and John Little's *Dauntlesses* in the "van" at about 10,000 feet and Johnny Curtis' *Wildcats* doing the "Thatch Weave" 2,000 feet above them. The Thatch Weave was named for Lieut. Comdr. Jimmy Thatch who introduced the weave into NAVY fighter doctrine during the early days of the war. The basic weave required a division of four fighters to break into two sections of two and weave back and forth, one crossing under the other at about a 90° angle on the course line so that each could see and protect the other from an attack from behind. The weave was generally used by fighters escorting bombers and torpedo planes and for self protection on fighter sweeps.

"Caught 'em just in time, Weej." Barbour patted Wujcik on the back. "Now they're deploying for the attack."

The fighters stopped weaving and maneuvered for positions from which they would make near simultaneous strafing runs on the sled. Massey's TBFs began a looping letdown in preparation for shallow glide bombing runs while the SBDs maneuvered to positions for their steep dives. By this time there was quite a crowd on the flight deck, awaiting the show.

"Here come the fighters," someone hollered. And here they came, three little bunches of four *Wildcats* each, making a big splash with their .50 cal. wing guns, bracketing the target.

"The bombers are in their dives," someone announced, craning to look almost straight up.

"Ooohhh." The collective howl went up as they all saw the big splash at the same time.

"Somebody went in," a voice cried.

"Who was it, for Christ's sake?"

"How the hell do I know?"

"Looked pretty steep to me," Wujcik offered. "Pieces came off the airplane before he went in."

"Might've been the Mach effect," Jay Smith suggested. "I've heard that can be a problem in steep dives."

"What the hell's that?," I asked.

"Compressibility – transonic air flow over the tail surfaces can cause loss of control." Smith explained. "I don't know much about it but engineers are finding out some of this stuff in trying to design higher speed airplanes."

"THIS IS THE CAPTAIN SPEAKING," came over the bull horn. "THAT WAS ONE OF OUR FIGHTERS THAT WENT IN – ENSIGN KING WAS THE PILOT – *PATTERSON* IS MANEUVERING FOR A SEARCH OF THE AREA." The destroyer – or "tin can" – was trailing black smoke, headed for the area of the crash at flank speed.

"Good evening gentlemen," I called out as I took the one step up to the unpretentious stage at the front of the torpedo pilots' ready room. Wujcik stood just inside the watertight door leading to the flight deck. As the chatter calmed down, I turned to Massey, seated in his easy chair; front row, aisle. "Who's goin' out tonight, skipper?

"I'm going, and you'll have Smith, Alston, and Manker, in that order." He turned to look at each one as he named them. "Just four the first time, to avoid confusion."

"Good – Now I'd like to cover some things that are different from daytime operations." I stepped to the chalk board where I had sketched the ship and the traffic pattern. "I guess this'll be your first night carrier work – except for you skipper." *Christ's sake, first time for me too. but no use spreadin' that word. Remember the infallibility of the LSO. I'm sure Massey'll catch me if I screw up.* "The pattern's the same as in the daytime but, as you know, judging your altitude over the black sea surface is difficult. We have part of a moon tonight and all the ships in the formation will be showing masthead lights. It won't be that easy when we get out in the fleet, right, Skipper?"

"That's right Harpo," Massey agreed as he grasped the opportunity to join me on the "stage." "Out there." He waved his arm in a sweeping motion. "All the ships will cruise in a completely darkened condition and on a cloudy moonless night there's no way to tell where the sky stops and the ocean begins." He grimaced. "We're lucky we've got some moon tonight."

"Then how do we find the ship and set up a pattern?," Manker asked.

"The ship'll give you a few blinks of the signal blinker." Massey imitated a signalman sending blinker with one of the big signal lights used for ship-to-ship communications during radio silence. "They're directional and not likely to be picked up by a sub. Then, as you get close you'll be able to pick up the silhouette of the ship against the sea reflecting whatever light there is in the sky."

"Then you set up your pattern with a masthead level fly-by, just like in the daytime." I pointed to the starboard side of the ship's sketch."

"Here's the critical point," Massey interjected. "Check your altitude, at this point! Subtract a hundred feet, and that's about your altitude for approach. Harpo will take it from there. But keep a constant watch on your altimeter since your visual references will be poor to nonexistent."

"Jeez, Skipper," Alston moaned. "That sounds like low altitude night instrument flying."

"You got it, Jim." Massey flashed an evil grin. "You'll have some visual cues – especially tonight – but don't depend on 'em. Use your instruments!"

"Now," I resumed. "Comin' downwind you'll be able to see a very faint blue light about amidships just below the port catwalk, here." I pointed to the point on the diagram of the ship. "But not until you get about abeam the bow. It's a narrow beam. Start your turn into the approach abeam the blue light."

"You've got to let down a little here so watch your altimeter very carefully," Massey warned.

"You'll be able to pick me up at the usual point in your approach." I used my right hand to simulate the approach. "But you won't see the deck edge lights until you're just about in the groove. They are very directional."

"You've seen these wands before – during night bounce drill." The two "wands" I held were made of aluminum tubing three feet long and two inches in diameter, with one side of the tube cut out to house an array of red flashlight lamps set one inch apart backed by the white-painted interior acting as a reflector. The lamps were powered by two "D" batteries in the handle of each wand. "You probably noticed on your day landings on the ship that I'm easier to see during the approach than in bounce drill. That's due to more relative wind across the deck, and that effect is even more noticeable at night." *At least that's what Iarrobino told me.*

"That'll help," Manker sighed. "I had a hell of a time seeing those little wands at Floyd Bennett."

"Now, We've got to be able to check your gear, flaps, and hook down," I began. "We've got a search light in the starboard catwalk to light up your belly just before you get to the CUT position."

"You can't do that," Massey countered. "You'll blind us just before we get to the ramp."

"No we won't, sir," I responded. "You'll be looking out the left side of the cockpit so you'll never know it when we flash the light."

"I don't want to risk it," Massey stated, flatly. "Here's what you'll do." I recognized an order when I saw one coming. "You'll bring us up the groove to the cut position, turn on the light and check ALL DOWN, and give us a WAVE-OFF. We'll take the WAVE-OFF and WILL NOT retract gear, flaps, or hook. The second time up the groove you'll give us a CUT, if we're okay, because you'll know that we'll have ALL DOWN.

"I think that's a bigger risk, sir," I countered, cautiously. Wujcik winced. "What if somebody raises the gear or flaps, both kind of automatic actions as you pour the coal on."

"No one will," Massey commanded, as he stared at each of his flight, in turn, as though to hypnotize them.

"But sir," I implored. "Charlie Iarrobino on *Ranger* says that's how they do it and it works fine."

"Well this isn't the *Ranger*, and you're not Iarrobino." He stamped his foot. "Damn it, Harpo! WE DO IT MY WAY!," Wujcik winced again.

"Aye, sir."

At the Landing Signals platform I called down into the catwalk. "Okay, Monahan. Y'got your signals straight with the search light operator over there in the starboard catwalk?"

"Yes sir. Callagee's all set up over there and we got our signals straight," Monahan hollered up to me. "Just a second, sir. Hey Robin." He yelled into his sound powered phone. "Don't forget, keep that light aimed at the belly of the airplane all the way up the groove, then, when I say 'FLASH', flip the lever for one quick flash. Got it? . . . Good."

"Uh . . . Monahan . . . there's a little change in procedure tonight," I warned. "Commander Massey's afraid we'll blind 'em with the light, so they're goin' to make one pass and we'll check gear, flaps, hook with the light. Then they'll take a WAVE-OFF, leave everything down, and come around again with the intent of getting aboard. We don't use the light on the second pass. UNDERSTAND?" I waited for the acknowledgment. Monahan gave Wujcik a quizzical glance, like he thought I was kidding.

Paddles!

Wujcik shrugged. "Commander Massey said, 'TRUST ME'."

How the hell do we KNOW they'll leave "everything down" while they come around for another pass. I could tell Wujcik and Monahan were thinking the same thing. Nobody said anything.

"Well. He's the boss, and they're his airplanes," I sighed. "Now get that squared away with Callagee, over there."

Monahan passed the word to Callagee and then: "Yeah . . . Yeah . . . I told ya, Commander's orders." Then to me, "Yes sir, he's got it – I think."

"Whoa! here comes the first one," Wujcik warned.

"Massey, I presume," I called over my shoulder to Wujcik as I held a HIGH signal. "He is smooth. I'll say that for him . . . now ROGER . . . yeah . . ."

"FLASH . . WHEELS – FLAPS – HOOK . . ALL DOWN," Monahan called out. The flash of light and Monahan's report all took up the better part of a second.

WAVE-OFF. The *Avenger*'s engine roared, thrusting it forward into the darkness.

"That worked Okay," Wujcik offered as the last TBF took a WAVE-OFF and disappeared in to the darkness. "Here comes Massey again."

"Remember, Monahan. No light this time," I yelled down to Monahan. "NO LIGHT! Got it?

"Yes SIR. No light," he grimaced.

"Remind Callagee, over there!," I ordered as I raised my wands for a ROGER.

"Aye, sir – Hey Robin . . . no flash this time – got it? . . . Right! NO FLASH."

"Perfect position, Weej, ROGER all the way." Then, CUT – Beeeeeeeeeeeeeep CLOP CLOP CLOP – CRASH.

"What was that LONG Beep," Monahan yelled.

"THAT," I paused, "Was the warning horn that sounds when you chop the throttle with the landing gear up . . . and that funny 'CLOP CLOP CLOP' was the propeller tearing up the flight deck."

"Shit! He must've put the gear up when he took the WAVE-OFF," Wujcik moaned.

"Yeah, must have," I shrugged. "Now 'Cobbs's got to clear the deck while those guys circle and wait." I waved at the sky.

I ran forward and jumped up on the *Avenger*'s left wing, Massey was saying to Tate on the right wing, "Feets, that's not the way to do it." A bit ironic, I thought, since Massey had told Tate, after a bad day at CarQual, that he should quit carrier flying before he killed himself.

Chapter 10: Shakedown

"You okay, skipper?," I shouted into Massey's ear.

"Yeah," Massey cringed. "The only thing hurt is my ego, and I guess that'll heal." He lifted himself out of the cockpit and I gave him a hand down onto the flight deck. "I'll get another airplane and, after they clear this one away, I'll take off and we'll finish night qualifications."

"Yes sir." *Leave it alone, dummy. He's the BOSS!* "We'll be ready." I turned to head for Landing Signals.

"Wait," Massey cowered a bit, averted his eyes. "We'll do it your way, Harpo," he whispered, and turned to walk forward to the ready room.

11

DEPLOY

The light of the half moon glistened off the waves of Lake Michigan as Peggy and I embraced in the front seat of my Dad's 1941 Plymouth coupe parked at the edge of the bluff two hundred feet above the beach.

"Did you enjoy the evening, darling?," I whispered, referring to our night of dancing at Lakeside Pavilion, out by Paw Paw Lake.

"I loved it, Johnny." Peggy gave me another kiss. "When can we do it again?" Ooh! There's that tingle again... more intense this time. "I don't know, honey." I mused, as I gazed out across the silvery lake. "I've got to get back to Willow Grove tomorrow and I understand we'll be deploying soon. When, nobody knows, but we know it won't be long." I shook my head. "No tellin' when I'll get back here."

"Well, I'm leaving for Palm Springs next week anyway," Peggy shrugged. "Dottie and Patsy are out there and they thought I could get a job there. Ought to be a lot of fun."

"You didn't tell me THAT."

"It doesn't make any difference anyway, with you going to sea," Peggy paused. "Does it?"

"Might make a LOT o' difference!," I exclaimed. "All the fast carriers seem to be headed for the Pacific, and they all stop in San Diego on the way," I gloated. "I can probably get a day or two to come up and visit you. That is if you won't give me the brush off like you did when I came up to Mackinac Island.

Chapter 11: Deploy

"I didn't do that," she ventured. "I thought we had a nice time there."

"'I didn't do that' you say," I grinned. "Remember your first words when I surprised you in Bennett Hall?" I paused, but there was no answer. "You said: 'What are you doing here?'."

I could feel Peggy's cheek flush and I gave her a nice long kiss. "That's okay," I soothed. "You're doing much better now."

"I do hope you can come up to see me in Palm Springs," she cooed. "I'll be nice. Honest." Then: "I think we'd better be getting home. It's late."

As we drove along Lake Shore Drive toward my folk's home Peggy began putting my shoulder boards back on. "Hey! There's your house," she yelped, as we whizzed by my parents' home.

I was so engrossed with Peggy I didn't notice, but I started to slow down and drew her into my arms and kissed her on the lips. "Hmmm," I sighed.

"LOOK OUT!," Peggy cried, she being the only one who could see ahead.

I could feel the car leave the pavement for the grass border and looked up to see the tree directly in our path. BRAKES . . . CRASH!

"Damn it!," I cursed, thinking first of the damage to my dad's car. Then, with some panic, "Are you okay, honey?"

"I think so. I don't hurt anywhere," she grimaced. "The way you were hugging me, I couldn't go anywhere."

We both laughed as we climbed out of the car to survey the damage – a smashed grill, but apparently no damage to the radiator.

The three of us stood next to the bus that would take me to Chicago Midway Airport for my trip back to Philadelphia. Peggy had taken an earlier bus home to Detroit. I took my mother in my arms and kissed her good-bye, through her tears. Then my Dad shook my hand. "Thanks for coming, Sonny, and especially for bringing Peggy." He said, squeezing my shoulder in a warm embrace. Then in his typical dead pan humor: "Come back any time, just bring your own car."

We all laughed, concealing our shared concern over my imminent entry into the war – somewhere.

Wow! here I am in the Navy's newest fighter, the F6F-3 Hellcat. What a thrill! What a MACHINE! That big P&W 2,000 horsepower engine really drives her. Top speed over 400 mph, I hear. Look at this; hydraulics everywhere: No more cranking the landing gear up and no more bruised knuckles from trying to catch the

Paddles!

crank handle on the way down; and two big push buttons to hydraulically charge and safe the six .50 caliber wing guns – amazing, I thought, as we cruised over lush green Pennsylvania farmland, Wujcik on my wing and "Doc" Herr and "Arky" Snowden forming my second section. We had taken off only minutes earlier from NAS Willow Grove, where VF-24 had transitioned to F6Fs in just three short weeks – probably a record. Wujcik and I had been pressed into service for this little ferry hop since some of the senior squadron officers were tied up with administrative matters. We were to taxi the airplanes to the Philadelphia Navy Yard pier where *Belleau Wood* was moored. They would be loaded aboard the ship for our deployment the next day.

"NAVY Mustin, this is NAVY 25837, four F6Fs over Camden, three thousand feet," I called, as we cruised down the Delaware river. "Request landing instructions. Over."

"NAVY 25837, this is NAVY Mustin, You're cleared for your overhead break, landing runway one four, wind east, ten to fifteen knots. Traffic is two SBNs at the break now.

"NAVY Mustin, 837 here, please check our special clearance to taxi directly to the NAVY Yard."

"Clearance confirmed, 837. Pick up the yellow jeep in front of operations."

"Roger, Mustin, taxi clearance confirmed."

Well! I've never seen an SBN in person – only pictures. SBN stands for "Scout Bomber by Naval Aircraft Factory", right here on NAS Mustin. Looks a lot like the SBA, made by Brewster, up north of here. They're both competing with the Curtiss SB2C to become the next fleet scout bomber. Yeah! it was an SBA that went in nose first on Floyd Bennett last winter. I remember I was the first one up on the airplane in the waist deep water, and the sight was appalling. The pilot had a gash in his forehead that went all the way back to his temples, and most of his blood was in his lap – and the passenger, a lieutenant in blues, was just a bag of broken bones, oozing blood. I learned to keep my cookies down on that one. OOps! Here we are.

"NAVY Mustin, this is NAVY 837, at the break."

"837, this is NAVY Mustin, you're cleared the break to downwind. Call turning base. Traffic is one SBN landing and one turning base."

We made our break, turned downwind, and, "NAVY Mustin, NAVY 837, turning base, gear down and locked."

"Cleared to land, 837. Turn off on the center taxiway and proceed to ops."

Chapter 11: Deploy

Well. There's the yellow jeep, as advertised. The man standing in the back of the jeep gave me the two fisted BRAKE signal and the signal to fold my wings. Four sailors rushed up to push my wings up to the fold lock position and we waited the couple of minutes it took for the others to join me on the taxiway and fold their wings. Then he waved us on as the jeep driver headed south along the aircraft parking apron until he turned right into one of the regular two lane streets on the station. Soon we found ourselves taxiing between two story houses built close to the street on either side. *Jesus! No wonder they folded our wings. If they were spread we'd be scraping the houses. Hmm. They'll have to take the SBDs a differ-ent route since their wings don't fold.* Sitting in our cockpits, we were eye to eye with the residents sitting on their second story porches, the men waving and giving us thumbs up, and the women blowing kisses as their drying laundry blew wildly in our slipstreams. We replied in kind. *I guess they know we are on our way to the war zone. What a thrilling send off for this small town kid from Michigan.*

"I get the impression this may be our last shore leave for a while," Wujcik commented, as we donned our whites for our evening on the big town, Washing-ton, D.C., in our Mayflower Hotel room.

Belleau Wood had anchored off the Naval Academy to give the middies a look at a REAL ship, and shore leave and liberty had been authorized for half the crew.

"Yeah," I groaned. "It'll take a couple o' weeks to get to San Diego." I bright-ened at the thought. "But when we get there I've got a date with Peggy in Palm Springs. Hot dog!"

"C'm on," Wujcik goaded. "Forget it for tonight, Harpo. I hear they've got some real live spots here," he enthused. "Let's find 'em."

25 July 1943 – We had just recovered the second training flights on the second day out of Norfolk, cruising south through choppy Atlantic waters. Wujcik and I were in the fighter ready room giving the usual critique of each pilot's approach, speaking from notes in the Landing Signals log.

"Doc – and you too Arky – you tend to approach too far to starboard." I used my hands to demonstrate. "I had to give you each a couple of WAVE-OFFs 'cause if I'd CUT you, you'd have landed in the starboard catwalk."

"Hell, I can't see you over the nose of this airplane," Doc complained. "It's not like the F4F. Little guys like me just can't see over that big nose."

"Same here," Arky chimed in. "On that last approach, all I could see was ocean on both sides of my airplane comin' up the groove. Shit, Harpo, I just barely caught the flash of your CUT."

"Yeah, I noticed you were a little wobbly comin' up the groove."

Ensigns Doc Herr and Arky Snowden were both about the same size and shape; not over five foot eight and short waisted, making them sit "short in the saddle" as cowboys say. Doc had a handsome round face with a curiously wrinkled brow, giving him a chronic quizzical look, and Arky actually resembled Leo Gorky, bad guy star of "Our Gang", with his pugnacious pout and piercing black eyes.

"Get a cushion, for Christ's sake," boomed Oveland.

Lieut(jg) Collin Oveland was the sixth senior pilot in the squadron, right behind Lieut.(jg)s "Stinky" Innis and "Dirty Eddie" March but was beginning to demonstrate strong leadership qualities and showing little sympathy for complainers. Collin had a movie star handsomeness with his fine Irish features, Clark Gable moustache, and perfectly combed blond hair. At five foot eleven he sat high enough to see over the nose of the Hellcat.

"I've already got two," Arky wailed.

"I don't know, Collin," the skipper interjected from his aisle seat in the front row. "I notice a big difference looking around the nose of this airplane. It's BIG. I'm tall enough that I don't have a problem, but I can sympathize with Doc and Arky." He paused. "Hell! I've never landed on a carrier this narrow. It takes some adjustment."

The skipper was soft spoken Lieut. Comdr. Johnny Curtis whose pursed smile and raised eyebrows gave him the appearance of someone continually enjoying some private humor. His prominent forehead gave way to sparse, graying brown hair.

"Yeah, skipper," Collin groused. "I guess the little guys do have a problem."

Curtis pursed his lips even further and did his best to frown as I sat down on the front of the little stage, facing him. "Harpo," he ventured. "Can you think of any way to avoid this problem?"

"I've been thinkin' about it Skipper," I began, cautiously. "Y' know, I've had some difficulty seeing Wujcik in bounce drill so I understand." I thought for a moment. "I've got an idea – but I don't like it very much."

"Well, let's have it," Curtis urged.

Jesus! Sounds like we're all learning together, I thought.

"Wait!," Herr interjected. "How about this, Harpo. Arky and I can approach up the starboard side, so we can see you, and then, at the CUT, we'll bank left and aim for the deck center line." With a glance a the skipper he appealed for approval. "How about it?"

Whew! I'm glad Doc suggested it. "Whoa!" I held up my hand, palm toward Doc. "Are you both SURE you can CONSISTENTLY make that left turn into the deck center." I challenged.

"I'm sure I can do that," Doc replied with a confident air.

"No problem, Harpo," Arky chirped. "Trust me." He raised his right hand as if making an oath.

"Is that okay with you Cap'n." I put the monkey on Curtis' back.

"For Christ's sake, Harpo," Curtis raged. "We've got to do SOMETHING. These guys have had three hops so far and had the same problem on every approach, RIGHT?"

"Yes sir," I replied, standing almost to attention.

"Then, DO IT!," Curtis ordered, emphatically. Then, eyeing Herr and Snowden very seriously, he lectured: "Now, listen up you guys. Don't forget what happens if you DON'T make that turn to the centerline – a SERIOUS catwalk crash, with you in it! GOT IT?"

"Yes SIR, Skipper."

"I got it, Boss."

The ships of the group hove to as the breakwater sheltering Limón Bay loomed close at hand and three small launches motored through the breakwater entrance towards us, bringing Canal pilots to the three carriers in the group; *Lexington*, *Princeton*, and our own *Beulah Maru*. The carriers would pass through the Panama Canal first, followed by their escorts.

"I guess we're going through in the order of our hull numbers." I mused as Wujcik and I stood on the forward end of the flight deck watching *Lexington* take up the lead. "First CV-16, second, CVL-23, and last but not least, CVL-24."

"Probably won't be the first time we'll be Tail End Charlie," Wujcik groused. "Might as well go below for a cup of coffee 'til we get to the locks."

Two hours later we were towed quietly into the northernmost of the Gatún locks by ten "mules", little locomotives on railroad tracks on either side of the lock. We watched *Princeton* rise slowly in the lock ahead of us as *Lexington* stood nearly at the level of Gatún Lake in lock number 3.

"Jesus," Wujcik exclaimed. "We can just barely see the top of *Lex*'s island. She must be up there a hundred feet."

Paddles!

"Eighty-five." It was Jack Barbour, the group intelligence officer.

"God damn, Jack," I exclaimed. "You know EVERYTHING!"

"Naw," Jack shrugged. "Just a little trivia here and there. Hey! Did you feel that."

"Yeah," Arky exclaimed with an amazed look. "We're goin' up, aren't we."

As *Belleau Wood* slipped smoothly through the placid waters of Gatún Lake, Wujcik and I strolled aft through the parked Hellcats to Landing Signals, drawn by some force that seems to pull NAVY people to their battle stations.

"God damn!," Exclaimed Wujcik. "Good thing we've got a pilot aboard. Hell! I can see land stickin' up all over the lake. No tellin' what would happen if we got out of the channel.

"Yeah," I agreed. "I guess they couldn't afford to fill up the lake all the way." Then, peering across at the verdant hillside: "Looks like they cut this canal right out of a tropical rain forest."

"And everybody got Malaria from the fierce mosquitoes, I hear."

"Not everyone, Weej," I teased. "They had to have somebody left to build the canal. Hey! what was that?"

A raucous cheer came up at the aft end of the flight deck.

"What the hell is all the yellin' about." Wujcik shouted as we both scrambled aft.

"I'll be God damned," I wheezed. "It's 'Hoot' with his friggin' fishin' pole – and he's hooked into something big. The way that rod's bent I don't know how the hell he'll ever boat whatever he's got, standin' there thirty feet above water level in that fantail gun tub."

Ensign Joe "Hoot" Gibson, one of our fighter pilots, was a true Southerner from Chattanooga, Tennessee, and an avid fisherman. He always looked happy – or surprised – I could never tell which, his thick lips frozen in a detached smile and his big blue eyes glowing with some discovery unknown to the rest of us. His kinky black hair crowned a square forehead, sans wrinkles. His broad southern drawl was a novelty to us Yankees.

"Oooooh!," came the collective groan from the crowd on the flight deck. Hoot had lost his catch.

"What the hell was that, Hoot?," I yelled down from the catwalk.

"Hey! Hawpo, Weej," Hoot hollered back. "The son-of-a-bitch took mah lure, damn it."

Chapter 11: Deploy

"Yeah. I can see," I called. "But what was it?"

"A great big groupah, ah'll bet." Hoot held his hands out almost at arms length and his eyes grew like saucers.

"Groupers don't grow in lakes, Hoot," I countered.

"Ya wanna bet."

As *Belleau Wood* cruised westward, four days out of Panama, I strolled aft along the flight deck, accompanied by Lieut.(jg) Harry "Dirty Eddy" March, one of the three fleet seasoned pilots VF-24 had. Harry was tall – about six foot four – with a definitely hunched posture, as though he were trying to get down the level of the rest of us. He was a happy soul, with his infectious smile and irreverent manner. But he could be very serious and direct if the situation warranted. We encouraged the pilots to come back to Landing Signals during recoveries to observe the operation from our vantage point, one or two at a time, of course. We were preparing to recover aircraft from all three squadrons. I didn't think there was much Harry needed to learn about carrier landings, but I welcomed his interest. *What the hell.* I thought. *Maybe I can learn something from HIM.*

"God damn, Harry. I've heard of the dark blue Pacific, but this is downright BLACK," I marvelled. "You've been out here before. Is the Pacific this black all over?"

"Yeah," March nodded. "Always this color on a clear day, but on cloudy days it changes to a dark grey color. Fascinating." He clapped me on the back, "Hey, have you seen the fluorescence in the wake at night, Harpo?"

"Naw, I don't get up here at night."

"You should, you know," March urged. "On nights like these the Milky Way doesn't seem to have any gaps – just solid stars. It'll knock your sox off . . . While you're at it, Harpo, take a look at the wake." He pointed aft at the big white wake. "The fluorescence in the wake varies in intensity, but it's always there on the Pacific, and it's like runway approach lights to line you up for a night carrier approach."

Son-of-a-bitch, I learned something already. "Hey, thanks a lot, Harry." Then: "Christ in the foothills, Harry. We've been on this course ever since we left the Canal. We've got to turn north pretty soon to get to San Diego, don't we?"

"Haven't you heard," Harry chided. "We're not goin' to San Diego. Hah! Sing it, Harpo; 'Pearl Harbor, here we come.'"

"What do you mean, 'not goin' to San Diego,'" I raged, watching my planned

127

Paddles!

rendezvous with Peggy fade. "Don't we have to replenish and get new orders there?"

"They just announced it in the ready room before I came up on deck," March crowed. "Hell, the whole damned command structure's moved to Pearl, and they've got more God damn supplies there than in San Diego, now."

"Well, shit!," I groused. "I was supposed to meet my girl friend, Peggy, in Palm Springs during our San Diego port stop. I guess I'll have to write another 'sorry' letter. Peggy gets a lot of those."

"Sorry, Harpo," March grinned. "War is hell." Then: "Hey! Here come the fighters." March pointed off the starboard quarter where eight *Hellcats* flew up the wind streaks with tail hooks down as the ship turned to port in search of the wind line and the ship's engines shook the fan tail.

"Hi Harpo. I see you brought an expert with you," Wujcik greeted us at Landing Signals. "God Damn! We might learn something from 'Dirty Eddy'."

"Shit, Weej. I already did. I'll tell you about it later."

"Gear, flaps, hook, all down, sir," Monahan shouted up from his station in the catwalk.

March stood immediately behind me, looking over my shoulder. "This first one's Bob Ross, I think."

"Yeah, it's Ross alright," I hollered over the swirling wind. "Roger all the way – typical Ross."

"Well," I gloated. "That went pretty well – nary a wave-off – and Doc got back to deck center, no problem. All we got left is Arky. He'll be comin' up the starboard side, just like Doc."

"Gear, flaps, hook, all down," yelled Monahan.

"Okay, Arky," I coached, as I gave him a left bank signal. "Not that far to starboard."

"Clear deck! Barriers up," came Callagee's assuring report.

"Shit!," I croaked. "Now he has to come back, making his visibility worse." Signal: FAST. "Okay now – nice – ROGER – okay – now – CUT! . . . Turn to deck center, You son-of-a-bitch. TURN!"

"God damn!," Wujcik yelled. "It's a catwalk!" Then: "Wow! Look at that!"

"The wire just jerked the whole empennage off," March marvelled. "He's headed for the stacks!"

As Arky smashed through the opening between numbers two and three stacks, we all raced for the starboard catwalk to see if he would get out. The plane guard

128

destroyer made a trail of black smoke accelerating to pick up Arky – we hoped.

"I'll be a son-of-a-bitch." March was elated. "The little fucker's already out and standin' on the wing.

The rescue was classic: The destroyer plucked Arky off the wing just as the crumpled *Hellcat* slipped beneath the waves.

The whole crew was topside, decked out in whites, as *Belleau Wood* steamed slowly through the entrance to Pearl Harbor, past the two tugs that had opened the submarine net for us. Off to starboard stood the Honolulu skyline, framed by the silhouette of Diamond Head, and to port, the steep promontory of Barbers Point decorated with verdant tropical growth. Four twin boomed P-38s passed us astern at about 1500 feet, heading for the Army's Hickham Field but giving no indication they'd seen us. Moments later we were greeted by a flight of four *Hellcats* buzzing along our starboard side, close aboard at deck level, on their way to a breakup over the red and white striped control tower on NAS Ford Island. Then we watched them, one-by-one, approach over our heads and land on the broad runway as our pilot guided *Belleau Wood* to port, around to the northwest side of Ford Island.

TOOO-EEE. "NOW HEAR THIS! FORM FOR PORT PARADE!," boomed the flight deck bull horn. "ATTENTION TO STARBOARD!"

"Air Department, FALL IN!" Lieut. Comdr. Mahchek, the Assistant Air Officer stood rigidly at attention on the flight deck just above 40MM gun mount number two as the Air Department lined up by division – V-1, V-2, and V-3 – from the forward edge of the flight deck, aft. "DRESS RIGHT!" Much shuffling of feet. "ATTENTION . . . AT EASE!" Very tall and emaciated, Mahchek had very sharp features, dominated by his large, beak shaped nose that inspired us to dub him "The Raven" as he leaned over his perch at Fly Control.

"THIS IS THE CAPTAIN SPEAKING," blared the bull horn. "WE WILL SALUTE THE WELCOMING PARTY IN ABOUT FIVE MINUTES . . . STAND BY."

"Jesus Christ! What the hell's THAT," cried Little Davy Kolb, pointing forward to the pier we were approaching.

"Left over from the Jap attack." Benny Freedman advised. "Wait'll you see the other side of the Island. *Oklahoma* still lies on the bottom with the main deck five feet under water – and all that's visible at *Arizona*'s pier are some spindly masts left over from her superstructure."

Paddles!

"Aren't they goin' to clear 'em out to make room for floatin' ships?," Davy asked. "Christ on a crutch!" It's been a year and a half."

"They got *Oklahoma* righted, and last time I was here they were plannin' to raise her." Benny looked down at the capsized hulk we saw at the pier. "No plans for *Utah*, there, or *Arizona* either." He bowed his head as though in prayer. "I guess they'll leave 'em as memorials to all the officers and men still down there. Anyway they've got to fix the ones that are fixable."

From the pier we heard the strains of "Aloha Oe" as the welcoming party struck up the NAVY band.

"ATTENTION ALL HANDS," the bull horn shouted. "HAND . . SALUTE!"

"Look at that piss ant band down there," Kolb whispered. "Two saxophones, one trumpet, a tuba, and a bass drum. Y' call that a welcome? Shee-it!"

"Better'n nothin'," Benny countered. "All the able bodies are out fightin' the war."

12

VP COUNTRY

"Sorry, suh." Purred the Chief Steward at the NAS Kaneohe officers' mess. "De unifoam fo' de ebenin' meal be whites, suh . . . But we gwine be open 'til twenty hundred so y'all's got plenty of time to change b'fo' we closes." He bowed slightly and his is broad smile revealed a complete set of sparkling white teeth.

"Change into WHAT?," I demanded. "On temporary duty ashore from a carrier we've only got room for one full khaki uniform, two or three pants and shirts, and our flight gear."

"Sorry, suh," the chief sympathized. "Cap'n's orders." Another ear-to-ear smile.

"Well, we'll fix that," I fumed. "Commander Massey'll be happy to hear that his pilots aren't allowed to eat in the officer's mess here." I tossed back at the chief as Wujcik and I made a bee line for Massey's quarters.

NAS Kaneohe was the operating base of Patrol Wing two, or should I say it was OCCUPIED by PatWing 2. The P-Boat drivers had set themselves up handsomely on Kaneohe, the most beautiful station on Oahu; boasting the best officers' mess in the islands, a beautiful championship golf course, and a gorgeous white sand beach on the north shore. They patrolled the whole central Pacific from here in their PBY *Catalinas*. Most of the married officers had their wives with them and occupied quarters on the station. They sure as hell didn't want their paradise marred by a bunch of boorish carrier pilots. *Hmm. Shades of my encounter with VP-17 and Lieutenant Proctor at NAS Key West last fall.*

Paddles!

"Yassuh, de duty offissuh called an' tol' us to let you gent'mens in." The Chief showed us to a table over in the corner away from the windows, in an area where he had already seated ten or twelve of our air group.

Oveland, Tabler, Wujcik, and I took our seats. "I guess this is the isolation ward," Oveland groused as he glared at the patrol pilots, all dressed up in their white uniforms, seated comfortably at the window tables. "Maybe nobody told 'em there's a war goin' on."

Back at Ford Island, I stepped up to the dispatcher's desk at the Carrier Air Service Unit (CASU). "I'm Lieut.(jg) Harper, the *Belleau Wood* LSO. I'd like to borrow an SBD or SNJ to get a little flight time."

Lieut.(jg) Sam Gallu stood behind me in quiet anticipation of the sight seeing ride around Oahu I had promised as we steamed into Pearl Harbor a couple of days earlier. Sam had been the director of Fred Waring's choir in civilian life and was now the ship's Signal Officer, in charge of all nonelectronic communications – semaphore, blinker, signal flags, etc. He was a rolly polly Italian about five foot eight with a perpetually happy face, featuring a Roman nose and a big smile. His olive complexion almost matched his sparse brown hair and his sparkling brown eyes radiated an enthusiasm for life and a love for people. Sam revelled in sliding his hand down my flat top crew cut from crown to brow and crowing, "You got a slidin' board head, boy."

"Sorry, sir." The dispatcher looked at his status board. "All I got left is one SO3C – It does have two seats, you know."

"I'll take it," I replied without a second thought.

The Curtiss SO3C *Seagull* was a seaplane observation plane flown off battleships and cruisers as spotters for shore bombardment and other scouting duties. I had heard that the Seagull was sorely underpowered with its twelve cylinder Ranger in-line engine, a truly gutless wonder. The guys that flew it in the fleet dubbed it "Kiwi" after the flightless bird of New Zealand. It was barely out of that class. The one they loaned me had a set of wheels in lieu of the single float used for fleet duty.

"Are you comfortable back there, Sam?," I called to over the intercom.

"Yeah. This is WONDERFUL!" Sam was absolutely delighted. "Is that a naval air station down there?"

"Yeah. That's NAS Kaneohe." I dropped the left wing further to give him a better view. "That's where the air group is based until our next cruise. Great place for Field Carrier Landing Practice, with the unobstructed approach over Kaneohe Bay." I levelled the wings and cruised across the bay to parallel the north shore of Oahu. "Hey, Sam. These rugged green canyons that drop down to the ocean are really gorgeous when you get up into them. Let's try this one." I had been all the way up this canyon and over the top in an F6F so I knew the terrain.

"Great," Sam called. "I'd love to see some of the interior."

Okay, J.A. Just ease her up this canyon. I've never flown the Seagull before but I've got enough time in the OS2U Kingfisher so I think I know how she'll handle.

"This is gorgeous, Harpo," Gallu called through the intercom. "Look at that pencil waterfall streaming down from that cliff up there."

I could see Sam through my rear view mirror, gawking up at the falls as we skimmed along close to the verdant canyon floor. *Oh oh! Canyon's gettin' steeper. And I've already got full throttle! This is REALLY a gutless wonder.*

"God damn! This is pretty," Sam chirped. "Look there, to the right. A real, honest to God Hawaiian grass shack. Like the song says. And there's a native wavin' to us." He waved back. "Hi guy."

Shit! We're stuck now. Not enough power to climb out and the canyon's so narrow I probably can't make a one-eighty without spinnin' in. Gotta try the turn, though.

"Yeah! That's neat." Sam was delighted. "Now we can see the little town down there. Real pastoral."

Shut up with your God damned poetry, Sam. We're just about to bust our asses and you're singin' about the beauty of the country side. "Tighten your shoulder straps, Sam." I called, as calmly as I could. "Just in case." *Oops! the stall buffet . . . and here comes the other side of the canyon. Gotta drop the nose just a touch. Whoa! We're goin to hit – HARD.* I must have closed my eyes for a moment.

"Hey! Why are we goin' back out of the canyon?," Sam wailed. "Just when it was gettin' beautiful." Then: "What was that shudder? Rough air?"

When nothing happened, I opened my eyes. *Whew! Back in the middle of the canyon! How the hell did I do that?* "Yeah, Sam, rough air." I sighed with relief. "I thought we'd cruise along the beach and look at the sun bathers." *That's sure as hell safer than what we just did. Wow! That's as close as I want to get to killin' myself – and good old oblivious Sam, too.*

"Got a couple of new fighter pilots here, Harpo," Wujcik greeted me as I sauntered into the VF ready room. "This is Ensign Schroeder, and that's Ensign Fleischer, over there."

"They call me 'Speed'," Schroeder announced, as his chest swelled with egotistical pride.

Fleischer stepped forward. "'Flash' Fleischer here," Fleischer sang out with an arrogant toss of his head.

"Well, I'll be God damned. Schroeder and Fleischer!," I exclaimed. "Sounds like a couple of renegades from the Luftwaffe. How about Schutzleutnant Schroeder und Fliegmeister Fleischer? Sieg Heil!" I teased and we shook hands all around.

I could tell "Speed" and "Flash" didn't know what to make of me, as they both took sidelong glances at Wujcik. I was enjoying it, but kept a serious expression.

"Take it easy, troops. He's only kiddin'." Wujcik clapped Schroeder on the back. "Hey, where're you guys from?"

"Hermann, Missouruh, on the banks of the wide Missouruh," Fleischer announced, proudly. "The heart of Missouruh wine country."

"Schulenburg, Texas, on the road to San Antone," Schroeder bragged. "In the big cattle ranch country."

"Who the hell ever heard of Missouri wine?," I sneered. "Hmm. Hermann and Schulenburg. Now I understand." My eyebrows went up. "Do those towns have German bunds? We had one where I lived in Michigan."

"Not that I know of, sir," Fleischer ventured, cautiously.

"Me neither, sir," Schroeder stammered, still a bit stunned.

"Okay, Speed, Flash. Call me Harpo." I eased their tension. "We've got a lot of work to do before our next cruise, and not even two weeks to do it in. Fortunately this is one of the best places I know of for bounce drill. Your approach is all over Kaneohe Bay with no obstruction. But look out for the P-boats." I referred to the PBY *Catalinas* flown by PatWing Two.

"Sounds super to me." Schroeder acknowledged, haughtily.

Hmm. God's gift to Naval Aviation. I thought. "There's just one thing to worry about," I warned. "The runway is only about fifteen feet above the surface of the water instead of seventy or eighty feet like on a carrier. So WATCH YOUR ALTITUDE! Now, Weej'll give you the FCLP briefing while I go see if I can scare up a couple o' airplanes for you."

Chapter 12: VP Country

Two days later: "Hey! These guys are pretty smooth for just coming out of CQTU," Wujcik called over his shoulder as he tapped a FAST at Schroeder, coming up the groove. Then: CUT . . CRUNCH . . ROAR.

"Yeah. Speed's generally on the fast side while Flash seems to like it a little low and slow," I mused. "Oops. Here he comes now."

"As usual, low and slow at the ninety." Wujcik fluttered a LOW at Fleischer. "Damn it! I don't think he can see the signals yet." He shook the paddles in the LOW position. "Come on. GET UP!"

"Jesus Christ! He's still settlin'." I instinctively shook a LOW at him with only the palms of my hands to show for it.

"Whew! That's better," Wujcik yelled. "He's got the nose up."

"Yeah, but he didn't add any throttle," I groaned. "Now he's settlin' fast. Oh Shit! He's goin' in."

The spectacular white splash settled back into the bay to reveal the *Hellcat* perched serenely in about five feet of water with the cockpit and wing completely out of the water. Fleischer clambered out of the cockpit onto the left wing and waved feebly, as though to signal: "I'm okay." The rescue boat was already on its way from its dock near the seaplane ramp.

Back in the ready room Wujcik briefed Fleischer, still drying off but uninjured, on the hazards of his low, slow approaches, as if he needed to be reminded after that experience.

"Hey Flash," I called, suppressing a Cheshire cat grin. "I've got a new nickname for you."

"Yeah? What's that, Harpo?"

"Splash."

We had been at the officers' club bar since night bounce drill had been canceled due to a thunderstorm that pummeled NAS Kaneohe with sheets of rain right after our evening mess.

"Hey! Bartender," Rover hollered, with a slight slur. "Another round here." CRASH! He smashed the dice cup down on the bar, upside down. "Lyer'sh Dysh or Horshes. What'll it be," he stammered, clearly beyond the tipsy stage.

"Liar's dice, I say," Collin yelled as he clapped his hand over Rover's on the dice cup. "Okay by you Harpo?"

"Hell yes," I asserted. "My game. Call 'em, Rover."

"ATTENTION ON DECK," someone shouted as Commander Massey burst through the swinging doors and headed straight for the bar, fire in his eyes. We all jumped off the bar stools and stood at a wavering attention.

"What the hell are you men doing in here, living it up?," Massey raged. "Night bounce drill is scheduled for tonight."

"It was canceled due to rain, sir," I ventured, stiffening perceptibly.

"I did NOT cancel it, Harpo, God damn it!," Massey bristled. "'POSTPONED' was the word. Postponed until after the rain. It's stopped raining now. Get 'em in the air!" He jabbed his finger toward the ceiling.

I shrank just a bit and offered: "But sir, I don't think . . ."

"Never mind what you think, damn it. Launch 'em . . NOW!"

"Aye, aye, sir." I almost saluted uncovered, and some of the pilots actually did salute, a reflex reaction.

The whole bar cleared out while I was saying "Aye, aye, sir", and I was right behind them. As we all headed for the flight line, I thought: *Let's see. The torpeckers are first. Jesus, Rover's stoned out of his gourd. I hope he can make it. Some of the others aren't much better.*

"Hey Rover," I called. "Don't just stand there, for Christ's sake. Get in the airplane!"

"Shit! Harpo," Rover moaned. "I can't find the fuckin' foot holds."

"Hey, Feets," I hailed Ben Tate as he headed for his airplane. "Help me get Rover in his airplane."

With Tate pushing and me up on the wing pulling, we poured Omark into his cockpit and helped him start his engine. "Are you okay, Rover?" I asked, as I helped him with his shoulder straps.

"Yeah. What the hell," Omark mumbled. "I could do this blindfolded."

Yeah. And it's a good thing, if true. He might as well be blindfolded, as drunk as he is. God! I hope we don't lose somebody tonight. I don't think Massey knew how drunk some of us were. Okay, J.A. Sober up and get with it. I thought as Wujcik drove us out to the end of the runway in the Air Group 24 jeep.

"God damn!," Wujcik broke the uneasy silence. "Has Massey gone batty? Somebody's liable to get killed tonight, drunk as they all are."

"Well, Weej," I said, gravely. "Now it's up to us to make sure they don't."

"Hey, Harpo," Wujcik yelled over his shoulder. "Here comes Rover again. He's been smoother'n lion shit, for Christ's sake. It's amazing! " He held a steady ROGER on Omark with the lighted wands. "ROGER all the way every God damned time." CUT . . . CRUNCH . . . ROAR. "Perfect!"

"Yeah, we knew he was good. But this is awesome!," I laughed. "Maybe we ought to get him drunk every time before he flies." . . . "Hey, here comes Tate again. Look out."

"Tate's high and slow again," Wujcik moaned as he stroked a few COME-ONs. "Damn it! I'm afraid to give him a high for fear he'll just keep comin' and put the landing gear up through the wings, He's so damned slow." WAVE-OFF. "Hell, he never answers any signals."

"Well, it's a God damned good thing he's high and not low or we might've lost him already."

"Oh oh! Here come the fighters," I announced, watching four *Hellcats* taxi to the end of the runway. "This might be a little hairier."

Minutes later: "Son-of-a-bitch! I yelled over my shoulder as I held a HIGH on Tommy Chuhak. "These fuckers are wilder'n a bunch o' scared quail. Tommy's not answerin' a thing and he's so damned high he's almost out o' range." I was so mad I made a motion to throw my right wand but wisely held onto it. "Shit! He thought that was a CUT. Here he comes. Crash crew, stand by." Fortunately Chuhak had enough airspeed to make a flare and the crash truck wasn't necessary. I was getting madder and madder at this unruly bunch of so-called pilots.

As the jeep came to a screeching halt at the runway's edge, Tabler and Thelen leapt out. "Hey, Harpo, y' want a ham 'n cheese sandwich," Tabler offered, straight faced. "Here."

Thelen stood by the jeep, suppressing a laugh. "Take it, Harpo. You need some nourishment."

"Here's one for you too, Weej." Tabler handed the sandwich to Wujcik as I picked up Speed Schroeder, coming off the ninety.

"Okay!," I snarled. "Wait'll I get through with this idiot." I held a FAST on Speed, then a left slant to get him back to deck center. "God damn, Speed, not THAT much. Can't you see the fuckin' runway lights, you dumb shit!" I screamed into the wind as I tried to get him to bank right. "Duck! The fucker's goin' to land right HERE!"

Wujcik and I took off running to the starboard side of the runway while Tabler and Thelen cringed behind the jeep. Schroeder added power to miss the darkened jeep by just a few feet.

Paddles!

I waved off the next *Hellcat* as we made our way back to the LSO position. "Yeah! Gimme the friggin' sandwich," I yelled at Tabler. "That's a bunch o' wild ass bastards you've got up there, Tab . . . Oh. Thanks." I bit off a big chunk of the sandwich and chewed fiercely. "Fuckers can't fly worth a shit! Can't see either I guess. The sons-o'-bitches never answer the signals." I shook my head in despair.

"What the hell do you expect, Harpo?," Thelen interjected. "They're all drunk as skunks."

"Well, sho am I fer Christ's shake," I slurred. "What difference does it make? Anyway, I think I'd better call 'em all down before they kill themselves . . . and us too." I chomped another big bite out of the sandwich and chewed.

"How'd ya like the sandwich, Harpo?," Tabler chided, grinning wickedly.

"Not bad," I fumed. "Better'n that bunch of untamed birdmen I've been tryin' to bring down to earth. What the hell are you grinnin' about?

"You don't mind the toilet paper, then, huh?"

"What God damned toilet paper," I seethed.

"In your sandwich, Harpo," Tabler giggled retreating slightly.

I opened the sandwich to find a folded sheet of toilet paper between the ham and the cheese. "You son-of-a-bitch! I already ate half of it." I pulled out the paper and threw it at Tabler while the three of them doubled over in gales of laughter.

13

FIRST BLOOD

Wujcik and I watched from the flight deck as Hickham Field buzzed with Army planes on our port and the lush foliage of Barbers Point slipped by on our starboard. Then, out in the open sea, *Princeton* and *Belleau Wood* joined the Task Force Eleven flagship, a heavy cruiser, and a destroyer squadron formed the protective screen. We were on our way to our first combat at sea. We wouldn't know where for a couple of days.

"Mr. Harper, come over here," Monahan called. "Look what the yard did to our net."

The escape net at Landing Signals provides for instant access to the relative safety of the catwalk under the platform in case an approaching airplane were to settle toward the platform. The net was loosely woven of steel cable, suspended from a heavy steel pipe frame jutting out to port from the Landing Signals platform. It had been secured to large steel eye fittings welded to the outboard edge of the catwalk and was covered with a canvas tarpaulin to limit injuries.

"Wow," Wujcik shrieked. "Look where the damned thing goes now. All the way down below the catwalk, against the hull."

I peered into the net, cautiously. "Anybody that has to jump in that thing is goin' to break something, I'll bet." I backed away. "Monahan, we've got to get the damned thing fixed like it was before."

Monahan peeked warily into the net. "Guess you'll have to talk to the First Lieutenant, sir."

Paddles!

"Who the hell is the First Lieutenant?," I demanded. "Sounds like a marine to me."

"No sir. The First Lieutenant is the head of the Hull department, in charge of all ship repair and modification," Monahan explained, patiently. "Lyons, I think his name is . . . er . . . Commander Lyons."

"God! I'm glad somebody around here knows something about the ship's organization." I was a little chagrined. "Let's find Lyons, Weej."

"I'm glad to meet you guys." Lyons offered his hand. "I've seen you two in the wardroom and back on the fantail waving those flags whenever I can get topside for flight operations." He gave us a sly smile. "You guys must need something pretty bad to get this far down in the bowels of the ship." His office was on the third deck.

"Yes SIR! We sure do." I leaned forward in my chair. "Somebody fixed our net so it's dangerous to jump into – scares the hell out of me, sir – goes all the way down below the catwalk. You've got to put it back the way it was before somebody breaks a leg, sir."

"Yeah, I know. The yard did that when we were in there for some minor modifications last week," Lyons explained. "The net change was a ComAirPac order. I guess some LSO didn't think the net did him much good the way it was put in." Lyons scratched his head and peered down at the papers on his desk. "Since the mod was ordered by ComAirPac we'd have to request permission." He eyed us quizzically. "Do you want me to do that?"

"But it's dangerous the way it is, sir," Wujcik pleaded. "Why don't you just do it on the Q.T." He whispered furtively.

"Yeah? But what if somebody gets hurt or killed in the short net?," Lyons mumbled, almost to himself. "All hell would break loose and my ass would be in a sling."

"Listen Commander," I leaned forward to challenge. "It's our asses that are on the line with that killer net. We're more likely to get hit by an airplane while we wonder whether to jump in or not." I leaned back but kept my eyes on Lyons. "Do you want me to talk to the captain?"

"Oh no, NO!" Lyons jumped out of his chair. "Don't do that. "No tellin' what the skipper would want to do." He sat down again. "Just let me handle it. I'll get it fixed for you . . . er . . . soon as I can."

"We'll appreciate it, sir." I stood up to leave. "Don't forget. As long as that net's the way it is we operate under a major hazard to life and limb." I said it with a smile but my eyes were serious. "If we get hurt, flight operations ceases, you know."

"What the hell's this big gun doin' in here?," Leo Dulacki demanded, with some derision, as I got ready for the next aircraft recovery.

"That's my antiaircraft weapon," I replied, proudly. The gun was a .50 cal. machine gun of the type used in the F6F. "I borrowed it from the squadron gunnery chief so I can shoot at attacking Jap airplanes like all you guys with your big 40 millimeters. I got a welder to install a makeshift gun mount back aft of Landing Signals. Hell, I have to keep up with you and your assorted weapons, Leo."

"Well then," Leo gave me a challenging leer. "Can you field strip it?"

"Well, the chief taught me how to do it but I haven't tried it by myself yet." I frowned as I put the gun on my desk. "UGH! – Let's see, I pull the bolt back . . turn this little toggle . . and then . . " BOING . . CLANK. "SHIT! There goes that friggin' spring the chief warned me about."

Dulacki doubled over with laughter. "I Just KNEW you were going to do that, Harpo. Happens to all the recruits."

"Did you see where that damned spring went, Leo?"

"Yeah, I got it." He reached into the corner behind his desk. "Here."

"Thanks." I grabbed the spring.

"AIR DEPARTMENT, MAN FLIGHT QUARTERS STATIONS FOR RE-COVERING AIRCRAFT," squawked the P.A. system.

"Oops! Flight Quarters." I jumped up out of my chair. "I'll have to finish this when I get back. See you later." As I left, Leo was laughing out loud.

"Is it Okay if I come back and watch you guys work a recovery?" Charlie Foster asked, catching up to me on the flight deck as I headed back to Landing Signals. Lieutenant Charles Foster was one of the Combat Information Center watch officers. Tall and distinguished looking, he had the marks of an Ivy League grad. Probably a product of Officer Candidate School and special training in communications and fighter direction, which is what CIC does.

"Happy to have you, Charlie," I invited. "Hey. How's the war goin'?"

"Pretty slow, Harpo," Foster grinned. "Our first strikes on Baker didn't meet any opposition at all, and reports from the Army landing force say everything's deserted. Looks like the Japs bailed out just in time."

"Then what are our fighters and torpeckers doin' up there?," I queried. "More trainin'?"

"Yeah, a little of that, I guess," Foster replied. "But we always need antisubmarine patrols, and we've got to protect the Army and ourselves from air attack from Jap bases up in the Gilberts and Marshalls until the Army gets their fighters in there."

"Oh. That's interesting," I commented as we arrived at the platform. "You've never been back here before, have you?"

"No. First time."

"You know Wujcik, here, don't you?"

"Yeah, Hi, Weej." They shook hands.

"There're a few things you need to pay attention to back here, Charlie," I began. "I'll be workin' this recovery and you may stand directly behind me, if you wish, or back against the wind screen, there."

"Hell. I'll just stand back by the screen and stay out of your way," Foster replied, awkwardly.

"Just be sure to stand still when an airplane's comin' up the groove," I cautioned. "Any extraneous motion up here can confuse the pilots."

"One more thing, Charlie," Wujcik interjected. "See this big net over here?" He took Foster's arm and led him to the edge of the platform.

"Wow!," Foster yelped, recoiling from the sight. "That's a net alright. What the hell's it for?"

"It's for us to escape to if and when an airplane threatens to land on the platform," Wujcik explained.

Foster peered down into the net again. "A guy could get hurt jumpin' in that thing. How many times have you used it?"

"It used to just go down to the catwalk. We've used that one a few times," Wujcik explained. "But we haven't used this deep one since the Pearl Harbor NAVY yard put it in last week."

"God damn it!," I fumed. "Lyons promised he'd have the damn thing tied up to the catwalk 'as soon as he could'. That was a week ago. We've got to talk to him again, I guess – or maybe the skipper."

Foster retreated from the edge. "I think I'll watch from the catwalk, if you don't mind."

"Well," I smiled. "At least they got my gun mount welded in."

The four *Hellcats* zipped by the island, broke formation, and entered downwind leg.

Chapter 13: First Blood

"Gear, flaps, hook, all down, sir," Monahan shouted up from his station in the catwalk.

"Clear deck, sir," Callagee called.

Wujcik stood immediately behind me, looking over my shoulder. "This first one's the skipper, I think."

"Yeah, it's Curtis alright," I hollered over the swirling wind. "I can tell already." Then, talking through the signals: "A little high." I gave him a HIGH. "Uh huh, Comin' down nicely. Nice alignment, just a slight turn in the groove. Now a little fast. Yeah, responding nicely. HIGH DIP to start him down. Now an early CUT."

"He's floating," Wujcik yelled, panic in his voice as Curtis floated up to a wheels-first landing around the fourth wire.

"GET THE TAIL DOWN," I yelled, in vain, as Curtis' hook bounced over all the wires.

"HE'S GOIN' IN THE BARRIER," Wujcik yelled in stunned surprise as the *Hellcat* nosed into the raised barrier and rolled right through, shedding the barrier cables like limp spaghetti, and continuing forward and to port, to rip the tail off a parked F6F and plunge over the side.

"DROP THE SCREEN," I commanded, as I waved off the next fighter. I wanted us to be able to see Curtis floating in the water.

"Aye aye, sir," Callagee yelled as he pulled the trip and the screen fell forward, flush with our platform, and we were blasted directly by the 35 knot wind.

"Yay!," Wujcik cheered. "He's still right side up." Curtis's airplane seemed to slide by, close aboard.

"Yes sir, but he's not gettin' out. Must be knocked out." I felt a bump as Monahan jumped up on the platform and headed for the edge of our net.

"Where the hell're you goin'?" I grabbed Monahan by the arm and yanked him back onto the platform.

"Damn it, sir. I could o' saved 'im." Monahan moaned. "I can tell he's not goin' to get out before his plane sinks. Damn! Too late now." Curtis and his airplane floated aft, sinking slowly as they were drawn toward the ship's boiling wake.

"For God's sake, Monahan," I shook him impulsively. "If you had jumped you'd have either busted yourself landin' on the airplane or you'd have drowned in that churnin' wake, or both. We sure as hell don't want to lose you. What do you think we've got the friggin' plane guard destroyer for?"

Paddles!

"Yeah. That can is almost up to him now." Wujcik rooted the destroyer on.

Belleau Wood turned ninety degrees to port and hove to as the destroyer stopped, dead in the water, at the spot where Curtis would be. After a few tense moments, the can began sending a blinker message.

"YEW . . ENN . . AYE . . BEE . . ELL . . EE . . UNABLE!," Monahan read the blinker signal. "Shit! They couldn't get him out. He must've sunk before the can could get there."

"THIS IS THE CAPTAIN SPEAKING," blared the ship's P.A. system. "I REGRET TO REPORT THAT COMMANDER CURTIS, THE FIGHTER SKIP-PER, WAS LOST OVER THE SIDE AND SANK WITH HIS AIRPLANE BE-FORE OUR PLANE GUARD DESTROYER COULD REACH HIM. WE'LL MISS HIM . . I SAY AGAIN. I REGRET . . ."

"God damn! I could o' saved 'im," Monahan mumbled quietly as he slipped on his shoes.

The vibration under our feet told me that the skipper was putting the ship back into the wind to recover the rest of our aircraft.

The bull horn squawked: "STAND BY TO RECOVER AIRCRAFT." And the ship heeled to port as she turned starboard to the wind line.

"You mean after losing the fighter skipper we just go on, business as usual, and recover aircraft?," Foster demanded, wide eyed.

"LAND AIRCRAFT!" A white flag replaced the red one at Fly Control and FOX was two blocked at the yard arm as the ship steadied into the wind and the barriers came up.

"Shit, yes, Charlie. What the hell do you think we do, leave everybody up there just because we lost one?," I shouted down at him. *Shit! Charlie. I don't feel good about it either.* "The memorial service comes later," I groaned.

"Yeah," Wujcik yelled into the buffeting wind. "We've got to get these guys aboard no matter what." I wondered what he was really thinking.

"Yeah, and here comes Speed," I announced, introducing Schroeder at the ninety.

"He's been lookin' better lately," Wujcik commented in my ear. "Got his speed pretty much under control."

"Overdid it this time, Weej," I hollered as I gave Speed a strong COME-ON signal. "Shit! Now he's settlin'." I shook a LOW signal at him and he raised his nose a little and added throttle. We heard the low murmur of the propeller in the low RPM cruise setting instead of the piercing whine given by a propeller in low pitch. "Oh oh! He's in HIGH PITCH!," I screamed. Then: WAVE-OFF.

Schroeder continued to settle and his left wing dropped, the first sign of a stall. "He's gonna hit the ramp!," I shrieked. "JUMP!", as the *Hellcat* settled directly toward the platform, left wing down.

My mind had already decided that I wouldn't jump in that deep net so I took off to starboard in my best fifty yard dash form while I heard Speed's engine roar into high RPM. As that thirteen foot propeller bore down on me, I ran faster. *Whew! That big propeller didn't miss me by much.*

Back at the platform Monahan was scrambling out of the deep net and Foster was cowering under the platform.

"Where the hell is Wujcik?," I yelled, peering into the net.

"I'm still down here, Harpo," Wujcik moaned from the bottom of the net. "I think I broke my leg. Are you Okay?"

"Shit! I knew one of us would break something in that damned net," I cursed. "Yeah. I'm Okay – a little winded – I ran across in front of the airplane. His propeller damn near got me, but I didn't break a leg." Then to Monahan: "Come on, men. Let's get him out of there." I had to wave off the next fighter.

"Oww!," Wujcik cried. "I can't stand on it. It's straight though. Maybe it's only sprained." He stood on his good leg and reached for the edge of the catwalk while Callagee shoved from below to get him up on the catwalk.

"God! I hope so," I grumbled. "Monahan. Tell 'em to send a corpsman back here – broken leg or sprained ankle."

"Aye, sir. right away." He looked up. "Here comes another fighter, sir."

"Let's get 'im aboard," I urged. "We've had too damned many delays already. Keep this up and they're all goin' to run out of fuel. How's he look?"

"Gear, flaps, hook, all down," Monahan yelled. "We got a clear deck and barriers." Callagee was still in the bottom of the net. Wujcik was under the platform, moaning.

Back in the fighter ready room Bob Ross was trying to rally the mourning squadron and assert his authority as its new skipper. Lieut. R. P. "Bob" Ross had come to the squadron from instructing duty at Corpus Christi as the next senior to Curtis and would now assume command under trying conditions. Bob was a big guy, about six feet tall and two hundred pounds, and his pudgy face showed a ruddy complexion to match the shock of auburn hair that fell over his broad forehead. His intense blue eyes made people pay attention. As squadron executive officer he had shown excellent leadership qualities and enjoyed the respect and friendship of most of the fighter pilots.

"Mr. Harper. Commander Dahl would like to see you and Mr. Wujcik in the Air Office, sir." It was the air office yeoman, Kempson.

"Bad day today." Commander Ted Dahl sat tall in his office chair, his sad eyes and heavy eyelids emphasizing the somberness of the occasion. His long face was topped by a bald pate fringed with sparse blond hair. He was a Swede from Minnesota and had a slight accent to prove it. He had served in Fighting six on *Saratoga*, aboard the cruiser *Houston* as a seaplane scout pilot, and in a patrol squadron – hell, he'd flown everything – before coming to *Belleau Wood* in the pre-commissioning party as prospective air officer. His kindly demeanor made us squirts look up to him, almost as a father. "First, we lose Curtis over the side – that was bizarre – then we almost had a crash at Landing Signals. Are you guys okay?"

Benny Freedman and Davy Kolb burst into the room. "Sorry we're late boss," Benny apologized, airily.

"That's okay Benny." Dahl waved at the couch. "Have a seat. We're just getting started."

"I'm Okay, sir," I replied. "But Wujcik sprained his ankle jumping in that deep net they gave us in Pearl."

"Sorry to hear that." Dahl peered at Wujcik with a look of sincere concern. "Can you work?"

"Doc Benson wrapped it for me, sir." Wujcik held up his foot. "He says it'll be a week or so before I can get around well enough to wave planes."

Hi Massey stuck his head in the door. "Are we late, sir?"

"No. come on in." Dahl invited with a wave of his hand. Then, to us: "I asked Hi and Bob to join us since we'll be talking about Curtis going through the barriers and, especially, what to do about it." Then to me: You should have that net fixed so it isn't such a hazard." Dahl urged.

"I asked Commander Lyons to fix it the first day out of Pearl, sir," I replied, cautiously. "He said he'd get it fixed as soon as he could."

"I'll speak to him," Dahl asserted flatly.

Go get 'im boss, I urged, silently.

"Should I see if I can get you some help out of Pearl, John?" Dahl gave me his Basset hound imitation, full of sympathy and concern.

"Not necessary, sir." I gave him a confident smile. "I can handle it okay –

unless some other idiot decides to land on the platform."

Dahl put his elbows on his desk and leaned forward, "What happened there, anyway?"

"Oh, Speed Schroeder decided to make his approach at eighteen hundred RPM," I replied. "Not good for recovering from low and slow. He just got it into low pitch in time to climb up over the ramp. His hook busted the window in our wind screen," I winced. "Wujcik jumped in the net and I went for the starboard side."

"That was close," Dahl frowned. "I saw you running for it . . . NOW. How did Curtis get through all three barriers. We've got to do something about that."

Freedman looked at Kolb expectantly.

"Looked like the propeller just knocked all the barriers down, and he just rolled right through." Kolb shook his head in disbelief. "I've never seen anything like it before."

"Maybe it's the airplane," Freedman offered. "This is the first barrier crash we've had with the F6F, so we really don't have any experience with it."

"It was the propeller that knocked them down," Kolb ventured. "Maybe if we lowered the barriers just below the propeller . . ."

"That's it," Freedman jumped up out of the couch. "Only we just carry the first barrier low to get under the propeller and trip the wheels, and we leave the other two full up."

Dahl eyed me for a reaction. "How does that sound to you, John?"

"Those guys are the experts, sir," I conceded. "Sounds like a good idea to me, though, since it might correct the problem as we see it."

Dahl scratched his chin and regarded Freedman. "Hmm. What are the potential consequences?"

Freedman sat down as though to retreat a little. "What do you think, Cobbs?" He threw the ball to Kolb – again.

"Well, sir," Kolb started cautiously, still assembling his thoughts. "If we flip 'em, they might go all the way over on their backs. Then we've got a problem clearing the deck." He paused to think. "On the other hand, the other two barriers, being full up, could hold 'em from goin' over." He glanced at Ross. "We'll just have to try it and see."

"Whoa! That doesn't sound good," Ross objected, glancing at Massey for support. "If we flip onto our backs, we're trapped, and if there's a fire, we're DEAD."

Paddles!

"Well, Bob," Dahl eyed Ross seriously. "We've got to keep your fighters from running through the barriers like Johnny did. We've GOT TO do something or we'll tear up more airplanes, and maybe get somebody else killed." He paused for effect. "Have you got any better ideas, Bob?"

"Okay. I guess we'll have to live with it," Ross frowned.

"As the commander says, we've got to do something," Massey interjected. "Then how about some special training for your deck rescue crew, Benny?"

"Good idea, Hi," Freedman smiled." We'll get it started right away."

Up on the bridge at Fly control as Air Department duty officer, I watched in awe as a carrier, two cruisers, and several destroyers appeared on the horizon.

"Who's this we're coming up on?," I asked the officer of the deck. "Some of ours, I hope."

"Yeah. Don't worry," Alexander drawled. "That's *Lexington,* with her escorts. We're joining them to strike some Jap held islands in the Gilberts."

Lexington's signal searchlight blinked a steady stream of dits and dahs and in a few moments our signalman came forward to the bridge.

"WELCOME TO TF-15 X FORM ACCORDING TO OP PLAN X POWNALL X," the signalman read from his pad.

"Well, thank you Admiral," Captain Pride saluted *Lexington* from his elevated arm chair at the starboard side of the bridge. "We're glad to be aboard, sir."

It was an inspiring sight: *Princeton* and *Belleau Wood* with their meager destroyer screen joining with the *Lexingtion* group to form a triangle of carriers in the center of the formation, with cruisers and destroyers taking up their supporting positions.

"You called, sir," I approached Commander Dahl at Fly Control in response to his call, delivered by the air department yeoman as I enjoyed the midday sun, stretched out on the forecastle. "What's up?" I bent over to tie my marine combat boots. "I came as soon as I could, boss."

Dahl gave me a suspicious look. "Listen, Harpo. We're going to receive the flag operations officer sometime in the next fifteen or twenty minutes," he sighed, with a hint of contempt. "He's delivering the Op Plan for our next target – IN PERSON.

"You mean he's flyin' aboard – HIMSELF?" I thought it very unusual.

"Yeah," Dahl frowned. "In an F6. They're getting ready to launch him now, over on the *Lex.*" He shook his head. "Well, at least he picked a time when all the decks are clear, waiting for our birds to return."

"Hey, Harpo," Wujcik met me at Landing Signals. "What the hell is the flight quarters for? Our birds won't be back for an hour or so."

"Admiral's Ops officer's hand deliverin' the friggin' Op Plan for the next caper," I announced with a cynical grin. "Christ's sake! He must be starvin' for flight time. Hell, he could've sent the Op Plan around on a destroyer. As it is the whole force has been on a course into the wind for twenty minutes," I shook my head. "Not smart in hostile waters. Well, here he comes." I took the paddles from Monahan. "I'd better take 'im."

The single *Hellcat* cruised by the starboard side, hook down, and broke smartly to enter the downwind leg.

"Gear, flaps, hook, all down, sir."

"Clear deck, arresting gear and barriers, set, sir."

"Log this: Fast start. Long in the groove." I signalled FAST. "Okay. Slowin' down nicely . . . Uh huh." ROGER, now HIGH DIP. "Yeah! Perfect." ROGER . . . CUT . . .

"LOOK OUT!," Wujcik screamed. "His hook's bouncin' – missin' all the wires."

"DAMN!," I moaned. "He landed wheels first. We've got a barrier!"

The fighter continued up the deck, tail high, hook bouncing, until the landing gear contacted the lowered first barrier, flipping the airplane up on its nose to hang there agonizing moments until it finally fell over on its back, fuel spewing from the belly tank.

"FIRE!," was the collective cry of the deck crew as the spilled aviation fuel ignited, enveloping the airplane in flames. Asbestos Joe was on the spot in seconds, dragging the pilot from the fire and rolling him in a blanket to extinguish the flames.

Running up the deck, Wujcik puffed: "God! He sure as hell didn't dip to the deck."

"Maybe he never landed on a CVL before," I scowled. "He just let it float."

Seconds later we reached the crash scene to view the pilot, stretched out on deck, face up. "God damn!," I gasped. "Look at that gash in his forehead."

"Shit! That's more'n a gash," Wujcik observed. "It's damned near back to his ears and oozin' brains." He bowed his head and half whispered, "He's gone."

"Must not have snugged up his shoulder harness," I offered. "Rose right up and smashed his head against the windshield bow – OUCH!" I looked over at *Lexington*, "Admiral's goin to be lookin' for a new Ops Officer."

"Hi, Charlie. How goes the battle?," I greeted Foster as I entered the Combat Information Center – CIC – where the fighter directors read radar returns and direct fighters to intercept enemy air threats.

He turned to face me from his watch station, seated at the cluttered communications console facing the circular Lucite plotting board with range circles and bearing lines etched to catch the light carried by the transparent Lucite. "Okay so far, Harpo – come on in." Foster waved me into the room. "The strike on Tarawa went pretty well from the sound of it. They're on their way back now." He looked perplexed. "Jesus! That was quite a show you put on back there the other day, Harpo." Foster wagged his head back and forth. "I hope every day isn't like that."

"Me too," I mumbled. "Like Dahl said, 'Bad day'. Fortunately we haven't had one like that before or since."

"Well. I think I'll watch from up on the bridge anyway," Foster grinned. "Too many bodies flyin' every which way back at your place. By the way, How's Wujcik?"

"Oh. Looks like he'll be back in commission in a couple of days," I sighed. "Sorry you didn't like our party . . . Hey! Have you seen any unidentified contacts . . . er – bogies?"

"No contacts yet." He pointed at the plot, devoid of any but friendlies. "But we've got a contact reported somewhere west of here by a PBY on patrol. We might see 'im pretty soon."

"Bogey bearing three one zero, sixty miles, sir," came the urgent report from the radar console. Immediately, the symbol for a enemy air threat took shape on the plot, grease penciled in by the plotter standing behind the plotting board, and glowing with light captured from the Lucite board. "Estimate angles five."

"Designate RAID ONE," Foster commanded. "Sounds like the reported contact." Then: "Hello Coké One, this is Coké. Vector three one zero, angles eight, BUSTER," Foster enunciated into his microphone, using the ship's call sign, Coké.

"Coké, this is Coké One, vector three one zero, BUSTER, WILCO," came the acknowledgment of the heading, altitude, and speed commands.

"Sounds like Bob Ross," I commented.

"Yeah. He took over Coké One when he took command of the squadron."

Chapter 13: First Blood

Foster picked up the phone, "Hey fly control . . . oh, Hello commander . . . uh . . . Sir, We just vectored the CAP out to intercept a bogey. I recommend we scramble the standbys . . . only two? . . . Well, that's better than none, sir.

"Ross's only got three you know," I offered.

"Yeah? What happened?

"Oh," I grimaced. "Fleischer lost power after launch and ditched about a hundred yards for'rd o' the ship. He got out okay and the plane guard destroyer picked him up. The "can" reports he's none the worse for wear." I couldn't suppress a little snicker.

"What the hell are you laughing about, Harpo?," Foster demanded. "We just lost another airplane and almost another pilot, and you laugh."

"Can't help it, Charlie," I attempted to subdue my mirth. "Fleischer's the guy who landed in Kaneohe Bay during FCLP last month. I dubbed him 'Splash' after that. Now everyone will be calling him 'Splash'." I spread my hands as though to frame a title. "'SPLASH FLEISCHER'! Has a nice ring to it, don't you think, Charlie?"

Foster gave me a sardonic grin, "You're BAD, Harpo."

"Hey, Charlie, you gave him the command: BUSTER," I squinted at the plot. "What's that mean?"

"We have four speed commands," Foster began, patiently. "SAUNT. . . "

"Raid One confirmed, sir. New bearing three two zero, sixty miles, course one two zero, angles four, speed two twenty."

"Hello Coké One. Vector three six zero, angles seven."

"Coké One here. Vector three six zero, angles seven, WILCO."

"Oh, yeah," Foster scratched his head. "Speeds . . uhh . . our commands relate to engine settings. There's SAUNTER, maximum endurance; LINER, maximum range; BUSTER, maximum climb setting, and GATE, full military power."

"New bogey, bearing two four zero, forty miles, sir. Estimate angles three."

"Well," Foster grimaced. "That looks more like the reported contact. Then where the hell did this other guy come from – designate RAID TWO." He picked up the phone again . . . "Did you launch the standbys yet, sir? . . Good. We just picked up another bogey and we need 'em . . . Yes sir. I'll try to reach 'em." Then: "Hello Coké standby, this is Coké, who are you?"

"Hey Coké, This is Coké Three, just gettin' my gear up," came Oveland's jaunty reply. "Coké Three-two's right behind me."

"Okay Coké Three. This is Coké. Vector two four zero, angles six, BUSTER."

Paddles!

"WILCO, Coké." Oveland was jubilant. "Two four zero, angles six, BUSTER. We're on our way."

"Raid One now bearing three four five, forty miles, course steady one two zero, angles four, speed two twenty," came the radar report.

"Coké One, this is Coké. Bogey now ten o'clock, down, three miles," Foster called.

"Raid Two now bearing two three zero, angles four, speed one twenty," radar reported.

"Coké Three, Coké. Vector one nine zero, angles six, bogey two o'clock down, four miles." Then: "Coké One, do you have contact?"

"Coké One here. No joy."

"Coké One." Foster's voice became urgent, "Vector one three zero, angles five, GATE! Bogey will be one o'clock down, two miles. Over."

"WILCO, Coké. We're GATE to angles five."

"TALLY HO! Bogey is Emily," Oveland exulted at sighting the four engine Jap flying boat. "Tab, break right, I'll go left, simultaneous high sides."

"Hey! Looks like we got one of 'em anyway," Foster was cheering.

"TALLY HO! Coké One's got a twin engine something," Ross howled. "Goin' like a scalded dog. Must be a Betty." "Betty" was the code name for a twin engine, land based, torpedo bomber. Then: "Buck, take the right side. Robby and I'll hold 'im on the left."

"Splash one Emily!," Came the jubilant announcement from Oveland.

"He's turnin' into you, Buck. Try for an overhead," Ross yelled.

"Got 'im skipper," Buck grunted under the extra "g"s. "Gives you and . . . UGH . . . Robby a tail shot."

"You smoked 'im, Buck. Pieces comin' off too," Ross called. "He's slowin' down! Oh! JINK, Robby. Tail gunner's blinkin'."

"I got the right engine burnin', skipper," Robby bragged. "Whoa! Just pulled up in time to miss 'im. We must've gotten both engines."

"Sombitch! He's goin' to ditch." Ross savored the victory. "Keep shootin' 'til they sink. Then: Coké, Coké one here. Splash one Betty!"

CIC was pandemonium. "We got 'em both!" The CIC crew screamed in unison – "FIRST BLOOD!"

14

SKINS

The air group had settled in at NAS Kahului, on the Hawaiian island of Maui and we were all billeted in the rustic BOQ, built in the best tradition of the "Little Grass Shack."

"Hey! What are you doin' in here?," I yelped as I reached for my towel. I had just stepped out of the shower, naked as a jay bird, and this little brown girl had me fixed in her curious gaze.

"I crean bafroom, suh," she bowed as I wrapped myself in my towel. "My name Lelani," she announced with a toothy smile. "You mine?" I knew that meant "Do you mind." Lelani was one of a bevy of housekeepers I had seen lounging in the lobby of the BOQ during rest periods, gossiping and giggling in their strange language. She was aptly named after a beautiful Hawaiian flower.

"Yeah . . . well . . . I guess not, if you don't." I stepped back in the shower to towel off. *God damn! This is primitive. I guess they're used to it with their big families. I never had a little sister so I'm not used to having young girls surveyin' my bare bod.*

"Yeah. One caught me takin' a leak yesterday," Arky grumbled as he lined up a shot in the BOQ pool room. "I told her to get her little brown ass lost." CLACK THUD CLACK PLOP! Arky sent the cue ball down the table to make a billiard off the cushion and sink the cue ball. "God damn! SCRATCH! . . . Shit! They must've robbed every cradle in Maui to find this bunch o' jail bait."

"Don't be such a hard head, Arky," I snickered. "They're just doin' their jobs for Christ's sake. Housekeepin' you know."

"Yeah?," Arky gave a lecherous grin. "Tryin' to find out what a white pecker looks like, I'd say."

"Hey you guys, listen up!," commanded Bernie Pirog, after announcing his entry with a violent slam of the screen door. "The CAG just got an invitation to a luau out in the country. It's for all the officers in the group." Pirog, one of the torpedo pilots, was the officer of the day.

"What the hell's a luau, Bernie?," "Frenchy" Endres demanded as he jumped out of the lounge chair where he had been reading. Endres was one of the dozen and a half new fighter pilots who had just come aboard in exchange for our nine SBDs – with pilots, to bring VF-24 up to twenty four plane strength.

"Hell, I don't know, Frenchy," Pirog scratched his head. "Some kind o' Hawaiian garden party, I gather." He glanced at the ceiling. "I hear this one's sponsored by some ladies' social group. CAG wants everyone to go."

"Sounds awful fancy to me," Freeman offered. "What the hell will we wear? I don't have my whites with me." Freeman, another of the new fighter pilots, had already been recognized for his fastidious dress.

"CAG says 'clean khakis, shined shoes, and a fresh shave'," Pirog stated perfunctorily. "Staff cars depart the BOQ at sixteen hundred. Pass the word!"

"Welcome to Maui," our charming hostess cooed as she placed a flower lei around my neck as a warm greeting to the sumptuous mountain estate overlooking the Pacific surf just north of Wailuku. "I'm Florence Kingsley." I found out later that Mrs. Kingsley was the president of the Wailuku Junior League which served the entire central valley of Maui. They had decided to greet the first NAVY air group into NAS Kahului with a traditional Hawaiian luau. The daily one hour afternoon shower had ended and the evening breeze carried the competing scents of exotic Hawaiian flowers and a pig roasting in a pit of glowing coals.

Now here's an unlikely sight. A bunch of scruffy aviators being greeted in turn by these handsome matrons, dressed in their garden party finest.

"Thank you Mrs. Kingsley," I bowed ever so slightly. "We really appreciate your hospitality. Then, sweeping the panorama of the estate: "Such a gorgeous home. Is it yours, ma'am?"

"Yes, thank you, young man. I do hope you will enjoy our luau," she smiled impishly. "And the lovely young ladies we have invited."

Chapter 14: Skins

I went on to meet the other hostesses in turn, the last of whom asked, "What's your name, young man?" Her eyelashes fluttered in a flush of romantic awe as she clasped my hand firmly. "And where are you from?"

"John Harper, ma'am." I tried to retrieve my hand but to no avail. "And I'm from Saint Joseph, Michigan."

"What a lovely Scottish name." She rolled her eyes. "And you're from MICHIGAN!" She threw her hands up in the air. "How absolutely exciting! I'm Hannah Larsson . . . with two esses."

"Swedish, isn't it?," I went along with the gag. "I'm half Swedish myself, ma'am. does that help?"

"'Does that help?' he asks," Mrs. Larsson shrieked. "It's marvelous!" She emoted as she took my arm and led me toward a small circle of girls locked in giggling conversation. "You must meet my daughter, Laura . . . LAURA!" It was a command.

Oh oh! Here comes the goon child who can't find a boyfriend without mommy's help. I feared.

Mrs. Larsson grabbed one of the girls by the shoulder and whirled her to face me, "I want you to meet Lieutenant John Harper, Laura."

Wow! This is no goon child. She's a real BEAUTY. I gaped.

"John's from MICHIGAN!," Mrs. Larsson emoted.

Big deal! I thought as I continued to stare and extended my hand. "Pleased to meet you – uh – Laura." It was an understatement.

"Happy to meet you Lieutenant Harper." Laura inclined her head and averted her eyes. Then, with her warm soft hand in mine, she raised her sea blue eyes in a kind of a challenge I didn't quite understand.

Ooh! There's that gnawing feeling in the pit of my stomach again.

Laura Larsson was about five foot six and a quick survey revealed a provocative figure on a lean athletic frame even her loose fitting flowered muumuu couldn't hide. Her fine Scandinavian features and creamy complexion were crowned by beautifully coifed silvery blond hair falling softly to her shoulders.

"Thanks Mrs. Larsson," I called as I watched my benefactor hurry back to her place in the reception line, leaving us blissfully alone. "I'm delighted to meet you, Laura." But please call me John." Then: "Hmm . . . Laura," I mused aloud. "What a charming name. "Has a romantic lilt to it." I eyed her expectantly.

Laura gave me a naughty grin, eyes flashing. "Well, then. Let's get acquainted." She whispered furtively as she took my arm possessively and led me off to the central table, laden with exotic fare from avocados to pineapples, surrounding the freshly roasted suckling pig. "Would you like something to drink . . . er . . . Johnny?" She looked up at me as if to say: "Is that okay?"

Hmm. Exploring the boundaries. "Good idea, Laura. What are you drinking?"

"They have a delicious punch." Her tongue swept her lips, making them even more irresistible. "Made out of pineapple, papaya, lime juice, and a little rum, made from our sugar cane. It's called grog, a good NAVY term." Lined up on the bar were several squat ten ounce glasses, filled with ice and the brownish green liquid with a stalk of sugar cane as a garnish. Laura picked up two of them and made a ceremony of handing one to me. "Have one."

"Mmmm. That IS good. Better'n the watery punch we get at garden parties back in Michigan." I savored the sweet, fruity drink, noting a barely perceptible bite. "The rum helps a lot." Then: "Now that we're gettin' acquainted, where are you from?"

"Me? Oh - I was born here - Can't you tell?" Laura gave me a haughty glance. "My dad came out here from Minnesota right after the war to establish a sugar mill down in Puunene and my mother followed him a year later," she related, proudly. Then: "Here, Johnny." Laura reached into a hand crafted pottery bowl and came out with an index finger full of something that looked like mucilage. "Have some poi."

"Hmm. Pretty tasty," I grimaced. "What's it made out of?" *Oops! I almost said; "What the HELL is this shit made out of?"* The only thing that tasted good was Laura's finger.

Laura laughed so hard she had to grab the table to hold her balance. "Taro root, Johnny. It's the primary staple of the Hawaiian diet." She was still laughing at me. "You know, like rice to the Chinese . . . er . . . You didn't like it, did you, honey."

Honey, is it. This is movin' pretty fast. "Well, not particularly." *Darling? No not yet.* "Are you in school, Laura?"

"Just graduated high school here in Wailuku." She drew her hand across her forehead. "Whew! I'm glad that's over. I'm going to Mills College in California next September." She was proud of that too. "That ought to be exciting."

"Speaking of exciting," I commented casually, glancing in the direction of the little Hawaiian combo playing something I didn't recognize. "Looks like our troops found something exciting over there." The hula dancer was gyrating to the strains of some Hawaiian tune plucked out by the little trio of steel guitar, steel string guitar, and ukelele, while a small knot of our aviators gaped.

"That's Sweetie Wilson," Laura confided, with a slight frown. "She's the top hula dancer in the islands." She pointed up to Maui's western mountains. "Lives right up there in the hills, I understand." She gave me a suspicious look as she took my hand. "Let's have some of this delicious Maui barbecue."

"No more poi, though. Okay?," I announced firmly. *Who needs a hula show when I've got Laura. Jesus, I think she likes me.*

"Boy! That was a scrumptious meal," I burped. "Excuse me." *Okay. Try it now.* "Hey . . . uh . . . honey . . . er . . . why don't we get another drink and take a little walk down to the cliffs and . . . er . . . enjoy the night . . . huh?" *And each other, I hope.*

"Wonderful, darling." Laura grasped my hand and made for the bar. "Two more grogs, please."

Laura and I strolled down the dirt trace toward the rugged cliffs, our arms around each other in a cautious embrace, and our silence interrupted only by the rumble of distant surf and the tinkle of ice in our glasses. Darkness fell suddenly, as it does in the tropics, transforming the night sky into a carpet of stars with the crescent moon silhouetting the jagged peaks to the west.

"Are you enjoying the evening, darling?," Laura cooed.

She said it, why can't I? I turned to look down at Laura and found her beautiful face upturned, pouting lips glistening in the starlight. I kissed them . . . and Laura kissed back . . . with enthusiasm! "Mmmm!" *Whoa! Talk about movin' fast. We're movin' now.*

After a long kiss that I could feel all the way down to my toes, Laura put both hands on my chest and pushed me away so she could speak. "Come on, Johnny. I want to show you something." She took my hand and started off down the path at a moderate trot.

"Hey! Where're we goin'?" *And what the hell is she goin' to show me?*

"There's a trail that cuts off up here." Laura called back somewhat breathlessly. "It goes all the way down to the beach. D'you want to go?" She didn't give me a chance to object with the firm grip she held on my hand.

"I'm ready for anything, darling." With our eyes now adapted to the darkness, we could already see the narrow beach, glowing with the reflection of the Milky Way.

Paddles!

After picking her way down the steep slit canyon, Laura threw herself onto a convenient rock near the ocean's edge and pulled me down to her for another long kiss, this one more passionate than the last. "This is where I change clothes when I swim down here." It sounded like an invitation. Then another long kiss. "Let's take a dip . . . darling." She whispered.

Cool it now, J.A. This could get out o' hand. "That surf looks pretty high, Laura. Probably a mean rip tide." *Hell. I'd just as soon stay here and see if I can parlay these kisses into something exciting.*

"Well, well. The NAVY Lieutenant is afraid of the ocean," Laura chided.

"No, no. Honey. I was just concerned about you." I stammered. "What would your mom say if you got lost in the surf?"

"Don't give it a second thought, old woman," she tossed her head defiantly. "I swim this surf all the time, and my mother knows it." She already had her muumuu off and turned her back to me. "Here. Unsnap my bra. And get those clothes off! Unless you plan to swim in them." As she pulled off her panties, her whole body shimmered with the perspiration of passion.

With everything off, my heart was pumping. I reached around to draw her to me for another kiss.

"Oh no you don't." Laura tossed back at me as she ran for the surf, her firm breasts bouncing invitingly. "Last one in is a swabbie!" SPLASH - SPLASH.

The second SPLASH was me. I swam hard to catch Laura just as a giant breaker drove us violently to the sandy bottom.

"Aargh . . . gurgle . . . Are you okay, honey?," I groped for Laura in the swift rip tide and she floated into my arms, her sensual body pressing hard against mine. *Whoa! I'm about to burst!*

"I'm just fine, Johnny Darling," Laura announced with a salty kiss. "Like I said. I do this all the time."

"All the time?," I queried. "Who with?"

"Just me. You're the first victim I've been able to entice," she giggled. Then sprang free of our embrace to catch the next wave.

I slid down the same wave just ahead of the foamy break, swimming hard to reach Laura's side and capture her in a new embrace. We held fast to each other as the big comber rolled us over and over, finally depositing us roughly on the beach. We just lay there in our passionate embrace as each succeeding wave rolled us over in the sand and a strange tingling sensation swept through my trembling body. Laura's sharp little screams sounded like a bird chirping.

Chapter 14: Skins

"Hey, Harpo," came a faint call from atop the cliff, barely audible over the crashing surf. "Where the hell are you?" It was Wujcik.

God damn! What a hell of a time for Weej to show up. I thought as I freed myself reluctantly from Laura's writhing embrace. "Right here, Weej." I waved both arms like a WAVE-OFF. "On the beach . . . Go away, will you."

"We're getting ready to shove off." He shouted back. "The CAG told me to find you . . . Hey! How the hell did you get down there anyway?"

"Never mind how I got here," I yelled. *Shit! No way to get dry. I'll have to put my clothes on while I'm soaking wet. That won't be easy . . . or comfortable either.* "Hold the boat, Weej. I'll be up in ten minutes . . . And watch your language – there's a lady present." *Probably can't make it any quicker than about twenty minutes, but that'll hold 'em anyway.* I bent down to cradle Laura in my arms for the short walk back to our dressing rock. "Got to go, honey. Maybe we can do this another time."

"Well, I hope so, darlin'." She gave me that naughty look and kissed my neck. "I've just about got you broken in."

Hmm. That gnawing feeling in my stomach is gone. I thought as I struggled to pull my trousers up over my wet legs.

"God damn! It's a good thing we've got connections," I called over the intercom to Wujcik in the back seat of the SBD, as we cruised back to Kaneohe. Weej had flown from Ford Island to NAS Kahului, Maui, so it was my turn.

"Yeah. Sam's a good one to know alright," Wujcik called back. "Hell, if it hadn't been for him we wouldn't know that we'll probably be away from Pearl for six months or more." Being in the communications department, Sam Gallu had a pipeline to fleet planning.

"Sure wouldn't want to be away that long without any booze," I crowed.

Our inter-island booze run had begun at the NAS Ford Island officers' package store where we picked up our rations of whiskey – three bottles each – which we promptly stored in a locker in the officers' club pool dressing room. We had stuffed our two aviator's green carryall bags – valises in civilian talk – and the biggest parachute bag we could find in the baggage compartment of the SBD before we took off from NAS Ford Island. Then, at the NAS Kahului officers' club we had drawn our rations of two bottles of whiskey and a case of beer, each.

Paddles!

"I wish to hell they made the baggage compartment bigger in this machine," Wujcik complained. "Havin' the beer up there on the glare shield between us bugs me . . . Hell, it damn near landed in my lap during take-off."

"I'll have to watch the braking on landing, I guess," I sympathized. "I wouldn't want that beer to knock me in the head. Christ! what'll we do if we get two more cases at Kaneohe?"

We would stop at the Kaneohe officers' club for lunch – best in the islands – pick up our rations at the package store, and take off again for Ford Island.

"Careful now, Weej," I cautioned as we stepped gingerly up the gangway to *Belleau Wood's* hangar deck, carrying the parachute bag between us and our carry-all bags in our outside hands. "We've got the bottles wrapped in scivvie shirts but the beer cans might clink a little unless we're real smooth."

"God! I hope seven bottles of booze'll fit in that little desk safe," Wujcik wondered out loud. "Trouble is, The parachute bag is stretched so tight with four cases of beer in it that it would take a blind man not to notice . . . For Christ's sake, we got the biggest parachute bag we could find."

"Don't worry about that," I scolded. "Worry about where the hell you're goin' to store two cases o' beer. I think 'Garg' has the duty this afternoon," I confided. "That's why I wanted to get back before sixteen hundred.

We knew Lieut. M. R. Kallman as "Garg", short for Gargantua, because of his imposing bulk and the thick brown hair he had all over his body. Hell! I never did know his first name. With all his mass, Garg was a pretty good looking guy, with his curious blue-grey eyes, a big Jewish nose, a full head of curly brown hair, and a broad, infectious smile. Outside of Sam Gallu, Garg was the friendliest guy on the ship. And he roomed just two doors forward of me on the oh-two deck.

"Whew! That's a relief," I whispered as we topped the gangway, a little winded. "Garg's still there."

"Good," Wujcik sighed. "This'll be easier'n I thought."

Grumman F3F-3 fighters over NAS Miami, ca. 1942. (U.S. Navy courtesy Robert L. Lawson collection)

Scorpions' Den, ca. 1942. (Original Kodacolor courtesy J.A. Harper collection)

Grumman J2F *Duck* amphibian, ca. 1942. (U.S. Navy courtesy Robert L. Lawson collection)

USS Ranger (CV-4) launches P-40s for Safi, Morocco, ca. January 1943. (U.S. Navy courtesy Robert L. Lawson collection)

U.S.S. Belleau Wood recovering TBF Avengers, ca. 1943. (U.S. Navy courtesy *"Flight Quarters" The War Story of USS Belleau Wood*) Below: The author's animated CUT signal, ca. 1943. (J.A. Harper collection)

Arky Snowden lands far starboard, ca. August 1943. (U.S. Navy courtesy J.A. Harper collection)

Arky loses his tail. (U.S. Navy courtesy J.A. Harper collection)

Arky through the stacks. (U.S. Navy courtesy J.A. Harper collection)

Arky the swimmer. (U.S. Navy courtesy J.A. Harper collection)

TF-15 Operations Officer lands long, ca. September 1943. (U.S. Navy courtesy J.A. Harper collection)

Barrier trips TF-15 Operations Officer. (U.S. Navy courtesy J.A. Harper collection)

Fire envelopes TF-15 Operations Officer's Hellcat. (U.S. Navy courtesy J.A. Harper collection)

TF-15 Operations Officer's body removed. (U.S. Navy courtesy J.A. Harper collection)

"Speed" Schroeder's 1800 RPM WAVE-OFF, ca. September 1943. (U.S. Navy courtesy J.A. Harper collection)

Japanese Betty bomber downed by *Belleau Wood* gunners, ca. September 1943. (U.S. Navy courtesy Jack Barbour collection)

Lidio Mariani loses his tailhook on ramp, ca. June 1944. Broken tailhook visible at the horizon in fourth frame. (U.S. Navy courtesy J.A. Harper collection)

Kamikaze strikes *Belleau Wood*, ca. October 1944. Below: Author is at the end of the starboard hose. (U.S. Navy courtesy *"Flight Quarters" The War Story of USS Belleau Wood*)

Hellcat lands long, another is at 8th wire, ca. February 1945. (U.S. Navy courtesy J.A. Harper collection)

Grinning "Arky" Snowden with Air Medal, ca. April 1944. (J.A. Harper collection)

Weej and Harpo on the beach at Majuro, ca. May 1944. (J.A. Harper collection)

U.S.S. Wolverine on Lake Michigan with FM-2 Wildcats, ca. July 1945. (Courtesy Robt. L. Lawson collection)

15

FRIENDLY(?) FIRE

"Looks like we're on our way to a big operation, this time," Oveland offered with considerable enthusiasm. "What do you think it'll be this time?," he mused as we picked up our napkins in their monogrammed silver napkin rings and strolled over to sit at our favorite table with its white linen table cloth and silver service ready for dinner. Present were Oveland's inseparable wingman, Tabler, with Jack Thelen, Hoot Gibson, and Tommy Chuhak.

"'Scuse me. Hey, Collins. What's for dinner tonight?," I called to our steward, who also served as room boy for my stateroom. Collins was a little guy, about five six and a hundred and thirty pounds, with fine features for a negro. A Jesse Owens with hair.

"Steak, french fries, and green beans, suh," Collins replied. "How d'you like yo steak, suh?

"Rare, thanks." Then: "Well, we won't know until a couple o' days out, anyway." I mused. "Hey! Too bad about Freddy. He wanted in the worst way to be in fighters and just when he got there, that had to happen. A real shame." Freddy Lamb had jumped at the opportunity to transfer from VT-24 to VF-24 during the shuffle when we traded our SBDs for twelve more fighters, and the CAG had approved it.

"I understand you were with him, Harpo," Tab inquired, with a sidelong glance. "What the hell happened?"

Paddles!

"We were takin' a couple of F6Fs back to CASU Ford Island for some mod," I began. "Freddy was leadin'. We broke over the tower, entered the downwind, and everything was okay." I used my hands to show our relative positions. "Freddy was on final and I was at the ninety when I saw him just roll over and go straight in." I touched my forehead with my right index and ring fingers. "I didn't think he'd just spun in from lack of airspeed cause he seemed to be in a safe attitude – besides, he rolled to the right. The F6F just naturally rolls to the left at the stall."

"Well," Oveland interjected. "The board said his right flap retracted. But they haven't figured out why.

"Well. That's comforting," Jack moaned. "I hope they let us know when they find out."

"How come we didn't get a replacement before we left Pearl?," Tommy beefed. "Hell, we were already short handed.

"Skipper requested one," Oveland offered. "He'll probably come aboard next time we're in port."

"Yeah," Hoot wailed. "Two or three weeks from now."

"Looks like two of 'em didn't make it back," Wujcik lamented as we walked up the deck after recovering the morning strike on Kwajalein.

"Yeah, one fighter and one torpecker," I replied, frowning. "I guess we'll find out who when we get to the ready rooms."

Tuffy Chase was describing the incident as we walked in, using his hands to describe airplane flight paths. "George was over to my right." Chase showed a steep dive with his right hand. "He was REALLY steep. The bombs barely got free of the bomb bay when his wings just folded." He made his right hand accelerate. "He went straight in – more or less in formation with his bombs. BIG EXPLO-SION!"

"Was it during his pullout?," Swensson asked.

"Oh no – Hell no," Chase shook his head. "He was still in his dive. And I mean DIVE.

"Did anyone get out?," Alston asked.

"No way!," Chase scowled. "We were down to about three thousand feet when his wings came off. No time."

In the passageway on the way to the fighter ready room I confided to Wujcik: "Agar's the guy who said 'you can even dive bomb with the TBF' during a discussion of structural limits after a fixed gunnery hop at Floyd Bennett," I winced.

Chapter 15: Friendly(?) Fire

"His emphasis was on DIVE BOMB! And he meant STEEP," I shrugged. "Well, he proved something today."

"Oh boy!," Hoot Gibson cheered as Collins served dinner plates to our wardroom table. "Mah favorite vittles – roast beef and baked patatah – and these cooks, heah, do a real good job on it. Sour cream for yo patatah, Hawpo?"

"No thanks," I took the sour cream and passed it on. "I just put a lot of butter and salt and pepper on it."

"You really mean 'a lot of butter' don't you," Jack taunted. That's . . ."

CLANG CLANG CLANG. TOOOEEEE – "ALL HANDS MAN YOUR BATTLE STATIONS – CLANG CLANG CLANG – ALL HANDS . . ."

The wardroom cleared completely in a minute or two, leaving me quietly munching my roast beef and baked potato as though nothing had happened. We didn't have any aircraft out so they didn't need me. When I had finished my meal I eased on forward to the forecastle, securing the hatch behind me.

"Hi, Leo. What the hell's goin' on?," I called to Dulacki up in 40MM mount number one, part of the Marines' gun battery.

"Raid reported comin' this way bearing three five zero – relative. Dulacki droned, peering forward through his binoculars. "I can see five of 'em right on the horizon, low, fifteen or twenty miles out. Whoa! Now there're six . . . look like Bettys circling to our port for a torpedo attack."

"I'm goin' down to CIC and see what's happenin'," I yelled up to Dulacki as I ran aft.

"Where's your gun, Harpo?," Leo chided. "Now's your chance for glory."

"No time, damn it." An excuse. "I just came from the wardroom. I hope you bag one if they get inside the screen."

I undogged the hatch, stepped through it, re-dogged it on the inside, and ran for the ladder. Down I went, two rungs at a time. "Hi. Charlie," I whispered, easing into CIC. "What's goin' on, anyway?

"Come on in, Harpo," Foster beckoned with a wave of his hand. "The picket destroyer reported visual contact with six bogies comin' this way about twenty minutes ago. Apparently they're right on the deck 'cause we don't paint 'em on radar. The CAP has been vectored over there and the flag has ordered a cease fire until the CAP I.D.s 'em."

"CIC, this is Fly Control," boomed Dahl's voice over the speaker. "*Patterson,* the forward screening destroyer, reports bogies on her port bow, five miles. What do you have, Charlie?"

Paddles!

"Nothing, sir," Foster scratched his head. "Apparently they're too low for surface radar . . ."

"TALLY HO!," we heard the CAP leader cheer over the speaker. "Cougar four, here. Six bogies on the deck. Look like *Bettys* to me." Then: "Cougar four-three, you and four-four take tail-end Charlie and move up. I'll take the leader."

"Cougar flight, HOLD . . ."

"SPLASH one Betty!," came the jubilant cry. "Cougar four-four got one of 'em."

"God damn it! Cougar flight. HOLD YOUR FIRE! Those are Army B-25s."

"Cougar four-three, here. They sure are givin' a realistic imitation of a formation of *Bettys* maneuverin' for a coordinated torpedo attack. I was convinced."

"Thanks Bill." No call sign but it was probably Cougar four-four.

"CIC, I see a big splash out there," came Dahl's voice again. "What's happening?"

"Yes sir, Commander," Charlie spoke cautiously. "CAP splashed one of 'em before the flight leader could order a hold fire. You see, sir, they're Army B-25s – probably returning from a raid on Kwaj to their base in the Gilberts."

"Oh."

CLANG CLANG CLANG – "ALL HANDS MAN YOUR BATTLE STATIONS – All hands . . . "

We had just finished debriefing the pilots who had returned from the afternoon strike on Saipan and Arky Snowden and I were already engrossed in our perpetual Acey Deucy game in the back seats of the fighter ready room.

"Fighter ready room, this is Fly Control." I recognized Commander Dahl's voice. "I want four pilots ready to launch as soon as we get the fighters respotted and rearmed. We've got bogies all around . . . and put four more on stand by to launch if we need 'em."

I leapt out of my chair and started for the door, "I'll see you later, Arky. I've got to get my gun. Who knows? I might get a shot at some of those bogies, if they get through the screen."

"Sounds like the hard way to me, Harpo," Arky chided.

"What the hell, Arky. It's the only way I can get some action since I can't fly with you guys," I yelled over my shoulder as I disappeared through the door on the run.

Chapter 15: Friendly(?) Fire

Jeez! This son-of-a-bitch is heavy. I thought as I hoisted the .50 cal. air cooled machine gun onto my shoulder and started out the door of my stateroom. CLANK. *Oh oh! Banged the barrel against the ladder. This seemed a lot easier when I was just going to gunnery drills.* I had taken the gun back to Landing Signals during gunnery drills to practice handling and firing the gun but now I was in a hurry. *Slow down, dummy! If you fall with this piece you're likely to become a casualty.*

As I stepped up onto the flight deck from the catwalk ladder a roar erupted from the bridge. "Hurrah! Gunner Harpo." Commander Dahl led the taunting cheer accompanied by loud applause and laughter. *They think my gun and I are funny, do they. Well, I'll admit there are bigger guns on the ship but I'll show 'em.* The applause and mocking laughter followed me like a wave as I strode aft, the up-turned faces of the 40MM gun crews signalling a mixture of merriment, respect, and encouragement. I saluted as I passed, as though I were in a parade.

"Hey, Callagee," I called, impatiently. "Where the hell is Monahan?"

"He seen you comin', sir," Callagee nodded. "Gone to get a box of ammo."

"Good – here." I handed him the gun. "Lets get this thing on its mount. Maybe we can bag one of those *Bettys.*"

POW POW POW POW . . . RAT-A-TAT-A-RAT-A-TAT . . . The entire starboard battery, 40MM and 20MM, opened fire all at once. "Damn! I can't fire across to starboard." *Hmmm. No ammo anyway.* I jumped up on the flight deck to see a stream of tracers, brilliant in the waning twilight, intersecting at the oncoming bomber just skimming the waves. *How in HELL does he just fly right through that hail of AA fire?* The thought just crossed my mind when a bright yellow flame issued from the port engine. "LOOK OUT! He's goin' to crash into us." I cried as I jumped back into the catwalk, the best cover I could find, then snuck a peek over the deck edge scupper to see the *Betty*, with its entire left wing blazing, climb just enough to clear the flight deck, then roll to the left and plunge into the water not fifty yards to port.

"Another one comin' on our port, sir," Monahan yelled as he set down the box of .50 cal. ammo. "Got through the screen without damage, looks like."

"Gimme that belt." I opened the breech plate on the gun, grabbed the end of the cartridge belt, slapped it into the gun, slammed the plate closed, and fired a test burst at the horizon. "Yeah! We're ready! . . . Hey. I didn't see him drop a fish."

"Neither did I, sir."

"Maybe he's got bombs . . . "

POW-POW, POW-POW . . . All the port side 40MM batteries opened fire on the Betty bomber as soon as it cleared the screen, their tracers lighting up the darkening sky and shell explosions sending geysers of sea water into the air all around the attacker. Next, the 20MMs opened up. The Betty just kept coming.

I took aim at the approaching aircraft and watched as projectiles splashed around it. *Hold your fire John A – a thousand yards ought to be about right – NOW!* I squeezed the makeshift trigger with my right trigger finger and held, watching my tracers arc toward the bomber, mingling with all the other tracers.

"You got 'im." Monahan clapped me on the back but I just kept on firing.

The brilliant orange fire started in the right wing root – probably a fuel tank – and grew until it enveloped the right engine nacelle. The *Betty* pulled up just as the other one had and rolled right. The flaming right wing struck the flight deck, causing the aircraft to cartwheel into the sea to our starboard, leaving most of his right wing smoldering among Cobbs' arresting wires.

Thirty minutes later: TOOOEE. "SECURE GENERAL QUARTERS."

Then: "THIS IS THE CAPTAIN SPEAKING. TBS MESSAGE FROM THE FLAG IS AS FOLLOWS: 'COKÉ, THIS IS BADGER. WELL DONE! PASS IT ALONG TO YOUR GUNNERY DEPARTMENT'." The captain paused. Then: "I ADD MY 'WELL DONE' TO ALL GUNNERS. YOU GOT THE ONES THAT WOULD HAVE GOTTEN US."

"Thanks skipper," I whispered to myself and aimed a salute at the bridge, assuming he included me in "all gunners."

God damn! I'd sure hate to have an engine failure here. I guess you'd call that a rain forest down there. Looks like a soft green carpet, with those dense vines connecting the tops of all the trees and supporting some kind of moss. Absolutely no terrain visible. Looks like it's been growing since the island came up out of the ocean. I had been catapulted from *Belleau Wood* two hundred and fifty miles north-northeast of the Espiritu Santo anchorage and I was cruising at 4,000 feet over the big peninsula that forms the northeast extremity of the island, Hog Harbor off to my left. The lush flora under my right wing spread as far as the eye could see and climbed the mountain range to the west until it disappeared into the clouds. The ship wouldn't drop the hook until about eighteen hundred, so this excursion would give me a whole day's head start on preparing the four replacement fighter pilots to fly their replacement *Hellcats* aboard whenever we got underway again. I knew the O'club would be full of familiar faces when I got through bouncing these guys.

Chapter 15: Friendly(?) Fire

"Bomber two tower, this is NAVY 25844, one F6F five miles north, request landing instructions."

"NAVY 844, cleared to runway 310, no traffic. Runway is pierced planking and taxiways are oiled dirt, soft in places from a recent rain."

Wow! What a roar. Sounded like landing the Duck on water, only more of a clatter. I marvelled as I landed on the pierced planking.

"Where're the guys that belong to those F6Fs out there?," I demanded as I stomped into the operations shack, my signal paddles under my arm.

"I think they're all in the pilots' lounge, sir." The sailor on duty pointed down a passageway that branched off to my left. "They said they're waitin' for the LSO from the *Belleau Wood.* Is that you?"

"Yeah." I started down the passageway. "Thanks."

"Good morning, gentlemen," I announced, breezily as I swept into the room. "I'm John Harper, the *Belleau Wood* LSO. Call me Harpo." I could see that the two big guys were full lieutenants. *Sure glad I pinned on these lieutenant's railroad tracks last October. Now I don't have to feel inferior when I meet other full lieutenants.*

"Hi . . . er . . . Harpo." The big redhead extended his hand. "McLaughlin here." We shook. "The string bean here is Holmgaard, Quinlan's over there, and that's Bennett."

Lieutenant McLaughlin was about six feet tall and a little pudgy at about two hundred, ten pounds. His blue eyes peered out from under bushy dark red eyebrows accenting his florid face – Ensign Holmgaard stood about six foot five and probably only weighed about a hundred and sixty-five pounds, a real string bean. His platinum blond shock of hair and fair complexion betrayed his Scandinavian heritage – Lieutenant Quinlan was a rugged six footer with a confident air, emphasized by his black Clark Gable moustache. Ensign Bennett was about five nine, with an athletic build and a blond crew cut.

"Glad to meet you." I shook hands all around. "We've got to get this done as quickly as possible, cause we don't know when we'll get under way. But I think we've got a couple of days, anyway." I eyed each one of them carefully. "You're all carrier qualified I presume." *Shit! I sure as hell hope so.*

"Yeah," McLaughlin spoke for the group. "Quinlan and I have both been in the fleet before." He surveyed the two Ensigns. "These two just came out of CQTU I understand. Is that right?"

Paddles!

"Yes sir. CQTU Norfolk," Holmgaard answered.

"San Diego, sir," Bennett reported. "Just last month."

"They put us together as a unit and gave us some FCLP at Barbers Point just before we boarded that jeep carrier . . . er . . . *Corregidor* to come out here." McLaughlin finished the story.

"Sounds good to me," I shifted the emphasis. "Let me review the signals with you so we'll all be on the same page – here have a seat." I stepped to the front of the room. "We've had some problems with guys comin' out of CQTU from time to time." I laid my paddles on the table and drew the standard flight pattern diagram on the blackboard. "Then I'll give you about a dozen passes to get acquainted – we've got time for two or three bounce drills today."

16

MIDNIGHT RIDE

"Hey. Harpo." Oveland clapped me on the back as Wujcik and I arrived at the Espiritu Santo O'Club bar after a day of FCLP at Bomber Two. "How'd it go with the new boys? . . . Hey – You need a drink."

"Yeah . . . scotch and water – double – how about you Weej? I'm buyin'." I had some catching up to do after that long drive down from Bomber Two. "Those guys are pretty smooth. We had two sessions today and they all responded pretty well."

"D'you think they're ready now?"

"Well, I think they'd be okay if we had to take 'em tomorrow." Wujcik frowned. "But we're goin' to give 'em a couple more sessions tomorrow morning."

I gulped my drink. "Haaa! That's pretty good scotch for bein' way the hell out here in the hinterlands." I slammed the glass on the bar, spilling some of the drink.

"Well," Wujcik pointed toward the lanai just outside the bar. "Sam's already struck up the choir."

Sam Gallu, drawing on his background with Fred Waring, had put together his own little choir of well oiled naval officers.

"Let's join 'em, Weej." I grabbed Wujcik by the arm. "You like to sing don't you?"

"Okay." Wujcik hesitated. "But I'm not very good."

"You think those guys are?" I gave a pull on his arm. "They sound like a flock o' sick sea gulls for Christ's sake. Come on." Then: "Oops! Hey bartender! Gimme another scotch and water, heavy on the scotch." And to Wujcik: "Have another one. Hell! You can't sing without some lubrication. Ha! Thanks bartender. C'mon Collin."

"My Wild Irish Rose. The sweetest flower . . ." Sam's choir started.

"Hey, Harpo!," came Sam's rowdy greeting. "Glad you made it. You can sing tenor harmony, can't you?"

"I can try," I ventured. "But I'm supposed to be a baritone so pick a little lower key, unless you want nothing but a screech from me."

"Okay." Sam raised his hands as though holding a baton. "HMMMMM." He set the key. "How's that?" I nodded okay. "Ah one, ah two, ah three. My Wild Irish Rose. The sweetest flower that grows . . . ."

"Hey Red!," I hailed Red Volz, fresh off *Yorktown*. "What the hell're you doing here."

"Hell, Harp," Volz drawled. "The whole damned fleet's here – well – three task groups anyway. Where the hell've you been? You're all dusty.

"We're gettin' four replacement pilots – with airplanes – so we've been bouncin' 'em up at Bomber Two." I pointed to Sam's choir. "D'you want to get in on the singin'? Sam used to direct the voices behind Fred Waring's band."

"Naw." Red didn't want to sing so we just stood around drinking, and talking about old times.

"Hey, did you hear that Stu Stephens got killed?," I groaned. "Now there's a great loss to the NAVY."

"Yeah. He finally got command of a TBF squadron and was trainin' 'em up for deployment at North Island," Red sighed. "Midair collision with one of his own, I understand."

"Here's to Stu Stephens." I raised my glass. "The best God damned LSO in the NAVY."

"Hear, hear!" Red bashed his glass against mine, drank it dry and slammed it on the bar. "Another scotch, bartender."

"One more for Stu." I banged my glass on the bar. "Scotch, rocks!"

And so it went through the evening, both of us trying to top each other with harrowing accounts of carrier operations, and drinking a toast to each succeeding tale of wild carrier approaches, wave-offs, and deck crashes.

"Everybody out! The club's closed!," the club officer announced.

Chapter 16: Midnight Ride

"Christ, it's only midnight," Red groused. "Just startin' to have a little fun."

"I've got an idea. I've got plenty of booze," I raved. "Let's go out to the old *Beulah Maru* and have a party."

"Great idea, Harp."

"Ish right up here, Ed," I whispered over my shoulder as I staggered along the passageway. Oops." I stopped suddenly when I saw Dr. List's light on next door to my stateroom. Red ran into me and we both damned near sprawled on the deck. "Just a shecond, fer Chrishake." I held my finger to my lips. "Shhhh . . That's the Inshpector's room. Maybe he'll join ush." I pulled back the curtain and peeked in. "Dr. Lisht?"

Commander List was our senior medical officer and he always enjoyed a good party. We called him "The Inspector" because one of his collateral duties was as the ship's health inspector. "Oh. Hi, Harpo." The doctor looked up from his book. "Just getting back from the club?"

"Yesh shir." I squatted down to face Dr. List and whispered furtively. "We're gonna have a party. "Y' like t' join ush . . er . . shir? Oh. Thish ish Ed Volz, *Yorktown*'sh LSO."

"Looks like you already had a party." The Doc flinched from my breath. "You guys probably ought to hit the rack. Never know what'll happen tomorrow."

"I know what'll happen," I said, falling backward into a sitting position on the deck. "I'm gonna shleep in. C'mon Inshpector, I got some booze in my shafe, next door."

"Okay, Harpo," List sighed. "But just one."

"Great! Hold it right there!" I held up my hand, palm to the Doctor and struggled to my feet. "I'll get the booze." I scrambled, too noisily, into my stateroom, hoping not to disturb Dulacki and, with the help of my flashlight, opened my personal safe and carefully slid out a bottle of White Horse Scotch. Back in the Inspector's stateroom: "I got it! Y' got any glasses, Doc?"

Sam Gallu came clattering down the passageway shouting: "We're gettin' underway at oh five thirty."

"Wait one fuckin' minute," I growled as I hauled Sam into the Inspector's stateroom by his shirt collar. "You're shittin' me aren't you, Sham?"

"Hell no, Harpo. Would I shit you?" His eyes cringed.

171

Paddles!

Hmmm. Wouldn't be the first time. Trouble is, as a communications officer he's sure to have the straight skinny. I let go his shirt.

Sam straightened his collar and held up his right hand as if taking an oath. "Straight from the captain's mouth. Honest! Pass the word."

I sobered up a little. "Son-of-a-bitch! I left our only set of paddles out at Bomber Two." I felt a little panic. "And my flight gear too . . . Shit! It's already oh two fifteen. I gotta get goin'. She ya later Inshpector." I scrambled down the passageway on my way to the hangardeck.

"Hey! Wait for me Harp." Red came stumbling after me. "I gotta get off this tub before you guys shove off."

I saluted the officer of the day as I rushed up to the quarter deck. "Request permission to go ashore, sir."

"You WHAT?" He was dumbfounded. "Hell, I can't let anybody off the ship, Harpo."

"But this is urgent," I pleaded. "I left our paddles ashore and we can't operate without 'em."

"Sorry, Harpo. You can't go." He held out both hands as though to hold me back. "Captain's orders."

No use talking to this guy. "Wait here, Red – hic – I'll get – hic – permission from the exec and I'll be right back." I turned on my heel and headed straight for the executive officer's stateroom at a dead run. I was sure he would give me permission to leave the ship, under the circumstances. I couldn't help staggering just a little as I rushed up to the executive officer's Marine orderly. "Lieutenant Harper to see Commander Miller." I announced, breathlessly.

"The commander's asleep, sir," was the formal response. "I suggest you try again in the morning, sir." The Marine sensed my condition and was being just a little patronizing.

"Thish thing can't wait, Private. That ish if we want – hic – gasp – to recover aircraft tomorrow," I announced with as much authority as I could muster, still puffing hard from my rapid climb up two ladders.

The Marine recoiled from the smell of my breath. "I'll see what I can do, sir." With that he disappeared through the curtains into the exec's cabin.

"What the hell does HE want in the middle of the God damned night," Miller thundered . . . "Okay, damn it! Send 'im in. I'm awake now."

I only staggered a little as I slipped quietly into the darkened room. and then, very softly: "Commander Miller, shir . . . hic."

Chapter 16: Midnight Ride

"Harper! You good for nothin' . . . you're drunk again, aren't you."

"Not any more, shir," I lied, and he knew it. *I'm not going to wait for him to ask.* "Shir, I was up at Bomber Two – hic – today – er – yesterday, I guess – an I lef our only set o' – hic – signal paddles up there." I took a deep breath and tried to stop swaying. "I gotta go get 'em shir, or we can't recover – hic – airplanesh."

"NO ONE is to leave this ship this morning," Miller announced, firmly. "And that includes YOU, Harper. You'll have to make do until you can get some paddles made."

"But shir . . ."

"You heard me, Harper, NO ONE," he roared. "And get in your bunk and sleep it off."

Back at the quarterdeck I gave the officer of the day a shaky salute and announced: "I have permission to leave the ship, shir." *Hell! I gotta get my paddles or we won't be able to operate.* "C'mon Red. We're off." Down the gangway we lurched, two steps at a time, and into the liberty launch. "Boat's loaded, Coxs'n. Shove off."

"Jesus Christ, Harp," Red moaned, as we roared through the Bomber Two main gate in the jeep assigned to *Belleau Wood.* "That was a hairy God damned ride up that canyon road."

"Yeah. I'm not used to drivin' on the wrong side o' the road like a God damned limey . . . 'specially at night." Espiritu Santo had been settled by the British so the rules of the road required driving on the left side. "The mud and ruts didn't help any either." I mumbled, skidding to a stop in front of the travel trailer that served as the parachute loft. "Good thing this jeep's got good tires. C'mon." I stomped up the three steps to the trailer door and grabbed the screen door handle. "Shit! They got the God damned place locked." I cursed as I drew my survival knife.

"Are you sure you want to do this, Harp?," Red scolded. "It's probably a court martial offense," he snickered as I carefully cut a short slit in the screen, reached in and opened the door.

"Aha! There they are," I crowed, putting my helmet on my head, slipping my gloves in my pocket, and stuffing the paddles under my arm.

"Good. You got 'em," Red cheered. "What the hell are you doin' now?"

"Just droppin' these guys a note to apologize for rippin' up their screen."

"You didn't sign it, did you?," Red grumbled.

"Hell, yesh," I whispered, heading for the jeep. "I wouldn't want to be anonymoush, would I?" VAROOM. The jeep's engine came to life. "Now, let's get the hell out o' here."

"Hey! slow down, Harp!," Red hollered as the jeep fishtailed in the deep ruts in the middle of the steep muddy road. "You're drivin' like a damned drunken sailor."

"Why the hell not? I am one," I yelled, trying to control the jeep's excursions. "This God damned mud is slicker'n owl shit." The left lane, where we should have been, was right at the edge of the steep canyon, with no guard rail.

"LOOK OUT!" Red's voice was tinged with terror at the sight of the two headlights coming around the corner toward us.

"Oh my God," I shrieked. "The son-of-a-bitch won't come out of the ruts." I wrestled the wheel until the jeep jumped out of the ruts and headed straight for the canyon."

"Whoa, Harp," Red screamed. "We're goin' over!"

"Relax, Red. Don't you have any faith?" I faked a calm I didn't have while fighting the jeep into the left lane and whizzing past the other vehicle at a frightening relative velocity. "Whew! That was close."

Red and I rushed onto the Navy landing and surveyed the docks. "Hey, Harp. No boats. What're you goin to do now?"

Jesus! It's already four thirty. They'll probably haul the gangway up around five. I began to feel some panic. BANG BANG. "Hey, in there," I called into the duty shack on the dock. "I gotta have a boat." BANG BANG. I pounded on the shack again.

The screen door opened and a bleary eyed sailor in his rumpled scivvies gave us a suspicious glare. "No boats any more tonight, sir. They're all out at their ships."

"Don't you have one here?," I appealed, urgently. "I gotta make it to my ship by five. We're shovin' off at five thirty."

"Sorry, sir," the sailor yawned. "You might try the fishin' dock down there." He pointed to a little pier about a hundred yards down the beach.

"Thanks, sailor," I called over my shoulder as I ran for the shore, Red in hot pursuit. "Sorry to bother you," I hollered even louder.

CLOMP CLOMP CLOMP. We made enough noise on the rickety dock to wake the dead. I noticed that there was no boat in the water but three or four dugout canoes were stashed on the dock. The smell of fish was overwhelming. The little hut looked like it might fall off into the bay at any moment. BANG BANG.

The torn screen door opened. "Wat yu wan? Mipela sreep. Yu kam tumora!," and he slammed the door.

"I think he said: 'tomorrow'." I yanked the door open again, almost tearing it from its loose hinges. "Urgent! Understand? Urgent!" I decided to try a little mock Pidgin English. "Me" I stabbed myself in the chest with my right finger. "Gotta get to ship." I pointed at *Belleau Wood*, out in the harbor. "NOW. Savvy? NOW!"

"Awwwh!" A toothless grin spread across his deeply lined brown face and his dark brown eyes sparkled. "Yu boskru bilong bikpela sip. HAUH!

It sounded like a statement to me, not a question. "What the hell did he say, Ed?"

"Damned if I know. Probably Pidgin English." Red scratched his head. "Let me try." Then, turning to the fisherman: "My fren." He enunciated, clapping me on the back. "Got to go to ship, there." And pointed to the ship. "NOW! Old man. NOW!"

"Unnastan!" The little man bowed five or six times. "Hauh! Unnastan! Boskru heah wango bikpela bot, deah. Hauh!

"Yeah! Yeah!," I exulted, jumping up and down. *Whew! Maybe I'll make it yet. Hmm. Wonder how much he wants.* I yanked out my wallet. "How much."

"Hauh!" The little man frowned. "Melican dollah . . . hmmm . . ."

Oh oh. Here it comes. Well, whatever it is I've GOTTA pay it.

"Okay Masta." The man brightened. "Wanpela ten faiv." And he put out his hand.

"I think he just quoted me a price, Ed." I shook my head. "What the hell was it?"

"Shit, Harp, I cant understand him either." Red looked curiously at the little fisherman. "I think I heard 'Five'. Why don't you offer him a fin?"

"Good idea." I pulled out a five dollar bill and offered it to the man.

"No Masta." He held out his hand, palm up. "I sai WANPELA TEN faiv, Masta." He announced impatiently and held up ten fingers, then five more.

"Oh. FIFTEEN dollars. Yeah! Okay! Fifteen dollars." *Whew! Four Forty-five. I think I'm goin' to make it.*

"Awwwh!" Ten fi dolla melican." He gave me that toothless grin with the sparkling eyes, and bowed again slowly. Then: "OKAY! Mipela bai go." He waddled over to one of the little fishing canoes and pushed it off the end of the dock, then turned and waved to me, paddles in hand. "Go now!"

Paddles!

"Aren't y' comin', Ed?"

"Naw. I'll just find a bunk over at the BOQ." Red waved. "See you some other time."

The combat air patrol had been launched shortly after old *Beulah Maru* cleared Segond Channel out of Espiritu Santo, but it didn't bother me. I was sound asleep in my rack. We now had a report that McLaughlin and his crew were inbound and Flight Quarters had been called. Wujcik and I strolled back through the arresting gear, leaning against the tilting deck as the ship turned into the wind. The whole of Rear Admiral "Black Jack" Reeves' TG 58.1 turned with us and plane guard destroyers took their positions astern *Enterprise* and *Belleau Wood*. *Cowpens* was not preparing to recover aircraft.

"You take 'em today, Weej." I handed him the paddles I had brought up from my stateroom. "You ought to know these guys as well as I do after the last two days of bounce drill."

"Yeah, but . . ." Wujcik eyed me carefully. "What the hell happened to you. You look ghastly . . . er . . . and what were our paddles doin' in your stateroom?"

"Remember we left 'em up at Bomber Two yesterday?," I leered at him. "Well, Red and I had to go get 'em this morning." I put my hand to my forehead. "Just got back in time to shove off. Transportation: Native dugout canoe. It's a long story."

"Scares me." Wujcik looked up to check the FOX flag at the dip.

"'Sweetie' Freeman is bringing back the airplane I took in to Bomber Two," I announced. "So there'll be five of them."

"Where'd Freeman get that "Sweetie" handle anyway?"

"Hah – remember that hula dancer." I did a little hula imitation. "The one who danced for us at that sedate luau we went to just outside Wailuku?"

"You mean that night when you got lost on the beach with that sexy blonde. Wujcik rolled his eyes. "Yeah. That was the best hula I've ever seen."

"Never mind me and the beach," I scowled. "Anyway – that dancer is Sweetie Wilson."

"The plot thickens." Wujick grinned. "Okay. I'll bite. Where the hell did she get the name 'Wilson'?"

"Okay. If you insist." I grabbed his arm. "Look. Her mom was your common everyday south sea island enchantress, living in Tahiti. She fell for this horny American explorer named Wilson and . . . er . . . produced Sweetie." I grinned wickedly. "Well, guess what? Mama never saw this Wilson guy again so she moved to Maui . . . and now Sweetie's hula is the toast of the Islands. Get it?

"Yeah. I get it." Wujcik scratched his head. "But what the hell's that got to do with Freeman." He was getting exasperated.

"Well, I understand Freemen had a private showing at her 'little grass shack' up in the hills," I shrugged. "Ipso Facto: He is now 'Sweetie' Freeman."

"Whoa!" Wujcik pointed aft at the approaching *Hellcats*. "Here they come."

The sound of the yodel announced the ship was ready to recover aircraft, the white flag came out at fly control, and FOX was two-blocked.

"Gear, flaps, hook, all down, sir," Monahan yelled, peering into his binoculars at the first *Hellcat* coming out of the ninety.

"Clear deck, cross deck pendants and barriers up," reported Callagee.

"Probably Bernie." I suggested that it was McLaughlin.

"Yeah. He always wants to line up with the starboard catwalk." Wujcik gave him a SLANT left. Then a FAST and a SLANT right. CUT. Power came off abruptly, Bernie dipped toward the centerline, pulled the nose up and grabbed the third wire. "Hey! That wasn't bad."

"Gear, flaps, hook, all down, sir."

"This is probably Holmgaard," I called into Wujcik's ear. "That's the order they were bouncin' at Bomber Two."

"Acts like him," Wujcik mused. "Perfect speed, attitude, and altitude. ROGER all the way . . . He's smooth."

"Clear deck. Barriers up!," Callagee yelled.

"ROGER! Nice gentle turn right onto the deck centerline. Now CUT." Wujcik turned to follow the airplane. "Well, DIP for Christ's sake, DIP."

"He's holdin' off," I screamed. "We've got a barrier."

"No! GOD DAMN IT!," Wujcik shrieked. "He's goin' into the planes up for'rd. LOOK OUT!" Instinctively, he looked away just as Holmgaard caught the top wire of the last barrier with his tailhook and didn't stop until his propeller had chewed off the tail of McLaughlin's *Hellcat* right up to the armor plate.

"WHEW! That was close," I squealed.

Wujcik looked up. "How the hell did he do that, Harpo?" His eyes were bugged out. "I thought we'd lose that whole pack of airplanes up for'rd." He hung his head. "Well. We did lose two . . . and it's my fault."

"God Damn it, Weej." I grabbed him by the shirt front. "I told you never to say it's your fault. NEVER! Do you hear me. NEVER SAY IT'S YOUR FAULT." The approach was perfect, like you said. Holmgaard just held off, pure and simple." I let go his shirt and gave him a pat on the back. "Besides. We really only lost one. The hangar deck crew'll make one good one out of those two busted ones. Wait and see." I looked into his eyes and whispered, "Forget it, Weej." Then: "Looks like Holmgaard just earned himself a new nickname: 'Homicide'. Listen." I enunciated carefully. "HOMICIDE HOLMGAARD. Hmmm. Poetic, don't you think?"

"Hey, you guys," Jack Thelen ragged Arky and me. "Don't you ever quit that piss ant Acey Deucy game?"

"The winner might," Arky muttered, tossing the dice. "But the loser always wants another game . . . Ahh! Double sixes." He gloated. "That makes my block solid."

"God Damn it! Jack," I swore, slamming the arm of the seat. "Get lost. You're bad luck."

"Not for me. Heh heh," Arky grinned. "Stay right here Jack."

"Well, our guys're gettin' their first look at Palau," Jack mused. "Did you see those crazy friggin' names? Babelthuap . . whew . . that's the big island – Koror's easy – that's where the main base is." He shook his head. "But how about Ngulu and Urukthapel? Took me all day yesterday just learnin' how to say 'em."

"Good thing we're using code names for the targets," Arky croaked. "Think how it might sound: 'Coké Four, you take Goo-Goo, Coké Five go for Babelthapel, and I'll take the one I can't pronounce . . . er . . . the one with the navalthuap base'. Har Har." He rolled the dice again. "ACEY DEUCY!"

TOOEEE. "NOW HEAR THIS. AIR DEPARTMENT MAN YOUR FLIGHT QUARTERS STATIONS FOR RECOVERING AIRCRAFT. NOW HEAR THIS. AIR DEPARTMENT . . . ."

I've got to get goin'," I announced. "That's the strike comin' back from those targets we can't pronounce."

"I'll save the game," Arky snickered. He was ahead.

"Don't bother," I frowned. "We can start over when I get back."

"No trouble at all, Harpo." Arky gave me that wicked grin as he set the Acey Deucey board carefully on the shelf at the back of the ready room. "Mind if I join you back at Landing Signals?"

"Naw, Come on," I yelled over my shoulder as I ran up the ladder to the flight deck, two rungs at a time.

Chapter 16: Midnight Ride

"Weej is goin' to take these, Arky," I advised, stepping over the number four arresting wire. "You can stand up on the platform behind him if you want to. I'm going to watch from the catwalk."

"Thanks. I'll join you in the catwalk."

"There they are," Arky yelled, pointing off to port and bracing himself against the ship's list to port as she turned to starboard, into the wind. "I thought we launched sixteen.

"We did," I affirmed. "Looks like Ross lost his number four." I grimaced. "That's Fleischer isn't it?"

Back in the ready room, Ross was describing the action: "We were goin' in on the airfield on Koror – Robby was tucked in tight on my left wing and Buck and Splash were split off to the right about a hundred yards." He showed the formation with his hands. "The AA was really heavy – bursts all around us." He exploded his fingers on both hands to emphasize the point."

"Yeah. Those Jap gunners were trackin' us right on," Buck affirmed. "We were all strafin' the AA battery but they kept right on firin'."

"We were gettin' down to about two thousand feet," Ross continued. "I saw a flash out of the corner of my right eye and turned to see Splash's right wing come off." He closed his eyes, tight. "He spiralled in just short of the gun emplacement, showering it with burning fuel. Splash got his target."

"So Splash made his last splash," I murmured.

Nobody laughed.

17

R & R?

I was getting an extended night's sleep after *Belleau Wood* anchored in Majuro Lagoon, near the southeastern extremity of the Marshall Islands. POW – TEWAAANG. "Hey! What the hell was that?" I rolled over and looked down at Dulacki's bunk. *Gone. Bunk neatly made.*

POW – CLANK. *Sounds like rifle fire . . . guess I'll have to find out for myself.* I jumped off my bunk onto the deck and stuck my head out of the port hole. *I'll be God damned! F6F fuselage hangin' tail down from the davit, spewin' water from every hole.* POW – WHUP – TEWAAANG. *I got it! They're tryin' to drop that hulk into the lagoon by shootin' the hawser that's holdin' it up. Leo must have one of his sharpshooters takin' pot shots. Hey I've got to get into this act. Ahh! Just the thing. That Garand M-1 is Dulacki's training piece for the week. PER-FECT!*

POW – CLACK. *Son-of-a-bitch! He hit something. I've got to get movin' before that shooter sinks the damned thing. Now where's the friggin' ammo?* I rummaged in Dulacki's locker. *Ahh! Here it is – Wow! A full mixture – ball, armor piercing, and tracer. Grab it and GO!* Up the two ladders and out onto the starboard catwalk I ran. POW – CLICK. The hawser frayed a little just above the Hellcat's propeller hub. *Damn! He hit the line. Now. steady the rifle on the rail. Nestle the front bead right in the rear sight notch – right on the hawser. STE-E-EADY. SQUEEEEEZE.* POW – TOIING. *Damn it! I missed. Hmmm. Just a little to the right. I could tell by the splash in the lagoon. Gotta aim just a hair to the left. Load another round.*

POW – CLACK. *Hah! He hit the cowling! Shit, he's not such a hot shot. Now, steady on the rail . . .*

"MISTER HARPER." It was Captain Pride's voice on the bull horn.

Shit! Now I'm in trouble. I waved at the skipper, up on the bridge, wondering what would come next.

The captain continued: "YOUR LINE OF FIRE IS DIRECTLY TOWARD MAJURO'S PORT FACILITY ON OUR PORT QUARTER AND YOUR RICO- CHETS COULD REACH IT."

POW – WHUP. *Ha! He missed again. But what am I in for now?* I saluted, jabbed myself in the chest with my index finger, pointed aft, and spread my arms in a pleading gesture. *Maybe he'll let me keep shooting if I move aft.* I thought.

"YES, MISTER HARPER. THAT WILL BE OKAY," boomed the bull horn "TAKE YOUR POSITION IN THE FLAG BAG." The "flag bag" on a CVL is an open area just to starboard of the island, three of four feet below flight deck level, where the signal flag racks are mounted and where signalmen assemble and hoist flag signals in response to orders from the signal bridge, above them.

The gun crew next to me applauded. *Whew! I lucked out . . . Whoa! It's a good thing there aren't any arresting wires up here.* I thought as I hustled aft to the flag bag. If there were, I'd probably trip over one of 'em . . . *Ahah! There's the marine that's been shootin' up the lagoon.*

POW – TWAAANG. "Damn! Missed again," the marine whispered to him- self just as I crouched down beside him. "Er . . . what're you doin' here . . . uh . . . SIR?

"Just tryin' to help out, Corporal." I smiled benignly. Then, levelling my rifle on the rail, I put the front bead just to the left of the hawser and squeeeezed. POW – THUD. "I got it" The hemp broke a little more right where the marine had hit it and the hulk turned very slowly as the line frayed.

"Good shot, Harpo." It was Captain Pride, kneeling right at my elbow. "Looks like you cut a strand."

Son-of-a-bitch! The skipper called me "Harpo" I thought proudly as I turned to face the captain. "Thank you, sir." Then turned back to aim.

"May I take a shot?," the captain whispered.

"Oh! Yes SIR!" I stood, retracted and locked the bolt, catching the ejected cartridge to reload it into the magazine, and handed the rifle to the captain.

Paddles!

"Chamber's open sir, magazine has three rounds,"

POW – THUD. "I got it!," exulted the marine.

Yeah, but in a different place. That didn't do anything. "Good shot, Corporal." I was humoring him. *Come on, skipper, get a hit.* I rooted silently.

Pride released the bolt, rested the forestock on the rail, and – POW – TWAAANG. "Damn! I missed," he cursed.

I leaned over to whisper in the captain's ear, "Aim just one bead left of the line, skipper."

"No. You take a shot." Pride offered the rifle. "It's your turn."

POW. "Damn!," the corporal cussed himself for missing again.

"Naw, skipper." I patted him on the shoulder. "I already got a hit. Go ahead." Then, as he took aim again, I whispered in his ear: "Remember. Just one pipper left."

POW – WHUP – TWANG. "Great shot, skipper," I cheered as another strand sprung free and the fuselage turned slowly and then suddenly dropped a couple of inches giving the ship a jolt we could feel. "I think it's going in!"

POW – WHUP – SPLOOSH. The frayed hawser sprang up violently to settle in a loop over the davit as the freed fuselage slid quietly into the lagoon leaving an ever widening pattern of bubbles at the surface.

"Great shot, Corporal," Pride cheered as he shook the marine's hand and handed Dulacki's M-1 back to me. "Bolt's locked open, Harpo."

"Same to you, Captain." The corporal didn't know whether to salute or not.

"Seems a strange way to dispose of dud aircraft, sir," I inquired cautiously as the Captain and I stepped up onto the flight deck. "Seems like they could've just fired it off the catapult."

"We thought of that, Harpo," Pride replied. "But they'd already cannibalized the landing gear, so there was nothing for the airplane to roll on or to attach the catapult bridle to. Here's what happened." Pride explained as we stepped up onto the flight deck. "After stripping the airplane of everything useful – wings, with guns, radios, instruments, and what all – Benny and his crew decided to hang the hulk on a length of hemp line, lower it into the lagoon, and let it fill up with water. The idea was that when they hoisted the water logged fuselage back out of the water it would be heavy enough to break the line, and the junker would sink to the bottom of the lagoon." Pride shook his head in disbelief. "Obviously they miscalculated . . . So we called out the marines."

"Well," I laughed. "We got a little target practice ourselves, eh skipper?"

Chapter 17: R & R?

Wujcik and I gaped over the starboard catwalk forward of the island watching Commander Dahl maneuver the seaplane under the wire cable bridle dangling from the davit. Benny Freedman stood up in the back seat, ready to handle the bridle. Captain Pride had been able to borrow the OS2U *Kingfisher* observation seaplane from one of the cruisers anchored with us in the Majuro Lagoon so we ship's officers could get our required four hours flight time for the month of April. I had flown the OS2U on wheels at JAX, but this *Kingfisher* carried a large, single float under the fuselage and one small float under each wing. *Hmm. It probably handles somewhat like the Grumman Duck I flew at Miami.* I thought as Benny Freedman secured the bridle hooks to the strong points on the *Kingfisher*'s fuselage. The hoist cable came taut and the *Kingfisher* was hoisted out of the lagoon, dripping water from the float, and placed gently in the boat trailer on the flight deck.

"We're next, Weej," I announced, as the gas gang brought out the fuel hose. "You get in the back seat for a few landings and take-offs and then we'll switch when you think you're ready to fly this thing." Wujcik had never flown a seaplane so he would be checked out on this flight.

The davit lifted us gently out of the boat trailer and over the side. Everything worked together to make this a simple operation. The ship streamed downwind from its anchor and the *Kingfisher* weathercocked into the wind, keeping us lined up perfectly by natural forces. I started the engine and was able to keep the airplane directly under the slack hoist cable until Wujcik detached the bridle and it was hauled safely away.

Okay, J.A. Pour the coal on – right rudder – get away from the ship before we have a collision. I turned on the intercom and picked up the mike. "Get on the controls, Weej," I instructed. "Notice that I hold the stick full back until she jumps up on the step – then I ease the nose down to a comfortable takeoff attitude. The machine will just fly off the water when she's ready."

Hey! This is a lot quieter than the Duck. I guess it's cause the float is separate from the fuselage. "Well. That took longer that I expected, Weej," I groaned into the intercom, as we staggered into the air.

"Yeah. I was beginning to wonder.," came Wujcik's shaky reply.

"Compared to the *Duck* this thing's a gutless wonder." I thought a second. "But not as bad as that weak dick Curtiss SO3C," I moaned.

I didn't know you ever flew one o' those," Wujcik commented.

Paddles!

"Yeah. God Damned near killed myself in one back on Oahu," I groaned. "And Sam Gallu too. Takin' that underpowered kite up a box canyon was the dumbest thing I've ever done. I'll tell you about it sometime." Then: "Have you ever seen such beautiful colors, Weej?" I referred to the myriad tones of green and blue that marked the lagoon's various depths, from the pale aqua in the shallows near the coral reefs, to a deep Pacific Ocean blue near the center where depths reach to hundreds of fathoms, with all shades of turquoise in between.

"Yeah. An artist would love this scene."

We cruised along at five hundred feet over the string of palm studded cays that formed the northeastern reach of the Majuro atoll, all relatively undamaged during the occupation. "Hey Weej." I called. "To see these quiet villages with their people going about their daily chores you sure wouldn't know a war was goin' on."

"Yeah. I guess the Army or Marines took this place while the Japs were busy defending Kwaj," Wujcik mused. "Hey! Look at the islanders out in the lagoon in their outrigger canoes . . . fishin' for dinner I guess."

After a few smooth water landings in a sheltered cove isolated near a deserted cay at the northern edge of the lagoon, with Wujcik following through on the controls, it was time for him to get some stick time. "Are you ready to make a few landings and takeoffs, Weej?" I called. We traded seats while the Kingfisher bobbed in the gentle ripples of the lagoon.

When our two hours were up I landed the *Kingfisher* to starboard of *Belleau Wood* and taxied to a position about a hundred feet abeam the island from which I would ease the seaplane carefully under the hoisting bridle hanging from the davit. "Whoa! what's happening? I cried as the aircraft slid dangerously toward the side of the ship. "Jesus Christ! The God damned wind's shifting." I kicked full right rudder and added power but we continued to drift toward the ship. "Hey, Weej. Get out on the wing and fend off. We're about to hit the gangway."

"God damn! I'm glad I've got this life jacket on," Wujcik groused as he climbed out of the cockpit. "I'll probably take a bath."

"Don't worry," I yelled. "The liberty launch is right there at the gangway. They'll pick you up."

"Thanks a LOT," Wujcik yelped as he scrambled out to the wing tip and pushed off of the gangway just as I got the airplane turning away from the ship . . . then climbed back into the rear cockpit, ready to handle the bridle.

Chapter 17: R & R?

Well, J.A., there's another instance where I needed to "sail" a seaplane. Hmm. Shades of Lieutenant Proctor at Key West.

Having avoided a collision with the ship, lining up under the bridle and being hoisted aboard was a piece of cake. But it took a little "sailing." Wujcik stayed dry.

"Hi, mate," I greeted the dispatcher at the Carrier Air Service Unit (CASU) at the Majuro air strip. "I'm looking for a Lieutenant Felt. Have you seen him?"

"Yes sir. He's been hangin' around for four or five days, now, flyin' our airplanes to keep his hand in. I think he's in the pilots' lounge." He pointed to the right. "Down the passageway, there."

"Thanks." Wujcik and I took off down the passageway. "Hi. Are you Robert Felt?," I inquired of the man in a sweat stained flying suit relaxing in one of the NAVY issue brown leather overstuffed easy chairs in the pilots' lounge.

The man put down his magazine and rose from the chair to extend his hand. "I'm him – are you the LSO off the *Belleau Wood*?"

"Yeah. I'm John Harper and this is Walt Wujcik, my assistant. Harpo and Weej to you." We shook hands around.

"Glad to meet you." Felt nodded. "Folks call me Knobby." Felt had a long face featuring a pair of deep set soft brown eyes and a high forehead topped by a full head of black hair. He stood about six foot two and was more legs than torso, at about a hundred and eighty pounds.

"Okay, Knobby. Sit down." I waved at his vacant chair while Wujcik and I pulled up a couple of chairs. "Bob Ross, our fighter exec said you were coming aboard as a replacement – I thought we should get acquainted."

Wujcik led off, "Have you been to sea before, Knobby?"

"No. Not until now," he grimaced. "I've been an instructor at Corpus ever since I got my wings. That's where I knew Bob Ross. He told me to expect you here."

"Okay. Where did you qualify in carrier landings?," Wujcik persisted.

"At the training squadron in San Diego. We went aboard the training carrier there . . . er . . . I don't know the name." The operational training squadron's mission was to collect aviators awaiting fleet assignment and fill in the gaps in their training to prepare them for duty in fleet squadrons requiring replacements. Felt had arrived in Majuro a week earlier with orders to VF-24.

"How many carrier landings did you get, in what kind of airplanes?"

"Eight . . . in F6Fs. I understand that's the standard."

Paddles!

"Right. That's the standard," I frowned. "But we're going to feel a hell of a lot more comfortable after we see you in a few bounce sessions." I stood up and spoke carefully. "I've arranged for a couple of airplanes from CASU. You and I will take off and rendezvous. Then I'll show you what our pattern around the ship is supposed to look like. Just follow me. Weej'll give us six or eight passes and call us down for a debriefing. Then you'll do it again with Weej leading and me waving. Then we'll keep doing it until you know it by heart. Let's go."

"*BELLEAU WOOD* ATTEYN-HUT!" Blared the bull horn, jolting the ship's company and air group to attention, arrayed as they were in formations by division and squadron covering the forward half of the flight deck facing to starboard, their freshly starched whites rippling slightly in the gentle tropical breeze wafting off Majuro Lagoon.

"DREYESS RIGHT!" The shuffle of feet and bobbing of heads brought each formation into precise alignment. "ATTEYN-HUT! . . . PARADE THE COLORS!"

The color bearers and color guard, with the American flag and ship's flag, stepped smartly from the base of the island to the scratchy strains of the recorded Star Spangled Banner, marched aft to a position abeam the third stack, and did an about face to retrace their steps.

"POST THE COLORS." The color bearers advanced to the small reviewing stand ten yards to port of the island structure, built for the occasion by the carpenters of the hull division, and placed the flags in their stands next to the small stage.

"STAND AT EASE!" There was a perceptible slump as the assembled ship's crew shifted their stances to relax and await the ceremony to come.

DING DING – DING DING. "CAPTAIN U.S. NAVY."

As Captain Pride emerged from the hatch at the base of the island followed by a taller captain, both wearing the ceremonial NAVY sword, we heard, "Division, ATTEYN-HUT!" From Lieutenant Ken Frazier, the Sixth Division officer. The pair returned Frazier's salute and began the deliberate march down the front rank with Frazier at the elbow of the guest captain, Captain Pride pausing before this man, and that man, to comment or ask a question.

"Division, ATTEYN-HUT!," came Dulacki's command to the marines of the Fifth Division at the moment the two captains had finished their inspection of the Sixth. And so it continued, the successive calls to attention as the two captains inspected each of the selected division in turn, finishing with the air group, then marching to the modest reviewing stand.

Chapter 17: R & R?

After the invocation had been delivered by Chaplain Pegnam, Captain Pride pinned medals on a number of the ships company and to nearly every pilot in the air group. The most emotion was shown by Arky Snowden, grinning from ear to ear.

The bull horn sounded forth again, "ATTENTION TO ORDERS!" It was Commander Miller, the executive officer. "To: Captain Alfred M. Pride – When relieved from command of U.S.S. *Belleau Wood* you are detached – Proceed and report to the Commander, Air Force, Pacific Fleet for further assignment to duty involving flying in the Aviation Establishment of the U.S. NAVY. And To: Captain John A. Perry – In accordance with reference (a) and applicable regulations, you are hereby designated Commanding Officer of United States Ship *Belleau Wood* (CVL-24), effective 1 April 1944 or the earliest date upon which you are able to assume said command – These orders in no way affect your assignment to duty involving flying in the Aviation Establishment of the U.S. NAVY."

Captain Perry turned and saluted Captain Pride announcing, "I relieve you, sir."

Captain Pride immediately returned the salute stating, "I stand relieved."

The Chief Quartermaster advanced from his position at the base of the island to present the ship's commissioning pennant and flag to Captain Pride, who turned immediately to present the flag to Captain Perry. Each saluted the other and the change of command was complete.

We had weighed anchor and I felt the gentle rumble of the engines as we joined other ships of the force departing Majuro for the next big operation. My attempts at perfecting "Poinsiana" on the clarinet borrowed from the ships stores were interrupted by a knock at my stateroom door, "The captain would like to see you on the bridge, sir." It was the quartermaster of the watch looking in on me with something of a pained look – probably due to the questionable quality of my "Poinsiana."

"Tell him I'll be there in five minutes," I responded, placing the horn carefully in its case and snapping the latch. "I've got to get dressed." *Hmm. I wonder where that fresh set of khakis is.*

"Yes sir." The sailor saluted and disappeared.

I had only seen our new captain, John Perry, from a distance at the change of command the day before but I noticed that he was a big man, possibly a head taller than Captain Pride, whose unsmiling face showed the strain of a long NAVY career in a dour expression absolutely devoid of a smile. I was, therefore, a little uneasy about my first meeting with the new skipper.

I approached Captain Perry, sitting calmly in the captain's chair on the starboard side of the bridge as *Belleau Wood* slipped quietly through the channel from the turquoise Majuro Lagoon to the blue-black waters of the Pacific. "Lieutenant Harper reporting as you requested, sir." I saluted.

The Captain turned his head to recognize me. "Oh! Harper. Good." He slid out of the elevated black leather command chair and casually returned my salute, his huge frame towering over me. Then he offered his hand. "Mel tells me you are called 'Harpo.' May I." He peered at me with his inquisitive blue-gray eyes while his lips remained frozen in an expression of anger, despair, or just plain boredom. I couldn't tell which. But his eyes smiled.

"As you wish, sir." I could hardly contain my elation that my captain would want to call me by my nickname. Hell, Pride only called me that once, and that was just a week earlier.

"Is there anything you'd like to tell me?" He leaned against the rail while the wind ruffled the khaki cap cover of his gold encrusted officer's cap.

"Uh . . . like what . . . er . . . sir?

"Like anything that's wrong with flight operations on this ship." His eyes cornered me. They didn't smile.

"Well . . . er . . . sir." *What the hell kind of stuff does he want to know?* "Things run pretty smooth around here, sir." I searched for something constructive, yet positive. *I've got it!* "I do think that we could expedite launches if we used the catapult more."

"Yeah. Benny suggested that too." Perry's eyes lit up. "What about recovery operations?"

"Well, sir. There are times when we seem to waste time when the flight is back because the ship isn't into the wind yet." I watched him carefully for some reaction but the stone face gave no signal. *God damn! I sure wouldn't want to play poker with this guy.* "I know you have all kinds of constraints due to the formation but it may be something to think about."

"Good idea, Harpo." Perry's eyes smiled. "I'll discuss it with the Exec and Air Boss." Then: "Tell me about your style at Landing Signals. I don't want to be surprised."

"My style, sir? Er . . . what do you mean?"

Chapter 17: R & R?

"I mean: Do you require precision approaches? How do you manage the landing intervals? Will I see a lot of WAVE-OFFs? Things like that." He froze me with a stern gaze.

"Oh. Yes sir. I understand. *Shit! I think I'm pretty God damned good. How do I make this sound modest? Hmm.* You know you've got two LSOs, Mister Wujcik and me. We're different, naturally. I certainly like a precision approach, but there aren't many of those. We've got these guys trained to get on deck and catch a wire from a range of positions and speeds so some of 'em might look a little hairy, but you won't see many WAVE-OFFs. Wujcik's a little more conservative than I am but you probably won't notice the difference." I thought for a second. "Er . . . intervals . . . Well, it's up to the pilots to keep a good interval – twenty to thirty seconds, we tell 'em – and we chew 'em out if they get over forty. I think our job is to get each flight aboard as quickly as possible." I watched for a reaction. *Aha! His eyes smiled again!*

"Sounds like you've got your eye on the ball, Harpo."

Hmm. He sure is in a good mood. Maybe this is the right time. "Er . . . Captain .. uh, how do I request permission to fly with the fighter squadron?"

"Just ask me." His eyes were laughing now.

"Well, sir. I was trained as a fighter pilot and taught fighter gunnery and tactics under Commander Jumpin' Joe Clifton at Miami and I want to get into combat. May I fly with VF-24, sir?" *Pray.*

"Aha! Mel told me you would ask that." His eyes were still laughing but there was a little sympathy mixed in. "As soon as we have three LSOs I'll okay it, but why would you want to leave the relative safety of Landing Signals?"

"As I said, sir. I was trained for air combat and I want to get into the action."

"Well." Perry almost smiled. "I have not and will not request another LSO so you'll have to wait until we get our next air group and hope an LSO comes with it. Until then, just keep doing what you've been doing. Mel tells me you're pretty good at it." Suddenly, he turned his gaze out to sea, almost as though he regretted the compliment. He was watching our task group form up as the low reefs of the Majuro atoll receded behind us.

"By your leave, sir." I saluted the captain's back, requesting permission to leave the bridge.

"Look at this, Harper." He ignored my request and turned back to face me, his expressive eyes showing a mixture of awe and pride. "This is just the second time we will have twelve carriers in the force, this time it's five *Essex* class and seven

189

Paddles!

CVLs, organized in three task groups." His eyes went misty as the pride washed over him. He turned back to the open sea, hiding his emotion. "Only months ago we were down to three carriers in the whole Pacific fleet."

"Yes, sir." I was taken by the drama of the occasion. "I recognize *Hornet* by her camouflage." I pointed over to our flagship.

"Yes, and we have *Cowpens* and *Bataan*." He swept his hand across the horizon where the two CVLs were kicking up wakes, maneuvering to their positions in the task group. "This is Carrier Task Group 58.1, Jocko Clark's first task group command since he made rear admiral after leaving *Yorktown*."

"We've got a feel for Admiral Clark's command personality, sir, having run with *Yorktown* quite a bit over the last few months," I commented.

"Carrier skippers are moving quickly into task group commands these days," Perry half shouted into the freshening wind. "I wouldn't be surprised to see your old skipper out here, commanding a task group. He'll put on the wide stripe as soon as he gets back to Pearl."

18

LOST SOULS

Task Group 58.1 steamed into the wind a hundred miles north of the north coast of New Guinea, all carriers recovering aircraft launched in the predawn darkness to strike Hollandia in support of General MacArthur's amphibious landings there. We had recovered all except one of ours and we knew the missing pilot was Knobby Felt. Wujcik and I had just arrived in the fighter ready room to debrief the pilots on their approaches and we encountered a heated exchange about what happened to Knobby.

"Hell, I never saw him after launch," McLaughlin was saying. "He never joined up. I haven't the slightest idea where the hell he went." Felt was Mac's section leader.

"Attention in the ready room," came the voice of our new air officer, Commander Joe Clymer, over the squawk box. "*Cabot*, over in fifty-eight point two, advises that they recovered Fagan six-three along with their air group returning from Hollandia. Who's Fagan six-three?" Captain Perry had brought the new call sign with him.

"Knobby Felt, sir," Ed Link, the fighter skipper, shouted at the speaker.

"Well. *Cabot* says they'll launch Felt as soon as they get their deck respotted . . . Is Harpo down there?"

"Yes sir, right here," I called into the box. "Wujcik's here too."

"Then stand by to recover Felt in twenty or thirty minutes."

"Aye aye, sir.

Paddles!

Up on the flight deck we watched as the lone F6F cruised in from the east and passed directly overhead, continuing westward.

"Hey! That must be Knobby. But where the hell's he goin'?," Wujcik shouted, into the wind. "Christ! We've got this giant "24" painted all over both ends of the flight deck. Can't he read?"

"Looks like he's joinin' the traffic pattern over at *Cowpens*." I was amazed. "They must've had some late returners they're still gettin' aboard. "Look at 'im, for Christ's sake. He's goin' to land over there, the dumb shit."

I ran forward, climbed hurriedly up the vertical ladder on the port side of the island, and stepped onto the bridge, then over to Fly Control. "Jesus! Commander. Knobby landed over on *Cowpens*. What're we goin' to do now?," I inquired breathlessly.

"Captain's maneuvering into a position where *Cowpens* can steam line astern and launch Felt directly at us so he can't miss again," Clymer snickered. "They're respotting their deck now so they can catapult him in about fifteen minutes. We'll just hold course into the wind until then." He couldn't hold back a belly laugh.

"Here he comes," Wujcik announced, pointing toward the Hellcat approaching from astern. "Hell, he's still got his gear and flaps down."

"Gear, flaps, hook, all down, sir," Monahan called, at the ninety.

"Clear deck, barriers up, sir," reported Callagee.

"Pretty smooth. Just a little high, as usual," Wujcik commented over his shoulder as he tossed a HIGH at Knobby. "You'd think he'd be a little nervous by now." CUT . . CRUNCH . . SREEEEE.

Back in the ready room Link loomed over Knobby, seated in one of the reclining chairs with his life jacket, helmet and goggles still on. The pair was surrounded by about half of the fighter squadron, curious to know what went on.

"Okay, Felt," Link sneered. "There's got to be some excuse for this circus. Where in God's name did you go this morning? – Huh? – Where?"

Gee, skipper, er . . ." Knobby stammered. "I don't know what happened. After launch I climbed out and rendezvoused in northeast quadrant, like you said."

"I said NORTHWEST, God damn it!," Link fumed. "D'you hear me – NORTH-WEST!"

Knobby cringed and looked around as though for an escape route. "Well, sir," Knobby continued, with obvious trepidation. "When it got light I noticed that the markings on the airplanes I was with didn't match ours.

"What the hell did you do then?," Link persisted.

"I didn't know what else to do so I just followed the flight in to the target." Knobby shrugged.

"What target?," Link demanded.

We went in on an airfield . . . er . . . Hollandia, I guess," Knobby struggled on. "I strafed a bunch of airplanes and bombed a hangar. The whole place was smokin' pretty bad when we left." A cautious smile showed he was proud of that.

Link wasn't impressed. "So you went back and landed on the wrong carrier." He scolded, spiking his remarks with derision.

Knobby flinched. "Yes sir . . . er . . . Gee, I didn't know what else to do."

"You knew it was the wrong ship, didn't you, Knobby." Link chanted quietly.

"Yes sir, but . . ."

"There's no BUT about it, damn it!," Link raged. "You should have found our ship, PERIOD."

Felt took off his helmet and began to get up.

"Oh no you don't." Link shoved knobby back in his chair. "I want to know why you landed on *Cowpens* when you got back here."

"Sir." Felt's eyes were pleading. "She looks just like *Belleau Wood*."

"Yeah!" Link was exasperated. "That's why they paint those great big fuckin' numbers on the flight decks, you idiot – Twenty-four for *Belleau Wood* and twenty-five for *Cowpens*." He backed off just a little. "Now, get with Chuhak and learn how to use the navigation equipment in your airplane." Tommy Chuhak was the squadron navigator.

Link turned to leave, then stopped and turned back to Felt, freezing him in his furious glare. "You might tell me why in hell you didn't raise your gear and flaps after you launched from *Cowpens*."

Knobby shrank visibly in his embarrassment. "They took me up on the bridge and the captain led me to the rail, pointed forward and said, 'Your ship is dead ahead – and we're both into the wind and at flight quarters. We'll launch you off the catapult. Proceed straight ahead after launch – do not retract your landing gear – do not raise your flaps – enter *Belleau Wood*'s traffic pattern – lower your hook and follow the LSO's signals to an arrested landing'." Knobby looked around at all the faces with bewilderment. "That's what I did, sir."

The ready room erupted in raucous laughter. Poor Knobby.

Paddles!

At Commander Clymer's request, we met on the bridge at Fly Control – Cobbs, Wujcik, and I were joined by our new flight deck officer, Lieut. Comdr. R. H. Prickett, known to us already as "Little Bobby" Prickett because of his diminutive stature and boyish manner.

"As you may have noticed, *Hornet*, *Cowpens*, and *Bataan* have already recovered all their aircraft," Clymer began. "Our air group had farther to go to their target so they won't be back for another thirty minutes, but the force has already turned to our new course, northeast to our next target, Truk, putting the wind directly at our stern." He looked around at the nodding heads. "Admiral Clark doesn't want to turn the whole force around just to recover our aircraft so we will be recovering on a course opposite to the task group course. Understand?

"Yes sir," I offered. "I notice the skipper's already sped up."

"Yeah," Prickett added. "We're leaving the other carriers behind."

"You noticed," Clymer smiled. "Good. Now comes the hard part." His smile turned to a frown. "When we reach the for'rd screening destroyers, and our aircraft have returned, Captain will turn us into the wind." He eyed each of us seriously. "At the minimum relative velocity between us and the force at about forty knots we have just nine minutes before we punch out of the other end of the screen into unpatrolled Jap submarine waters."

"Oh oh!," I grimaced. "We've got sixteen fighters and six torpeckers out . . . Hmm. The way I figure it, landing intervals need to be less that thirty seconds each . . . and NO WAVE-OFFs."

"You got it, Harpo," Clymer smiled, wickedly. "How're you going to do it."

"Whoa, boss." I raised my arms as though to stop a train. "This is a team effort, sir. Everybody's got to do his part."

"What do you suggest?"

"Intervals are up to the pilots, you know." Excuse me but I was lecturing. "I'll go down to CIC, call the pilots, and tell them to tighten up their intervals, just a smidge though, cause we can't stand a WAVE-OFF." I turned to Little Davey Kolb. "Cobbs, you and your crew's got to do everything you can to get each airplane out of the gear quicker!" Prickett was next. "Mister Prickett – your plane directors and spotters have to work 'em up the deck quickly so Cobbs can get the barriers up." I took a deep breath. "Don't forget that when I tell the pilots to shorten their intervals they might get down to fifteen seconds. But we have to handle it. NO WAVE-OFF."

Chapter 18: Lost Souls

Everybody nodded and Joe Clymer smiled with questionable satisfaction. We hadn't done it yet!

Back at Landing Signals I held Wujcik by the shoulder and looked into his eyes. "I hope you'll excuse my arrogance, Weej. I'm goin' to take all of these."

"Oh . . . yeah, Harpo," Wujcik reacted positively. "Hell, I know it's your responsibility whether you wave 'em or I do." His eyes said he meant it. "I'll be cheerin' for you."

"Thanks Weej." *Now you can't let any of them go astray, J.A. You've got to anticipate and catch any problems early . . . Y'hear? ANTICIPATE! No WAVE-OFFs allowed!*

The TBMs came first since they were getting low on fuel. "Gear, flaps, hook, all down, sir," Monahan called.

"Clear deck, barriers up, sir," reported Callagee.

CUT . . SCRUNCH . . SHREEEEE. The wire went out. "Well, there's the first one. Twenty-one to go."

"Gear, flaps, hook, all down, sir."

God damn! That was quick. Looks like they took my request for shorter intervals seriously. I hope it doesn't get any closer than this. Okay – a little high – come on down – good. ROGER. "Hey Callagee! how's the deck?"

"He's taxiin' over the barriers now, sir."

Cut position now – Got to hold 'im – Hurry. I thought, as though I could command the first TBM pilot to taxi faster.

"Clear deck . . ."

CUT . . "Get it down, damn it! You're long." I yelled, as though he could hear me. *Whew! Number six wire. Close.*

"Gear, flaps, hook, all down sir."

Eight minutes later: "Hey! We got twenty of 'em," Wujcik cheered. "Two more to go."

"Gear, flaps, hook, all down, sir."

"And we're bearin' down on that destroyer." I looked up the deck. "What the hell happened to that last F6F. He's not movin'." SLANT LEFT *Flick a FAST.* "Where is he now, Callagee?"

"Now he's movin', sir. I'll let you know."

Signal FAST . . . Maybe I can slow 'im down enough to make it. I glanced up the deck to see the *Hellcat* cross the eighth wire. *Not enough . . . God damn! I got 'im too slow.* COME-ON. I looked up the deck again. *Just over the barriers now.* CUT . . .

"Barriers up, sir," came Callagee's belated call.

Be there. I Prayed . . . SCRUNCH . . . *Whew! Fourth wire . . . First CUT without barriers . . . I sure as hell don't want to do that again.*

Immediately after we got the last fighter aboard, *Belleau Wood* heeled to starboard and we could feel the engine vibration as Captain Perry turned sharply and ordered flank speed to catch the other carriers.

The bull horn boomed, "THIS IS THE CAPTAIN SPEAKING. MY CONGRATULATIONS TO ALL AIR DEPARTMENT PERSONNEL TOPSIDE, AND TO THE AIR GROUP. YOU HAVE DONE THE NEAR IMPOSSIBLE, WITHOUT INCIDENT, AND WE REMAINED SAFE WITHIN THE DESTROYER SCREEN. YOU ARE A TEAM TO BE RECKONED WITH. I SAY AGAIN: MY CONGRAT . . ."

A cheer went up all along the flight deck, joined by all the gunners in the gun tubs, and a chill went up my spine when I thought how close it was. Then I choked back my pride and shook Weej's hand. We both ran forward to share the moment with Cobbs and Prickett.

"God damn!," Wujcik cursed. "Three missing.

We had launched twenty fighters and nine TBMs for the massive strike on Truk, the central Pacific bastion of the Japanese Navy, but we could only see seven TBMs coming up the wake to the break position and nineteen fighters orbiting overhead.

"Emergency, sir," Monahan boomed. "One of the torpeckers is badly damaged – crew wounded – pilot losing blood." He listened again to his sound powered phones. "The wounded one's comin' aboard first."

The hull vibration signalled the captain's effort to produce more wind across the deck, easing the wounded pilot's task.

"Gear, flaps, hook, all down, sir."

"Clear deck, sir, barriers up."

"Lookin' good, so far," Wujcik commented cautiously as he held a ROGER. "I hope he doesn't pass out in the groove."

"Hey! something's dripping off the bottom of the airplane, just aft of the torpedo bay," I cautioned. "I hope he's not runnin' out o' oil."

Chapter 18: Lost Souls

"Don't slow down!," Weej hollered, waving a vigorous COME-ON. "Damn it! Now he's settling." We heard some power come on, but the engine was sputtering. "God damn! Is that all the power you can get?" Now he shook a frantic LOW. "Come on, God damn it! More power!" The engine sputtered again and the big Avenger settled onto the deck, without a cut. CRUNCH! He rolled up to the first wire with his propeller windmilling. "Whew! That was close. That must've been a bad oil leak."

"Maybe so. But that wasn't oil drippin' off the belly," I cringed. "It was BLOOD – look." The plexiglass around the little .30 caliber tail gun formed into a kind of a bowl which, by now, was filled to overflowing with BLOOD – the torpedoman's blood. A string of bullet holes in the side of the airplane explained the crew's wounds.

In a moment two corpsmen extracted the inert torpedoman from the belly of the airplane onto a stretcher and another helped the bleeding pilot off the wing as the turret gunner popped his emergency hatch and hopped out onto the wing, apparently unscathed. In another moment, the flight deck mule – a tractor – hooked up to the airplane and began towing it forward, leaving a widening reddish brown trail . . . of blood.

With recovery of all strike aircraft complete, Task Group 58.1 turned out of the wind, back to base course, and Wujcik and I strolled forward to debrief the pilots. The deck crew was just beginning to respot aircraft aft.

"ATTENTION ON THE FLIGHT DECK!," boomed Clymer's voice over the bull horn just as Weej and I were about to descend the ladder to the ready rooms. "WE HAVE AN APPARENT EMERGENCY. RESPOT THE DECK FOR IMMEDIATE RECOVERY – ONE F6F." Then: "HARPER AND WUJCIK. RETURN TO LANDING SIGNALS – ON THE DOUBLE!"

We stopped dead in our tracks and looked aft to see Monahan wave off the *Hellcat* with his gear, flaps, and hook, all down. His erratic flight path indicated that he was having some difficulty controlling the airplane.

I saluted the bridge, acknowledging the command. "Maybe it's Tex," I shouted, hopefully, as we broke into a run. Tex Odom was our missing fighter.

"Didn't look like our markings, though," Wujcik countered, sadly.

"What's goin' on, Monahan?," I gasped, as we arrived at the platform.

"Fly control says it's a straggler comin' back from Truk, sir. Not one of ours," Monahan shouted, excitedly. "Looked damaged when he went by here. Oops! Here he comes, again, sir. Gear, flaps, hook, all down." He jumped down into the catwalk.

"No deck, sir," Callagee called. "Still airplanes in the wires."

"Hell! We're not into the wind yet anyway." I started giving a WAVE-OFF very early and the *Hellcat* came up the groove, very fast. "Jesus! Look at that. Blood all over his face." I cried as he whizzed by, banking left and gesturing frantically, indicating he had to land – NOW! "Tell Fly Control this guy won't last long . . . and get us into the wind ASAP."

"Fly Control says Captain's maneuverin' to get clearance from the other ships, cause he'll have to steam THROUGH the formation to recover this guy."

"Clear deck, sir. Barriers up."

"Here he comes again, still erratic as hell." I gave him another WAVE-OFF. "God damn! look at all the holes in that airplane! Tell Fly Control we've GOT TO get into the wind. We're liable to lose this guy, and I don't think he'll survive in the water." I gave the paddles to Wujcik and turned to wave at the bridge and point dramatically up the wind line.

Suddenly the ship listed sharply to port as the captain turned into the wind, across *Bataan*'s course line, but well clear. The yodel sounded and Fox was two-blocked, even before we were into the wind.

"There he is." I pointed to port. "Turnin' off the downwind – in good position, considerin' our maneuvering. You take 'im, Weej. I'll go for'rd with Cobbs in case he needs help after he gets aboard." I took off on a dead run to join Dave Kolb on the starboard side at the eighth wire sheave.

"Hey, Davey!," I yelled. "This guy's wounded – GASP – how badly we can't tell – GASP – blood all over his face." I took another deep breath. "Get the plane pushers ready in case he can't make it up the deck. I'll man the brakes after we get him out of there – if necessary."

We turned to look astern. "Hey! I think he's goin' to make it." Cobbs cheered as Weej signalled CUT. CRUNCH . . . WHEEEEE. Cobbs gave him two clenched fists but he drifted aft slowly and the tail swung to port.

A dozen plane pushers, responding to Cobbs' call, grabbed both wings and held the airplane in place while I jumped up on the wing. "Are you okay?," I yelled in the pilot's ear.

"Hell no! I'm hit." He grimaced through all the blood. "Get me out of here!"

Jesus Christ! This is a grim sight. Blood all over the God damned cockpit and the pilot's right thigh oozin' fresh crimson through the jagged tear in the leg of his flying suit. No wonder he couldn't hold the right brake. "Here. Let me get you unstrapped."

"Hurry up! I think I'm goin' to pass out," the pilot gurgled.

Come on J.A. . . . first the seat belt and shoulder harness . . . then the parachute harness . . . now straddle the cockpit on the canopy rails and lift. "Ooof! Come on, a little help here." I yelled at the plane director who had just jumped up on the left wing.

"I got his legs, sir . . . UGH! – Hey, you! Get up here. We need help."

With me lifting under his arm pits and the two sailors dragging his legs out of the cockpit we moved the pilot onto the left wing.

"Oww! Watch it with that leg, God damn it," he moaned. "It hurts like hell."

I slid down into the cockpit to get on the brakes and I reached for the throttle. The engine was still idling. "Oww! God damn it!" I raked my left hand on the jagged aluminum projecting inward from the hole in the side of the airplane. *Well! I guess I'll contribute a little of my blood to this gory scene . . . Wow! What a disaster! Most of the instruments shattered and shards of plexiglass from the canopy scattered all over . . . I've got to safe the guns – gun switches off – check! Both charging handles to "SAFE."* CLICK – CLICK. "STAND CLEAR THE GUNS!" I commanded, waving my arms to signal movement toward the wing tips. "Whoa! Come back," I yelled, as I punched in the two charging handles, placing all guns on SAFE.

But nobody listened, running forward as if for their lives, all peering fearfully to starboard.

Looking to starboard, I saw what they were running from: *Cowpens'* bow was exactly abeam my position, so close to our side that the union jack was obscured by our gun tubs. "Stand by for collision!" I yelled at myself. *Oh shit! We collide and I'm swept off the deck, flipped upside down, and deposited on Cowpens'fo'c's'l. OUCH! God damn! I can't even taxi for'rd with all the people on deck. I'm stuck! SCREWED!* I thought, as I hurriedly secured the safety belt and shoulder harness and waited for the shock.

Ahah! Feel the engine vibration? Captain's tryin' to swing the stern away from Cowpens . . . I think it's workin'. . . Positions stayin' the same . . . Yeah! Now we're movin' apart. Shit! I can even see Cowpens' jack staff. WHEW! That was close . . . Too close.

19

THE SMELL OF WAR

Belleau Wood streamed from her anchor chain in a light breeze on Kwajalein Lagoon on a balmy May morning. I checked ignition magnetos, left, right, and both. The plane director in his yellow shirt and helmet waved both arms toward his rear, directing me, in my stripped F6F, to the launch position on the catapult. When I was in precise position, he showed me two fists and pointed with both hands to the catapult officer, Lieut. David Greenberg, standing on the deck centerline stripe forward of my right wing. I knew from experience that the catapult bridle would be attached to the hooks under my wing roots and the holdback release cylinder to the holdback fitting on the tail. Then, when Geenberg jabbed forward with his right index finger, a signal to the catapult crew, I could feel the catapult shuttle pull forward up to the prelaunch tension setting. I caught the thumbs up signal from the catapult crew chief up forward in the port catwalk and looked back to see Greenberg giving me the two finger engine run-up signal. Advancing the throttle handle to obtain full manifold pressure, I wrapped my fingers around the throttle hold fitting while holding the throttle in the thumb crotch and checking RPM at 2800. I raised my right hand in a salute to Greenberg and immediately grabbed the stick, jammed my elbow into the soft cavity in front of my pelvis, and forced my head back against the head rest.

"UUGGHH!" *Jesus Christ! What a jolt.* The breath was driven out of me and my head snapped back further into the head rest by the violent acceleration from standstill to sixty-five knots in just sixty feet. Recovering from the shock, I raised the landing gear handle and instinctively put the airplane in a right climbing turn, raising the flaps at about ninety knots.

Wujcik followed in another stripped *Hellcat* and, after he was snugly in formation on my right wing, I headed for the string of cays that formed the eastern boundary of Kwajalein atoll. We were delivering a couple of flyable duds to the Carrier Air Service Unit – CASU – at the air station on Kwajalein Island at the southeast corner of Kwajalein atoll. The two F6Fs had been stripped of everything but the bare essentials to prepare them for delivery, not to mention lightening them for the catapult launch at anchor with little or no wind across the deck. We had no guns or ammo aboard, no belly tank, and we each had just 100 gallons of fuel. *Hmmm. The clock's gone too. Yeah! That's usually the first thing to go.*

As we turned north to cruise along the cays at about 300 feet, I signalled tactical frequency and punched the button on the throttle to use the newly available throat mike strapped around my neck. "Hey Weej. Look at those little islands." What devastation!"

"God damn!," Weej exclaimed. "Not a coconut left standing."

"What do you say we drop in on Roi," I suggested.

"Hell, it's probably all bombed out," Weej protested. "Anyway, why do you want to do that?"

"I checked," I gloated. "Apparently the Army and our P-Boat buddies have been using the airfield since right after it was occupied in February. Hell, the runways are reported usable and the O'club is open." That was an invitation I couldn't resist. "Let's stop in for lunch at the Club and then take a look around Roi and Namur . . . See what a war zone looks like."

"Okay, but we don't have much fuel and we've still got to get back to the Kwajalein strip where CASU is."

"No sweat, Weej. With all those operations going on they've got to have fuel. Are you with me?" I looked over to see Weej giving the "thumbs up." "Goin' to tower frequency," I advised. Then: "Roi tower, this is NAVY 40418, two F6Fs five miles southeast at five hundred feet. Request landing clearance."

"NAVY 418, this is Roi mobile. You guys took care of the tower. Now it's nothin' but rubble. Our crushed coral runways are almost as good as concrete. Duty runway is two four. No traffic at the present time."

"Roger, Roi mobile, NAVY 418 here. Acknowledge runway two four. Hey! You got any aviation fuel down there? We just catted off *Belleau Wood* with only a hundred gallons."

Paddles!

"Got fuel, 418. You're cleared to the break. Watch the Jap airplane wreckage on south side of the runway. Still no traffic."

"I don't know why you swabbies want to wander through this God forsaken island," the marine groaned. We had met Marine Captain Charlie Inkster during lunch at the O'club and indicated our interest in touring Roi and Namur, entirely out of curiosity, obviously. Inkster was a compact package about five ten and a muscular hundred and eighty pounds. Hell, we could see his muscles rippling through his meticulously pressed khaki shirt and he wore his piss cutter cap at a jaunty angle revealing his boot camp hair cut. He walked at ram-rod attention as though he expected to encounter a general at the next turn in the road.

As we crossed the short causeway between Roi and Namur, the contrast between the efficiency and comparative cleanliness of the partially restored air base on Roi and the complete destruction of the housing and plant life on Namur was startling. There wasn't a coconut palm left standing.

"Well, this is Namur." Inkster spread his arms as if introducing one of the wonders of the world. "Where most of the Jap garrison and air detachment were housed."

"Whiff, whiff." Wujcik sniffed the air. "What the hell's that smell?"

"Rotting bodies," Inkster answered with a sneeze.

We could see that the bodies had been sprinkled liberally with lime, and the buzz of hovering flies was only partially muted by the sound of the surf on the north beach. "Japs, I presume," I ventured.

"Both kinds, I'm afraid." Inkster concealed his emotion by turning his head and marching onward. "I lost a quarter of my company, right here," he whispered with unconcealed reverence.

"Jesus! Cap'n." I was amazed. "It's been over three months since you guys took this place. Are you just going to leave all these bodies lying around?" *Stinking up the place*, I thought.

"No other choice," the marine replied, almost apologetically. "They cut my garrison back to just twenty men and no one ever sent any corpsmen to police up the rest of the bodies. So all we can do is leave them there to rot." He rubbed his nose. "After a while they won't smell any more. Hell, we don't use this island for anything anyway," Inkster sighed. "So we just don't come over here."

He eyed us curiously. "Seen enough?"

We certainly had.

Chapter 19: The Smell of War

Cruising back down Kwajalein's eastern chain of coral islands the tactical channel was strangely quiet for quite a while. Then I heard the radio click. "Jesus, Harpo." Wujcik called in an uncharacteristically hoarse voice. "That Namur was a disaster." A little gulp came over the radio. "I hate to think what it was like three months ago."

"War is hell, they say." I tried to lighten the conversation. "Now we know how it is on the ground: BRUTAL." *Thank God we're in the NAVY where we can commute to the war from the comfort of our clean white sheets and civilized meals in the wardroom, where all our deaths are clean, and where we never see the enemy close up, dead OR alive.* "We're lucky to be in the NAVY, Weej."

"God! I never knew how good we've got it." Then, in a kind of a whisper, "Until today when we breathed the smell of war."

Hmm. "The Smell of War." Sounds like the title for a book.

The anchor detail had just been secured after establishing our mooring in the Majuro Lagoon where the fleet was being assembled for the next assault in Admiral Nimitz's Island hopping campaign to drive the Japanese presence from the Pacific. I sat in my stateroom trying to play "Tangerine" on the clarinet I had drawn from ship's Morale Activities locker. Dulacki had the watch so I could play (?) without complaint.

TOOOEEEE. "NOW HEAR THIS! LIBERTY AND OFFICERS' SHORE LEAVE WILL BE AUTHORIZED TOMORROW FOR SECTIONS ONE AND THREE." Blared the P.A. system. "LIBERTY LAUNCH DEPARTS FOR RECREATION ISLAND AT OH EIGHT HUNDRED – BEER ON BOARD. NOW HEAR THIS! LIBERTY AND . . ."

Hmm. Liberty launch jammed with officers and men of all description. Ugh! It'll be bad enough on the way over, but on the way back – PEW! – Even a fresh breeze won't be enough to blow away the smell of fifty or so sweating bodies. Hmm – "The Smell of War"? Naw, not like Namur. Couldn't be that bad. Anyway, I've got to find a better way . . . I could paddle over there in one of the ship's life rafts . . . Naw – Shit! I'd have to entice eight or ten guys to go with me . . . I got it! LIFE RAFT! Yeah! Rubber life raft that goes in an airplane . . . Naw. Those one man life rafts don't have any propulsion. It'd be back to paddlin' – alone . . . HOLD IT! The TBF three man life raft has a sail, lee boards, and a rudder. Hot damn! I could sail one of those over to the island easy. Hell! That R & R island can't be more than about four or five miles from here, along the northern chain of Majuro Atoll. With

Paddles!

a good breeze I can make it in an hour or so. Hmm. fifteen hundred. Get your ass in gear J.A.

Down on the hangar deck I made my way, under and around the airplanes, to the flight equipment locker. "Hey 'Scar'," I hailed Storekeeper Second Class Skwarkowski, one of the many Polacks who formed the commissioning party at Camden. "How about loaning me a three man life raft for a day?"

"Scar" inclined his six foot three frame toward me to rest his tattooed forearms on the counter that topped the bottom half of the dutch door guarding the equipment stores. His shaggy eyebrows rose to force furrows in his broad, heavily tanned, forehead and reveal a pair of inquisitive blue eyes peering at me around his generous Slavic nose in obvious disbelief. He actually had a large scar tracing an ugly red line from the left corner of his broad mouth to his ear lobe, making him look very menacing – but he was a gentle giant. "Pardon me, sir." Scar scratched his head. "But what the hell would you do with a three man life raft?" He stood up straight, as if at attention. "Oh! No offense, sir. Just curious."

"You know we're set up to invade the recreation island tomorrow," I began.

"Yes sir." His eyes lit up. "I'm goin'. How about you?"

"Yeah. I'm goin'." I watched as his eyes softened just a little. "That's what I want the life raft for. To sail over."

"SAIL OVER? You can't do that! . . . er . . . sir?" He made it into a question.

"No sweat, Scar, if you'll just loan me one of those life rafts." I smiled invitingly. "I used to race on Lake Michigan." *Try a little blarney J.A.* "D'you want to go with me?"

Scar stood up with a start. "Oh n – n – no . . . sir," he stammered. "But you can have the life raft. Just be sure to get it back to me tomorrow afternoon." He turned abruptly and disappeared into the jumble of shelves and equipment.

"Hey, Harpo," little Davey Kolb yelped. "Liberty launch is shovin' off for the recreation island in ten or fifteen minutes. Are ya comin'?"

"Not right now, Cobbs." I smiled to myself as I peered out onto the lagoon to see that the wind was almost perfect – fifteen or twenty knots from the west, or southwest – just ripples on the lagoon. "I'll see you over there." *In about an hour and a half. heh, heh.*

"No you won't, Harpo. Not unless you get on this boat." Kolb's tone was urgent. "C'm on! This is the only boat that's goin'."

Chapter 19: The Smell of War

"Don't be so sure." I looked down the gangway to see the launch nearly full. *Ugh.* And there was my little life raft, all fitted out with lee boards, rudder, and furled sail, tied up aft of the liberty launch. "Don't worry. I'll see you there."

"Don't say I didn't warn you," Kolb hollered over his shoulder as he took the gangway two rungs at a time, his open Khaki shirt billowing behind him.

The launch had been gone about five minutes. "Shove me off, will ya," I yelled at the sailor standing on the float at the base of the gangway. "Thanks." *Okay, J.A. Just let 'er drift astern until you're clear of the ship.* I coached myself. *Okay, clear – now step the mast – Oops – Not so quick, idiot. You forgot the lee boards . . . Okay. Lee boards locked down. NOW step the mast . . . Now, over the thwart to the aft compartment.* SPLOOSH! "Owww!" *God damn! Slipped and hit my head on the tiller. Shit! Now the sail's luffing out to starboard – can't get hold of the sheet. Helm hard alee! Son-of-a-bitch! It worked! Got the sheet! Now turn out of the wind to the north.* I laid the tiller over full to port. *Shit! Nothin's happenin'. . . with no jib she won't turn out of the wind . . . Ahh! Now I remember. y' gotta scull 'er around.* "Ugh . . ugh . . ugh." *Hot dog! There she comes . . . Sail's filling . . . Boy! Now I've got enough way on to hold course . . . Now where the hell's that friggin' island . . . Ahah! There's the liberty launch – I'll just watch where she goes.*

The sail filled nicely on the port reach and I seemed to be able to hold course quite well with only moderate force on the tiller. We were on a broad reach that would take us to the R & R island without tacking, and I had the sensation that we were overtaking the launch. *NO WAY! This thing can't make that kind of speed.* WRONG! With only me aboard, the little raft skimmed across the rippled surface of the lagoon and, with this wind angle, even the lee boards produced very little drag. Soon I was hearing cheers and jeers from the launch, and about an hour later I was on the beach, greeting the crew as they splashed through the gentle surf of the lagoon carrying all manner of beach paraphernalia and, most important of all, cases and cases of beer. *Where the hell they ever got the beach chairs and umbrellas I'll never know.* "Hi, Cobbs. How was the ride?," I snickered.

Under the watchful eye of the master at arms, the beer was whisked to the low concrete block building that served as the beach club where the boisterous crew crowded to get their first ration. *Hmm. Probably the first building built after the island was secured . . . NO! The second. Right after the officers' club. Typical NAVY operation. Makes the crew happy though, and that's the objective.*

Paddles!

A small group of sailors set up a net and began a rowdy game of beach volley ball while another group headed for the tepid waters of the lagoon, leaving their chairs and umbrellas behind. A few hardy characters from VF-24 headed for the Pacific side of the island with their snorkeling gear. Some had spear guns in hopes of bagging some edible ocean fish. Weej, Cobbs and I tried, with limited success, the native way of climbing some coconut palms, left undisturbed by the peaceful capture of Majuro Atoll. *This is sure as hell nothing like the battle for Kwajalein.* I couldn't forget that smell. Opening coconuts was an even greater challenge, which we soon abandoned before we cut off a finger.

A couple of hours later we were back on the beach soaking up the sun when some of the VF-24 snorkelers burst onto the beach from the palm grove. "Is there a doctor here," screamed Hillner limping from a bloody wound in his right shin while helping Thelen the best he could. One of the spears they were using for fishing had penetrated entirely through Jack's left calf with an equal length protruding from each side of his leg. The scivvie shirt wrapped around the wound was partially soaked with blood.

"No doctor here, Jack," warned Lieut. Alexander, the senior officer present, I presumed. "We've got a corpsman. I'll get him over here," he grimaced. "I bet that hurts."

"Fucking well right it hurts, God damn it." Thelen's mouth was twisted by the pain. "I've gotta have some morphine . . . or something." He sagged to a sitting position on the sand.

Alexander scampered off in the direction of the beer hut. "Master at arms to the beach club," he commanded, as loud as he could.

"How the hell did that happen, Jack?," queried Wujcik, eyes glued on the bloody spear.

"Shit! I was just snorkeling along on the surface, lookin' for fish, when this big ass breaker picked me up and rolled me over – and over. I must've shot myself with the God damned spear while the wave was shakin' me every way but loose." Jack moved his leg to a more comfortable position but the tip of the spear scraped the sand in the process. "OWWW! Son-of-a-bitch! That hurts like hell. For Christ's sake, don't anybody TOUCH the friggin' spear." Then, turning toward the beer hut: "Where the hell's the morphine?"

"Yeah. I bet it hurts," I sympathized and handed him a can of beer I'd been nursing. "Here. Have a beer . . . So what the hell happened to you, Al?"

Chapter 19: The Smell of War

Hillner reached down to feel the long laceration, deep enough to expose his shin bone in places. "Got caught in the same monster wave, I guess." He curled his hand in a big arc to emphasize the size of the comber that hit them. "It drove me to the bottom and scraped me along the coral reef. I didn't think it'd ever let me go."

"That sure is an ugly wound," I cringed from the sight of the yellowish fluid oozing out of the jagged gash that looked like it might have been half plasma.

Then: "Corpsman Hopkins! Report to Mr. Alexander at the club hut. ON THE DOUBLE. Pass the word." The Master at arms bawled out as he strode among the sun bathers and out to the water's edge, repeating his call for the corpsman.

"Here he is, Hopkins," Alexander announced, leading the corpsman through the growing knot of onlookers. "He's got a spear stuck in his leg. Needs attention – BAD."

"Hmm. That is bad," Hopkins mused as he removed the bloody scivvie shirt. "Here. This morphine'll ease the pain a little."

"God! I hope so," Jack cringed as Hopkins jammed the needle into his left thigh and squeezed the little tin foil tube dry.

"Uh . . . sir." Hopkins stammered. "Er . . . I'm goin' to have to remove the spear . . . uh . . . sir?" It sounded like a question but Hopkins meant that he really had to take the spear out.

"No! NO!" Thelen yelped at the thought of even moving the spear. "Don't you DARE even touch that fuckin' spear, God damn it!"

"But sir . . ." Hopkins spread his arms in a pleading gesture.

"Never mind the 'but sir', damn it, leave it alone, I said. Oww!," Jack moaned.

"But the boat won't be back 'til seventeen hundred, sir," Hopkins pleaded. "That's six hours from now. Er . . . and another hour and a half to get back to the ship, sir. By the time you get to sick bay you'll have a roaring infection."

"That may be." Thelen glared at Hopkins. "But nobody's goin' to touch that damned spear without a general anesthetic."

"But sir," Hopkins continued to plead. "You might lose your leg."

"Hold it!" I held my hands up, palms toward the two of them. "How about I take him back to the ship in my special rescue vessel." I wasn't kidding.

"Sounds risky to me," Alexander offered. "What if you tip over . . . er . . . or the boat leaks . . . or . . ."

"No problem." I spread my arms in a gesture of absolute confidence. "Hell, I got over here quicker that you guys did, and with the wind like it is I can get back just about as quick – NO SWEAT!" I turned to Thelen, who was holding his leg as though he could soothe the pain. "What do you think, Jack?"

"But he needs attention, right now, sir," Hopkins pleaded.

"Any delay will make it worse," Alexander chimed in.

Thelen burst in: "To hell with it! This friggin' morphine isn't doin' much for the pain and I'm not goin' to sit around this hell hole for six hours when I can get back to the ship – even if it takes two hours." He punched the air with his fist. "Let's go Harpo!"

"If you insist, sir," Hopkins surrendered. "But let me get some sulfa into that wound before you shove off."

"Okay," Thelen conceded. "But don't you even touch that spear – Owww! Just the thought makes it hurt – BAD."

"Here, sir." Hopkins handed Thelen a gauze bandage. "You better put this on, yourself." He obviously didn't want to get chewed out for irritating the wound. "Let me put a tourniquet on there to keep down the bleeding.

"Hell," Thelen grinned. "Can't bleed much if we leave the spear in there, hey?" Then he flinched from another twinge of pain. "Oh. Okay. go ahead. If I don't like it I'll just loosen it."

"Okay. Are you ready to go?," I asked, standing up beside Thelen.

"Hell yes," was Jack's resolute reply. "Let's get the hell out of here."

"Hey! How about me?," Hillner yelped.

"Sorry Al." I felt bad about leaving him. "I can only take Jack in any kind of comfort. You'll be okay until the boat comes back. Hopkins here'll put some sulfa on it."

"Yes sir. I'll be right back," Hopkins assured Hillner.

Back to Thelen: "A couple of things we've got to do before we shove off, Jack." I looked into his eyes and squeezed his shoulder.

"What do you mean, things to do," Jack wheezed suspiciously.

"Here. Put on this shirt," I ordered as I took off my shirt and put his left hand in the arm hole.

"Naw, Harpo," Jack grimaced with another twinge. "I'm okay."

"Well, you won't be after an hour out on that windy lagoon; and losin' blood like you are." I pulled on his arm. "Put on the God damned shirt, Jack," I ordered. "The other thing is . . ." I hesitated. "I've got to wrap the head end of that spear with your scivvie shirt. That thing could sink us if we hit a little rough water; and you're in no shape to be in the open water."

Chapter 19: The Smell of War

"Wait a minute, sir," Hopkins put in. "Lets just put a couple of Band Aids on that spear point. That won't weigh down the spear as much."

"Thanks, Doc," Jack sighed. "But you put 'em on, Harpo. I don't trust the sawbones here. OWWW! Hell I can't even trust you, can I." He looked up at me. "Are you done, you God damned sadist?"

"Hopkins, you take that side," I ordered. "I've got the side with the spear."

"OWW! OOOH! That hurts like hell." I could feel Jack writhing with pain as we lifted him. "Take it easy for Christ's sake." Tears stained his cheeks.

"Best we can do, I'm afraid," I soothed. "It'll feel better when you get in the boat." I didn't know why it would, but I said it anyway.

We eased Thelen very gently into the forward compartment of the life raft, draping his legs carefully over the midships thwart.

"How's that, Jack . . . Are you ready?" I squeezed his shoulder.

"Shove off, Cox'n. Boat's loaded." Jack managed a weak smile and wriggled gingerly into a position of relative comfort, under the luffing sail.

"Hey, Hopkins," I yelled over the soft murmur of the surf. "Get some help and push us out beyond the surf."

"Aye, aye, sir."

Out beyond the gentle surf of the lagoon I started forward, as quietly as possible. "Hold on, Jack. I got to get the lee boards down and I'll probably rock the boat a little."

"You would, wouldn't you. OWW!," Jack cringed with a sudden surge of pain. "I was right," he cheered feebly. "You are a friggin' sadist."

"You'll be more comfortable once we get out of this surf and under way." I tried to comfort him as I locked the lee boards down and stole back to the stern. *Now. Scull it around and get us on the starboard tack . . . Okay. Underway now and slippin' smoothly over the little ripples.* "Are you okay, Jack?"

"Yeah! Hey, that's pretty smooth." Jack wiped his forehead. "I'm feelin' awful hot. I don't know why I've got your shirt on."

"I hope it's just sunburn, Jack, not fever. We've got about an hour to go so keep the damned shirt ON." *God damn! I think the wind shifted a little to the south, and this damned little sail won't hold a tack any closer than about forty-five degrees out of the wind . . . Can't get too close to the wind or we'll lose water speed . . . Whoa! I can't approach the ship on a port tack, anyway. That'll put me on the wrong side . . . Better do the port tack first.*

Paddles!

"Stand by to come about." I announced, and jammed the tiller hard alee and slid over to sit on the port side. *Oh oh. Not a sound from Jack . . . I guess the morphine got to him . . . Well, he'll be more comfortable if he's unconscious . . . Ah! Sail's filling and we're slidin' along nicely . . . If I can hold this course, the starboard tack back to the ship will be a short one . . . Son-of-a-bitch! Jack's leg's turnin' blue. I've got to loosen the tourniquet. Eeeaasy.*

"OWW! Hmmmm . . ."

Yeah! That'll be okay . . . Hmm. I guess he passed out again.

"Ahoy *Belleau Wood*," I yelled up at the gangway.

"Uh . . . hey! What the hell's goin' on?" Jack rolled over a little to see forward. "OWWAHH! SON-OF-A-BITCH, THAT SMARTS!" He rolled back gingerly.

"We're here, Jack," I bragged. "Just relax."

First, the marine on watch and then the officer of the deck appeared at the top of the gangway. "Ahoy the life raft. Identify yourself." The watch had been relieved since I shoved off so these guys didn't know about me and the life raft.

"Harpo here," I called. "Got a fighter pilot with a bad leg wound." I pointed into the bilges. "Alert sick bay and get a couple of corpsmen down here with a stretcher – ON THE DOUBLE!"

"Aye aye! Stretcher comin'," the officer yelled back before disappearing into the hangar deck.

"Hey Sergeant!" *I think I promoted him, but that'll get his attention.*

"Corporal, sir," came the smart reply. "What do you need."

"Send a mooring party down here," I demanded. "I can't tie this thing up with this R & R casualty on board."

"Aye aye, sir. Right away." He saluted and disappeared.

"Stretcher's on the way, Harpo," announced the officer.

"Is that you, Lasater?," I called, as we eased to within about fifty yards of the gangway.

"Yeah. It's me, Harpo."

"Okay, Al, you better get that mooring party down here – QUICK. I don't want to have to go around – with this cargo." I luffed the sail a little to slow down.

"C'm on, Corporal." Lasater led the marine down the gangway two rungs at a time just in time to fend us off.

"Sorry, Al," I called out. "Hell! No way I could get this little raft to sidle up the float like a real sailboat would. Thanks for catching us."

Chapter 19: The Smell of War

"No sweat, Harpo," Lasater called as he steadied the stern of the raft while the corporal cleated the bow painter.

I looked up to see two corpsmen hustling down the gangway with the stretcher. I leaned over and spoke softly. "Okay Jack – stretcher's here – we're goin' to lift you out of the boat. It might hurt a little."

"Uuuhh . . . OWW! Careful with the God damned spear, will ya? . . . OWW!"

20

HEAVY WEATHER

I rolled the dice on the Acey Deucy board. "Hah! Acey Deucy! Here we go." I crowed as I assembled a solid block straddling the end of the board.

"God damn! Harpo," Arky moaned "You've got those friggin' dice trained."

"You noticed," I grinned. "Stand by for a skunk."

TOOOEEEE. The boatswain's pipe screamed from the ready room speaker, "NOW HEAR THIS. AIR DEPARTMENT, MAN YOUR FLIGHT QUARTERS STATIONS FOR RECOVERING AIRCRAFT."

Wujcik stuck his head in the door. "Hey, Harpo, let's go . . . Hey! Don't you guys ever stop playin' that dumb ass game?"

"On my way, Weej." Then: "Save that game, Arky." I ordered, as I made for the hatch leading to the port catwalk.

"No need, Harpo." Arky flashed his evil grin, showing the gap between his two front teeth. "We can start over when you get back."

"Oh no you don't." I hesitated at the hatch. "Save it, God damn it!"

"Here come the fighters, sir." Monahan pointed to the flight of Hellcats just passing to starboard of the island. "Eight of 'em."

The last of the six TBFs was just turning off the downwind, so the timing was good.

"Yeah. We've got the Sours and McLaughlin divisions," I announced as I held a ROGER on the last torpecker.

Chapter 20: Heavy Weather

"Bill Sours and Sweetie looked pretty good," I hollered over my shoulder. "Here comes Herr."

"Gear, flaps, hook, all down, sir."

"I notice Doc's holdin' his approaches closer to the centerline," Wujcik commented in my ear.

"Yeah. He stopped that slight overshoot so now he can ease right to the centerline instead of having to come back." I picked him up with just a tapped FAST signal . . . Power eased slightly . . . LOW DIP . . .

"Clear deck, sir – barriers up!"

"Hmm. Perfect," I mused. then: ROGER . . . CUT . . . SCRUNCH . . . SHREEEE. "Yeah! almost on the centerline."

"Gear, flaps, hook, all down, sir."

"Here's Mariani," Wujcik shouted in my ear.

"Yeah, damn it! I wish to hell he'd learn how to get settled down earlier," I grumbled, and picked Irish up with a steady FAST signal.

"Clear deck, sir. Barriers up."

"Whoa!," I hollered reflexively when we heard Lidio yank the power off and I went to a frantic COME-ON . . . NOTHING! "He's sinkin' fast. STAND BY THE WIND SCREEN. Add power, Lidio!," I screamed as I banged the paddles on the platform in a frantic LOW . . . then WAVE-OFF. Finally FULL POWER came on and all we could see was the belly of the *Hellcat* coming at us, left wing down, as Lidio horsed the nose up. I was staggered by the sudden blast of wind released when the wind screen dropped.

"HE'S GOT THE RAMP!," I shrieked. "HIT THE NET!" I went into the net right on top of Wujcik and rolled toward the relative safety of the catwalk. We heard the crack of something hitting the ramp, and then the roar of the *Hellcat* passing overhead.

"Whew! That was close." I peeked over the edge of the platform to see Lidio's airplane, still in a left turn, gaining altitude and airspeed. "Looks like he's okay."

"Hey!," Wujcik yelled. "Here comes Bernie."

We both jumped up on the platform and Callagee raised the wind screen for us.

I picked up McLaughlin with a FAST. "How does he look, Monahan?" I hadn't seen Monahan throughout this whole episode.

"Looks okay, sir," Callagee called. "Gear, flaps, hook, all down." He turned to look up the deck. "And you've got a clear deck and barriers."

"Good, now a little high," I commented with a HIGH DIP. "Hey! I see Bernie found out where the centerline is." ROGER . . . CUT . . . CRUNCH. "What the hell happened to Monahan?"

"Bumped his head tryin' to get under the platform, sir," Callagee shouted. "I've got wheels, flaps, hook, all down, sir. You'll have a clear deck." Then: "Monahan's still in the catwalk, groanin'."

"Well, we can't stop now." I picked up Holmgaard with a ROGER. "Smooooth Homicide," I purred, holding a solid ROGER.

"Sure glad he learned to dip for the deck," Wujcik called in my ear.

"Clear deck. Barriers up, sir."

CUT . . CRUNCH . . SHREEEE.

"Whoa!," Wujcik screamed. "Look at that!"

I turned to port to see a big white splash full of airplane parts. "Jesus Christ! Must've spun in turnin' at the ninety."

"Yes sir." It was Monahan emerging from the catwalk, blood oozing from a nasty gash on his forehead. "I was watchin' him all the way from the downwind. He was slow as hell, sir. Then he tried to turn too steep." He mimicked the airplane with his right hand. "SPLASH! He hit left wing first and just cartwheeled in."

The plane guard destroyer belched a cloud of black smoke as she accelerated toward the crash position.

"Who the hell was that?," Wujcik shrieked.

"I'm pretty sure it was Knobby," I frowned. "He always flies Bernie's section lead. Hey! What the hell happened to Lidio? There's only one left, and that's got to be Bennett."

"Fly Control says Mariani lost his hook on the ramp, sir," Monahan reported, adjusting his sound powered phones. "They're sendin' him over to *Yorktown*. Here's the next one, sir . . . Gear, flaps, hook, all down."

"Good," I crowed, as I picked up Bennett with a little SLANT LEFT and a tap FAST. Red'll get him aboard okay on that big deck of his. Anyway, we don't need any more incidents today." HIGH DIP . . . CUT . . . CRUNCH.

"THIS IS THE CAPTAIN SPEAKING," boomed the flight deck bull horn. "BELL REPORTS A FEW AIRPLANE PARTS STILL FLOATING. NO SIGN OF THE PILOT." USS *Bell* was the plane guard destroyer. "I'M AFRAID WE'VE LOST LIEUTENANT FELT."

Chapter 20: Heavy Weather

"What the hell happened to Doc and Arky?," I demanded as Wujcik and I burst into the fighter ready room after recovering the Guam strike.

"Just as we were pullin' up from our last run a bunch of Zekes jumped us." "Zeke" was the code name for the front line Japanese Navy fighter. "We got 'em in a weave and splashed four of 'em but one of 'em flamed Arky." Oveland gestured with both hands. "Then the damned Zeke pulled up and headed back to Orote." Collin made a chandelle maneuver with his left hand.

"Cowboy and I tried to catch him but he ducked into a cloud," Tab apologized.

"So what the hell happened to Arky?" I was getting impatient.

"I thought he was goin' right in but he kept it in a gentle glide, trailin' black smoke, with Frenchy right on his wing and Doc and Cracker weavin' up above to keep the Zekes off him. Tommy and I strafed the antiaircraft battery on Facpi Point to keep 'em quiet while Arky went over, still in that gentle glide, smokin' like a God damned stove. Then he bailed out about two miles off shore."

"So he got out okay?" I was relieved. *I sure as hell don't want to lose my Acey Deucey partner.*

"Yeah. He was in his raft when we left." Then to Cowboy Mayer: "Hey! Don't take your flight gear off. We're goin' to launch as soon as they can clear the catapult and refuel and rearm four airplanes. Gotta get back there and relieve Doc. They'll be runnin' low on fuel by now."

An hour later: "Well, we got Doc, Cracker, and Frenchy back," Wujcik shouted as we staggered forward against the thirty-five knot wind. "Maybe we can find out what happened to Arky."

"Hold it! Weej." I grabbed his arm and pointed out to the north where the incoming *Hellcats* were just four little black spots against the high overcast. "Here come four more. Must be Collin." *God damn! That was quick – Hmm. – Wonder what that means.*

Back in the ready room after recovering Collin's division, everyone was talking at once. Collin was telling Doc: "Right after you left . . ."

"Yeah. Good thing you got there when you did." Doc gave a sigh of relief. "We couldn't have stayed much longer and still gotten back to the ship."

"Well. Not five minutes later a submarine surfaced right next to Arky's life raft," Collin enthused. "Whew! That was a relief. Looked like Arky had it made."

Paddles!

"Yeah," Tabler chimed in. "But just then the big shore battery on Facpi Point opened up and bracketed the sub with big geysers of water." He flung his hands in the air imitating a shell burst. "The sub just disappeared in a big white splash."

"Shit! I thought she'd been sunk," Chuhak added. "And I couldn't see Arky in all the white water."

"Yeah. I couldn't either, by then." Collin shook his head. "So we went over and made a couple of strafing runs on the shore battery but I don't think our fifties made much of an impression on that concrete bunker." Collin shrugged. "But when we got back, the sub had her periscope up lookin' for Arky. That was encouraging."

"Yeah, but Arky wasn't in his boat any more," Tab groaned.

"So what the hell happened to him?," I demanded.

"I guess he must've gotten bounced out of his boat by the water bursts from the shore battery," Collin shrugged.

"But he's got a life jacket," I said, hopefully.

"Yeah, but . . . you know," Doc started. "He never did put out any dye marker and he never waved at us." He looked down at the deck. "I think he was wounded pretty badly when he got hit and really couldn't do much for himself."

"Gone, huh?," I whispered.

"Yeah," Doc sighed as tears welled up in his eyes. "Arky's gone."

I felt a pang of melancholy deeper than I had ever felt before. I guess I was closer to Arky than to anyone else in the air group. *Goodbye Arky. I hope you find a good Acey Deucy partner wherever you're going.*

"Did you bring a waste basket, Cobbs?," I whispered to Kolb as he, Wujcik, and I assembled in the air conditioning spaces up on the oh three deck to tap some of the beer Weej and I had brought aboard at Pearl . . . just a little relaxation after a hectic day on the flight deck.

"No." Kolb eyed me with wonder. "What the hell do we need a waste basket for?"

"To cool the beer in," Wujcik hissed. "What the hell do you think?"

"And bring some towels too," I added. "For insulation."

As Kolb stole out and down the passageway, Wujcik worked on the fire extinguisher and I broke open the case of beer I had smuggled up from my stateroom.

"I guess all you do is pull this pin and turn the valve," Wujcik mumbled.

"Here's the waste basket and towels," Kolb whispered as he closed the hatch.

Chapter 20: Heavy Weather

"Are you ready with that fire extinguisher, Weej?," I whispered as I stacked eight cans of beer in the towel insulated waste basket.

"Yeah. Here." Wujcik stuck the nozzle down into the cluster of beer cans. SHHHH. The CO_2 formed a small white cloud around the waste basket.

"Whoa!," I wheezed. "We don't want to freeze the damned things."

"Hey! What's goin' on in here?," came a gruff voice from the partially open hatch.

I turned to see "Garg" Kallman, leering at us his crooked grin. *Damn! Caught in the act.* I thought. Then: *No! He had the watch when we brought the beer aboard . . . He must know.* "Er . . . Hi, Garg . . . uh – come on in . . . and secure the hatch, will you?"

"Didn't you know that you've got to report the use of fire extinguishers?," Kallman demanded as he carefully dogged the hatch shut and ogled my case of beer.

"Here, Garg." I picked a can out of the basket. "Have a beer . . . No. I never thought about that problem."

Wujcik picked a can out of the basket, opened it, and took a swig. "Jeez! We can't report it or they'll know we're havin' these beer parties."

Kallman drew on his can of beer. "Ahhh! That's good." He raised the can and admired it as a long lost friend. "Hull Department's got to know so they can keep 'em filled up for any fire emergency . . . "Don't worry. I'll take care of it . . . and nobody'll be the wiser." He gave me a sidelong glance. "I figured that was beer you guys brought aboard back at Pearl." He snickered wickedly. "I could hear the cans tinkling in that parachute bag."

"Here's to the Hull Department." We all raised our cans and drank.

"THIS IS THE CAPTAIN SPEAKING," boomed the speaker outside our stateroom. "ADMIRAL CLARK ADVISES THAT WE'VE BEEN DETACHED FROM THE MAIN FORCE TO PROCEED NORTH TO THE BONIN ISLANDS TO DESTROY JAP AIRCRAFT STAGED THERE FOR ATTACKS ON U.S. MARINES LANDING ON SAIPAN. ALL AVAILABLE AIRCRAFT WILL BE LAUNCHED FOR THE STRIKE. MAKE EVERY BOMB, ROCKET, AND BULLET COUNT! THIS IS THE CAPTAIN SPEAKING."

"We're goin' to launch aircraft in THIS weather?" Dulacki was skeptical because the ship was rolling and pitching so violently that all loose gear and furniture had to be lashed down to keep it in place. We were on the edge of a Typhoon.

Paddles!

"When Admiral Clark says 'GO', We go!," I declared, proudly.

TOOOEEEE. "NOW HEAR THIS. AIR DEPARTMENT, MAN YOUR FLIGHT QUARTERS STATIONS FOR LAUNCHING AIRCRAFT."

"Gotta go, Leo," I said, leaping out of my tethered chair. "With this weather they might need me topside."

Up on deck, airplanes were directed forward, one by one, to the catapult, but launching them wasn't the usual BANG BANG, twenty second interval, routine operation. Greenberg had to hold each launch until the violent pitch and roll of the ship reached a condition that would permit a safe catapult launch. Otherwise he could have launched them downward, directly into one of those monstrous waves, or upward at an angle that would have guaranteed that the aircraft would have spun in. This tortuous process continued until Greenberg had gotten the eight fighters of the first strike up and the five TBFs and six fighters of the second strike all safely airborne.

"Okay, Weej," I yelled into the gusting wind. "Dave got 'em all up safely. When they come back we're goin' to have to get 'em aboard without anyone bustin' his ass. That'll be a piece of magic. Too bad we don't have Talos here to help."

"Talos?" Wujcik's eyebrows shot up. "What the hell is that?"

"A magician friend of mine," I frowned "Bad joke. Forget it. Talos got killed on a bombing run out of Norfolk."

Wujcik eyed me quizzically as though he thought that might be a bad omen. "Anyway, I sure as hell hope this weather calms down by then." He shuddered.

Four hours later, the call to flight quarters brought us up on the flight deck to recover the two strikes on Chichi Jima and Haha Jima that Dave Greenberg had so masterfully launched.

"God damn! I've never seen anything like this before," Wujcik shouted into the howling wind. "I think it's worse than when Dave launched 'em; and it looks like they're about an hour late returning. They'll probably be low on fuel. Especially the torpeckers."

"Hell, I'm havin' trouble just standin' up," I hollered back. "Jesus Christ! The fantail must be goin' up and down twenty or thirty feet and we're rollin' about twenty-five degrees, port and starboard. These guys have never seen deck motion like this. I hope they remember to bank to the high side of the deck as she rolls – like we told 'em."

Chapter 20: Heavy Weather

"Yeah. And the friggin' wind must be fifty knots on the surface." Wujcik pointed out at the violent sea. "Look at those monster white caps."

"They look more like tidal waves than white caps," I grimaced. "Skipper's goin' to have to maintain only minimum steerage way on and that'll make the ship wallow . . . Hell! That's what she's doin' now. I hope to hell these guys remember to turn off the downwind abeam or for'rd of the bow, not abeam the island, as usual."

We ducked in behind the wind screen. "Jesus! That's not much better," Wujcik screamed. "Wind's whippin' from every which way back here."

"God! It's goin' to be hard to hold onto the paddles," I complained as Monahan handed them to me.

"Here comes the first strike up the starboard side – all eight of 'em," Wujcik crowed. "Glad to see that."

Twenty-five minutes later: "Whew! What a struggle!," I sighed with relief. "All eight aboard with no damage – Just lots of WAVE-OFFs – Now where the hell are those other guys?"

"Looks like we've got some of 'em." Wujcik pointed aft at the five TBFs straining to catch the ship against the gale force wind. Look at those friggin' torpeckers comin' up the starboard side. They look like they're standin' still."

"Yeah!," I growled. "And we're goin' to have one hell of a time gettin' 'em on the deck. Ah, here comes one now. flyin' sideways at the ninety."

"Gear, flaps, hook, all down, sir," Monahan shrieked into the swirling wind.

"Clear deck, barriers up, sir." Callagee barely made himself heard.

Five minutes later: "Well, Weej, we got Alston's section okay. Only four WAVE-OFFs." I hollered over my shoulder. "God damn! We had Tuffy goin' like a scalded dog and he still barely made it to the second wire." I marvelled as I picked up Feets Tate coming out of the ninety.

"Too bad you had to wave off Brownie," Wujcik called in my ear. "That was a perfect approach."

"Yeah, but the deck was comin' up so fast he would have driven the gear up through the wings when he hit." I shook my head. "This is a contest between gettin' the right deck position and them runnin' out of fuel. I sure as hell hope we win. They wouldn't last long in that sea."

"Gear, flaps, hook, all down, sir."

"High and slow, as usual," I groused as I picked Tate up with a HIGH.

Paddles!

"Hell! I don't think he's gainin' on us," Wujcik yelled.

"Clear deck, barriers up, sir."

Weej was right so I shifted to a COME-ON and we could almost hear the power come on. "God damned Tate!," I railed as I shifted back to a HIGH. "If he ever gets here he's goin' to be too high anyway."

"Now he's comin' down," Wujcik shouted. "But he's not gainin' on us at all now."

Back to a frantic COME-ON. "Come on, Feets, God damn it! Speed up! You can't land 'til you get here," I yelled into the wind while shifting to a HIGH again.

As Tate crept up to the ramp I was still giving him a frantic COME-ON alternating with an exaggerated HIGH.

"Deck comin' up," Wujcik yelled. "Rollin' to level." We helped each other reporting deck position during rough weather.

Shit! This might be perfect. I thought as Tate struggled against the wind, still too high at about twenty five feet and, by now, just about over the first wire looking back at me.

"Deck's at the high point, Harpo," Wujcik shouted. "Level goin' to starboard."

"Hell! This is the best we're goin' to get." CUT.

Tate's TBF did its falling leaf act with the deck falling away and touched down ever so softly between the first and second wires. Amazingly, he rolled forward only about five feet and didn't even come close to catching the second wire. I hadn't noticed it before but the plane directors had to be careful not to taxi the TBFs forward too fast, lest they take off in the process. A very touchy situation.

Later, as we recovered the remaining fighters I marvelled to myself. *Boy! What a contrast. The TBFs seemed to hang in the air aft of the ship and we had to coax them up the groove. Now these fighters seem so quick. But they get bounced around by the wind gusts so badly that they can't get settled down on approach. Well, we got all but three of 'em.*

"Gear, flaps, hook, all down, sir."

I picked up the next *Hellcat* with a ROGER and gave him a little SLANT LEFT. "How's the deck, Weej?"

"Just startin' back up, Harpo," Wujcik measured his words. "Rollin' to port, now."

"Sounds good. Keep it comin', Weej." A little tap FAST now. "He's lookin' good."

Chapter 20: Heavy Weather

"Clear deck, barriers up, sir."

"Deck passing level, comin' up . . . just startin' to roll back from a port list." Wujcik reported.

Lookin' good, buddy . . . Just hold that. ROGER. "How's the deck?"

"Deck at the high point now – rollin' starboard past level."

PERFECT! Take him NOW! CUT.

"Whoa!," Wujcik screamed. "He's rollin' with the deck, and his tail's too high to catch a wire."

"BARRIER!," I yelled. "No! . . . NO!" The fighter drifted to starboard right through all three barriers and smashed into the island in a shower of sparks which ignited the splattered fuel. In a moment the island structure and the flag bag to starboard were engulfed in flame. "Somebody's goin' to die in this one – Damn it!"

Asbestos Joe got the pilot out of his flaming *Hellcat* but a corpsman and a signalman died in the raging fire. Red Volz took our other two chickens aboard *Yorktown*'s big, stable deck.

21

NIGHT LIGHTS

It was a very dark, moonless night with the inky sea showing no white caps in the light breeze and the wake fluorescence was at a minimum. The strike against the Japanese fleet, launched over five hours earlier, would be returning with a very low fuel state, especially the torpedo planes. I recalled the huge banner spread across the front of the torpedo ready room shouting, "GET THE CARRIERS."

"Whoa!," I yelped as we took our positions back at Landing Signals in preparation for recovering the strike aircraft. "This looks like a big city at night."

Suddenly, every ship in the formation had turned on all external lights and the carriers had illuminated their flight decks with flood lights.

"Fly Control says the admiral ordered all lights on to recover as many of our returning aircraft as possible," reported Monahan.

"Pretty risky," Wujcik mused. "We're still only a couple hundred miles from Jap fighter bases on Guam."

"I imagine the Admiral's got some night fighters up," I suggested. "That'll help." Then: "Hey, Monahan. Is your starboard catwalk crew ready with the searchlight?"

"Ready, sir," Monahan called up to me. "Callagee's got the duty. But with all this light we may not need it."

"Well. They're recoverin' aircraft over on *Hornet* and *Yorktown*. I wonder where the hell our guys are," Wujcik thought aloud as we tested our new ultra violet light to be sure it worked okay.

Chapter 21: Night Lights

We had graduated from the thin, battery powered, night signal wands to a flight suit decorated with fluorescent cloth and illuminated by an ultra violet light mounted in the catwalk aft of the platform. Our daylight paddles were already fluorescent, so they complemented the suit just fine. We wore a pair of goggles fitted with light shields to protect our eyes against the so-called "black light."

"Maybe they like those big decks better," I laughed. "Chickens."

"Well, finally," Wujcik groaned. "Here comes somebody." The single red running light streaked past the starboard side and the white tail light came into view as the airplane passed our position. Then, out past the bow, the lights rolled left for the turn onto the downwind.

"You've got a clear deck, sir.," Monahan reported. "Barriers up."

"This guy's set up pretty well," I commented as I picked up the *Hellcat* with a FAST signal. "His approach light is showing red, but I can see just a hint of amber. A perfect start. Now a little high. Yeah! Comin' down nicely." ROGER . . . The searchlight illuminated the belly of the airplane for a half second.

"Gear, flaps, hook, all down, sir."

CUT . . . SCRUNCH!

"We got him," I yelled in my exhilaration. "Find out who that was, Monahan!"

"Jesus! is that all we get?," Wujcik groaned. "Looks like your buddy Volz's got plenty of business over on *Yorktown*."

"Fly Control says that was Hillner, sir.

"Fer Christ's sake," I thought aloud. "We send out six fighters and four TBFs and get back one measly F6F. Not a good average."

"Well," Wujcik scowled. "The TBFs will be very low on fuel after five and a half hours, including combat. Maybe they all had to ditch."

"Yeah," I hesitated, not wanting to say it. "Or maybe they got shot down."

"God, I hope not," Wujcik objected to the thought. "Hey! Here comes another one." A touch of relief edged his voice as another single red light disappeared behind the island chased by the little white tail light. "Looks like they're comin' back one by one."

"Clear deck, sir, and you've got barriers."

"God damn!," I yelled. "This one's better'n Hillner – ROGER all the way."

At the blink of the searchlight Monahan yelled, "GEAR, FLAPS, HOOK, ALL DOWN, SIR!

CUT . . . CRUNCH . . . SHREEE.

"We've got another one at the ninety, sir."

Paddles!

"God damn!," Wujcik hollered in amazement. "This son-of-a-bitch didn't even bother with a break. He must be real low on fuel."

"You've got a clear deck, sir. Barriers comin', one . . . two . . . three . . . BARRIERS UP!" Monahan called. "That last one was Oveland, sir."

"This guy's comin' okay," I called, starting with a ROGER. "Now a little high. Oops! I gave 'im a HIGH and he went higher."

"Japs have opposite signals, you know," Wujcik cautioned. "I told you we're too close to Guam to turn the lights on."

"Yeah!," I called. "I just gave him a LOW and he came down." Then: "Gimme the searchlight . . . NOW!

"Jesus Christ!," Wujcik screamed. "Look at those meat balls. Looks like a Val to me."

Suddenly the ship went absolutely dark. "What the hell happened?," I hollered. Since my eyes were adapted to the light we had before, the ship looked like a gigantic black hole in the starlit sea.

"I told Fly Control it was a Jap," Monahan crowed. "I guess they darkened ship, sir."

"They sure as hell did!"

CLANG CLANG CLANG. "ALL HANDS MAN YOUR BATTLE STATIONS." CLANG CLANG CLANG.

As the Val's engine noise passed over our heads our whole task group went black.

"God damn! That was quick."

As dawn broke the next day all four carriers in the group launched patrols into their assigned sectors and the cruisers catapulted their OS2U *Kingfisher* scout planes to search for survivors of the battle.

With our patrols airborne, I scaled the island ladder to emerge on the bridge at Fly Control and salute Commander Clymer. "Ready to relieve air department watch, sir."

"Good. Now here's the situation:" Clymer began his report to the oncoming duty officer. "Four F6F combat air patrol and three TBFs airborne. Twelve ready fighters are spotted topside and two flyable VF are on the hangar deck. We have no flyable TBF in reserve. Missing pilot status is as follows: Tabler and Omark recovered aboard *Lexington* over in fifty-eight point three and Christensen and Rogers are aboard *Yorktown*. Transfers will be arranged sometime today. Brown, Tate,

224

Chapter 21: Night Lights

Luton – with their crews – are unaccounted for, as is Barr from VF. The entire force is now turning to a northwesterly course and deploying in task group line abeam to sweep the ocean area between here and the battle location in search of survivors."

"Aye, aye, sir," I acknowledged the information. "I guess those ships hull down both port and starboard are two other task groups."

"Yes, and you'll notice that the destroyers have formed a modified screen, spread out abeam to cover more ocean area." Clymer pointed across our port quarter toward a couple of destroyers kicking up wakes as they moved into their search positions.

"And I noticed that the cruisers launched their scout planes."

"Admiral Mitscher wants to use every resource we have to find our missing pilots and air crews and return them to their ships," Clymer announced pridefully. "And the gentle breeze and moderate sea state give us reason to hope that the search can be successful."

My mind said a little prayer. Then I saluted again. "I understand the situation, sir. I'm ready to relieve you."

Clymer returned my salute. "You have the watch." Then he peered into my eyes with an intense curiosity. "Tell me about that airplane you identified as a Japanese."

"Well, sir," I began as I organized my recollection of the incident. "He started out with a nice position but he didn't have an approach light – I figured it was shot out – so I couldn't tell speed very well."

"So how'd you know it was a Jap?"

"He was answering signals backward and Wujcik remembered that the Jap signals are opposite to ours. Then's when we hit him with the searchlight. You should've seen those meat balls." I made a big circle with my hands. "He had his gear and hook down and was responding pretty well to my backward signals so I figured we could get him aboard. Then all the lights went out." I sagged with disappointment. "We could've captured him, sir."

"Jesus Christ, Harpo," Clymer exploded. "Haven't you heard about the Japanese suicide pilots?"

"SUICIDE PILOTS?" My amazement showed. " No sir."

"Barbour tells me the Japs are trainin' up a special corps of pilots to dive right into our carriers – with or without bombs." Clymer punctuated his rage by imitat-

225

ing an airplane's dive into a carrier with his hand. "Suicide pilots devoted to their emperor!" He frowned and peered fiercely into my eyes. "He could have crashed on the flight deck." He made a bomb burst with his hands. "And killed a lot of the crew – including you, probably – and put us out of commission."

"Well." I was embarrassed. "It's a good thing the lights went out . . . I guess.

"It's a damned good thing Monahan reported the Jap on the approach – before he got closer." Clymer became pensive. "Well, we dodged that one, but I'm sure we haven't seen the last of that suicide tactic."

TOOOEEEE – "NOW HEAR THIS! FOURTH DIVISION STAND BY TO RIG BREECHES BUOY TO *BRADFORD*, CLOSE ABOARD, STARB'RD SIDE."

I scurried around to the starboard side of the bridge and looked down to see a destroyer cruising with us, holding a position only about twenty-five or thirty yards abeam. POW. The First Division's boatswain's mate fired his line throwing gun across *Bradford*'s number two gun mount. Immediately, her crew scurried to capture the lead line to haul in the suspension line and secure it to a position at the bridge level.

"Hey, McVeigh," I called to the officer of the deck. "Lend me your binoculars for a minute, will you?

"Okay . . . here." He lifted the strap off his neck and handed me the glasses. "What the hell're you searchin' for?"

"There're a couple of guys in flight suits over on that can." I put the binoculars to my eyes. "I want to see who they are."

"Probably had to land in the water last night," McVeigh suggested.

"For Christ's sake!," I spouted. "It's Buck and Chris. They landed over on *Yorktown*. I wonder why the hell didn't they just fly back?"

TOOOEEEE. I heard the duty boatswain's mate inside the bridge. "NOW HEAR THIS. AIR DEPARTMENT, MAN YOUR FLIGHT QUARTERS STATIONS FOR RECOVERING AIRCRAFT."

"Here're your glasses, Mac." I pulled the binocular strap over my head and handed the glasses to McVeigh. "Gotta get goin'."

Commander Clymer was just stepping off the ladder onto the bridge at Fly Control. "Okay, I'll take over. Anything change?

"Nothing, sir, except we just got Rogers and Christensen back," I frowned. "Via destroyer. Looks like we lost a couple of F6F's in the confusion last night."

Chapter 21: Night Lights

Then: "You have the watch, sir." I saluted and disappeared down the ladder to the flight deck.

"Well, that's progress," I commented as Wujcik and I strolled forward after he had recovered our patrols and Omark and Tabler, returning from *Lexington*. "I guess that leaves four still unaccounted for."

Back in the fighter ready room everyone was waving their arms, demonstrating one or another strafing run or dog fight. "Hey! Chris," I yelled over the din. "What the hell happened to your airplanes, for Christ's sake?"

"Shit! Harpo," Chris moaned. "*Yorktown* was so damned loaded with everyone else's airplanes that they didn't have any place to park us."

"Yeah? So what the hell happened?

God damned if they didn't just roll our airplanes over the side at the deck edge elevator." Chris gave a sardonic laugh. "And after we worked so hard to get 'em back."

"You mean, perfectly good airplanes in the drink." Wujcik was astonished.

"Well, they did take the clocks out," Rogers grinned." Standard procedure, you know."

Over in the torpedo ready room Tate had just gotten back off the destroyer *Knapp*, who had picked him and his crew up after they had to ditch inside the screen – with all fuel gauges reading zero. He and Omark were regaling the rest with their battle and survival stories.

"Anybody hear anything about Brownie?" Omark demanded. "I found him just at twilight. His airplane was really torn up and his running lights weren't working. I think he was wounded pretty badly 'cause he kept wandering off course, dropping one wing or the other. Then it got real dark and he slipped into a cloud." He bowed his head and sighed. "I never saw him after that."

Tate chimed in, " Hey, Rovah! That sounds awful fishy to me, cause ah saw Brownie get hit just aftah he dropped his fish. Then there wuh two or three parachutes. Hell! Ah figgahed he and his crew'd just bailed out. Then, aftah ah got clear o' the Jap force, ah'll be dawg if ah didn't find Brownie a-flyin' along, very low to the watah." He used his hands to show a two plane formation. "When ah joined up ah could tell that he'd been on fiah by the soot all ovah his belly, and he had a BIG hole in his left wing. From what ah could see, he was bleedin' like a stuck pig. Ah tried to lead him back toward ouwah fleet but ah lost him." Tate screwed up his bushy eyebrows and looked down at the deck. "Ah figgahed he probably wouldn't make it back."

"Well, apparently he made it for awhile, anyway, since I found him later, around sunset," Omark reminded him.

"That matches up, fellas," Jack Barbour interjected.

"What do you mean, 'matches up', Jack?," Omark demanded.

"We've got a report from *Baltimore* that one of their scout planes picked up Brownie's crew near where the Jap fleet was last night," Jack replied, with confidence.

"Great!," Shouted Tate. "But what the hell happened to Brownie?"

"No word yet on George." Barbour averted his eyes. "One of his crew . . . er . . . Babcock I think, reported that they'd been hit real bad and their airplane was on fire when they bailed out."

"Jeez!" Tate grinned. "Then they must've been floatin' around raht in the middle of the Jap fleet, all naht. Sheeit! They had a ringsahd seat."

"Hear anything about Luton?," Omark asked, urgently. "Hell, I never saw him after we started our diving turn down through that hole in the clouds to attack the carrier."

"Yeah!," Jack smiled. "They've got Luton – AND his crew – over on *Boyd*. I guess he ran out of fuel last night and they all bailed out."

Then: "Hey wait, you guys. There's good news," Barbour radiated enthusiasm. "Babcock and Platz report that all three of your torpedoes struck home and the carrier sank in about an hour. *Hayataka* class, they think. Congratulations! That's NAVY Cross material . . . Hey Feets. What the hell happened to your hand? That's the biggest bandage I ever saw on a finger."

"Not much of a fingah in theyah though, Jack." Tate glowed with pride as he continued. "Aftah ah dropped mah fish ah turned to fly raht down the stawb'd side of the carriah." He used two hands to demonstrate. "As close as ah could get so they couldn't train theyah guns on me." He held his right hand out as though gripping the stick, with the big bandage on his index finger protruding at a grotesque angle. "All of a sudden this AA round comes through the sahd o' the cockpit and, POW! Blows up raht on top of the stick." He opened up his right hand dramatically. "OUCH! That smawrts." What was left of his finger was sensitive to abrupt movement.

"Okay." Barbour eyed Tate skeptically. "How come you didn't get wounded anywhere else?"

Chapter 21: Night Lights

"Well, now, Jack," Tate drawled. "You didn't see mah legs befowah they put the bandages on. Ah'll be pickin' shrapnel out of 'em fo' months, they tell me. Hey!" He reached up to pick his flying suit off the peg. "Look at the legs." The pride welled up again.

"Jesus Christ!," Barbour exclaimed. "I see what you mean. God! You must be hurting all over."

"Yeah." Tate grimaced, then continued his story to a rapt audience. "But then, aftah ah got past the Jap carriah two Zekes bracketed me." Tate demonstrated the attack with a swoop of his bandaged right hand. "As soon as one of 'em started a run on me ah turned into him and put the pippah on him and pulled the triggah on the stick." He slapped himself on the forehead with his left hand. "That was the first tahm ah knew mah fingah was shot off . . . along with the triggah on the stick. God almighty! Ah couldn't fiah mah wing guns . . . But the Zeke broke off." Tate wiped his forehead. "Then, mah gunnah repoted that the turret gun was jammed – Ah thought we wuh gonnahs . . . Then, those Zekes just kept makin' runs on me and I kept turnin' into 'em until I gained enough altitude to slip into a cloud – Hallelujah! Ah don't think those Zekes evah got a shot." He breathed a great sigh. "It was just aftah that I found Brownie." Then, to Omark: "What ah want to know is how the heyell you got back without runnin' out o' fuel, Rovah.

"It was close." Omark frowned. "My engine quit cold just after I caught a wire on the LEX. Christ! They had to drag me for'd with the friggin' mule." He wiped his brow. "A gallon or two less and I would've been in the drink with you, Feets . . . or worse yet hit the ramp on approach."

Ensign Marcellus "Harry" Barr was finally picked up by one of *Charleston's Kingfishers* and had been transferred to *Belleau Wood* by breeches buoy just an hour earlier. "Shit! I thought I was goin' to be one of the missing." Barr regaled us at the evening meal in the wardroom. "Boy! was I glad to see that OS2U land by me."

"What the hell happened?," Tabler queried. "Last time I saw you, you were buzzin' along just fine until we went into that cloud. Were you hit?"

"Not then, Tab." Barr shook his head. "But all of a sudden, just as I was comin' out of the other side of that cloud, I got hit with a burst of gun fire." He made a sweeping turn with his right hand. "I turned into the son-of-a-bitch . . . and you know what?"

Paddles!

"WHAT?" The whole table was hooked.

"It was a fuckin' F6F, for Christ's sake." Barr shook his head. "How do you like that . . . shot down by another F6F. What kind of a hero's medal do I get for that?"

The whole table broke into spontaneous laughter. . . then everyone fell silent. *Probably all thinkin' about Brownie . . . I guess he's gone.*

22

MAGIC CARPET

Hey! Here I am leading my squadron into battle. I fantasized. *You dreamer you . . . Shit! you couldn't battle a Piper Cub in this stripped down excuse for a fighter.* The eight of us had just catted off *Belleau Wood* in the repairable casualties of the big battle off Guam. I had the log books for delivery to the Carrier Air Service Unit. Anything that was not absolutely essential to the short flight to Ford Island was stripped from these tired birds – guns, gunsight, IFF, belly tank, and . . . oh! The clock, naturally. I led the flight over the Ford Island tower in two echelons of four and broke to the downwind leg, then into the easy, descending left turn toward the runway threshold. *Hmm . . . there's the hole in the ground where Freddy went in . . . I'll be damned! Still some charred airplane parts scattered around.*

We all landed safely and, with a little guidance from the ground crew, parked our airplanes in a neat line southwest of the control tower.

Well, there goes my "squadron," I thought, with a little lump in my throat as the seven VF-24 pilots gathered their gear and made for the BOQ. *I'll sure miss those guys . . . been with some of 'em for a year and a half . . . Now they're leavin' and we're gettin' a whole new batch.* I waved and some of them waved back. *Just think. I may never see those guys again.*

As I entered the Carrier Air Service Unit office on the second deck of the hangar at the south corner of NAS Ford Island, I was trying to perfect my speech to whomever it is that accepts these airplanes. *Hmm. Here's a list of CASU personnel, right on the bulkhead . . . Let's see.* I scanned the list, using my index finger to take a bead on each name. A*ha! "Transfer Officer – Lieut. Rosenthal" . . . Yeah. That's the guy I want to see . . . Now. How do I pose this proposal – or request? I've got to find a benefit for him . . . okay! I think I've got it.* "I'd like to see Lieutenant Rosenthal," I announced to the Yeoman Third Class behind the gray steel desk. "I've got some aircraft to transfer."

"Yes, sir. He's in." The Yeoman pointed down the passageway to his right. "Second door on the left."

"Come on in," was the response to my knock.

"Good morning, Mister Rosenthal." I reached across the desk to shake his hand. "I'm John Harper, LSO off *Belleau Wood.*" The placard on my flying suit announced my rank so I stayed humble.

"Call me Ben, John – and have a seat." He raised his sparse eyebrows. "Coffee?"

"Yeah, thanks." I took a seat in the upholstered mahogany conference chair. "Just sugar." *I'll be God damned. These shore swabbies certainly can kumshaw office comforts.*

Ben Rosenthal's high forehead glowed with a deep tan below a head of curly black hair – too long for NAVY regulations – and his prominent nose separated two bulging cheeks that met the specification for jowls. If he stood up, he would probably top six feet and he could tip the scales at two hundred twenty pounds or more – overweight and out of shape. Lounging in his plush, reclining executive's chair, his smallish hazel eyes projected a jolly disposition, a relief to me. "What've you got for me, John?"

"Eight F6Fs," I stated, reaching in the parachute bag for the pile of log books. "All flyable duds from the big battle in the Philippine Sea. We just flew 'em in from the ship this morning."

"I'll be damned." Rosenthal scratched the back of his head. "How'd you ever get that many battle damaged airplanes on a little CVL?"

"Actually, only two of 'em were ours," I began. "When we were detached to return to Pearl, the rest were flown over from the other carriers in our task group – Jocko Clark's 58.1," I announced proudly."

"Yeoman Doyle!," Rosenthal shouted through his open door.

In the blink of an eye the yeoman appeared at the door. "Yes sir?"

Chapter 22: Magic Carpet

"Here." He pointed to the pile of log books I had put on his desk. "Take these logs and check 'em for completion." Rosenthal chuckled. "Before I sign my life away." Then, to me: "So you've been out in the big battles." His curious hazel eyes examined me as some sort of oddity. "So tell me a sea story." His manner was jaunty and anything but fawning – but I sensed a sincere interest.

"Yeah." *Not too arrogant, now.* "Our fighters did their share in the 'Turkey Shoot' – Twelve kills and still counting – and we only lost one." I paused as I remembered Arky. "Pretty good average, don't you think?" *Now Arky's just a friggin' statistic. Shit!* "And our torpedo squadron sank a Jap carrier." *You don't have to mention Brownie.*

"God." Rosenthal put his elbows on his desk and fixed his eyes on me. "What a tribute to two great airplanes. So what did you do?"

Great airplanes, Hell. How about a little credit to the pilots, you God damned . . . No NO, don't say it. Say something nice, you idiot! "What did I do? . . . Well – my assistant and I got 'em back aboard safely – most of 'em, that is." I tried not to look proud. *Now I've got to soften him up.* "Hey, by the way. I've done business with your operations at Majuro, Kwajalein, and Eniwetok – great people." *Let's see how he responds to "your operations."*

His chest swelled perceptibly with pride in his organization. "What kind of 'business'?"

"Well, lets see." I looked up at the overhead. "We delivered worn out airplanes to the Kwaj CASU and . . . uh . . . we borrowed airplanes from all three of 'em to get in our flight time." I looked him in the eye. "Very cooperative people you have." *Hit 'im with the "you have."*

Yeoman Doyle stepped to the door of the office. "Logs are all in order, sir . . . er . . . as far as they go." The sailor took a sidelong glance at me and placed the log books on Rosenthal's desk. "Flight time has been logged up to about a week ago . . . but nothing since."

"I'm sorry." I nodded to Rosenthal. "I haven't logged today's flight . . . but they really haven't been flown since we got 'em aboard last week." I tried to be apologetic. "I'll do it right now." I reached for the top log book.

"Never mind, John." Rosenthal smiled. "Doyle'll do it. How much time was it?" His manner was protective.

"Point seven hour," I stated, positively.

"Point seven aye, sir." The yeoman took the logs and left.

Hey. Rosenthal's opening up nicely. Now is the time. "Uhh . . . Ben?" I leaned back in my chair and glanced over as Rosenthal eyed me suspiciously. "What would you say if I asked to borrow two of those airplanes for a month . . . er . . . transportation for the Landing Signals staff while we work our new air group on FCLP at NAS Kahului."

Rosenthal cocked his head and held up his index finger, then picked up the phone on his desk and dialed a number. "Let me check something." I could just barely hear the ring in his ear piece.

Sounds encouraging, but maybe I need more justification. I pulled my temporary orders out of my shirt and showed them to Rosenthal as he listened. "Er . . . at the same time I'll be workin' up the Night Combat Training Unit at Barbers Point for night qual . . ."

Rosenthal held up his hand for quiet and spoke into the phone. "Hi, Bill . . . Goin' strong . . . Yeah that's right . . . Hey! What kind of backlog have you got for O&R? . . . F6Fs . . . They're all mod threes . . ." He looked to me for confirmation. I nodded. "Oh yeah?" He looked up and gave me a wink. "I'll be damned . . . uh huh . . . Just got six of 'em back from the fleet battle in the Marianas . . . "

Hah! I see how he does it. Reports six and keeps two . . . FOR US!

"All serious battle damage, I understand . . . Okay. I'll send 'em over . . . Thanks." He hung up the phone and leaned forward to give me a thumbs up. "No problem, John. Bill tells me O&R is up to its gunn'ls with TBFs and SB-Deuceys, and Mod five F6Fs are comin' in here by the boat load. They just park the damaged 'threes'." He permitted himself a smug grin like the benefactor he was. "D'you know which ones you want?"

"Strange you should ask." I muffled a gleeful giggle as I reached in my hip pocket for my personal log. I tore out a page and handed it to Rosenthal. "Here. These are the bureau numbers." I stood up and offered my hand. "Thanks a lot, Ben."

"Hold it, John." He held up his left hand. "You can have 'em, but I want you to keep the logs religiously, and run the thirty and sixty hour checks on schedule. Y' got that?" It's the first time saw him frown. He was serious.

"Yes SIR! I understand . . . and WILL COMPLY!" I was elated at the opportunity.

Rosenthal shouted: "Doyle!"

"Yes sir?" Doyle was at the door.

"Get me the logs for 25884 and 40262."

Chapter 22: Magic Carpet

"Aye aye, sir." Doyle disappeared for a moment and returned with two log books. "That 262 is overdue for a thirty hour check, sir."

"Okay. Thanks." Rosenthal dismissed the yeoman. "Now, I want you to get a thirty hour check for that 262 as soon as possible." He eyed me with some concern. "What's your plan for getting that done? Uh . . . since you are something of a nomad."

"262'll be my airplane and my first stop will be the Pac Fleet night fighter school at Barber's Point." I tried to toss off the urgency. "That'll only be a ten or fifteen minute flight and I ought to have enough leverage to get a thirty hour check done – since they depend on me to get their gang night qualified aboard ship." *I'd better give him some more assurance.* "Once I get to Kahului I won't have a problem. I'll be with our new air group there."

"Sounds good to me, John." Rosenthal lifted his six foot bulk out of the swivel chair and reached across his desk to shake my hand. "See you in thirty days . . . Right?"

"Right!"

"Come on in, Harper." Captain Griffin stepped briskly around his desk to extend his hand. "Welcome aboard . . . am I glad to see YOU!" He announced with sincere enthusiasm. The skipper of night fighter training was very youthful – in spite of his balding pate – for a captain, He was just about my size and shape – five foot ten, a hundred and fifty pounds – and in superb physical condition. His handshake would have been bone crunching if I hadn't used my big man handshake technique – SQUEEZE FIRST! The directness of his deep set blue eyes revealed a firm and resolute commander with a fairness that demanded respect. "First name's John isn't it?"

"Yes, sir," I acknowledged. "I'm glad I can help. I understand you need to night qualify your current batch of neophyte night fighters."

"Yeah, badly – Hey. Have a seat." Captain Griffin returned to his grey steel desk chair. "God! I requested an LSO about a month ago. All my students already have their orders, but they've got to get night qualified before they can report. What are your plans?"

"Tell you what, skipper." I leaned forward in my chair. "I've got to start working with our new air group down at Kahului, too." *This ought to get me a thirty hour check.* "So I'll work with them part of the day and fly up here in the afternoon to work with your pilots at night."

"How are you going to make that commute every day?," Griffin scowled. "I don't have any spare airplanes you can use."

"That's okay, sir." I smiled, without smugness, I hoped. "I've got a battle damaged *Hellcat* back from the wars. The CASU let me keep it for a month."

"Well that's a relief," the captain sighed.

"Yes, sir." I eyed him carefully. "Only she needs a thirty hour check before I can fly her again, and I should get over to Kahului tomorrow morning, first thing."

"Hell, we can handle that – Hey Cooper, come in here," he called to his yeoman.

"Yes, sir. What do you need, sir."

"Find Mister Forrester and tell him I want to see him." He didn't have to add the "On the double", 'cause Cooper knew that was what he meant.

"Aye aye, sir." Cooper scurried off on his errand.

"We'll fix that problem, Harper," Griffin announced with confidence. "But we've got another problem." He leaned forward to capture my eyes in his intense gaze. "I've got a commitment from *Ommaney Bay*'s captain to qualify my guys – but only for the rest of this week. D'you think we can do it by Friday?"

This time squeeze worried me a little. "Are all your guys ship qualified, in type, sir?" The "type" was F6F-5N.

"Yeah. We did that a month ago." His frustration showed. "Then we had to wait three weeks for another ship. Now I have to firm up a date and time before Friday." He eyed me very seriously. "D'you think we can do that?"

"Hmm." I mused. "Er . . . can I have 'em for bounce drill tonight, sir?'

"Hell, yes!" The captain's eyebrows shot up. "If you want to work on Sunday night."

"Hell! You know how it is at sea, sir." I guessed he'd probably forgotten. "Out there, you don't know Sunday from any other day, 'cept for the services on the hangar deck – if we're not operating . . . Right, sir?"

"Yeah, I guess." He scratched his temple. "It's been a while for me."

"You called, sir," announced the big burly lieutenant(jg) who nearly filled the doorway. The front of his wrinkled khaki shirt parted between buttons over his voluminous stomach where smudges of grease combined to give him away as a former chief petty officer and now the maintenance officer.

"Yeah, Forrester." The captain remained seated. "Meet John Harper, our night qual LSO."

I rose to shake his hand with the friendliest smile I could muster. *Better use the big man handshake again. This brute could really crunch my hand.* "Glad to know you."

"Harper's got a war weary F6 he's usin' for transportation." Griffin continued without inviting Forrester in. "Needs a thirty hour check – TODAY!

Forrester turned to me. "Where is it, sir?"

"Parked out in front of Ops . . . transient aircraft parking, I guess. It's got a red prop spinner – Bureau Number 40262."

"We'll get right on it, sir." Forrester saluted the captain and turned to leave.

"Careful of the baggage compartment . . . er . . . Forrester." I almost called him "Chief." "My gear's still in there."

"I'll have it delivered to operations, sir." He turned to leave.

"Whoa!," I called after him. "Could you send it over to the BOQ? Looks like I'll have to bunk there every night this week."

"Yes sir. I can do that." He turned and hustled down the passageway, discernibly shaking our part of the wood frame building.

"Thank you, sir. Now, back to your problem." I scratched my ear. "I think you could schedule the ship for Thursday night if I can bounce 'em every night 'til then."

"We'll schedule bounce drill every night!," Griffin stated with certainty, and sat back in his chair, relieved. "I'll set up the ship for Thursday night, then."

"Whoa! I wouldn't do that quite yet, sir," I cautioned. "Let me look at 'em tonight and I'll let you know tomorrow."

"Let me know TONIGHT!" He banged his fist on his desk for emphasis. "I'll be here!"

"Good." His intensity pleased me. "Oh. By the way, skipper. I'll need a log yeoman to record my comments during all night bounce sessions."

"You'll have 'im, John."

The next morning I flew over to Ford Island to rendezvous with Wujcik and together we flew down to NAS Kahului in our two borrowed birds. First priority after landing at Kahului was to collar the CASU maintenance officer in the main hangar.

Stenciled letters on the textured glass door panel announced "MAINTENANCE OFFICER" and the little brass placard mounted on the steel door below the glass told us that Lieut. H. J. Franklin was our man. I knocked.

"Door's open." The door was ajar but I sensed a deep weariness in the voice – a bad start. "Come on in," the voice invited.

I smiled broadly. "Mister Franklin?" He nodded, wearily. Then: "Hi. I'm John Harper and this is Walt Wujcik," I announced lightly, hoping to ease the tension I heard in Franklin's voice. "We're the LSOs off *Belleau Wood*, down here to work with our new air group – Twenty-One."

Franklin shook hands without enthusiasm and looked at us with suspicion. "Okay. So what do you want with me?" He didn't invite us to sit down.

"Well, sir," I began, using extra courtesy. "We've got two F6F flyable duds from the war zone that your Mister Rosenthal, at Ford Island, let us keep for the duration of our stay here in the islands."

Wujcik sensed the cool reception. "They're for transportation to Pearl and back," he offered.

"Yeah. And I have to get back to Barbers Point every night this week to bounce the night fighters," I added for good measure. "We'd appreciate it if you could arrange periodic checks on our airplanes." *Now. Ease the pain.* "Actually, my airplane's in good shape – just had a thirty hour check yesterday at Barbers Point."

"That God damned Rosie – did it again," Franklin raged, and I could see the wheels turning as he calmed down. "Well. I guess I might as well." His weariness was tinged with misgiving. "I sure as hell don't want that CAG of yours jumpin' my ass again." He glared mournfully at Wujcik, then at me. "I'll appreciate it if you will schedule your checks a couple of days in advance."

"We certainly will," I purred. "And thanks very much for your cooperation."

We headed for the hangar that sported a nice fresh sign proclaiming: "CVLG-21."

"God damn!," Wujcik exclaimed. "This place certainly is a far cry from the wilderness it was . . . what? . . . nine months ago? Look at this, for Christ's sake." He swept his hand across the line of buildings facing the runway. "Hangars and everything."

Wujcik pushed open the steel framed glass entrance door and we stashed our gear behind an empty desk. The first door down the hall was labeled: "CAG-21", for Commander, Air Group 21. We went in.

"Is Commander Casey here?"

"No sir." The yeoman stood. "He's in the VF ready room down the hall, second door on the right."

Chapter 22: Magic Carpet

"Thanks," I said as I turned to leave.

"Sir?" The yeoman stopped us. "Are you reporting for duty?"

"Yeah." I turned to face him. "I'm Harper and this is Wujcik, LSOs off *Belleau Wood*, down here to work with the air group." I undid two buttons on my shirt and withdrew a manila envelope. "Here're my TDY orders."

The yeoman accepted both sets of orders. "Thank you, sir. I'll get 'em processed."

We entered the VF ready room to find it set up much like a classroom – chairs with writing surfaces placed in neat lines facing the blackboard at the front of the room. Ten or twelve men in flight suits stood and sat in three little groups waving their arms in the universal language of fighter pilots.

"Commander Casey?," I called into the room.

The man sitting in the front row rose to his full height of about six foot eight. "Casey here." He responded as he stepped forward to greet us. "You must be the *Belleau Wood* LSOs." Casey's lean frame towered over even the six foot two Wujcik, and I had to crane my neck to talk to him. He had a long face with a lantern jaw, squinty eyes, and a built in grin, all of which made him look a little supercilious.

"Yes sir." I offered my hand. "I'm John Harper – call me 'Harpo', and this is Walt Wujcik – AKA 'Weej'."

"You can call me 'Vince'." Casey's grin turned into a friendly smile as we shook hands.

Hmm. I think I'll wait a bit before I address the commander as "Vince."

Casey looked to his left. "Oh. This is Harry Hassenfratz, my fighter exec." As we shook hands I noted that Lieutenant Hassenfratz projected a very serious mien, assuring us that he was the strict disciplinarian of the squadron. God knows they needed one with Casey's jaunty air. Harry's wiry build conspired with his pinched features and straight blond hair to project a Prussian image. His light gray eyes peered at us with barely concealed disdain. "Happy to know you – both." He didn't quite say "I think."

"Come on into my office where we can talk." Casey gave us another broad smile as he led us back through the passageway and past the yeoman we had met earlier to his Spartan office overlooking the parking apron sprinkled with a few fighters and torpedo planes. "Have a seat and tell me your plans for getting us ready to go aboard." Casey folded himself into his well used Steelcase desk chair and lit up a cigar as we took our seats facing his gray steel desk.

"I understand we've just got two weeks before the training cruise, sir," I warned.

"We'll need to schedule a couple of sessions of FCLP each morning. Then, after a week of that we'll need a few night bounce drills. We can handle six per flight."

"That's about what I expected, Harpo," Casey drawled. "Just get with Keely and he'll schedule it for VF and coordinate with the VT flight officer." He sat back and drew on his cigar. "Don't forget to ring in our LSO, Frank Lynch. He's been workin' with both squadrons.

"I'll get it scheduled, Harpo," Wujcik offered. "And I'll get hold of Lynch to work with us. I know you've got to get back to Barbers Point this afternoon."

"What's this Barbers point shit?," Casey challenged.

"Just a minor conflict that shouldn't last beyond this week, sir," I began, in a casual tone. "I've got orders to night qualify a bunch of pilots out of the night fighter school at Barbers Point, Captain Griffin's outfit." *It shouldn't hurt to throw a little rank around.* "I've got to bounce 'em every night this week and then we'll go out and qualify 'em on the ship Thursday night. I just bounced 'em last night. I'm pretty sure they'll be ready. After that I'll be back here full time."

"Well . . . er." Casey squirmed a little and his eyes squinted more than usual with disapproval. "That's a hell of a note." I could tell he was weighing his options against Captain Griffin. "So we're gonna have all this bounce drill here without you?"

"No problem, sir." I gave it a confident air. "Wujcik's fully qualified, and we want to give your guy, Lynch, as much work as possible. Anyway, I'll be back every day to work with 'em on some of the bounce drills."

Casey's eyebrows shot up so we could see his light blue eyes for the first time. "How the hell are you gonna do that, Harpo? Have you got a magic carpet?"

"I guess you could call it that, sir." I grinned. "It's a shot-up F6 from the Turkey Shoot. I borrowed a couple of 'em from CASU for Weej and me."

"Well, I'll be damned." Casey blew a cloud of cigar smoke. "LSOs on a magic carpet."

Escort carrier *Ommaney Bay* (CVE-79), had slipped out of the channel south of Pearl Harbor shortly after dawn, accompanied by a bevy of destroyer escorts – or DEs – those little undersized warships with paper thin hulls and three inch guns designed specifically to keep enemy submarines away from escort carriers with cardboard thin hulls. Now the force was steaming smartly southward at about twelve knots to commence whatever exercises were planned. I would wait in the stateroom I had commandeered until my night fighters would arrive from Barbers Point

– twelve hours hence. Sensing an opportunity for a little sleep, I took off my marine combat boots and flopped in the lower bunk.

"Mister Harper, sir?" A tentative voice interrupted my snooze.

Without moving a muscle, I opened one eye to see the silhouette of a sailor peering in at me. "Yeah. That's me." I wheezed. "What's up."

"The air officer wishes to see you on the bridge, sir," the sailor announced in a stage whisper.

"Yeah? – When?," I sighed, sitting up in the bunk. "Oww!"

"What happened, sir." The sailor called from a safe distance.

"Never mind." I rubbed the knob on my head and checked my fingers for a sign of blood. "I'm not used to these lower bunks." My weary eyes began to close again and I croaked. "What the hell time is it, anyway?"

"Ten hundred, sir."

"So when does the commander wish to seem me?," I groaned.

"Now, sir."

"Commander Richardson?," I called as I stepped off the ladder and approached the officer at Fly Control. I knew of Richardson as the author of "I Fly for Vengeance" the autobiographical account of his experiences as a NAVY carrier scout bomber pilot in the early Pacific sea-air battles. Thus the nick name "I Fly."

"I'm Richardson." "I Fly" replied crustily as a smile stretched his ample cheeks and wrinkled his tanned forehead under a shock of straight blond hair. "Ah! You must be Harper, the night fighter LSO . . . uh . . . where've you been since we shoved off?"

"In the sack, sir." I rubbed some sleep out of my eye. "Thought I'd get a wink or two before my charges get here. Hell, it's only 1015. They won't be here for hours." Emphasis on "hours."

"True." Richardson gave me an evil grin. "But we've got two flights of qualifiers comin' out." He thought it was funny, interrupting my sack time.

I eyed him quizzically. "You don't need me for that, sir." It was almost a question. "Your own LSO can handle that . . . er . . . right?"

"We don't have an LSO, son. Lost him to some CV slippin' through Pearl on the way to the big show." I didn't know whether he was laughing or crying. "It's just a couple of flights of six – one of SB2Cs and one of F4U-1D *Corsairs*." Richardson eyed me like a new found bonanza. "You can handle that, can't you?"

241

Paddles!

OH oh! Now he's playin' ego games – Christ's sake! I've never brought either one of those airplanes aboard ship – Hell! I've never even seen one in the groove. Oh well. It's no use tellin' him. He's committed. "Yes sir . . . er . . . when'll they be here?"

"Air plot says the first flight just launched from Barbers Point – be here in about fifteen minutes."

"I'll get my paddles and be back at Landing Signals in ten minutes," I started down the ladder. "Uh . . . Sir . . . Do I have a talker and a spotter?"

"Yeah." Richardson gave me a doleful grin. "Talker-spotter – one man – we're a little undermanned."

Strolling aft on the flight deck an avalanche of thoughts crashed through my mind. *I've got to question this talker-spotter – see if he knows what the hell he's doin'. Play it safe on these beasts and hogs – high and fast – I'd rather have a barrier than a ramp. There's no hurry – the screen of DEs, such as it is, sticks with us – plenty of time for WAVE-OFFs. Just take your time.* "Hi! I'm Harper, your borrowed LSO," I called down to the man wearing the sound powered phones standing in the catwalk below the Landing Signals platform. "Commander Richardson said I would have a talker-spotter."

"I'm him, sir." The boyish face reflected a touch of awe as he held his right sound powered earphone away from his ear. "Airman Potter, sir." Potter's fresh crew cut and unfaded dungarees marked him as a recent graduate of boot camp. *My God! What a contrast to Monahan – from combat wise old salt to a wet-behind-the-ears recruit. I'll have to check everything myself and take no chances – NO CHANCES!*

I sat down on the platform and let my legs dangle over the catwalk. "Have you ever done this before, son?"

"Yes sir. Mister Cranston was aboard for a couple of days last week." Potter held up his binoculars. "He taught me to check wheels, flaps, and hook down on airplanes in the cross leg – over there." He pointed off our port quarter. "And call out 'clear deck' when there's no airplane in the arresting gear and all the wires and barriers are up." Potter recited, proudly.

I had never heard of Cranston. "Good!," I exclaimed. "But don't forget the wind screen trip line," I scolded. "Hold onto it all the time and be ready to trip it if an airplane gets too low and comes at us."

"Yes sir. I've got it right here." He showed me the line. "Sir! Fly control says the first flight of *Helldivers* is inbound, five minutes out." The yodel sounded, Fox was two-blocked and the white flag fluttered at Fly Control. Potter turned to check the first airplane in the pattern.

"One more thing, Potter," I shouted at his back, and when he turned around I handed him the 5"x7" green ledger I brought along for the purpose. "You'll have to keep the log too – just write down what I call out after each approach . . . Oh – Here's a pen."

"Aye – er – sir." He took the book and the pen and looked up at me in a confused state. *Got him snowed I guess.*

Potter put the binoculars to his eyes. "Wheels down, flaps down, hook down, sir," Potter announced.

I picked up the first SB2C with a ROGER to see what he would do. "Gimme a call on the deck, Potter."

"Clear deck, sir."

"Barriers?" I looked around to check the deck myself as I gave the *Helldiver* a HIGH DIP.

"Barriers up, sir."

ROGER. *Pretty smooth. I see why they call the SB2C "The Beast." What an ungainly hulk it is, comin' up the groove – and the wide tread on the landing gear – INTIMIDATING!* CUT . . . CRUNCH. *Ah. Fourth wire. Just about right. I could slow 'em down a little – but why tempt fate.* "Potter – Log 'OK,' and circle the numeral four – for fourth wire."

Potter was still writing when the next Beast came out of the ninety but he whirled around in time to report: "Wheels, flaps, and hook down, sir – the first one's still in the gear, sir." We heard the roar of the Helldiver's engine on takeoff. "Clear deck, now sir – barriers comin' up."

And so it went – Potter learning as we went along – and me checking everything – We had a few WAVE-OFFs.

"Nicely done, Harper." Richardson smiled as we stood together on the bridge watching the six F4Us disappear into the haze toward Oahu." You got all those SB-Deucey and *Corsair* pilots qualified, with hardly a glitch."

"Yes sir. Fortunately there was no hurry as there would be if we were running with a task group . . . er – it would sure help a lot if you could assign one more man back there . . . Talker – airplane spotter – deck spotter – and log yeoman is a little overwhelming for a young seaman, sir." *Hmm – I guess I'd better tell him.* "Sir? .

. . I think you should know that I've never brought either one of those machines aboard ship before.

"For God's sake, Harper," "I Fly" sputtered. "Why didn't you tell me that in the first place?"

"I knew you were committed, Commander," I said. "I didn't want both of us to have to worry about it."

"God!," Richardson exclaimed fearfully. "I hope you know something about these night fighters coming out at dusk."

"Yes sir," I replied confidently. "They'll be F6Fs. I've probably got five or six thousand F6F landings on a narrow CVL – including some at night ." I shuddered a little when I thought of that night. "And I've been bouncin' these guys at Barbers point for the last four nights. We know each other pretty well."

"Well, I'm sure glad to hear that." "I Fly" was relieved.

"Hi Harpo," Wujcik greeted me as I sat down at the table in the newly constructed officers' mess at Kahului. "How'd it go with the night fighters?"

"Hey! I'll tell you. "Those friggin' night fighters were slick as grease," I exulted. "Those guys are the cream of the crop. But that *Ommaney Bay* air officer really threw me a curve." I frowned. "Before we got around to the night fighters he brought out a bunch of SB-Deuceys and U-birds for sea qual. You know I've never seen any of those comin' aboard."

"What the hell," Lynch chimed in. "Didn't they have their own LSO?" Lieut.(jg) Francis Lynch, the air group LSO, was about six feet tall – a little pudgy – and had the ruddy face, green eyes, and tawny hair of a New England Irishman.

"It turned out they didn't," I grinned. "I just had to learn fast." Then: "Did I ever tell you how glad I am to have you with us, Frank?"

"No," Frank replied quizzically. "Why is that?"

"Skipper said I could fly with VF-21 if they brought an LSO with them." I related with a grin. "You're it! Besides, Casey said it's fine with him . . . uh . . . thanks again for coming." I looked around the table and saw a familiar face. "Hey Charlie." I got up to shake Charlie Foster's hand. "When'd you get down here?"

"Just came down today to do a little mock fighter direction with VF-21." Foster sat down and shoveled in a bite of potato.

"Glad to have you aboard, Charlie. *Hmm. That gives me an idea.*

Chapter 22: Magic Carpet

The next day, down at the motor pool, still housed in a Quonset hut, I stepped up to the only desk in the office. "I'm Lieutenant Harper, the Landing Signal Officer off *Belleau Wood*. I need a car."

The storekeeper first class showed me a doleful stare that told me he had heard that song before. "Yes sir. I get that request frequently from transient officers." He nettled his brow. "We're pretty short on wheels right at this time, sir. Do you have an authorization?"

Pump it up, J.A. Build a story. "Actually, I'm the commander of the detachment off *Belleau Wood*, down here to work with our new air group."

"Yes sir?" He responded doubtfully, summoning all the courtesy he could muster and posing the next question with obvious skepticism. "What do you have in your detachment?"

Make it good, J.A. "My detachment is comprised of two landing signal officers, one fighter director officer, and two airplanes – F6Fs."

"TWO FIGHTER AIRPLANES?" The sailor was agog. "Off your ship?"

Wow! That impressed him. Let's try this. "No. CASU Ford Island loaned 'em to us for our transportation between here and Ford Island."

I could almost hear the gears grinding in the storekeeper's head as he opened the tattered gray loose leaf notebook. He was not about to be outdone by the CASU. "Let me see." He mused as he ran his finger down the hand written listing. "Hmm. I don't have a jeep or a command car, sir," he announced, obviously trying to help. "Would a weapons carrier be okay?"

Now that you've got him, don't let him off too easily. "Does a weapons carrier carry people?" I inquired, haughtily.

"Oh, yes SIR!" The petty officer jumped out of his chair and stepped smartly to the key rack. "A weapons carrier is made to carry a whole squad of infantry . . . and their weapons, too. Here, let me show you." He grabbed the keys off the hook and marched briskly out the door and toward a motley assortment of olive drab vehicles parked in an uneven line in the dirt parking lot.

"Here she is, sir." The storekeep introduced the small army type truck with a fatherly pat on the right front fender. "Built by G.M. along the lines of their one-and-a-half ton pickup." He led me around to the canvas covered cargo bed of the vehicle, clambered in and gave me a hand up. "You see. These bench seats lift up for access to the weapon storage bays underneath."

Whoa! That weapons storage could hold enough beer to get a whole battalion drunk . . . or a whole squadron? I took the keys, climbed into the driver's seat and cranked up the beast. "Thanks, Chief. Just what I needed," I called as I drove away inspecting all the levers on the floor boards. *I'll be God damned! Four wheel drive . . . creeper gear . . . son-of-a-bitch. I could go anywhere in this boat. Hmm – Sweetie Wilson's?*

"Hi, Sweetie. I'm John. Remember?," I hollered out of the cab of the weapons carrier as a dozen eager pilots bailed out of the covered cargo bed. "Long time, no see."

"Yah. six monf maybe. Hawh?" Sweetie stood, hands on hips, giving me a quizzical look. "Who these guy? I no see befoe."

"Our new air group, Sweetie." I hopped out of the truck and gave her a hug. "And we brought a few cases of beer."

"Too many guy, Johnny," Sweetie scolded. "What we do with so many guy, Hawh?"

"We can have a little luau . . . drink a little beer . . . you do a couple of hulas . . . and we'll get acquainted." We walked arm in arm toward the three thatched huts that made up their little compound. "Then we'll leave you a case or two of beer. How's that?"

"Okay, Johnny." She smiled up at me. "New guy get 'quainted. Yah . . . heah, you 'member Mama . . . an' my sistah Passion Frowah, ovah deah."

I nodded to the obese sister and bowed to take Mama Wilson's hand as a sinister looking polynesian man emerged from one of the huts. "Mama's new husband." Sweetie whispered. "No probrem."

Mama, in her brilliantly flowered muumuu, sat cross legged on a mat of woven palm fronds, her voluminous stomach hiding all but her knees and toes, dwarfing the little ukulele she held in her fat hands, and hinting at a body weight close to three hundred pounds. At a signal from Sweetie she began playing the little ukulele and Sweetie danced her famous hula to the raucous cheers of the little circle of pilots seated cross legged on the ground. Passion Flower brought out a couple of bowls of poi to make it an authentic, if austere, luau.

Picking my way back down the rutted mountain road in four wheel drive was made more difficult by the pilots who chose seating on the front fenders and hood in preference to the crowding of the cargo bed – Hell, I almost lost a couple of 'em on some of the bigger bumps in the road. The boisterous singing didn't help any either. *Well, I did my duty to the new air group. Now I can get back to something more enjoyable – body surfing with Laura. Hmmm.*

23

AIR COMBAT

Cruising west from Pearl I could look out our port hole and see two of our four screening destroyers and a *Boston* class cruiser, all heading west with us to join the Central Pacific fleet for the next major sea-air battles.

At last! Mail from the states. Mom's letter reads like everything is fine, except they can't get any gas for their cars, or new tires, either, without ration stamps – and there aren't enough of those, she says. Says she got a job at the State Employment Office . . . And Pop's gettin' more buildings to design so he had to hire a 4-F draftsman . . . Ah! another warm, fuzzy, letter from Mike in Brooklyn. A letter a month so far. Hmm. – I think she loves me . . . But what the hell happened to Peggy Green? So far just one letter in the year I've been out here. I wonder if my letters are gettin' through to her. Oh well. No use worryin' about it. Just keep on writin' . . . Nothin' from Peggy Rogers either . . . Oh well. At least I've got Mike . . . Oh ho! And Laura. I think we've got something goin' there. That night on the beach at Waihee last week was something to remember – The "grog" she brought in a thermos, the sea food salad, and oooh! Another sensuous swim in the north shore surf . . . These photos she sent bring it all back . . . Mmmmm!

"Hey, Harpo," Commander Casey called from his front row seat as I hunched over to get through the hatch into the fighter ready room. "Come on over here and have a seat." He motioned to the seat next to his.

"Thank you, skipper," I purred as I slipped into the plush ready room seat. "What's up?"

Paddles!

"You've asked to fly with us in combat." It was a statement that required an answer.

"Yes, sir," I affirmed. "Captain Perry has approved it based on the fact that we have three LSOs now . . . and if it's okay with you."

"Yeah, but the Captain laid a number of limitations on us," Casey began. "First; you're not allowed to fly strikes – just CAP; maximum one flight per day; and he wants to keep you on the ship in heavy weather – just in case."

"Yeah," I groused. "I knew he'd put some restrictions on it – anyway, I'll take what I can get – but is that going to be too much trouble for you?"

"Oh, no!" Casey raised his right hand and flashed his crooked grin. "It's okay with me – I'm glad to have you." He slapped me on the shoulder. "But we'll have to schedule you as a substitute section leader – even though you're senior enough to have a division. Okay?"

"Hell yes, skipper." I grinned like a Chessie cat. "Like I said, I'll take what I can get, thank you . . . uh . . . by the way. Would you approve my transfer into your squadron?"

Casey gave me a wry grin. "Yeah, Captain Perry said you might want to do that too – said it was okay with him if I trade Lynch for you . . . and that's okay with me." Then there was a sort of a welcoming smile. "Just write up a request and I'll sign it."

Belleau Wood swung at anchor in Seeadler Harbor on the island of Manus, just north of New Guinea, for a short respite in the fleet's steady westward push. As the sun sank in the west, I stood at the head of the gangway and watched the familiar tow head bound out of the boat and take his lean six foot frame up the gangway, two rungs at a stride. "Hi, Jonny. Glad you could make it. Come on." We shook hands and I reached up to squeeze his shoulder with my left hand. Then, to the Officer of the Day: "This is Captain Burton, Seventh Cavalry, U.S. Army." I announced proudly. "He's my guest."

Jonathan Rowall Burton had been my roommate in the ΣAE house at Michigan State College where he had majored in horses – in and out of the R.O.T.C. Jon had lost some of the youth and innocence that had marked his handsome Anglo-Saxon features, but he still projected a shy, almost self deprecating manner.

"God damn! Harp. You're lookin' good," Burton exclaimed. "Uh . . . even with the moustache. What the hell is that for – tempting girls?"

"Hah!," I laughed. "See any girls around here? But I'll tell you something. We

248

just got our mail today and there was a letter from Peggy Green – you remember her – my girlfriend at State?" I was ecstatic. "First letter in almost a year – How's your love life?"

"Jeez, Harp." Burton grinned. "I didn't know you were that stuck on her." Then, trying his Aussi accent: "Oi ran across a lovely Austreyelian guhl in Brisbane that I loik a lot." His eyes softened as he thought of her and shifted back to "American." "I think I'll marry her . . . if I ever get out of this thing alive."

"You've got the right idea, Jonny," I crowed, giving him a slap on the back. "Next time I get back to the states I'm gonna get married . . . to someone . . . Peggy, I hope."

"Wow!," Burton exclaimed, as we entered the wardroom for dinner. "Is this your mess hall?"

"Please!," I cried, feigning pain. "Officers' mess on a ship is . . . " I paused for effect and lifted my chin haughtily. "The Wardroom."

"Well! Pardon me!," Jonny snickered as he bowed in mock obeisance.

I stopped at the linen swathed buffet and picked up two silver ringed linen napkins and handed Burton the one with the unmarked ring. "Here. This is yours for tonight."

"God damn! You swabbies sure have it plush – white table cloths and all." Burton's eyes widened as we sidled over to my regular table." Do you guys live like this all the time?"

"Yeah," I affirmed, jauntily. "Except when we're in a Typhoon."

I stepped to my usual place at the table, hauling Jonny by the elbow. "Hey, you guys. I want you to meet Captain Jonny Burton, my college room mate, horse cavalryman, and hero of the Seventh Cavalry's invasion of Los Negros," I announced, holding Jonny's hand high.

"Here's to the Army . . . and Custer's cavalry," crowed Lieutenant Billy Biggers, the blond fighter pilot with the whalers moustache and laughing green eyes. Billy had a lean, wiry body and a face to match.

"Hear! Hear!" Everyone at the table saluted, raising their water glasses in a toast.

"Aww . . ." Jonny sputtered. "That's too much, Harp."

"Here, Jonny," I began the introductions as we took our seats. "I want you to meet the aces of Fighting Twenty-one." Everyone laughed 'cause no one was an ace – yet. "There's Billy Biggers, your toastmaster . . . Terry Rice is the big guy at the head of the table, and that's his wingman, Johnny Nellis – call him 'Nellie' –

sittin' next to him . . . and my assistant LSO, Walt Wujcik, is sitting next to you." There were head nods all around and Wujcik and Burton shook hands as our mess steward delivered our dinner plates.

Burton's eyes widened and his mouth dropped open. "What's this? He poked at his steak. "T-Bone steak and fries? Incredible! You guys really know how to live."

"That's your treat for the day," I scolded. Then: "Hey, Jonny. What's happened to you since you left State?"

"You know I got orders to the Seventh Cavalry at Fort Riley – Custer's old outfit." He began, with a nod to Biggers. "The answer to my wildest dreams – horse cavalry."

"Yeah," I recalled. "You had just gotten 'em when I last visited the campus to take Peggy to her junior prom." I savored the memory.

"You mean you guys are still ridin' horses?," Rice growled in his usually gruff manner. The reason I called Lieutenant Terry Rice "the big guy" was because of his big face, jowls and all, with the fierce gray eyes and the perpetual frown, contrasting with his lean, muscular, six foot body.

"We were then." Jonny's pride showed. "Our colonel was able to maintain the horse cavalry tradition even when all the other cavalry divisions were mechanized or converted to infantry. Hell, we brought our horses with us to Australia when we joined MacArthur's Army.

"What the hell did you do with the horses in the war zone?," Rice demanded in his Oklahoma drawl.

"Played Polo," Jonny answered, apologetically.

"POLO?," Biggers exclaimed as the table erupted in derisive laughter.

"Hey! Don't laugh, fellas." I held up my hands for quiet. "Don't forget the Seventh landed on Los Negros last month . . . without horses – Right, Jonny?"

"Right, Harp." Burton looked down at his plate and swallowed deeply. "That was rough . . . God! I thought the Marines were supposed to do all the amphibious landings. We found out the hard way that the colonel had spent too much time with horse training and not enough on infantry tactics." He swept a tear away with some embarrassment. "I lost half of my company . . . including a couple of shave tails fresh out of West Point." His composure returned. "But there are no more Japs on Los Negros . . . no live ones, anyway."

"Hey, Collins," Rice growled again, pointing his spoon at the dish the steward had just placed before him. "What the hell is this?"

Chapter 23: Air Combat

"Butter Pecan, sir," Collins answered proudly as he placed a dish at Burton's place.

"Ice cream?" Burton was ecstatic. "ICE CREAM! Jesus Christ!" He lifted his eyes to the ceiling and raised his arms as though in prayer. "I must've gotten killed on Los Negros and gone to heaven – You know how I love ice cream, Harp." He peered at me in mock contempt. "You did this on purpose. Didn't you?"

"Sure did Jonny." I clapped him on the back. "I remember when we used to drive down to that little ice cream parlor on Lansing's east end in your 1937 Chevy, get a gallon of ice cream each, and just sit in the car and eat the whole thing . . . out of the carton – Yum."

"Fagan Seven, this is Fagan," the voice of our fighter director squawked in my ears as Terry Rice led his division in lazy circles at eighteen thousand feet and maximum endurance settings awaiting instructions from CIC. "Vector three one zero, angels fifteen, BUSTER. Over."

"Fagan. This is Fagan Seven," Rice replied. "Turning vector three one zero, goin' to angels fifteen – BUSTER. Wilco."

Rice's division, complete with me as section lead, had been launched a half hour earlier as Combat Air Patrol for the northwest sector while other task group aircraft struck Okinawa. Nellis flew Rice's wing and Ensign Art Manger, fresh out of advanced training, was my wingman. I pulled my plotting board out and turned the frosted plexiglass disk over the Mercator grid to a heading of 310 degrees and marked my progress while taking a few whiffs from my oxygen mask.

Cruising BUSTER in a combat spread at fifteen thousand feet Rice reported, "Fagan. This is Fagan Seven. Comin' up on a solid cloud deck – tops about angels nine. Over.

"Roger, Fagan Seven. New vector two nine zero, hold angels fifteen at BUSTER. Fagan Seven three, break to vector three zero zero, angels five, BUSTER, and report cloud base. Acknowledge."

"Fagan Seven, here. Turning to two nine zero, angels fifteen Wilco."

"Fagan, this is Fagan Seven Three, vector three zero zero, angels five – BUSTER. Wilco," I acknowledged, rolling into a steep glide and finding my new heading. Manger stuck to my right wing.

"Fagan, this is Fagan Seven Three, cloud base is angels seven. Over."

"Fagan Seven Three, this is Fagan. New vector three five zero, angels six, GATE. Fagan Seven, vector three six zero, hold angels fifteen, GATE. Acknowledge!"

Paddles!

"Fagan Seven Three here, on vector three five zero, angels six, comin' to GATE. Wilco!" I turned the plotting board vector to 350° and made another mark.

"This is Fagan Seven, now vector three six zero – angels fifteen – Wilco GATE."

"Fagan Seven AND Seven Three. Bogey is eleven o'clock, four miles, crossing port to starboard, speed three twenty, angels uncertain."

"TALLY HO! This is Fagan Seven Three," I screamed into the mike as I rolled right, into a shallow dive, keeping the target in sight. I could feel the blood coursing through my temples. "TALLY HO one twin engine bandit – angels four – turning port – Very fast! Over." I turned sharply to follow the sleek, olive camouflaged aircraft, turned the gun charging handles to FIRE and punched them both in, then flipped the gun switches on. The momentary rumble I felt through the aircraft structure when I touched the trigger on the stick told me all six guns were firing – but when I looked around, Manger was GONE!

"Hey, Harpo! Terry here – Fagan acknowledged your TALLY HO – did you get it?"

"Naw," I gasped, my heart racing in anticipation of the kill. "I must be below radio horizon. You'll have to relay." I took a deep breath. "Tell 'em I'm on his tail, closing." Another breath. "Looks like a 'Fran' – You know, that twin engine Jap recon bird . . . but I lost Manger. Over." I flipped the water injection switch on to eke out a few more knots while adjusting my plotting board heading index.

"Fagan. This is Fagan Seven. Fagan Seven Three identifies bandit as a 'Fran' . . . advises Fagan Seven Four detached . . ." Then: "Fagan's got it, Harpo. Hey! Where the hell are you?"

Shit! How the hell do I know. "Under the clouds, Terry – but we must be pretty close," I wheezed. *God damn! This son-of-a-bitch is goin' like a striped ass ape . . . I'm barely gainin' on 'im . . . better drop my belly tank . . . Yeah. That's better. I'm closin' on 'im now . . . Down to a thousand feet now . . . Whoa! What was that?* It looked like a blinking flashlight in his tail. *God damn! it's the tail gunner. And I'm his target. Jink, for Christ's sake. JINK!*

"Fagan Seven Three, this is Seven Four. Where are you?" It was Manger.

"Heading Three Four Five, angels one, balls to the wall," I screamed. "Drop your tank – water injection – come on!" I was still jinking to avoid the tail gunner's fire and closing . . . at a snails pace it seemed.

"Mister Harper," came Manger's plaintive wail. "If you don't answer, I'm goin' home."

I put the pipper on that tail gun and measured the wing span in my sight –

252

Chapter 23: Air Combat

Almost there. Oh oh! He's blinkin' again – JINK! "Hey, Art!," I yelled. "Drop your belly tank and hit water injection. Heading three five five now – angels ONE! – COME ON!"

Hmm. No answer. I guess he's goin' back to the ship. Pipper back on the tail gun – Ahah! Range right – FIRE! The tracers crossed on my side of the "Fran" but some of them slammed into the tail, blasting pieces off the fuselage. *Hey! No more blinks from the tail. I must've gotten the tail gunner . . . Now move in a little closer . . . Pipper on the right engine. Now – FIRE! Hah! Feel the guns rattle – Tracers goin' into the engine – SMOKE! – I got 'im! – Keep firing – now pipper on the cockpit – Whoa! Tracers goin' out in circles now – STOP FIRING! Oh Shit! Target fixation – probably burned out all six barrels, you dumb ass!* I kicked the gun charging handles frantically – hoping – hoping – then touched the trigger – POP POP POP. *Shit! Just one gun firing. Well, right engine's smokin', he's slowin' down, and losin' altitude – down to seven hundred feet – gotta finish 'im off – try a beam run.* I pulled out to his port side and ahead, turned into my run, put the pipper ahead of the port engine and squeezed off three short bursts with my one gun. *SMOKE! Squeeze again! Nothing. Pull up – charge guns – try again. Both engines smokin'. How can he hold altitude? Into my run now – pipper on the cockpit – squeeze!* POP POP POP . . . *Nothing – charge guns – squeeze – still nothing. God! I hope I don't get jumped on the way home. Well. Let's watch 'im go in. He can't hold it much longer.* I took a position above and to the right to watch him splash. *Now he's down to about a hundred and twenty knots – can't last much longer . . . Oops – fuel gettin' low – and I'm probably a hundred and fifty miles out . . . Why the hell doesn't he go in? – Hell! I'd better get goin' or I won't make it back.*

Reluctantly, I banked right to a heading of one six five and took one more look back, only to see the "Fran" cruising along with both engines trailing smoke. *Maybe that one got away . . . thanks to my buck fever.* Doing the reverse plot on my plotting board told me I should shave my heading to one four five. "Hey, Terry. Harpo here – I got both engines smokin' but he wouldn't go down." I winced at the admission I had to make next. "I'm out o' ammo and low on gas, heading one four five, climbing to angels ten so the ship's radar can paint me."

My heart was still pumping so hard I could feel it in my toes. *Cool down, J.A. You're actin' like the first time you shot a rabbit with your .22 – freaked out! You're still racin' the engine at forty inches. CUT BACK!* I levelled off at ten thousand feet and eased back to 28 inches and 1,800 RPM. *Oh Oh! Oil all over the friggin' windshield – must have an oil leak – Hey! Engine settings back up to 35*

Paddles!

inches and 2,500 RPM – How'd that happen – Come on, J.A., settle down – ease her back. I took a deep breath, reset to lower power settings, and turned on the YE beacon. *Yeah! I got a SUGAR on the YE. Hmm. What the hell does that mean?* I fingered the daily YE beacon code I had taped to the instrument panel. *Okay. I'm in the 270 degree sector. Heading to the ship, 090. Stay calm now, J.A.*

The wakes of the task group ships were barely visible in the gathering dusk as I approached the destroyer screen. BOOM! I felt a jolt. *What the hell was THAT?* I looked down to see one of the destroyers blink at me – a BIG blink – like a SEARCHLIGHT! *Whoa! They're shootin' at me. Get the hell out o' here.* I banked sharply and dove away from the task group. *Those bastards! . . . Shootin' at a friendly . . . Oops! I forgot my IFF. That's why they're shootin'. Okay, idiot. On with the IFF.* I groped for the guarded switch and flipped it up – then cautiously turned back toward the force, descending to a thousand feet to find *Belleau Wood.* Then down to masthead level – hook down – past the island. *Ahah . . . FOX two blocked – they're ready for me – Oops! still fast – 180 knots – Slow down. God Damn it! – Gear, flaps, down – still 120 knots downwind – SLOW DOWN!* Out of the ninety Wujcik gives me a steady HIGH – then shakes it for emphasis. *Look at your airspeed, idiot! Still ninety knots.* Wujcik is shaking a FAST – Then WAVE-OFF. Full throttle, gear, flaps, up. *Settle down, DAMN IT! It's gettin' dark fast and you're low on fuel. Keep this up and you'll end up in the drink . . . Now. Down to ninety knots on the downwind. God! I feel like I'm gonna spin in. Oops! Forgot the flaps – Gear, flaps, down, now – feel the lift – But you've gotta slow down some more out of the ninety.* Wujcik shakes a HIGH – Then a FAST – HIGH again – FAST – CUT. *God damn! Weej. I'm still high and too fast. You shouldn't have cut me – Deck's waaay down there – Dump the nose, J.A. . . . . Oww! Here comes the deck – Tail down, HARD! Oh SHIT! We're climbin' – over the barriers – stand by to die, J.A.* WHUP . . . CRUNCH. *Thank you, God. Or whatever sea god puts wires in hooks.* Badly shaken by this close call, I sat frozen in my seat until Cobbs jumped up on the wing.

"Guns safe, Harpo?"

"Oh – uh – yeah." I gasped as I turned the charging handles to safe, punched them in, and snapped the gun switches off. *Shit! I forgot to turn on the gun camera.*

Down in the ready room, Rice, Nellis, and Manger were waiting for me. "Glad you made it," Rice growled.

I stomped over to the trio. "God damn it! Manger. Where the hell did you go, for Christ's sake?"

Chapter 23: Air Combat

Manger closed his eyes and flinched from the shower of spit I had released. "When you sped up, I couldn't keep up, sir." He took one step back. "Then I saw a big splash in the water and I thought you'd been shot down." He took a sidelong look at Rice. "I'm sure glad you made it, sir."

"That splash was my belly tank, damn it! . . . Yeah. I made it alright." I raged. "But no thanks to you. Hell, I answered all your calls."

"Radioman checked my radio when I got back, sir – receiver crapped out."

"Hmm." *Well, nobody mentioned that I blew out at least five gun barrels and probably an engine, with only a probable to show for it – and no pictures at that. I wouldn't blame 'em if they grounded me. I'll see what's scheduled for tomorrow . . . Well, I'm scheduled to fly CAP with Rice's division AT 0940 . . . They could change that . . . I'll check tomorrow.*

The next day, I eased into the ready room and took a peek at the flight schedule. *Hmmm. Another strike on Formosa and I'm still scheduled for launch with Rice's division at 0940.*

"Hey, Harpo!," Rice grumbled. "Get your God damned gear on. We're launchin' at 0930.

I'll be God damned. I'm not grounded . . . and Rice seems pleased to have me in his division . . . as pleased as he ever gets. "Shit! I thought it was 0940, Terry."

"Some son-of-a-bitch changed it," Rice groused. "Get your ass in gear. We're briefin' in ten minutes and . . . uh . . . save us the airplane this time, will you." He gave a mischievous snicker and a staged frown – first time I'd seen him laugh. "Your last combat adventure cost us a new engine, six guns, a belly tank, and a few bullet holes to fill." He slapped me on the back. "But Intelligence reports the Japs lost a *'Fran'* south of Kyushu last night . . . right where we were . . . Nice goin."

"Thanks . . . See you in ten minutes." I shouted over my shoulder on my way to my stateroom to change. *I'll be God damned! He seems to think my performance was okay . . . Well. He doesn't know how badly I screwed up.*

Up on CAP again, Rice's division circled lazily in the northwest quadrant at twenty thousand feet, oxygen masks clamped firmly in place. Keely had swapped our wingmen so Manger was on Rice's wing and Nellis was on mine.

"Fagan Seven – this is Fagan. Vector three one zero – angels fifteen – BUSTER. Acknowledge."

"Fagan. Fagan Seven here – Vector three one zero – angels fifteen – BUSTER

– Wilco." Rice wheezed into his oxygen mask as he turned sharply to the specified heading and accelerated during the gentle glide down to fifteen thousand feet as Nellis and I slid out to the left in our combat spread.

"Fagan Seven – This is Fagan – Vector two eight five – angels ten – Acknowledge."

"Fagan Seven here. Vector two eight five, angels ten. Wilco." Then: "Harpo – Double your spread."

"Harpo here. Double spread. WILCO," I confirmed as I kicked the gun chargers in the "Fire" position, flipped gun and camera switches on, unclipped my oxygen mask, and noted the heading on my plotting board. *Pretty cool, J.A. – a hell of a lot better'n my "Fran" chase.* I slid my section left about a half mile, adding power to hold a beam position on Terry until I resumed the commanded vector.

"Fagan Seven. This is Fagan. Bogey one o'clock down, five miles, crossing right to left. Over."

"TALLY HO!," I called as I banked sharply left, checking Nellis stuck on my right wing. "This is Seven Three – bandit is single engine recon machine . . . *Myrt* I think . . . heading two four zero, angels eight. Whoa! Now turning right." I pulled in behind the two seater and noticed I was closing rapidly. I felt calm. *Okay, J.A. – Pipper on the right wing root – fuel tank – QUICK SQUEEZE!* BRRRIPP. The short burst converged right over the wing root. *Yeah! Perfect range. Now lower the pipper just below the wing root – QUICK SQUEEZE!* BRRRIPP. Flame engulfed the right side of "Myrt's" fuselage and a few chunks of metal flew by the side of my canopy. *Whoa! LOOK OUT!* I flinched as Nellis slid in just over my propeller, firing continuously and spraying .50 cal brass, right in my face, it seemed. *Oh Shit! There goes my propeller. PUSH DOWN! Hey, look. We got 'im.* Myrt's right wing snapped off at the flaming root section and flew by, just missing Nellis and me as the Myrt entered a violent spin downward – toward the white caps – still flaming brightly.

"Fagan – Fagan Seven Three here – Splash one *Myrt*," I reported, coolly. "Got one parachute – we're goin' in to strafe 'im."

"Fagan Seven Three – BREAK OFF! BREAK OFF! Flag's sending a can out to capture the survivors. Rejoin Fagan Seven – ACKNOWLEDGE!"

"Fagan Seven Three here – Break off – WILCO!" I looked around to see Terry and Art right behind us so I slowed down to let them pass and then rejoined.

24

NO JOY

"SCRAMBLE FOUR FIGHTERS!," came the order over the squawk box in the ready room where Rice's division stood by in full flight gear, ready for the scramble order. "FOR YOUR INFO: CAP HAS ENGAGED A LARGE FLIGHT OF BETTYS ESCORTED BY MANY FIGHTERS HEADED FOR FORMOSA – NOW ABOUT SEVENTY MILES OUT. GO GET 'EM!"

"Let's go!," Rice growled, and the four of us ran for the exit hatch and the catwalk ladder leading to the flight deck.

My heart pounded as I moved furtively among the airplanes to conceal myself from Captain Perry's view. *Hot Damn! Another opportunity. Hell! This could be another Turkey Shoot – with me in it! Don't stop me now, skipper.* I thought as I pulled down my goggles as a disguise and climbed into the *Hellcat*. The plane captain helped me with the shoulder straps and I thought: *Okay, J.A. Turn on the gun camera NOW, so you don't forget it again.* I flipped the gun camera switch up.

"STAND BY TO START ENGINES," blared the bull horn. "STAND CLEAR OF PROPELLERS."

Yeah! I'm gonna make it. And It'll be the battle of my life. I could actually hear my heart pumping.

"MISTER HARPER," the bull horn shouted. *Oh shit! Caught in the act.* "LEAVE THAT AIRCRAFT! MISTER TURNER WILL TAKE YOUR PLACE."

I felt the energy drain from my body as Turner ran toward me in full flight gear. *God damn! Skipper sure is being cautious. You'd think Weej couldn't cut it.*

Paddles!

He can! I unbuckled the seat belt, slid off the wing and crept dejectedly back to the ready room.

The next day, I sat in my airplane going over the check-off list, second in line for the catapult – Terry Rice had already been launched. I searched the cumulus dotted sky for any sign of the large enemy raid from Clark Field which, according to the ready room announcement, posed an immediate threat to the task group. *Don't stop me now, Skipper.* I prayed.

The flag had ordered all flyable aircraft launched immediately to blunt the approaching threat and to save them from possible damage aboard their ships. Over half of our aircraft had been launched an hour earlier to strike airfields around Manila. The scene on the flight deck was one of sheer pandemonium; with fighters roaring off the catapult even as pilots ran to their aircraft, dodging the planes taxiing forward, while the deck crew continued to bring airplanes up on the after elevator. Some of the fighters were still armed with HVARs – High Velocity Aircraft Rockets with 5" armor piercing warheads – for the next strike. I would be launched as Rice's section leader, as usual, with Ensign Hugh Tate on my wing. Hugh was an admiral's son, but was only nineteen – with brash adolescent ways – the teen aged wonder.

On the catapult now . . . feel the bridle tension . . . Two fingers from Dave Greenberg . . . full throttle – grab the throttle hold fitting – salute – stick in neutral and right elbow in my gut. SHHWOOONK. *Airborne! Hold level flight – gear up – gentle bank right – flaps up. Now where the hell's Nellie . . . There, dead ahead, and Terry's just starting to make his left turn for the rendezvous . . . Ahh! here comes Tate, just off the cat.*

BANG! BANG! Two sharp jolts. *God damn! There goes a Betty the other way and all the ships are shootin' at him – just missed me!.* "Hey Terry. This is Harpo. The ships are shooting at everything in sight – and a *Betty* just went by me goin' the other way. We better get outside the screen – quick."

"Flight. This is Terry. Power to GATE – Follow me – Lets get the hell out of here." Rice led us outside the screen and into our rendezvous sector, climbing to angels fifteen. Nellis was tucked in tight on Rice's left wing and Tate was glued on my right wing – a pretty sight.

BOOM! BOOM! The explosions rocked our aircraft and left two small black clouds close aboard to starboard where the five inch shells had burst. As Rice banked sharply and dove away from the force we could look down and see the destroyer blinking at us. BOOM! BOOM! Black clouds burst right off Nellis' left wing.

"BREAK UP! BREAK UP!," Rice yelled into the radio. "Every man for himself!" Then: "Fagan. This is Fagan Seven. Tell that God damned can to stop shootin' at us. Over."

"I'll get that son-of-a-bitch!" I recognized Tate's shrill scream. "I've got six HVARs and I'm gonna put 'em all on that friggin' can." He had one of the airplanes armed with HVARs and had peeled off into a dive toward the offending destroyer.

I banked sharply to follow him. BOOM! BOOM! – Two more bursts – right between Tate and me. "Hold your fire, Hugh, God damn it. HOLD YOUR FIRE! Get back on my wing and we'll get the hell out of here . . . THAT'S AN ORDER. ACKNOWLEDGE!"

"Fagan Seven. This is Fagan. Word's goin' out to the screen but we're under attack by many *Bettys, Vals,* and *Zekes.* Vector two five zero to intercept the rest of the raid . . . uh . . . BUSTER!"

"Fagan, Fagan Seven here. We're already at GATE, and we're scattered to avoid all gettin' shot down by one shell from that damned can . . . oh . . . What are bogey angels?" Then: "Flight. This is Terry. Acknowledge vector and hold GATE . . . RENDEZVOUS ASAP!"

"OKAY – OKAY!," was Tate's reluctant reply. "But what the hell am I gonna do with these friggin' rockets?"

"Jettison 'em, for Christ's sake, Hugh," I yelled as Tate slid back under my right wing. "We're goin' vector two five zero for the big dog fight." I saw Tate's six rockets fall away. *Whew! That was close. God! Tate could've wiped out the whole crew of that destroyer. Well . . . They could've shot us down too . . . if their aim had been better.* "You got that, Fagan? This is Fagan Seven Three."

"I got it Fagan Seven Three. Bogies all around . . . angels seven to twelve – hold vector two five zero. Over."

"TALLY HO! This is Fagan Seven. Three Vals headin' your way. Stand by."

"I have you in sight, Terry . . . Slow down . . . I'll join up." It was Nellis.

"I'm in my run, Nellie. Pick a target and go on in!"

"TALLY HO! Fagan Seven Four's got a straggler." I looked around to see Tate peel off sharply and head for a dot on the horizon. I followed.

"This is Fagan Seven. Splash one Val . . . Oops!" Gunfire was audible over Rice's radio. "Scratch that . . . splash TWO Vals!"

Paddles!

"Fagan Seven Two here," Nellis screamed. "Splash one Val."

"Fagan Seven Four, here. NO JOY." He was disappointed. "It was a damned F6 . . . goin' the wrong way."

The rest of the flight brought the same results for Tate and me – NO JOY.

It was the day after the Army landings on Leyte and there we sat, sucking oxygen at eighteen thousand feet, circling at maximum endurance power settings, Nellis on Rice's wing and Jim McFadden on mine. We could see *Belleau Wood* hooked up to the fleet oiler on her starboard while a destroyer drank from the oiler's starboard hoses.

I'll be damned. No action in three and a half hours. Not a sign of a bogie anywhere in the area. Ho Hum. Looks like our strikes up and down the Philippines must have cleaned out all the Jap aircraft in the area. Well, another half hour up here and we get relieved.

"Hello Fagan Seven – this is Fagan – expect a thirty minute delay in your relief due to refueling operation just getting underway. Acknowledge."

"Fagan Seven here. Thirty minute delay. WILCO."

Damn! Thirty more minutes up here. Hell, if they leave us up here much longer we won't have enough fuel to respond to a vector. Hmm . . . Look at those clouds building up just west of us . . . Gonna be a big ass thunderbumper. God damn! I thought I could hold it but it looks like I'll have to figure out how to use this relief tube at eighteen thousand feet – while flyin' formation . . . Whew! That's cold.

Thirty minutes later: "Fagan seven. This is Fagan. We're launching your relief now. Begin your descent. Over."

Yeah. I see the four fighters comin' off the catapult . . . But the ship is headed straight for that big thunderstorm . . . That's normal, since wind blows away from the base of a thunderstorm . . . Oh oh – There she goes – zip – right into the thunderstorm.

"Hello Fagan Seven. This is Fagan. Your relief is airborne, climbing to station. Aerology advises we'll find favorable winds west of the storm – Ship's course now two eight five, speed twenty – Call when you're west of the storm – Over."

"Flight. This is Fagan Seven. This thunderbumper's too wide to go around. I'll hold angels fifteen and vector two eight five through the storm. Stick with me." Rice headed straight for the mass of gray and white.

God damn! This air is rough . . . feels like we're goin' up and down fifty to a hundred feet . . . Whoa! visibility close to zilch . . . just occasional glimpses of

Chapter 24: No Joy

Terry's airplane and I can't see Nellie at all . . . Oops! they disappeared . . . better get some separation . . . ease right to vector . . . How the hell do I know, with the directional gyro swingin' plus and minus twenty degrees. "This is Harpo – I lost you, Terry – Goin' to vector two nine five – as close as I can hold it – for separation . . . Mac's still with me." CRASH! *Oww! Lightning! Just off my left wing . . . didn't hit me 'cause all I felt was a big jolt – no buzz . . . Oh oh! How's Mac?* I looked back to starboard. *Ahh! Still there!*

"Roger Harpo – I'll hold two eight five – See you on the other side. I lost Nellie – but he'll get through okay."

"Hang in there, Mac," I called as I looked down at McFadden's upturned face, only about fifteen feet below me, lighted by distant lightning. *No answer . . . Must be too busy holdin' position to call.*

At last! Blessed sunshine . . . Hah! There's Mac, stuck right there on my right wing – now about twenty five feet away. "Nice goin' Mac. You stuck tight," I called . . . still no answer. "Fagan – This is Fagan Seven Three – In the clear now – with Fagan Seven Four – Y-E says you bear about one five zero, true – right in the middle of the storm."

"Fagan Seven Three – This is Fagan – Fly Control advises we are still in the storm – Orbit your position and wait – we'll be out soon. Where's Fagan Seven? Over."

"Fagan Seven, here. Still in the cloud, heading two eight zero. Fagan Seven Two separated."

"This is Fagan Seven Two. still in the cloud, heading two seven zero."

By the looks of the wind streaks and white caps we'll have to wait 'til the ship takes a position well clear of the storm before she turns back to recover us . . . Jeez! We've already been up over five hours. We could get low on fuel before old Beulah can take us aboard . . . just circle in the clear and keep her at max endurance, J.A. I looked over to Mac and gave him a thumbs up – it was a question. To my relief Mac returned my signal. *Hmm. I guess his radio must've gone dead.*

Out of the corner of my eye I noticed Mac was rocking his wings violently. When I looked, he was pointing emphatically to the south. *Ahh! There's the ship, just coming out of the storm.*

"Hello Fagan. This is Fagan Seven Three. Have you in sight about five miles south of our position, in the clear."

"Roger, Seven Three – Bridge advises we're maneuvering for wind position – Expect Charlie in five or ten minutes. Over."

Paddles!

"Roger, Fagan. Ten minutes. We're lettin' down. Over."

Down to masthead level . . . flight deck still wet and glistening from the heavy rain . . . FOX at the dip . . . but she's still goin' down wind . . . Kickin' up a good wake . . . probably about thirty knots – good . . . Ahh. turnin' to port now . . . Okay, J.A. maneuver for the wind streaks . . . Wonder where Terry and Nellie went . . . Up the wind streaks now . . . Hook down. I looked over at Mac and got a thumbs up as his tailhook came out. *Ship's just about there now . . . Break . . . downwind . . . gear down . . . flaps . . . at the ninety . . . Hmm. Lynch is wavin' – Weej behind him . . .* ROGER . . . HIGH DIP . . . CUT . . . SCREEEE . . . *I'm down – taxiing forward . . . Rain on the windshield – not much time for Mac . . . Get out of the gear, quick!* I looked back to see Mac comin' up the groove in good position – perfect interval.

Out of the airplane I ran for the ready room – through heavy rain by now – as the ship heeled sharply to port, turning to get back out in the open to recover Terry and Nellie.

Back in the ready room I was just hanging up my rain soaked helmet and life jacket when Mac burst into the room. "Hey, Mac. Nice goin'. You stuck to me like glue through that whole storm – and it was rough in there."

"Had to stick, Harpo." McFadden shook his head. "My God damned radio crapped out sometime in the middle of the flight so I didn't know what the hell was goin' on." His hands shook when he tried to light a cigarette. "It was pretty God damned quiet up there anyway with no bogies, but when the ship launched our relief and disappeared into that thunderstorm I knew there had to be some conversation I wasn't hearing. Then when you guys headed for that big cloud I knew I had to stick on your wing come hell or high water or I'd never find the ship. Shit! My Y-E wasn't workin' either. Must've been some electrical failure."

Twenty minutes later Rice and Nellie got back aboard just before the ship plunged back into the thunderstorm. *Hmm. Five and a half hours. Longest flight I've ever logged.*

25

KAMIKAZE

It was a beautiful, crystal clear day on the Pacific. We had launched the second Combat Air Patrol of the day and I was lounging on the forecastle in my swimming trunks soaking up the midday sun. We weren't launching strikes anymore since General Douglas MacArthur, Commander-in-Chief Southwest Pacific, had ordered the Pacific Fleet to cease all air strikes in the Philippines. I guess he reasoned that the squadron of P-38 *Lightnings* installed at the newly secured Tacloban Airfield on Leyte was enough to protect his toe hold in the Visayans. One squadron to replace the entire air power of Halsey's Third Fleet fast carriers and the jeep carriers of Kinkaid's Seventh Fleet. This order freed the Japs to repair the runways at Clark Field and bring in more aircraft to make a last stand in the Philippines. We had already lost *Princeton* just a week earlier – sunk by a Japanese bomber based on Luzon. Still, MacArthur held to his order, further flaunting his ego. The latest ready room joke was spawned by the report that the Japanese had actually organized their inexperienced pilots into the "Kamikaze Corps" named for the legendary Kamikaze – *Divine Wind* – which saved the Japanese from defeat in an earlier war. The story went like this:

The Japanese admiral briefed the room full of young pilots on their duty as Kamikaze – "Dive your planes into the American carriers to the glory of Emperor Hirohito. Any questions?" One young ensign at the back of the room rose to ask: "Admiral, SUH! What'a you, out'o you fuckin' mind?"

Paddles!

Raucous laughter greeted this dark humor but we all knew that such attacks would be more difficult to defend against.

Toooweee. "GUNNERY DEPARTMENT, MAN YOUR GENERAL QUARTERS STATIONS," blared the Forecastle speaker.

"Hi Leo," I called up to Dulacki when he arrived at the Marines' 40MM mount on the forecastle. "What the hell's goin' on?"

"Big raid comin' in from up north," Leo called back. "Hey! You better get your ass in gear. We'll be at General Quarters in a few minutes."

"Thanks, Leo," I yelled as I made for the water tight door leading into officers' country.

CLANG CLANG CLANG. "ALL HANDS, MAN YOUR BATTLE STATIONS!" CLANG CLANG CLANG. "ALL HANDS . . ."

Up the ladder I went, two rungs at a time. Then down the passageway on a dead run . . . into my stateroom. *Off with the trunks . . . scivvie shorts on . . . shirt . . . pants . . . socks . . . boondockers . . . never mind lacin' 'em . . . battle helmet? Hell! It's up in the ready room – and so's my life jacket. Come on! Up the ladder and into the ready room.* "Where'd everybody go?" I asked Art Manger, the only pilot in the ready room.

"Oh, hi Harpo." Manger tossed me a greeting as I whizzed by toward the bulkhead hook that held my steel helmet and life jacket. "We're launchin' eight fighters right now . . . " CLANK – WHOOSH – CLONK. The catapult was just above our heads. "There goes another one – Then we got orders to man all airplanes to get 'em in the air in case we get hit."

I picked my helmet off the hook and got it half way down on my head when: WHUMP – The room shook and things fell off bulkhead hooks. "What the hell was THAT?" I screamed, buckling the chin strap on my helmet.

"God Damn! We must've gotten hit," Manger wailed.

Up on the flight deck the scene was something out of a war movie – the brilliant orange flame that engulfed the fighters parked aft produced a billowing column of black smoke, trailing off downwind, off our starboard quarter. .50 cal ammunition was exploding, throwing bullets and shrapnel in every direction and endangering the TBFs parked in a line along the starboard side.

"Hey, Mister Harper!," the yellow shirted plane director called. "Get up in that cockpit and man the brakes, sir!" He pointed to the TBF closest to the raging fire.

Chapter 25: Kamikaze

"Okay, 'Ski'." I was ready to help. "But what the hell happened?"

"Kamikaze! . . . Hit right in the middle of all those airplanes back there." Then Ski pointed off to our port quarter. "They got the *Franklin* too."

I climbed up on the wing root and turned to port to see a pillar of black smoke issuing from the yellow glow, amidships on *Franklin*. Then, with me in the cockpit of the TBF the crew pushed it forward out of range of the blazing debris.

Back on deck, along the starboard side, I noticed an unused fire hose. "Hey you guys. Get your asses over here." I shouted at two sailors gaping at the spectacular fire consuming the parked F6Fs. "Grab hold of this hose and help me fight the fire." I picked up the nozzle and aimed it aft. "Turn on the water!," I ordered one of my helpers. *Whoa! what a jolt. The high water pressure sure makes this hose hard to handle.* "Grab the hose, you guys! We're goin' aft."

The three of us struggled aft down the starboard side, fighting the writhing hose as I attempted to aim the nozzle at the fiercest part of the fire. We found our way through a gap between two airplanes that had almost stopped burning. "Okay. Hold it right here, men!" I shrieked, as I played the stream of water on the deck under the hottest part of the fire, only about thirty feet away.

"It's awful hot in here, sir," one of my sailors wailed. "I think I'm gettin' burned." I knew why he said "in here." We were surrounded by fire and exploding ammunition.

I turned to glare at the complainer. "Hold your position, God damn it! We'll be a hell of a lot worse off than a few burns if we let this magazine explode."

"Knock it off with the water." Some Chief Petty Officer yelled at me from aft of our position. "You gotta have foam to fight this fire. The water just adds oxygen, uh . . . sir."

Hmm. This hose doesn't have foam, does it. Maybe that's why it wasn't in use. "Screw it, Chief," I screamed back. "I'm goin' to keep this God damned deck cool. The rocket magazines are just below us, you know, and if they blow, the ship's a goner." I continued to spray the deck below the main concentration of the fire.

All of a sudden our hose went limp – the water was off. I dropped the nozzle, turned, and ran forward to find the valve to my fire hose turned off. I started to open it again.

"You'd better leave it off, sir." I recognized the chief from the hull department. "The First Lieutenant ordered all hoses without foam turned off."

"Why, For Christ's sake, Chief?," I challenged. "I'm tryin' to keep the magazine cool."

Paddles!

"We're runnin' low on water pressure, sir," the chief explained. "We've got the fire cooled off pretty well now so we want to concentrate on smothering it." He patted me on the shoulder. "Thanks for the help, sir."

I turned to see my two helpers looking on. "Hey, Chief, get these mens' names. They were helping me back there in that inferno. They deserve some kind of medal."

"Aye, sir." The chief pulled out his pocket note book as I started off to the port side to see what kind of damage Landing Signals took.

"Hey! Mister Harper." It was Corpsman Hopkins of the Majuro spear incident. "Could you help me with this guy. He's burnt bad, sir." He had a stretcher all laid out next to the wounded man.

"Sure. What do you want me to do?"

"We've got to lift this guy onto the stretcher and get him to the burn clinic we've got set up in the wardroom. You take his arms and I'll take his legs." Hopkins directed as he reached down to grab the man's ankles.

The man's face was burned beyond recognition and most of his clothes were burned off. Patches of charred skin had peeled off his arms and chest, revealing raw flesh, oozing plasma. The odor, like a chicken barbecuing on the grill, seared my nostrils. I grabbed him under the arm pits where he wasn't burned, and lifted. Hopkins hoisted his legs.

"OWW!," the man screamed, reacting to the rough canvas stretcher against his skinned body. As we eased forward along the flight deck, he lapsed into a groaning delirium, interrupted occasionally by a scream of pain. Then, as we descended the last ladder to the wardroom, the man convulsed violently, screaming garbled obscenities, and reached up to grab the chain bannister, leaving a grisly residue of skin, flesh, blood, and plasma on the chain. "OWW! Oh . . . ohhh . . ." He shrieked as he fell back on the stretcher, unconscious. When his hand fell from the chain the naked tendons of his palm glistened in the faint light of the passageway.

The wardroom was a startling sight. The severely burned lay on sheets covering our dining tables while plastic bags of plasma hung from the overhead, dripping their contents into the victims' veins. The less severely wounded found themselves on the deck, but not without a sheet. Doctors and medical corpsmen moved among these moaning bodies, administering morphine and assessing each individual's chance to live.

The constant moaning and groaning and the pervasive odor of barbecued flesh was too much for me. I had to have some fresh air.

266

Chapter 25: Kamikaze

"Hold it, Harpo!" It was Doc Benson. "You need some attention to those wounds of yours."

"Wounds?" I didn't know I had any until I looked down at my right arm and leg. Most of my right sleeve was burned off and a trail of blood spread down from a long tear in my trouser leg. "I'll be God damned! I am wounded . . . Well. Fix it quick, Doc. . . I've got lots to do topside."

Back up on the flight deck, I pursued my curiosity as to the condition of the Landing Signals station, stepping gingerly around smoldering airplanes along the port side aft and onto the platform. *Not bad here. With the wind over the port bow the flames would have been swept to starboard. I'll bet there are a bunch of dead ones over there. Hey! There's my machine gun on its mount – and the ammo box is almost empty – God damn! Callagee must've gotten some shots at that Kamikaze. Jeez, I hope he's okay.* Callagee had taken over as my talker-spotter when Monahan left the ship at Eniwetok. *Well . . . I wonder what happened down on the fantail . . . I think I'll go down and find out . . . Still a lot of smoke down there though.* I grabbed a gas mask from our emergency gear locker under the platform, put it on, and started down the long ladder to the oh two deck.

Whoa! Look at the God damned bodies – all over the friggin' deck outside the aircrew ready room. Check pulse on this guy. Hell, I can't feel a thing, my own pulse is thumpin' so hard. Hmm. He's still warm and limp though. Get 'im up on deck in the fresh air and maybe he'll revive . . . Whew! How the hell do I do that? . . . Fireman's carry – Yeah – Stand 'im up against the bulkhead. "Ugh!" CLUNK. *Now let him flop over your shoulders.* "Owww. This son-of-a-bitch is heavy." I moaned. *Now up the ladder . . . awful narrow – don't know if we'll fit . . . Yeah! Just barely.* "Oof!" *Damn! I can hardly breathe with this friggin' mask on. Oh! The light's fadin'. . . . I feel dizzy. I'm passin' out. Damn! . . . don't fall backward.* I put my free hand on the step above me and waited, gasping frantically for air. A moment later: *Jesus! I'm still conscious – Guess I'll just keep goin' . . . Hmm. What happened? Light comin' on again. I guess our bodies blocked the light from behind for a while . . . Whew! In the catwalk now. Flop this guy on the flight deck.* Pop CLOP! *Oh oh! That was his head hittin' the deck. God! If he wasn't dead already he might be now. Where the hell's a doctor when I need one. Shit! I'll just go down and get another one.* Down below, I did my fireman act again and struggled back up the ladder, again experiencing the fading light, and flopped my second victim on the flight deck next to the first.

Paddles!

Ah! There's Chaplain Pegnam. I yanked the gas mask off. "Hey! Padre. Can you tell if these guys are alive? I got 'em down by the after ready room – and there're a couple more down there." I wheezed. "I'm puffin' so hard I can't feel anybody's pulse but my own."

"No wonder you're puffing – carrying these big guys all the way up two decks – and breathing through that gas mask." The Chaplain kneeled down by my first victim and lifted his eyelid. "Hmm. No reaction." He murmured. Then he grasped the man's wrist and looked at his watch. A moment later he looked up at me, his eyes already grieving. "Sorry, Harpo . . . He's dead." He checked the other man's vitals and turned to me, his eyes downcast. "This one's dead too – smoke got 'em I suppose." He put his arm around my shoulders in his best counselling manner. "No use going down there again, Harpo . . . Sorry."

The next day, standing at attention on the flight deck, we honored ninety one of our shipmates, one by one, with a formal burial at sea, the stars and stripes fluttering over each shroud until it slipped silently into the sea to the sound of taps and the traditional prayer – "Ashes to ashes . . ."

Belleau Wood rested at anchor in Ulithi Lagoon with *Franklin* and a few other ships damaged during the action around the Philippines. We were off-loading ammunition, airplane parts, and other supplies that could be useful to the remaining ships of the task force. The inspectors from the repair ship had already declared our damage too extensive for local repair so we were bound for Pearl, or possibly some shipyard in the states.

Ah! Finally! Some mail from the states. Yeah, here's one from my mom . . . concerned about keepin' my money in a safe deposit box where it doesn't earn any interest . . . I don't care, mom. Remember when I lost all the money in my savings account when the banks closed during the depression? I don't trust 'em . . . So dad's got more work than he can handle . . . hired another 4-F draftsman . . . wants me to join him when the war's over . . . Hmm. Do I want to be an architect? . . . Ah Here's one from Mike – regular as clock work . . . Rationing is getting to them – especially since some people get all they want – The Mafia and politicians . . . as usual.

"Mister Harper, sir?" It was the captain's yeoman with what looked like more mail.

"Yeah. What've you got?"

Chapter 25: Kamikaze

"A response to your request for transfer, sir . . . I think." He handed me the envelope and turned to leave.

"Hey. Thanks . . . I think?" I tore open the envelope.

"Yippee!," I screamed. "Look at this, for Christ's sake."

At that, Sam Gallu and Garg Kallman pulled the curtain on my door aside and both eyed me like I was some madman. "Hold it down, Harpo," Gallu ordered, with a silly grin. "What the hell happened? Did one of your harem submit to marriage? Or did one of your rich uncles just die?"

"No no. Nothin' like that," I exulted. "Listen to this you apes. 'From: Commander Air Force, Pacific Fleet.' Then it says 'Forwarded, recommending approval'."

"Approval of WHAT?," Kallman demanded. He was unaware of my request.

"My request for transfer to VF-21 – Hot Damn! Now I get to fly regularly . . . and on strikes, too!"

"What the hell do you want to do that for, Harpo?" Sam looked flabbergasted. "They're gonna be transferred to another carrier to go right back out again." A "cat ate the canary" grin swept over his face. "And we're goin' back to the states . . . Heh heh."

26

FOG

Peggy and I sat in the lounge atop El Cortez Hotel in San Diego sipping our Cuba Libras and watching the brilliant hues of orange change to red as the sun descended into the shimmering Pacific.

Three weeks earlier, battle scarred *Belleau Wood* had limped into San Francisco bay and into Hunters Point Navy Yard for the repair of the extensive Kamikaze damage . . . and of the hole punched in her starboard side by an errant TBF from *Hornet*'s landing pattern one night.

There was a lighted Christmas tree in the corner of the lounge and some wreaths on the walls. We would have our first family Christmas far from home and family . . . alone together.

God damn! Where the hell are my orders to VF-21? All I got when I reported back off leave was a set of TDY orders to come down here and work with Air Group 30, slated to come aboard Belleau Wood when we head west next month . . . Jesus! VF-21 got off the ship in Pearl a month ago . . . Hell, they could be long gone by now on some other carrier and here I sit nursin' a new air group . . .

"What're you thinking about, Johnny?" Peggy broke the silence that had fallen between us.

"Nothin' much, honey . . . er . . . just thinkin' about how many things have happened in the last couple of months." I looked out across the ocean – wistfully, no doubt. "First, I get your nice long letter in September . . . Next, I get to fly with VF-21 and shoot down one Jap and smoke another . . . Then we get hit by a Kami-

Chapter 26: Fog

kaze and lose a hundred men, killed and missing overboard – what a mess . . . Then we cruise back to San Francisco with stops in Ulithi and Pearl . . ." *Yeah! With a chance to fly down to Maui and spend a memorable evening at the beach with Laura – my final fling . . . Forget her as a wife though – she's too wild to tame.* "The high point was marrying you in Detroit . . . and our extended honeymoon on planes and trains, trains and busses . . . and in the Embassy Hotel." I laughed at the start-stop nature of our honeymoon travel and the government imposed five day limit at the Embassy.

Peggy joined in the laughter. But then: "What did you go to New York for?" she asked with a suspicious glance.

"Oh . . . I thought it would be easier to go all the way to New York first and then see you and my mom on the way back . . . er – I wanted to see Mary Louise and Ray, anyway. *Yeah. And check on Mike in Brooklyn as a candidate wife. Hell, she was the only one who wrote to me regularly – once a month . . . But I didn't think I could handle a Catholic wife.* "Boy! That was a LO-O-ONG trip in that DC-3 . . . We must've stopped every two hundred miles . . . Took us twenty-four hours, coast to coast."

"Poor baby," Peggy chided. "And you had to look in on all your old girl friends, I suppose."

"Well . . . er, yeah," I stammered. *Now. Counter attack!* "But darling. How could I know that you would marry me? You only wrote me three letters in two years . . . By the way – How come you wrote me that letter after all those months? . . . And it was so warm!"

Peggy averted her eyes. "I have to admit, it was Barb . . . er, you remember Barbara Godfrey – my roommate at the Theta house. When she and I got together back in Detroit she said I'd better write you a nice long letter . . . before you forget about me, she said . . . so I did."

"Well. I hadn't forgotten you." *That's a relief. We're talking about her now.* "But I was beginning to wonder."

Change the subject, dummy. "You know, honey." I began softly. "We're without transportation and I have to commute to Otay Mesa every day to work with our new air group. We'd better go down and buy a car . . . tomorrow."

That was another great leap for both of us and I could see the concern in Peggy's eyes. "How can we afford it, Johnny?," she wailed. "We don't have any money."

Paddles!

I reached over and placed my hand on hers. "I saved quite a bit while I was at sea – enough for the down payment . . . and we can handle the monthly payments with my salary." *Hmm. Better nail it down with a benefit.* "Anyway, you'll need transportation when I'm at sea."

Peggy gave me another suspicious glance.

The 1940 surf green twelve cylinder Lincoln Zephyr was our wedding present to each other – more than we could afford.

I hugged Peggy with my right arm as I drove our Zephyr one-handed up the narrow serpentine track to NAS Brown Field on Otay Mesa, just north of the Mexican border, the temporary home of Air Group 30. Dinah Shore sang "You'd be so easy to love" on the radio.

"Thanks for inviting me to come down here with you tonight," Peggy purred. "I'd be lonesome without you."

"I love having you come with me, darling," I whispered, kissing her cheek.

"LOOK OUT," Peggy screamed as we approached another sharp turn.

I looked up to see the edge of the narrow road with only deep canyon beyond and grabbed the wheel with both hands to skid the Zephyr back on the road. "Whew! That was close," I groaned.

"You're too romantic in the car," Peggy scolded. "Remember what happened in your dad's car? You could kill us on this road." She moved away from me to sit squarely in the right seat.

As we entered the cinder block Officers' Club building, Peggy holding my right arm, I announced, "There's someone here you know, honey. I'll see if I can find him."

"Whom would I know here?" Peggy was very dubious.

"Dave Philips," I quipped with a sly grin. "You know, that buddy of your friend Lee Cahill over at the Phi Delt house at Michigan State."

"I don't believe it."

"You don't huh?," I smirked. "There he is, at the bar . . . Hey! Dave! Say hello to Mrs. Harper."

"Peggy Green!," Philips exclaimed as he hopped off the bar stool. "For Pete's sake. I didn't even know you two were married. CONGRATULATIONS! We've got to celebrate this . . . Bartender! champagne – three glasses."

Ensign David Philips of VF-30 was a cross between Spankey of "Our Gang" and Alfred Neuman of MAD Magazine – "What? Me worry?" – with his unruly shock of auburn hair, prominent ears, and freckles. Hell! His face was practically one big freckle. His blue eyes twinkled with mischief through his shaggy, orange eyebrows. His lean, boyish, frame stood awkwardly as though he were embarrassed about something.

"Whoa! Dave." I held up both hands. "I've gotta bounce the torpedo squadron tonight so I can't touch it. But you and Peg go ahead . . . We're goin' to have dinner before I go out on the field. Can you join us?"

"Okay, party pooper." Dave's wry glance skewered me. "Bartender! Hold the champagne." He put his arm around Peggy and helped her up on a bar stool giving me an impish grin. "Oh, yeah. I would like to join you for dinner . . . What time's your bounce drill?

"Twenty hundred."

"Okaayy! Plenty of time," Philips laughed. "What'll you have, Peg? I'm buyin'."

"Hmm . . . Cuba Libra, thanks . . . Oh! Do you mind, Johnny?" Peggy cooed.

Naturally I mind, damn it. "Sure. That's okay." I mumbled as I took the bar stool next to Peggy. "I'll just have a Coke."

"Hey! I've got an idea," Philips began. "Er . . . do you play bridge, Peggy?"

"Yeah, sometimes," Peggy chirped. "But not very well, I'm afraid."

"Great!," Philips exulted as the bartender slid our drinks across the bar. "I'll get a couple of guys from the squadron and we'll play a few hands while John is slaving over a hot runway – how about it?" His eyes lit up with the thought. "Then we'll celebrate your matrimonial bliss when John gets back – Okay?"

Hmm. That's better'n some options I could think of. "Good idea," I offered, without enthusiasm. "Hey Dave. Do you play Acey Deucey?"

"Squadron champion," he boasted, raising his glass in a toast"

"Good." I encouraged his ego as we clicked glasses. *Well! Maybe I've got a replacement for Arky . . . Come to think about it I haven't played Acey Deucey since we lost Arky.*

Wujcik was still on leave but Frank Green was the air group LSO so the two of us would handle the night FCLP. When we got out to Runway Two Six after briefing the pilots, the electricians had already set up our ultraviolet light and an extra light by which to record comments. We had no searchlight to check wheels and flaps so we depended on the pilots to call in at the ninety and report gear and flaps down. Frank manned the radio – receiver only.

Paddles!

The six TBM-3s taxied out and took off one by one at about a one minute intervals, the landing interval I had specified – longer than on the ship so as to stay out of the previous airplane's slipstream.

"Four five five's at the ninety," Green reported. "Gear and flaps down." He checked his list. "That's Joe Zalewski, a pretty good head."

"Yeah, I see." I signalled HIGH. "Good speed . . . just a little bit high . . . Okay." ROGER . . . CUT . . . CRUNCH – ROAR. "Yeah! Pretty smooth – small 'hi', Okay." I called out my comments for the log. "Hell! I don't blame these guys for stayin' a little high for this runway with all the obstructions on the downwind."

"I've got four four one at the ninety, gear and flaps down." Green looked at his list. "Says here that's Bill Willert."

"Got 'im," I answered, showing a LOW. "Well, so much for those obstructions – Willert's low – speed good though." I came up to a ROGER – then COME ON. "Damn! Pulled up the nose without addin' any gun." I rowed faster with the COME ON. "Come on with the power, God damn it! – Ahh, that's better." ROGER . . . HIGH DIP – CUT . . . CRUNCH – ROAR. "Low at ninety – no gun at low – gun at ramp." I dictated.

"Four three nine reports gear and flaps down." Green called. "That's Jake Reisert – a smooth cookie."

"Yeah. Perfect set up . . . ROGER all the way." CUT . . . CRUNCH – ROAR.

"Comment: 'VG' for very good," I called to Green.

Twenty minutes later: "These guys are pretty smooth, Frank. Did you train 'em?"

"Taught 'em all they know, Harpo." Frank's silly grin looked a bit grotesque in the stark beam of the writing light. Then he pushed his ear phones in with both hands. "Okay. Willert's at the ninety. Gear and flaps down."

"Well, that's better altitude." I signalled HIGH DIP. "Perfect speed." ROGER . . . CUT . . . CRUNCH – ROAR.

"Now we've got Reisert, gear and flaps, down." Then: "Whoa. Wait a minute. These guys are out of order now." Green yelled with some urgency.

"Shit!" I stamped my foot on the sandy tarmac. "That's all we need – some son-of-a-bitch wanderin' around loose up there. I'm goin to call 'em all down before we have a midair." I picked up Reisert with a ROGER and gave him an animated call-down signal . . . then a CUT."

"Hey, Frank. Give me the earphones. Then when Jake gets back here tell him

274

to call the flight and tell them we're calling them all down – securing FCLP – er – and tell 'em we'll see 'em in the ready room."

"NAVY Brown Field. This is NAVY 68451 in the bounce pattern." The earphones crackled. "There's a big fire due west of the field about three miles . . . Looks like a fog bank rollin' in out there, too."

"Hello Paddles. Four five four at the ninety. Gear and flaps down."

"NAVY 451. Brown tower. Understand fire three miles west. Fire truck on the way.

"Who this comin'?," Green hollered.

"Four five four – and there's a fire reported west of the field. Sounds like somebody went in."

"Jesus! I wonder who." Green perused his list. "Okay! Four five four is Guhse . . . These three are in order. Okay – I'll see you later." He took off on a dead run toward Reisert's *Avenger*, just taxiing up beside us.

Guhse landed, then the earphones crackled again: "Hey Paddles. You've got four four six, gear and flaps down."

Green was breathless when he got back. "Jake says . . . gasp . . . the only one who didn't answer was . . . gasp – Zalewski."

"God!," I swore into the wind. "I'm sure as hell glad we're gettin' these guys down before the fog gets here . . . Sounds like Joe went in out there . . . Not much chance he'll make it."

"Paddles. This is four five one. Gear and flaps down at the ninety."

"Hey, Frank." I took off the earphones. "Four five one comin' next – Here. Take the earphones." ROGER for four five one . . . then CUT. "Well, that's five. If Joe were in order he'd be comin' in right now. What do you hear?"

"I've got Bill Willert at the ninety." His frown looked especially ominous in the writing light "No sign of Zalewski."

Back in the ready room Dodson was describing the fire and the fog to the rest of the flight and everyone was bemoaning the apparent loss of Joe Zalewski when the skipper, Fred Tothill, burst into the room.

"That fire was Joe's airplane, all right," Tothill announced. "But I've got good news, men! Joe's alive and on his way to San Diego Naval Hospital now."

"Jesus! I can't believe anyone could survive a crash like that." Willert expressed everyone's thoughts. "Especially with the fire . . . He must be hurt, BAD."

"Somehow, he was thrown clear of the crash – IN HIS SEAT." Tothill cringed.

275

Paddles!

"I understand he has two broken legs, a broken arm, and a lot of cuts and bruises, not to mention a few burns," Tothill sighed. "The corpsman who's with him says he ought to make it, but he'll be in the hospital for a long time."

"Where the hell have you been, John?" Philips waved a cocktail glass at me. "Here's a Manhattan for you – probably warm by now – you're already two behind."

"Thanks Dave." I took the glass and bent over to kiss Peggy noting that her eyes were just a little glazed. "How're you doin', honey?"

"I feel wonderful!," she chirped as she raised her glass in a toast. "I missed you, darlin' . . . What happened, anyway?"

"Oh, one of the torps flew into a fog bank west of here and splatted all over the landscape." I grimaced at the thought. "Sounds like the pilot'll be okay though – ambulance is takin' him to the big Naval hospital in San Diego."

"Do I know 'im?," Philips asked.

"Probably – Joe Zalewski?"

After knocking down four or five Manhattans in less than an hour our VF-30 drinking buddies decided to make a wedding gift of a dozen of the empty cocktail glasses so Dave and two others trailed us to the Zephyr and passed the glasses in while I cradled them on the back shelf with some napkins – also commandeered from the club.

"Hey Dave," I called in a stage whisper. "We got thirteen."

"Good. Now you've got a flyable spare," Dave snickered wickedly. Then he slapped me on the back and gave Peggy a kiss on the cheek. "That was fun, Peg. I hope we see you again before we shove off." Then he turned serious. "Now take it easy goin' down that so-called road in this fog – visibility zero, you know.

As the Zephyr crept down the winding canyon road I knew I was in no condition to drive – especially on an unmarked road with no guard rail in the dense fog. But my survival senses had come to my rescue. I felt myself sober up and all my reflexes sharpen as they had when we fought the fires after the Kamikaze attack. Peggy was slumped onto my right shoulder, having fallen asleep seconds after we left the Air Station main gate.

27

DARK DAY

Belleau Wood slipped quietly into Ulithi Lagoon in company with an impressive array of warships reporting back for duty with Admiral Mitcher's Task Force 58. Among them, *Saratoga*, three *Essex* class carriers, a heavy cruiser, and a covey of destroyers. Those of us on the flight deck were stunned by the massive naval force that lay before us in the Ulithi anchorage, now the primary forward base for the Pacific Fleet.

"Wow! Look at all the ships," I exclaimed. "Must be eight or ten carriers . . . and look at all the battleships, for Christ's sake."

"I count ELEVEN carriers, Harpo," Wujcik announced, proudly. "And the five of us make sixteen. Must be somethin' big brewin'."

Yeah. Something big alright – and I'm stuck on this tub, wavin' paddles.

Two blows had been dealt to my ambition to get into combat with a fighter squadron. The first was the official correspondence I had received just before departing San Francisco. The BuPers endorsement to my request for transfer to VF-21 read in part:

"2. In view of your experience and training and the current shortage of landing signal officers, request of reference (a) is not approved."

The second blow was our new skipper, Captain William G. "Pinky" Tomlinson. Captain Perry had called me over to his table at the Ford Island O'Club last week

Paddles!

to introduce us and announce that Tomlinson was taking command of *Belleau Wood*. It was immediately clear why Captain Tomlinson was known as "Pinky." His strawberry blond hair topped a broad, pink, forehead, reddened by sun, I presumed. His expressionless brown eyes seemed to regard me as a Naval Academy first classman would regard a plebe – with a mixture of curiosity and contempt.

"I'm sorry," Tomlinson had said without conviction. "I couldn't possibly allow you to fly with the fighter squadron." Then with a disapproving glance at Captain Perry: "That would be endangering the operational readiness of the ship."

"Even when we have two other qualified LSOs aboard, sir?," I asked, giving Captain Perry a pleading glance.

"We may need all three of you where we're going, Harper." His eyes hardened and I knew it was over.

"The captain's right, Harpo." Captain Perry agreed, his eyes signalling sympathy – and just a hint of embarrassment.

Suddenly I realized that Captain Perry had taken a significant career risk to let me fly . . . *And I damn near blew it for him chasin' that Fran almost to Kyushu . . . How could I thank him enough?* "Well, I'd better be going." I stood up and reached to shake Captain Perry's hand. "Thanks for a great cruise, sir." I tried to signal my deep appreciation with my eyes and an extra squeeze of his hand – I thought he got it. "And good luck with your next command." Then I reached to shake Captain Tomlinson's hand. "Glad to have you aboard, sir." He knew I didn't mean it.

Wujcik shocked me out of my reverie. "Hey Harpo! Let's go ashore and get some flight time."

"Good idea, Weej." I reveled in the thought. I hadn't been getting much flight time since the Kamikaze. "Where's Frank? We ought to take him too."

The intrepid trio of LSOs, Green on my right wing and Weej loose on the left as section leader, had spent most of the hour touring the reef cays that bounded the Ulithi Lagoon in three old F6F-3s borrowed from the local CASU. The "threes" were made obsolete almost a year earlier with the introduction of the F6F-5 to the fleet but they were still retained at forward CASU bases as replacements for combat losses and therefore were available to ship's officers for flight time.

Now, circling above the anchorage, I marvelled at the extent of the naval power assembled here. "There's old *Beulah* down there," I called on the tactical channel. "What do you say we give her a little greeting." I looked around to see Frank and Weej smiling and giving the enthusiastic thumbs up, then peeled into gentle glide and aligned our flight path with *Belleau Wood's* port side. I looked around to see both Frank and Weej tucked in tight. *Okay, J.A. Level now . . . just above deck level . . . Yeah! That'll put those guys right at deck level – and puts Frank just a couple of wing spans from the catwalk . . . Hah! look at all the guys wavin'. . . . Okay. We'll give 'em a loop – Hmm. 290 Knots – Yeah, that's enough – pull up gently.* I looked around to check Weej and Frank. *Yep! They're still stuck – tight. Remember how this airplane does a snap stall without warning if you get too slow at the top . . . On my back now – Weej and Frank still there.* I craned my neck up to see the ship directly below us. *Oh oh! Airspeed bleedin' fast . . . Easy now . . . pull just hard enough to get over the top . . . Aarrgh! She flipped . . . in a spin now . . . only three thousand feet to the water . . .* The image of the three of us spinning into the lagoon flashed through my mind. *Nose down, HARD . . . two thousand feet . . . kick right rudder . . . one thousand feet . . . Ahh! ninety knots – spin stopped . . . FOUR HUNDRED FEET! . . . PULL OUT.* The airplane came out of the dive right over the ship, at masthead level. I looked around fearfully, expecting to see a couple of splashes in the lagoon, but there they were – Weej to my right and Frank to my left. I pulled up and closed my eyes. *Thank you God, for saving the three of us from my foolishness.*

The second day out of Ulithi was a beautiful day on the blue-black western Pacific, with a moderate sea state, a twenty knot surface wind, and a clear blue sky – ideal conditions for carrier operations. At the sound of Flight Quarters Wujcik and I met at the port catwalk ladder outside the fighter ready room and bounded onto the flight deck for the stroll back to Landing Signals among blue helmeted plane pushers moving the last aircraft forward of the barriers and the green shirted arresting gear crew raising the barriers and arresting wires to their operational positions. Four hours earlier we had launched twenty fighters and eight TBMs – to support a marine amphibious exercise on Tinian, I understood. *Probably getting ready for the next hop up the island chain toward the Japanese Empire.* It was time to recover them.

"God Damn, Harpo. This is the most ships I've ever seen in a task group," Wujcik mused as he looked out across Rear Admiral Jocko Clark's CTG 58.1, bristling with four carriers, two battleships, and three cruisers, not to mention the ever present screening destroyers. "Where do you think we're going next?"

"Apparently that's a deep, dark, secret . . . but I understand the air group has been briefed on targets around Tokyo." I put my finger to my lips. "Shhhh."

Paddles!

We were just stepping over arresting wires on our way to Landing Signals when a raucous cheer arose from the 40MM gun mounts on the port side. "What the hell's that for?" Wujcik demanded, as we stopped at the sixth wire.

"Damned if I know." I was as puzzled as he was, so I stepped over to the nearest fire director. "Hey, John!," I called to Lieut. John Alexander, the Second Division officer. "What the hell's all the racket?"

The gun crew began pointing at us and chanting: "ANGELS . . . ANGELS . . . . ANGELS . . ."

Alexander came over to the scupper at the edge of the flight deck and cupped his hands around his mouth to shout: "They're cheering you guys for the great air show you put on the other day. Just like the Blue Angels they said – especially the star burst."

"Star Burst?," I exclaimed, with a sheepish glance at Wujcik. "Hell! We just spun out of the top of a loop." *Yeah! My near fatal folly.*

Captain Tomlinson maneuvered the ship to hold his position as the entire force turned slowly into the wind so all four carriers could recover aircraft. Meanwhile, however, with the wind still off the starboard bow, we were being peppered with pea sized cinders and diesel smoke from the stacks arrayed along the starboard side, amidships. The FOX flag flew at the dip, signalling preparation for flight operations . . . Frank Green met us at the platform.

From downwind came the two flights of four *Avengers*, each in right echelon formation with hooks down, flying up the wind streaks on the sea to anticipate the ship's position into the wind.

"Why don't you take these torpeckers, Frank," I offered. "Weej and I'll split the fighters." I pointed to the five divisions of *Hellcats* circling at about fifteen hundred feet.

Moments later, the first division of *Avengers* passed the ship on the starboard side at masthead level as the signalman two-blocked the FOX flag and the bull horn roared: "PREPARE TO RECOVER AIRCRAFT."

"Okay, Weej, you got yours," I called, leaping up out of the catwalk after the twelfth Hellcat had come aboard. "I'll take the rest." Taking the paddles from Wujcik I called to Green: "Who's this?" And started him with a FAST.

"Roy Gillespie's division."

"Gear, flaps, hook, all down, sir," Callagee reported.

"Okay. Pretty steady . . . A little fast . . . okay." ROGER . . .

Chapter 27: Dark Day

"Clear deck, sir."

CUT . . . CRUNCH. "Now who?," I called over my shoulder.

"This is Wescott," Green replied. "Then you get Curry and Rhodes."

Okay, Wescott. Don't crowd the port side. I gave him a SLANT STARBOARD and took a few steps out onto the flight deck to push him toward the centerline. HIGH DIP . . . CUT . . . CRUNCH. *Good. Second wire.*

"Gear, flaps, hook, all down, sir," Callagee called.

"The last one's movin' out o' the gear slowly, sir," Osterhout called.

"Got it!" I yelled, picking up Curry with a HIGH. "Keep talkin'. We'll work this guy and see what happens . . . " *Now FAST. Damn! He pulled the nose up and climbed.* HIGH!

"Still no deck, sir," Osterhout called. "He's crossing the seventh wire now."

Approaching the cut position, now . . . Still high and fast . . . Its goin' to be a wave-off.

"FOUL DECK SIR," Osterhout shrieked. "FOUL DECK!"

CUT . . . "No! WAVE-OFF. WAVE-OFF!," I screamed as I flailed the paddles in a frantic WAVE-OFF. But carrier aviators are taught that CUT and WAVE-OFF signals are mandatory and non-reversible, for some very good reasons. I turned to look up the deck only to see Wescott just crossing the ninth wire as Curry's *Hellcat* soared over my head, still high and fast.

Suddenly, this nightmare was unfolding in slow motion so every instant in the progress of Curry's landing was painfully burned into my senses as each frame emerged individually and serially.

I watched in horror as Curry floated up the deck. "TOO FAR," I yelled at no one in particular.

Curry touched down fast, at about the fourth wire – not catching a wire – then bounced and landed squarely atop Wescott's *Hellcat*.

Fire broke out immediately, fueled by the aviation fuel from the smashed belly tanks, and the two aircraft slumped into a flaming mass of aluminum debris. Fortunately, Asbestos Joe, our fire rescue man, was able to extract Curry from his flaming aircraft but nothing could be done for Wescott.

Watching the inferno I wondered: *How – FOR GOD'S SAKE HOW – After two years at sea and over eight thousand carrier landings under my belt – could I possibly give a CUT while thinking WAVE-OFF?* I had no answer, no excuse.

The blazing aircraft, now hardly recognizable as airplanes, were on the port side of the flight deck, just forward of the ninth, and last, arresting wire. With my head swimming with regret and recrimination, I began the painful walk forward to confront Captain Tomlinson and Commander Clymer. What would I say? What COULD I say? I stopped to watch as the fire crew began spraying the fire with fire extinguishing foam.

I remembered Stu Stephens, back at NAS Miami – Bless his soul – telling us that landing signals is a lonely job because the LSO was not a member of the air group and needed to remain aloof from the pilots while developing and maintaining their confidence in his competence and judgement during carrier approaches. *Remember! An LSO must maintain the myth of infallibility in the interest of efficient flight operations.*

So I was alone on the flight deck with the feeling that no one, not a soul, was there with me, while images of all the previous deck crashes I'd been a party to brought more self denigration as I questioned my culpability in those events. Still I made my way at a deliberate pace toward the island, staying to starboard of the flaming wreck.

"MISTER HARPER, STAND CLEAR OF EXPLODING AMMUNITION!" Came the urgent warning over the bull horn.

I felt some .50 cal. slugs hit me on the left shoulder and arm but felt no pain – bullets have little velocity without a gun barrel to build the chamber pressure – but I kept coming – alone . . . and slowly because I was not eager for my encounter with the skipper and others. As long as I walked on deck I was protected from their scorn . . . and alone.

What, IN GOD'S NAME, will I say? Hell! After this fiasco, the air group will lose any confidence they may have had in me – and confidence is ESSENTIAL! – But we're probably approaching the most important operation of our careers, an attack on Tokyo – And I still want to get into combat with a fighter squadron.

I stopped to look up to the bridge, imagining the disdain that must exist. *Shit! I don't want to talk to anyone – Especially not to anyone from the air group.* I started walking toward the island again – slowly. *I know what I have to do, damn it! Request that I be relieved of LSO duty immediately and transferred to another command as soon as possible . . . There's no other choice!* This was my DARKEST DAY.

In the week that followed, I stayed in my stateroom except for meals, during which I kept away from air group pilots; and flight operations, which I watched from the signal bridge at the aft end of the island. The first NAVY raids on Tokyo

Chapter 27: Dark Day

– Jimmy Doolittle's AAF Raiders of the old *HORNET* were the first – had been conducted in a string of bad weather days with leaden clouds reaching down at times to obscure the ship's masthead. Then came the raids on the Bonin Islands in support of the marine landings on Iwo Jima flown in equally bad weather.

At the conclusion of recovery operations of the day, I saw Comdr. Clymer approaching out of the corner of my eye. "Hey, Harpo!"

I didn't want to talk to him so I kept my eyes glued on the plane guard destroyer returning to his station in the screen. "Yes sir."

"Did you know we just lost Bob Lindner?," he probed, cautiously.

"No sir." I didn't want conversation. "But I noticed that one was missing when they returned . . . uhh – what happened?"

"Shot down over Chichi Jima." Then: Can you come down to my office, Harpo?," Clymer began. "I think we need to talk."

"CAN" I come down to his office? Sounds like an invitation but coming from my boss – it's an order.

"Yes sir. When?," I assented reluctantly. "Er . . . talk about what, sir?"

"Now, if you don't mind." He ignored my other question. "Come on."

I did mind but I didn't think I had a choice.

Lieut. Comdr. Doug Clark and Wujcik stood as Comdr. Clymer entered the air office with me straggling reluctantly behind. Clark had assumed command of Air Group 30 and VF-30 immediately after Lindner was shot down.

"Thanks for coming, gentlemen." Clymer took his seat behind his desk and the rest of us sat down in a tight semicircle. "You asked for this meeting, Weej, so would you introduce the subject?"

Wujcik kept his eyes on Comdr. Clymer. "As you know, sir, we've had a very hectic week," He began. "Three and four strikes a day in sea conditions pushing the margin of safe flight operations. I've been doing all the waving because I don't think Frank is ready for conditions like this." He stole a glance at me. "As I said before, sir, I need some help."

Clymer fixed his gaze upon me. "You know you're the only one who can help in conditions like this, Harpo." He was very serious. "Will you?"

"How can I help, sir?," I protested. "The pilots can't possibly have any confidence in me any more, and . . ." *Why the hell don't you just give Frank the paddles. There's got to be a first time.* I thought.

"Hey, Harp," Clark interrupted. "No problem. You've got the experience to handle these conditions and the pilots know it – we need you back."

Paddles!

"But what about Wescott?," I asked defensively, averting my eyes.

"Just an operational accident." Clark shrugged. "Weej needs help and you're the one who can help him . . . Come on!"

Just an accident . . . Jesus! I wish I could think that way . . . Well, what can I say to such accolades . . . or are they saying 'stop pouting, get off your ass, and help' . . . but can I handle it? Hmmm. I guess I should try. "Okay" I said, almost in a whisper.

Clymer broke the oppressive silence. "You will report to Landing Signals for the first recovery tomorrow." It was not a question.

"Aye, sir."

Back to the Tokyo area the next day we had catapulted every flyable airplane into an icy wind storming off the mountainous waves streaked with white foam. Salt spray had drenched the catapult crew as the ship dove into each successive wave. With that hairy operation completed, Wujcik and I retreated to the wardroom to warm up with a cup of coffee.

"God damn!," Wujcik swore as he threw his flight jacket onto a spare chair. "This weather's worse than when we were up here last week – Reminds me of the sea state on our first strikes on the Bonins last year." We exchanged glances, both remembering the fiery *Hellcat* crash in the flag bag.

"Yeah," I agreed. "Only it's a hell of a lot colder this time. I damn near froze my ass just watchin' those launches. I wish to hell I had some long johns."

"You seem to be feeling better today," Wujcik ventured.

"Yeah." I watched the little bubbles float around on the surface of my coffee. "You guys gave me back some confidence."

"That's good." Wujcik seemed relieved. "Then you can work on gettin' these guys aboard when they get back." His face was grim.

"Tell you what, Weej," I challenged, as I peeked over the rim of my coffee mug. "Let's let Frank handle 'em."

"FRANK?" The shock spilled Wujcik's coffee all over the front of his shirt. "He's never waved 'em aboard in weather like this," he protested.

"Neither had you before you got into this Tokyo fiasco," I pressed.

"Yeah, but I'd watched you a lot."

"Yeah – and Frank has watched you a lot." I let it all out. "Look, Weej. Clymer put in a request for my transfer. Shit! I'll probably be gone the next time we hit

284

port and then you won't have me to pick up the slack in rough situations. You've got to turn Frank loose!"

"Jesus! On a day like this?" He looked scared.

"You've got to do it sometime, Weej," I countered. "Listen! You've briefed the pilots on how to handle a pitching and rolling deck. Right?"

"Yeah." He looked suspicious.

"And Frank was there. Right?"

"Yeah . . . but . . ."

"Yeah, but – nothin'. That means he knows as much as you do about how to do it. Right?

"Well . . . er . . . Yeah. I guess . . . but . . ." He squirmed a little.

Here's what we'll do, Weej." I slammed my empty coffee mug on the table. "Frank'll wave. You stand behind him and talk him through the signals, and I'll call out deck motion – No sweat, Weej – We can do it!" I was beginning to feel like Wescott never happened.

"Well. I guess we can try it." His face was a worried frown.

"Maybe we just give him the torpeckers . . . Give him some confidence . . . What the hell. You've got to start him sometime."

Back at Landing Signals the three of us watched the eight TBMs struggle up the near gale force wind. FOX was already two-blocked, and flapping frantically. I took the paddles from Callagee and handed them to Green, remembering Ben Tate's unarrested landing in similar weather.

"Who me?" Frank was startled. "In this weather?"

"Fly control says all the TBMs are real low on fuel," Callagee interrupted. "Commander Clymer says do your best to get 'em aboard, first pass. They won't last long in this icy water if they have to ditch."

"Oh!," Frank winced. "If we have a crash, the rest will have to ditch – I'd better not try this." His body seemed to shrink as he handed the paddles back to me.

"Oh no you don't, Frank. You've got to try it sometime," I challenged, refusing the paddles. "Weej and I'll be here, talkin' you through it."

Frank took all of Tothill's flight of eight TBMs with only four WAVE-OFFS and I got all the fighters aboard safely – but with the flaming image of the flag bag crash searing my memory the whole time.

285

28

BRITISH HOSPITALITY

After two days on Guam searching for transportation back to civilization with little success, I threw open the front door of the Apra Naval Operating Base Officers' Club, scrubbed my muddy boots on the welcome mat, and shook the rain off my cap before hanging it on a hook in the entry hall. A familiar form sat on a bar stool, nursing a tall frosty drink. "Hey, Cobbs." I clapped Dave Kolb on the back. "What the hell are you doin' here?" Kolb's was the first familiar face I'd seen since I flew into Agaña airport two days earlier.

"Just arrived this afternoon, Harpo," Kolb enthused as we shook hands like long lost buddies in spite of the fact that we had been together on *Belleau Wood* just a week earlier. "Not a bad flight – an R4D with regular airline seats. Hell. We even had a box lunch on the way. How was your flight up here?"

"Don't ask," I grimaced. "First I had the friggin' boat ride from the ship through sea conditions I didn't think could exist in a lagoon. Shit! I was soaked to the bone by the time I got to the airfield." I shuddered at the thought. "And then they told me my flight was leaving immediately – no time to dry off. That old C-46 had the typical Army canvas bench seats along the side and no heat. Those Army shit heads put that clunker up to about twelve thousand feet and I froze my ass all the way . . . Hey, bartender! Scotch and splash over here."

"Sorry about that," Kolb offered. "You look okay, now."

"I'd feel a hell of a lot better if it'd quit rainin'." I shook some more rain water off my sleeves and hands and took a big gulp of my drink.

Chapter 28: British Hospitality

"McVeigh's here too." Kolb flipped his thumb toward the tall dark man coming toward us. McVeigh seemed to glower at us with his beetle brows but I knew his stern manner was just a façade.

"Well, I'll be God damned! The *Beulah Maru* crew is here! I shook McVeigh's hand. "Sit down and have a drink, for Christ's sake. We've got to toast this occasion."

Lieutenant William B. McVeigh – Don't call me "Bill" – was a proud New Englander apparently bred of Pilgrim stock and a product of Ivy League education. His smug manner and droll humor conspired to distance him from his peers – as was his wish. He had been a division officer in *Belleau Wood*'s gunnery department. "How come you're still here, Harpo?" Mac got right to the point.

"Well, I'll tell you, fellas. Transportation is really tight around here." I took another sip. "Any God damned airplane headed east is stuffed full of the walking wounded from the Iwo Jima campaign – God! That must've been bloody – and there are enough of those to last weeks." I shook my head. "And any ship with a doctor on it is reserved exclusively for the more serious Iwo casualties. And if you think you can get back on some Army bomber, forget it." I gave them a thumbs down. "I've been up to Anderson Field twice now, and all their bombers are headed north to Japan – No chance."

"That bad?" McVeigh didn't want to believe it. "So what the hell do we do now? Get drunk and forget it?"

"Hey!," Kolb brightened. "We've got orders, for Christ's sake, that ought to do it."

"Orders, schmorders," I groaned. "Our orders get us to the end of the friggin' line – ZERO priority! . . . But all is not lost, folks," I announced with a wry grin. There's an LCI in the harbor." I paused for effect. "Without a doctor – shovin' off in a couple of days for Pearl – I've got reservations and I can probably get you guys on."

"LCI?," McVeigh croaked. "Do you know what an LCI is for Christ's sake?" He shook his head in disbelief. "It's a 'Landing Craft Infantry', a God damned landing craft for delivering infantry troops to an invasion beach."

"Yeah, I know," I answered with some impatience. "I was out there yesterday. This one's a 'Flag' conversion. You know, kind of a command ship for a squadron of those things – or flotilla – whatever. The quarters are not too bad."

"Those rusty tubs can't make over eight knots." He threw up his hands. "We'd never get to Pearl . . . Besides, they don't even have a wardroom."

"Is that all the thanks I get for workin' my ass off in your behalf." I gave them a sardonic grin and slurped my drink.

"Oh, no. Harpo," Kolb cried apologetically. "We appreciate it."

"Shit, Dave," McVeigh glowered. "He didn't even know we were coming."

"Right, Mac. I didn't." I picked up my drink and swirled it around, making the ice cubes jingle, while a satisfied smile developed on my lips. "I've got a contact that might just work."

"Better'n that friggin' LCI I hope," McVeigh groaned. "Flagship my ass."

"Here's the deal." I put my arm around Kolb's shoulders and lowered my voice. "There's a British carrier in the harbor."

"So what?," Kolb challenged.

"I'll tell you WHAT," I whispered. "The U.S. NAVY won't ask the Brits to take on any Iwo refugees." I affected a British accent: "For diplomatic reasons, of course . . . I think I've got a contact who'll get us aboard."

"Who the hell's that?," McVeigh demanded.

"Shhh!" I put my finger to my lips, glanced furtively around the bar, and whispered: "There're a couple of dozen guys lookin' for a ride and there isn't much room." I'm goin' over to see the CAG off *Ticonderoga* tomorrow." I looked around again and found no curious onlookers. "I'm told that he got his whole friggin' air group on that British carrier. I'll see if he'll take us."

I found the small house trailer on Orote Point Naval Air Station taken over from the Japs about six months earlier, after the island had been secured. Hell! There weren't any buildings left. The paper sign taped to the trailer door announced: "CVG-80 – COMDR. A. O. VORSE, CAG." I knocked.

"Come in," came a gruff voice from inside.

"Good morning, sir," I saluted as I entered. "I'm . . ."

"Sit down, son." The commander invited in a fatherly manner, waving at the single chair. "Go on." Vorse was a big man with a big face and straight, reddish, hair slicked back from his broad forehead. His gray-blue eyes seemed receptive.

"I'm John Harper, the LSO off *Belleau Wood*, sir . . ."

"Glad to know you, Harper." Vorse permitted a thin smile. "Why do you want to see me?"

"Sir . . . er – I was told that you have an arrangement with that British carrier out there to transport your air group to Pearl." I paused for a response.

Chapter 28: British Hospitality

"Who told you that?" He lurched forward in his chair and glared at me while his tone implied that it wasn't true.

Jesus! I don't want to finger that guy in the Apra Harbor Master's office. "Oh. Some guy at the bar over at NOB, sir – didn't catch his name." I stared back into his eyes and challenged: "Is it true, sir?"

Vorse squirmed in his chair and looked out the tiny window while he collected his thoughts. Then he sighed heavily. "Why is that of interest to you?"

Not very hospitable, but I've got to try. "Sir, three of us were just detached from *Belleau Wood* down at Ulithi – I was her LSO for two years. We're looking for transportation back to Pearl. You know how bad the situation is here on Guam." I leaned forward and gave him my best pleading manner. "I wondered if you would take us aboard with your air group, sir."

I could see him begin to fume. It was not a good sign. "Listen, mister." He started with hostile formality. "We're already imposing on those Britishers." He took a deep breath. "And I'm not going to impose any more – NO! You and your mates can't come."

"But sir, you already have over a hundred . . ."

"Forget it, Harper. I'm not taking you."

"But there's no other way, sir," I pleaded.

"I said NO!" Vorse stood up and I knew the conversation was over.

"Yes sir." I stood up and opened the door to leave.

"One more thing, Harper." He froze me in my tracks with his harsh tone. "You will not, I repeat, WILL NOT ask the British to take you. Do you understand that?"

"Yes sir." I turned and slunk out of the trailer.

"Permission to come aboard, sir." I saluted the officer of the day on the hangar deck of H.M.S *Ranee*, a British escort carrier lying at anchor in Apra Harbor. I had left McVeigh and Kolb back at the B.O.Q. so as not to appear too presumptuous.

"Permission grahnted, suh," was the British accented response along with the palm forward salute. "And what might we do for you, suh?"

"I have orders to return to the States and I understand from the Harbor Master that you are going to Pearl Harbor."

"And you wish to go with us, I presume." He smiled and bowed slightly.

"Yes sir. And two of my shipmates if possible."

"I understand." He turned to the quartermaster of the watch. "Find the First Leftenant and bring him heah."

Paddles!

"Aye aye, suh." The sailor was off on the dead run.

Five minutes later: "How do you do, suh. I'm Leftenant Hopwood." He extended his hand and we shook. "How may I help you?" Hopwood displayed the manners of an English country gentleman – very formal, yet congenial. He was a compact little man – about five foot eight and a hundred sixty pounds. A tousle of reddish brown hair escaped from his cap to cover part of his freckled forehead and his bright hazel eyes signalled welcome.

"I'm Lieutenant Harper." I was aware of the formality of the Royal Navy. "I was "Paddles" for two years aboard USS *Belleau Wood*, a CVL, until I was detached last Friday." *Maybe that'll impress him.* "I wondered if you could get me and two of my shipmates aboard for the trip back to Pearl."

"It may be possible." Hopwood frowned as though making some calculations. "We've already a hundred and thirty-some of your flyers going already – Air Group Eighty, I believe. We had to billet most of them on the hangar deck." His eyebrows shot up in a display of discovery. "Oh, yes. Commahnder Vorse must have sent you."

"Oh! No SIR!" *Damn! It's bad enough I'm out here against Vorse's explicit orders. Don't make it worse.* "As a matter of fact he asked me not to impose upon you." *Hmm. "Asked" is a slight understatement.*

"Oh! It's no imposition, suh – not at all." He inclined his head in a sign of hospitality. "Please! Bring your mates out and we'll find a way to accommodate you."

"Thank you very much for your consideration." I bowed a little as we shook hands. "I can be back in an hour and a half. Will that be alright?" I couldn't suppress a broad smile.

"Perfect!" Hopwood laughed at my excitement. "Ahsk for me – Hopwood."

Just an hour and fifteen minutes later the three of us were back on *Ranee*'s quarterdeck lugging our meager baggage. "Mister Hopwood," I reached out to shake his hand. "I'd like you to meet Lieutenants McVeigh and Kolb, my shipmates from *Belleau Wood*.

"Delighted to know you, gentlemen." Hopwood shook their hands. "I'd like you to meet Leftenant Hanford-Smith. He's offered to help."

"Yes. We've tried to find you gentlemen acceptable billeting." Hanford-Smith bowed slightly from the waist. "Now. We must know who of you is the senior."

Chapter 28: British Hospitality

"We'll be happy to sleep anywhere," Kolb blurted out. "Hangar deck . . . even the flight deck. We're just happy to be aboard."

"We're all Lieutenants," McVeigh stated, flatly. "So we have equal seniority." None of us knew why they were asking who was senior and none of us knew the answer.

"We understand, suh," Hopwood interceded. "We have satisfactory space for all three of you. But we must know who is the senior."

Hanford-Smith surveyed us in anticipation.

"Well," I sighed. "I guess we have to compare dates of rank." I looked for answers from McVeigh and Kolb.

"1 October 1943," Kolb reported.

"The same," McVeigh frowned at the perceived imposition.

"Me too," I laughed. "Then we ARE all the same seniority."

"Then what are your ensign dates of rank?," Hanford-Smith persisted.

McVeigh squirmed and challenged their questioning as courteously as he could. "Is all this necessary, gentlemen? As Dave said, we'll be happy to bunk anywhere."

"Please, gentlemen," Hopwood interceded again with courteous firmness. "We must have that information in order that we may properly accommodate you."

"Yes," I started. "My ensign date of rank is 14 October 1941." I eyed Kolb for his response.

Kolb's brow wrinkled in an expression of deep thought. "Well . . . Ah . . . It's in December forty-one sometime . . . eleventh, I think."

All eyes turned to McVeigh. "Ah, yes." He stretched himself to be taller than he already was. "The third of September 1941 . . . Hmm, I guess I'm the senior." He couldn't conceal his satisfaction.

"That settles it then," Hanford-Smith exulted. "You, Leftenant McVeigh, shall have the navigator's cabin."

"The navigator's cabin?," McVeigh exclaimed. "Where's he going to sleep?"

Hanford-Smith laughed at the shock shown on McVeigh's face. "The navigator, suh, must stay in his sea cabin whenever we're underway." Then he gave McVeigh a wink. "When I told him of your plight he offered his cabin to whomever of you is the senior."

"Well, thank you very much." McVeigh shook his head in disbelief. "I'm overwhelmed. Please thank the navigator for me."

"You may thank him yourself, suh," Hopwood offered. "You shall meet him in the wardroom from time to time."

Paddles!

"Thank you. I will."

"Now." Hopwood would billet Kolb and me, I presumed. "Mister Harper, I have an extra bunk in my stateroom." He smiled hospitably. "You may have it."

"That's too much, sir," I protested. "I'll be putting you out."

"No." Hopwood held up his hand to quiet my objection. "I should have a mate, you know. And what better than a fine American naval flyer?"

"You're too kind. Thank you." I nodded my appreciation. "But how about Mister Kolb, here?"

"Don't worry, suh," Hanford-Smith interceded, putting a hand on Kolb's shoulder. "Mister Kolb shall be my mate. I also have an extra bunk." Then before anyone could speak: "Come now." He announced to Kolb. "We'll show Mister McVeigh to his quarters and swing by my stateroom and get you settled."

Kolb and McVeigh reached for their baggage.

"No," Hopwood objected. "Your luggage will be sent up to your quarters, gentlemen." Then to me: "Come now, mate. I'll show you your accommodations."

"Tea suh," came the sound of a cockney accent waking me from a deep sleep.

I felt a shaking of my arm in the upper bunk of Hopwood's stateroom. "Uhh . . . What?" I opened one eye to see the sallow face of the young steward just at the level of the bunk.

"Tea suh." He raised the steaming cup to the edge of the bunk. "And a good morning to you, suh."

I raised up on one elbow, a look of bewilderment spreading over my face. "Uh . . ." Yawn. "Thank you." Then, rubbing the sleep out of my eyes: "What time is it?"

"Just ahftah sev'n bells, suh." The steward left me with my tea.

Hmm. Seven thirty. I peeked over the side of my bunk to see that Hopwood's bunk was empty. *What a gentlemanly way to start the day – waking up to tea served at bunkside . . . Well, the U.S. NAVY just didn't inherit enough of these gentlemanly ways from the Royal Navy.* I never cared particularly for tea, but that cup certainly tasted good.

"Hi. Cobbs." I found Dave Kolb on the forward end of the flight deck surveying the gray windswept sea while keeping his cap firmly in place with his right hand. "Didn't see you at breakfast this morning."

"Hell. Hanford-Smith was up and at 'em at oh six hundred – took me to breakfast with him." He gave me a baleful grin. "What did you think of the fried bread – ugh! Just bread drenched in lard."

"Actually, I think that was bacon grease – but it sure made for soggy toast, didn't it." I made a sour face. "Boy! I hope our P-Boat buddies are covering us. Those two destroyer escorts don't make for very good anti-sub coverage . . . and we don't have any airplanes at all on this tub – much less ASW birds . . . "Hey. Have you seen Mac?"

"Naw. He's probably still crapped out in his luxury accommodations," Kolb groaned.

"Well, let's get him out of there," I laughed. "You know where the navigator's cabin is – lead on!

"What the hell's all the commotion about?" McVeigh groaned as we burst into his sanctuary and turned on the light. He opened his eyes and immediately closed them again and clapped his hands over them. "Turn off the fuckin' light, God damn it. You're gonna blind me."

"Christ's sake, Mac," I protested, snapping off the light but holding the curtain open. "It's damn near eleven hundred."

"What the hell do I care," McVeigh croaked, rubbing his eyes. "I'm not goin' any . . ."

TOOWEEE. "UP SPIRITS . . . UP SPIRITS." Announced the Boatswain's mate over the public address speaker.

"'Up spirits'?," McVeigh gasped. "What the hell does that mean." He looked about the room as though he might see a ghost or two.

"Spirits, Mac," I snickered. "That's British for booze."

"Yeah," Kolb chimed in. "Hanford-Smith tells me that's a call for section leaders to draw a ration of grog for their men."

"Well, I'll be dipped." McVeigh got up on one elbow and scratched his tousled head. "These Brits think of everything don't they?" Suddenly, he threw his legs out of the bunk and sat up straight. Fortunately there was no upper bunk. "Hey! Don't British ships permit booze in their wardrooms?"

"I understand they do, yes . . . encourage it, actually," I agreed. "But if you don't get your ass movin', you'll miss luncheon . . . with ale, gin, or whiskey – your choice."

McVeigh leapt out of his bunk and grabbed his towel. "I'll be ready in half an hour, men." He disappeared down the passageway shouting over his shoulder. "I'll meet you there!"

Paddles!

"What would you like, Harper?," Hopwood invited. "We've whiskey if you like – but only scotch – cahn't get bourbon you know – gin of course – and various English brews – at room temperature, I feah." He apologized, recognizing that Americans like their beer iced. "I recommend Hahlf and Hahlf, an even mixture of pale ale and Guinness stout – What say you?"

We sat at the tiny bar in one corner of the wardroom. "Half and Half sounds good to me . . . Oh oh!"

As the towering form of Comdr. Vorse approached I tried to make myself invisible behind Hopwood. "Hey, Harper." He greeted me with a gratuitous smile and a slap on the back. "I . . ."

"Commander Vorse!," I interrupted and returned his smile. "How nice to see you, sir . . . uh – Here – Meet Lieutenant Hopwood, Royal Navy." I wasn't going to tell him what kind of quarters we got. "Commander Vorse, CAG-80."

"Harrumpf," Vorse scowled at me. Then smiled at Hopwood. "Delighted to meet you Hopwood . . . Uh – Harper," he glowered. "I need to talk to you – over here." He grabbed my arm and dragged me toward another corner of the wardroom. "You'll excuse us, Hopwood?"

"Oh, yes of course, and it's nice to meet you, suh." Hopwood gave a casual salute and smiled. "Wouldn't want to intercede in U.S. NAVY business, now would I."

"What the hell are you doing here, Harper?" Vorse hissed.

"Er . . . goin' to Pearl, sir." I smiled weakly and gave him an innocent look.

"Damn you!," Vorse hissed louder, releasing a spray of saliva. "I TOLD you – EXPLICITLY – not to impose on these folks." The veins stood out on his neck and his hands shook.

I pulled out my handkerchief to wipe my forehead and tried to back away from Vorse, but I was stuck in the corner. "But sir, they said we weren't imposing at all . . . said we're very welcome."

Vorse's face turned red and he jammed his fists into his hips. "God damn it! I ORDERED you not to even go out to this ship in the harbor." He moved closer so I had to look straight up to return his glare and I was squeezed farther into the corner. "You violated the direct order of a superior officer, MISTER Harper . . . You'll hear from me when we get back to the States." He gave me one more nasty glare, turned on his heel, and stomped off to a table occupied by four lieutenant commanders – his squadron commanders, no doubt.

Chapter 28: British Hospitality

"Here's your Hahlf and Hahlf." Hopwood eyed me quizzically as I sat down on the bar stool. "What was that about?"

Oh . . . er – the commander just wanted to welcome me aboard.

Hopwood's glance told me he didn't believe me. "Here's to the U.S. NAVY."

"Gulp." I drank the foaming brown brew. "And here's to Hopwood and Hanford-Smith, Royal Navy, our saviors." Clink.

29

PADDLE WHEELS

The two month odyssey which would carry me from good old *Belleau Wood* to my new duty station – somewhere – was nearly completed. The frigid C-46 ride from Ulithi to Guam – the restful passage to Pearl aboard H.M.S. *Ranee* with plenty of time to think about my lost confidence, only slightly recovered after satisfactory performance during the last Tokyo raids – and thoughts of my chances to fly combat with a fighter squadron waning as the Pacific war seemed to wind down – then the PB2Y-2 Coronado flight into the arms of my dear Peggy in San Francisco – and our unforgettable second honeymoon high up in the Mark Hopkins Hotel on Nob Hill – thence, via Lincoln Zephyr through Michigan and New York to . . . Fayetteville, North Carolina.

"Well, I guess our Zephyr was due for a little trouble after all those miles, honey," I sighed as we sat at the Prince Charles Hotel bar sipping a couple of Manhattans.

"A LITTLE trouble, you say," Peggy exclaimed. "The whole bottom of the car fell off. Is that just a LITTLE trouble?"

"Please don't exaggerate, honey," I grumbled. "The drive shaft just fell out, that's all."

"Just the drive shaft, huh? So how long does it take to fix THAT," she scolded, obviously suspicious.

"The guy at the shop said he'd have it fixed by tomorrow." I took a sip of my Manhattan and glanced at Peggy. "I hope he's right. I'm already a week late reporting to JAX." I shook my head. "They're liable to toss me in the brig for AOL whenever we do get there." I smiled a silly grin. "Will you bring me a cake – with a saw in it?"

"Don't be silly, Johnny." Peggy caressed the nape of my neck with the fingers of her left hand. "They'll understand."

"I hope." I looked up as though praying. "What a place to be on V-E Day – Fayetteville, Nawth Carolina." I gave a derisive laugh. "Radio says they're having a grand old party up in New York."

"Well we'll just have our own party," Peggy toasted, raising her glass and pursing her lips for a kiss. "Right here together."

I kissed her – then: "Peace in Europe!," I sang out, clicking my glass to hers. "And it helps to have Hitler dead in his bunker with no other fanatic immediately available to destroy the world." I turned to watch the rain streak the window and obscure the city, and murmured: "Hmm. I guess that means we can really gang up on the Japs now – so the war in the Pacific can't last much longer." *Yeah – and me with orders to more Landing Signals – probably training new ones – hmm – I guess I'm out of luck – No fighter squadron for me. Well, to hell with it. I've got Peggy. I guess I'll just relax and enjoy it.* "How'd you like to go to Miami, honey?"

"You sure make it sound fabulous." Peggy's eyes lit up. "Can we?"

"I don't know." I scratched my temple. "I'll put in for it – see what happens." I placed my empty cocktail glass on the bar. "Are you ready for dinner?"

"Benny the Birch!," I exulted on entering the LSO ready room at NAS Miami. Birchfiel's was the only face I recognized in the room – way back from VC-24 – Floyd Bennett and *Belleau Wood*. "How'd you get sucked into this LSO racket?," I queried as we shook hands.

"Hell! I put in for it," Benny grinned. "Safer'n flyin' around with all those Jap gunners trackin' you." He grimaced. "Y' know we formed VB-98 when we left the *Belleau Wood* and spent a year beatin' up the Japs from Munda to Kavieng in our Speedy-Ds."

"Safer, maybe." I looked up at the schedule board and thought of Wescott. "But It'll do things to your mind." *And spirit?* I thought.

Benny dismissed the thought. "I'm married now you know."

"Hey! That's great." I reached up to clap him on the back. "Anyone I know?"

"No. She was my girl friend back home in San Jose." He gave me a smug look as though it had been some kind of a coup. "Pat's her name."

"So am I – married, that is." The thought of Peggy brightened my eyes. "Hey! we ought to get together for dinner or something."

"Good idea." Benny smiled his approval. "And we can play golf over at La Gorce Country Club."

"LA GORCE?" I was startled. "Isn't that some plush club over on Miami Beach?"

"Yeah. They've got a special deal for us NAVY types." He couldn't hold back a smug grin. "Five dollar green fees – play any time. D'you want to play?"

"Hell yes! I'd love it. Does your wife play?"

"Oh yeah! All four of us can play. I'll arrange it." He assured me as he went to check the schedule. "Looks like they've got you and me goin' up to Perry Field to bounce a bunch of TBMs this afternoon."

"Perry Field?" I looked around for a chart of the area. "Where the hell is that? I don't remember a Perry Field."

"It's the new one up by Hollywood." Benny stepped over to the area chart. "Up here. It's a cartwheel design – six concrete runways sixty degrees apart with a circular perimeter taxiway."

"My-oh-my! Ain't you fancy?," I laughed. "That's a far cry from the grass fields we used to have here . . . progress, I guess."

After the completion of the second FCLP session at Perry Field, Benny the Birch and I stood on the concrete taxiway briefing the pilots on their performance, backed by the six TBMs parked, wings folded, along the taxiway.

"Okay, if there are no more questions you may return to base," Benny announced and the pilots headed for their airplanes.

"Hey! What the hell are we doin' with these guys, anyway?" I asked as one of the TBM engines coughed to life. "They're ready!"

"They're required to have at least six bounce sessions before we can send 'em to CQTU." Birchfiel shook his head. "We can't cut their FCLP short even if they're ready."

"God Damn!" I shook my fist as the first TBM taxied by. "The friggin' bureaucrats are takin' over the NAVY. Maybe they think the war's over, for Christ's sake . . . I can tell you it's not. They need pilots out there . . . and LSOs too." I kicked at the ground in disgust. "Next thing you know we'll have to wear ties to morning muster. Friggin' canoe school weenies are movin' in, I'm afraid . . . pisses me off."

Chapter 29: Paddle Wheels

I looked at Benny as the second TBM went by and the first started down the runway for takeoff. I raised my voice over the engine noise. "By the way, Benny, how come you're still here? You've got this bounce drill down pat."

"All I've got is these damned torpeckers." Benny watched the second TBM run down the runway. "I've got to go to some CQTU where they've got all types – Glenview, I guess."

"What the hell's at Glenview?," I demanded.

"Hadn't you heard?," Benny ogled. "They've got two paddle wheel carriers on Lake Michigan and CQTU's got a few of every fleet operational type. That's what I need.

"Well. I'll be damned." I scratched my temple. "Learn somethin' every day." Then: "So? Have you requested orders?," I demanded.

"The boss tells me they'll send me when they think I'm ready." Another TBM sputtered by.

"Well. You're READY God damn it!," I raged. "And I'm goin' to tell him . . . HEY! HOLD IT!" I yelled as the third TBM ran up his engine for take-off. "That son-of-a-bitch hasn't spread his wings." I took off on a dead run waving my arms in a frantic wave-off. "HOLD IT! GOD DAMN IT! HOLD IT!" But nobody heard.

"Shit," Benny panted. "He can't see us around those folded wing roots." He was waving too but the pilot just kept advancing his throttle. "He's goin' . . . God damn! There he goes!"

As the big *Avenger* accelerated down the runway the elevators flipped down and up with the pilot's attempts to raise the tail. Reaching a speed well above takeoff airspeed, but with his wings folded, he just blasted off the end of the runway raising a giant cloud of dust which completely obscured the airplane.

We listened. "Jesus! He's not reducing power," Benny yelled. "I hope he doesn't think he's goin' to take off."

"It's a damned good thing there aren't any buildings out there." I waited for the inevitable crash and explosion. "He's got to run into something pretty soon." Then we'll have to get the crash crew out here to scrape him up off the landscape."

"There he goes!," Benny yelled, pointing to the right side of the dust cloud. "Still at full throttle – tryin' to get back to the concrete without bogging down, I guess."

"God!," I exclaimed. "That's goin' to be one bent up Torpecker ...even if he gets it back here without flippin' over."

It was clear that the pilot was concerned about rolling over as he continued his gentle right turn – still at full power – bouncing over the hummocks and pot holes covering the unprepared ground around Perry Field.

"I'll be a son-of-a-bitch!" Benny started to laugh. "He made it."

The pilot cut back the power as he rolled back on the concrete runway and proceeded to taxi back to our position. The airplane stopped and the pilot slouched down in the cockpit in his deep embarrassment. I waved him toward the taxiway and signalled him to park the airplane and cut the engine. We got the chocks under the wheels and waited for the pilot to get down off the wing – He just sat there. Benny and I doubled over with laughter.

I climbed up on the wing of the dusty *Avenger. Easy now, J.A. This kid's got to be really shaken up.* I slapped him on the shoulder. "Hey! How the hell did you do that?" A left handed compliment was the best I could do.

"Sorry, sir." He gave me a sorrowful look and his hands shook as he reached for the cockpit rail to get out. "I don't think I'd better fly back."

"You can ride back with me, son." *SON? How'd that come out of my mouth? Must be gettin' old . . . Yeah! Twenty-four year old father Harpo – Hmmpf!* "We can't fly this airplane anyway 'til it's inspected for structural damage." I helped him out of the cockpit and Benny gave him a hand off the wing.

"Do you think I'll get grounded, sir?" The kid moaned as he climbed into the back seat of my SNJ.

"I don't know." I tossed over my shoulder as I climbed into the front seat. "That'll be up to the board."

With orders to temporary duty at CQTU Glenview, Illinois, Peggy and I had driven up from Miami in the Zephyr which, by now, was operating pretty reliably. I had left Peggy at the Library Hotel in Evanston to come out to the station and check in. As I entered the ready room I heard a raucous greeting.

"Harpo! God damn! What the hell are you doin' here?" Hugh McLinden, ex of VC-24 at Floyd Bennett and on *Belleau Wood,* leapt out of his chair and came toward me with open arms.

"Up here to fill in for Tim Timberlake," I began. "I understand he got hit by an airplane. So what are you doin' here, Mac?"

"Son-of-a-bitch! Am I glad to see you. "I've been here for three months . . . learnin' how to be an LSO."

"Three months?," I exclaimed after Mac stopped shaking me. "What the hell are you waiting . . .?"

Chapter 29: Paddle Wheels

"Shit! Harpo," Mac frowned. "I finally got qualified in TBFs last week but I hardly ever get to wave any fighters."

"What are you doing tomorrow?," I asked.

"This is what I hate about this fuckin' job," Mac frowned. "I've got to board *Wolverine* at Navy Pier tomorrow morning at oh five hundred." He shook his head. "She shoves off at dawn each morning."

"Well," I grinned. "How about that. I'm bringin' the first group out tomorrow. I'll see you there, Mac."

"Hello Gulo," I called to *Wolverine*, somewhere on Lake Michigan. "This is SeaCue three four, one SNJ and five FM-2s, angles five, over point Oboe for CARQUAL. Over." I was the SNJ. *Pretty clever of them, makin' this big white marble temple the navigation point of origin for CARQUAL flights. God! You can see the damned thing for miles – even in poor visibility – right there on the Lake Michigan shoreline, north of Chicago.*

"SeaCue three four. This is Gulo. Vector zero six five – fifty five miles. Acknowledge!"

"Wilco, Gulo. Zero six five, fifty five." I looked around to check the five *Wildcats*, one on my right wing and the others making up a division of four, off to my left.

As the Chicago skyline sank below the horizon behind us the blue green surface of Lake Michigan stretched to the eastern horizon, showing only occasional white caps and wind streaks marking the wind at about fifteen knots from the northwest. I adjusted my heading to zero six zero.

Twenty minutes later: "Hello Gulo. This is SeaCue three four. Have you in sight, bearing zero three five, three miles, over." I could see FOX at the dip and *Wolverine* was lined up pretty well with the wind streaks, making a broad wake with those side mounted paddle wheels.

"Roger SeaCue three four. Gulo course is three zero five – Prep Charlie – Acknowledge!"

That was my invitation to enter *Wolverine*'s landing pattern so I began a gentle let down and turned to position myself abeam the island at masthead level. The fighters followed. "SeaCue three four here. Wilco Prep Charlie."

"Fox flight leader. This is Gulo. Orbit angels one until advised – Acknowledge."

"Gulo. This is Fox one nine. Wilco orbit angels one."

301

Paddles!

I looked around to see my wingman break off and join the division of four *Wildcats* as they climbed back up to a thousand feet. *Look at that silly ass flattop – flight deck looks like it's right on the water – Hmmm. They tell me it's only about twenty-five feet above the water – Compare that to Belleau Wood and you get one third the altitude cushion . . . Hmm. Shades of Splash Fleischer.* As I approached *Wolverine*'s starboard side from astern I could see McLinden waving at me from the LSO platform. I waved back. *Hmm. Flight deck looks wider than a CVE – I'll be damned! It's almost as wide as Yorktown. Hell. This'll be the widest deck I've ever landed on . . . Break now. She's supposed to be about five hundred feet long – almost as long as Belleau Wood.*

At the ninety now . . . I think I'll test Mac a little – start off a little high and slow – emulating Feets Tate. Ahh – he gives me a COME-ON first – perfect – add a little throttle – nose down a little – check airspeed – right on – now I get a HIGH – now pull off too much power – Wow! He was right there with the COME-ON – like he could hear the power – GOOD – now add power and lower the nose – just a little too much – gettin' close now – yeah! LOW-DIP – I just get the nose up and – CUT . . . SCRUNCH – RUMBLE – RUMBLE – SCREECH.

"Okay, sir. I'll take 'er from here." It was one of the plane directors standing on my wing. " You're wanted at Landing Signals ASAP!"

"MISTER HARPER!" The bull horn screamed as I hopped off the wing of my SNJ. "REPORT TO THE BRIDGE IMMEDIATELY."

Striding forward to the island structure I noticed that the ship was turning to starboard, out of the wind, but with no heel to port as would be the case on *Belleau Wood* . . . *Wolverine* had a broad beam and low center of gravity. I clambered up the inboard island ladder and onto the bridge level.

"The Captain wants to see you," the air officer announced as he returned my salute.

"Over here, Harper." I heard the gruff voice from the starboard side of the bridge.

I stepped over to the big man just sliding out of the captain's chair and extending his hand. *I'll be damned. It's Bagdanovich. Hell, the last time I saw him he was still a lieutenant.* Lieut. H. P. Bagdanovich had been the chief flight instructor at NAS Miami when I got there in November 1941 as an Aviation Cadet. "Bags", as he was known, was a big bear of a man with an infectious smile, a full face, big slavic nose, and inquisitive blue eyes to go with his full head of blond hair. He hadn't changed in four years. Except now he was a captain.

Chapter 29: Paddle Wheels

"Captain Bagdanovich? God! It's been three and a half years, sir."

"Call me Captain Bags. Everyone else does." He grinned, shaking my hand vigorously. *It's a damned good thing I used my big man handshake.* "I remember you from Jumpin' Joe's organization at Miami. I thought it was probably you when I saw your name on the plan of the day." Then came an evil glint in his eye. "I didn't think you were going to come up to pay your respects."

"But sir, I . . ."

"I know." Bags smiled benevolently. "You thought we should get on with qualifying these fighter pilots, didn't you?

"Yes, sir." I noticed that the ship had completed 270 degrees of turn to starboard.

"Helmsman. Come to three zero five," Bags commanded. Then: "First things first, Harper." He laughed. "Now, get your ass down there and qualify some pilots . . . We can talk later."

Back at Landing Signals: "What the hell happened to you Harpo?" Mac greeted me with a slap on the back.

"Captain Bags wanted to talk to me."

"I knew that," he smirked. "I'm talkin' about that lousy approach of yours." His black eyes surveyed me skeptically. "Lost your touch?"

"What do you mean, lost my touch?" I eyed him with mock scorn.

"What do you mean, what do you mean?" Mac pointed aft where planes approach. "You were all over the God damned sky out there."

"Yeah," I grinned. "And you gave ALL the right signals . . . just testing, Mac."

"Testing, my ass!" Mac grabbed the paddles from the talker. "Here. D'you think you can handle these FM-2s?"

"Hell yes, Mac. But I haven't seen an F4F in the groove since our shakedown in forty-three – and FM-2s are probably a little different anyway." I looked him in the eye and handed the paddles back. "You take 'em."

"D'you mean it?" Mac's eyes lit up like a couple of searchlights. "I told you I've never waved any fighters before."

"There's a first time for everything, I hear . . . Remember the SNB out of Norfolk" I gave him a wry grin . . . "You wave – I'll coach . . . heh heh."

Back in Miami we were just getting resettled in our little Miami Shores bungalow after our month long excursion to Glenview. The doorbell rang – I opened the door – only to see Ray Eden peering at me thorough the screen.

Paddles!

"Hi-ya pal," Ray chanted in his usual flamboyant style. "How are things in the windy city, pal?" He shook my hand as he doffed his pith helmet and stepped into our modest living room.

"Okay, Ray," I offered cautiously. "What's up?"

"Er . . . Got a call from the Wilsons – your landlords up in Indiana." He sang the last phrase and rolled his eyes. "Said the neighbors called to tell 'em that 'their' yard was growing out of control . . . Remember? You promised to keep the yard in good condition."

"Who is it, Johnny!," Peggy called from the bedroom.

"Never mind, honey," I called. "It's just Ray Eden . . . I'll handle it." *Damned civilians!* "God damn it, Ray," I raged. "NAVY says go to Glenview, I go to Glenview." I collapsed in a living room chair. "Have a seat."

"I know," Ray sang as he flopped on the couch. "But you've got to do something about it . . . uh . . . it's in the contract, you know."

"What the hell do you think I am, Ray? A God damned gardener?," I steamed. "I've got work to do you know . . . and my work is a hell of a lot more important than mowin' this damned lawn."

"Whoa, Pal." Ray held up his hands as though in surrender. "We can work this out, easy . . . I know. I'll send over a gardener."

"What the hell do you think I'm made out of – money?," I roared. "Hell! We can't afford a gardener." I thought for a minute. *Must be the price you pay for being married . . . Hmm . . . contract . . . I guess I gotta do something.* "Okay, damn it. Tell the Wilsons the yard will be okay."

"Yeah, but what're you goin' to do?" Ray wanted an answer.

"I'm goin' to mow the God damned lawn, Ray . . . What the hell did you think I was goin' to do?

"When?" Ray eyed me suspiciously.

Persistent son-of-a-bitch, isn't he? I squirmed a little. "Okay . . . today! If I can find the friggin' lawn mower."

"Don't forget to prune the bushes, too." Ray persisted as he made for the door.

God damned civilians . . . I hope to hell I never have to be one. I slammed the door as Ray retreated to his car.

"Well. It's about time we finally got the Birchfiels over for dinner," I called to Peggy from the living room. "Can you believe it was almost three months ago we invited 'em."

Chapter 29: Paddle Wheels

"Well. That Chicago trip really cut into things," Peggy called back. "Hey! would you come out here and make the tartar sauce?"

"Is that what you put on deep fried shrimp?," I asked as I slunk into the kitchen. "Hey! Did I tell you that Mac finally got certified and has orders to a training squadron at Barbers Point? Great news . . . er – How am I supposed to make this tartar sauce, anyway, honey?"

"It's easy. Here's the recipe." Peggy shoved a recipe book across the kitchen table. "Oh! Wasn't that a nice commendation you got from Captain Bagdanovich."

"Yeah. Real nice." *"Nice" is the wrong word. Hell! It's the biggest morale boost I've had in months – some senior officer thinks I'm good at Landing Signals – and he wrote it down – God! What a relief.* "Hey! This says mayonnaise, pickles, and onions. That's pretty simple." . . . I started rummaging in the refrigerator. "Only we don't have any onions."

"No onions?," Peggy screamed. "Well! You'll just have to go to the store and get some."

"No time, honey." I kept rummaging. "They'll be here in a half hour . . . Hey! There's some garlic here. Why don't we just use that.

"Sounds okay to me, Johnny."

Hmmm . . . Warrior to sous chef in six short months.

Minutes later, I threw the front door open at the sound of the door bell. "Hey Benny." I grabbed Benny the Birch's hand to haul him into the house. "And Pat!" I drew Mrs. Birchfiel to me for a polite embrace. "God! We didn't know we'd be celebrating a momentous occasion – V-J Day. Come on in and have a seat."

"Hi, Birches," Peggy sang out as she danced in from the kitchen. "Johnny went and got some champagne for the celebration. I'll bring the glasses."

"I'd LOVE some of that bubbly," Pat beamed.

"Champagne's bad for my innards," Benny frowned. "Got any scotch?"

"Scotch and soda." I scratched my head. "I should've remembered . . . Yeah – I can do that." POP. I opened the champagne, aiming the cork at the ceiling over the fireplace.

Peggy poured the champagne and I mixed the scotch and soda. Then, back in the living room I chanted: "HERE'S TO PEACE!" We all clinked glasses and cheered.

PEACE! What the hell's that . . . My whole adult life has been spent in war . . . What do I do now? Stay in? . . . Then I could keep flyin' . . . Hell, the NAVY is

Paddles!

*being taken over by the canoe school crowd – ties at morning muster – humbug –
and no chance at air combat . . . Test pilot, maybe? That's exciting . . . Or get out?
. . . My dad wants me to be an architect and join him – I guess Peg would like that
. . . I'll have to get a degree no matter what I do . . . Hmm – Peace – What to do?*

Appendix

AIR WAR AT SEA ABOARD USS *BELLEAU WOOD* (CVL-24)

A contemporaneous log kept by LT John A. Harper, Landing Signal Officer.

DATE	SHIP MOVEMENT	MISSION EVENTS
23 MAY 1943	Enter Chesapeake Bay	CVLG-24 training exercises
01 JUN 1943	Enter Norfolk NavYard	Ship modifications
09 JUN 1943	Dep Norfolk NavYard	Shakedown cruise, Gulf of Paria, Trinidad
04 JUL 1943	Enter Philly NavYard	Final ship Mods. Loaded CVLG-24 aboard
23 JUL 1943	Dep Philly Navy Yard	Transited Panama Canal westward
08 AUG 1943	Arr Pearl Harbor	CVLG-24 to NAS Kaneohe for training
25 AUG 1943	Dep Pearl Harbor	Supported Baker Island occupation
19 SEP 1943	At sea	Struck Tarawa Atoll
22 SEP 1943	Arr Pearl Harbor	R&R at Chris Holms' residence.
29 SEP 1943	Dep Pearl Harbor	Cruising west
05 OCT 1943	At sea	Struck Wake Island
10 OCT 1943	Arr Pearl Harbor	CVLG-24 to NAS Kahului, Maui
20 OCT 1943	Dep Pearl Harbor	Two day training cruise. Return Pearl
31 OCT 1943	Dep Pearl Harbor	Two day training cruise. Return Pearl
11 NOV 1943	Dep Pearl Harbor	Cruising west
19 NOV 1943	At sea	Struck Makin Atoll, Army Occupied

Paddles!

DATE	SHIP MOVEMENT	MISSION EVENTS
05 DEC 1943	At sea	Struck Kwajalien Atoll
08 DEC 1943	Arr Pearl Harbor	CVLG-24 to NAS Kahului, Maui
20 DEC 1943	Dep Pearl Harbor	Another training cruise. Return Pearl
05 JAN 1944	Dep Pearl Harbor	Another training cruise. Return Pearl
16 JAN 1944	Dep Pearl Harbor	Cruising west
29 JAN 1944	2 days off Marshalls	Struck Taroa, Maloelap, Kwajalien.
04 FEB 1944	Arr Majuro Anchorage	Fuel, Ammo, provisions, R&R
12 FEB 1944	Dep Majuro Anchorage	Cruising west
16 FEB 1944	At sea	Struck Truk Base. Lost LT Swensson, CO VT-24
22 FEB 1944	At sea	Struck Saipan. Attacked by Jap *Bettys*
28 FEB 1944	Arr Majuro Anchorage	Fuel, Ammo, provisions, R&R
07 MAR 1944	Dep Majuro Anchorage	Cruising south-west
11 MAR 1944	Arr Espiritu Santo	Replacement pilots bounced at Bomber II
15 MAR 1944	Dep Espiritu Santo	Cruising north
20 MAR 1944	At sea	Struck Emirau Island. Army occupied
30 MAR 1944	3 days at sea	Struck Palau, Yap, Ngulu, Ulithi, Woleai
06 APR 1944	Arr Majuro Anchorage	Note 1
13 APR 1944	Dep Majuro Anchorage	Cruising west
21 APR 1944	At sea off New Guinea	Struck Hollandia, New Guinea. Army landed
29 APR 1944	2 days off Truk Atoll	Struck Truk Naval Base
01 MAY 1944	At sea	Struck Ponape Island
03 MAY 1944	Arr Kwajalien Anchor	Fuel, Ammo, provisions, R&R
13 MAY 1944	Dep Kwajalien Anchor	
14 MAY 1944	Arr Majuro Anchorage	
19 MAY 1944	Dep Majuro Anchorage	Practice cruise with *Iowa* & *New Jersey*
06 JUN 1944	Dep Majuro Anchorage	Cruising west
11 JUN 1944	At sea	Struck Guam. VF-24 got 4 Jap fighters
16 JUN 1944	At sea	Struck Chichi Jima and Haha Jima. Bad WX
19 JUN 1944	At sea off Guam	Turkey shoot. Bag: TF 58, 329; VF-24, 10

Appendix: Air War at Sea Aboard USS Belleau Wood (CVL-24)

DATE	SHIP MOVEMENT	MISSION EVENTS
20 JUN 1944	At sea	Struck Jap fleet. VT-24 sank Jap CV *Hiyu*
22 JUN 1944	At sea	Got word we were being relieved
27 JUN 1944	Arr Eniwitok Anchor	Departed same day enroute Pearl Harbor
02 JUL 1944	Arr Pearl Harbor	CVLG-21 at NAS Kahului, relieves CVLG-24
16 JUL 1944	Dep Pearl Harbor	3 day train cruise, CVLG-21. Ret. Pearl
22 JUL 1944	Dep Pearl Harbor	Cruising west
29 JUL 1944	Arr Eniwitok Anchor.	Staging west
31 JUL 1944	Dep Eniwitok Anchor.	Cruising west
03 AUG 1944	8 days off Guam	Harassed Jap troops on Guam
13 AUG 1944	Arr Eniwitok Anchor.	Fuel, Ammo, provisions, R&R
29 AUG 1944	Dep Eniwitok Anchor.	Cruising west
06 SEP 1944	At sea	Struck Palau. Nothing there.
09 SEP 1944	7 days, Philippines	Struck Mindanao, Cebu, Negros
16 SEP 1944	2 days at sea	Supported Morotai landing; Struck Celebes
21 SEP 1944	Arr Seeadler Harbor	Fuel, Ammo, provisions, R&R
24 SEP 1944	Dep Seeadler Harbor	Cruising west
10 OCT 1944	At sea	Struck Okinawa. LT Harper downs a Fran?
11 OCT 1944	At sea	Struck Northern Luzon; VF sweep
12 OCT 1944	At sea	Struck Formosa. LT Harper downs a *Myrt*
15 OCT 1944	4 days off Luzon	Struck Manila. Japs attacked. 100 downed
20 OCT 1944	3 days off Leyte	Supported Army landing on Leyte
24 OCT 1944	2 days E of Luzon	Attacked & decimated main Jap naval force
30 OCT 1944	At sea off Leyte	CVL-24 hit by Kamikaze. Out of commission
01 NOV 1944	Arr Ulithi Anchorage	Damage assessment, fuel, R&R, provisions
11 NOV 1944	Dep Ulithi Anchorage	Cruising east
21 NOV 1944	Arr Pearl Harbor	More damage assessment
23 NOV 1944	Dep Pearl Harbor	Note 2

Paddles!

DATE	SHIP MOVEMENT	MISSION EVENTS
29 NOV 1944	Arr San Francisco	Repair and O'haul at Hunters Point NavYard
20 JAN 1945	Dep San Francisco	CVLG-30 loaded aboard at NAS Alameda
26 JAN 1945	Arr Pearl Harbor	Note 3
29 JAN 1945	Dep Pearl Harbor	Cruising west
07 FEB 1945	Arr Ulithi Anchorage	
10 FEB 1945	Dep Ulithi Anchorage	Cruising north-west
16 FEB 1945	2 days off Tokyo	Struck Tokyo and environs
20 FEB 1945	3 days off Iwo Jima	Supported landings on Iwo Jima
24 FEB 1945	4 days off Tokyo	Some strikes on Tokyo but WX very bad
01 MAR 1945	At sea off Okinawa	Struck Okinawa. Lost 5 pilots
04 MAR 1945	Arr Ulithi Anchorage	LT Harper flies island CAP
07 MAR 1945	At Ulithi Anchorage	Orders detached LT Harper from CVL-24

Notes:
1. CAPT John A. Perry relieves CAPT Alfred M. Pride, 12 APR 1944.
2. CVLG-21 was detached sometime, somewhere, during this period. I have no record of exactly when and I can't remember whether they were with us to San Francisco.
3. CAPT Wm. G. Tomlinson relieves CAPT John A. Perry, 26 JAN 1945.

BIBLIOGRAPHY

Alexander, Lt. John W. et al., *Flight Quarters: The War Story of the U.S.S. Belleau Wood*, Los Angeles: Cole Holmquist Press 1946.

Anon., *U.S. Navy Carrier Fighters of World War II*, Carollton, Texas: Squadron/ Signal Publications, Inc, 1987.

Brown, Captain Eric, *Wings of the Navy*, Second Edition. Annapolis: Naval Institute Press 1987.

Jensen, Lt. Oliver, USNR., *Carrier War*, New York: Simon and Schuster 1945.

Miller, Ann Woodward, *History of World War II*, Iowa Falls, Iowa: Riverside Book and Bible House 1945.

Reynolds, Clark G., *The Fast Carriers: The Forging of an Air Navy*, Annapolis: Naval Institute Press 1992.

Also from the Publisher

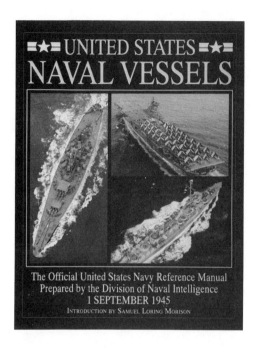

UNITED STATES NAVAL VESSELS
The Official United States Navy Reference Manual
Prepared by the Division of Naval Intelligence
1 SEPTEMBER 1945
Introduction by Samuel Loring Morison

This book comprises four manuals compiled from official sources during World War II. Manuals such as those in this book, were distributed widely through the fleet and used constantly as a standard reference. The Office of Naval Intelligence published a library of manuals that covered our own Navy as well as British, French, Soviet, Japanese and German Navies, among others. The first part of this book comprises the manual entitled **ONI 222 - US: UNITED STATES NAVAL VESSELS**. In the official introduction to this manual, Commodore Thomas B. Inglis, USN, Acting Director of Naval Intelligence states, "It is a graphic and statistical picture of the U.S. Navy at its peak in numerical strength. The information in this manual is corrected to and as of 1 September 1945." The second part of this book is a study compiled by the Statistical Section of the Office of Naval Intelligence. Entitled **THE UNITED STATES FLEET (From Pearl Harbor to Oct. 1, 1945)**, the purpose of this study is two fold. As it states in the introduction, "the purpose of the present table is A: To provide a compact and readily intelligible overall view of the United States Fleet. (1) Before the onset of War, (2) At the end of the war, (3) At the present time, and (4) As presently being built for the future, and B: To present a summary of the changes which have taken place in the United States Fleet, documented by the names or hull numbers of the vessels whose status have changed." The latter includes those ships sunk during the war and converted/reclassified to other uses. The final part of this book is a reprint of a 1 December 1944 document entitled **INDEX OF UNITED STATES FLEET**. This document was prepared by Commander, Air Force, Pacific Fleet. Excepting unnamed ships and craft, all vessels are included. They are listed individually by their classification, followed by their name, in tabular form under their class name. While this document does not include unnamed ships, such as those found in the Patrol Vessel and Amphibious categories, the manual does include a separate section for **LANDING SHIPS, CRAFT AND VEHICLES**, with characteristics and illustrations, at the end of the document.

Size: 8 1/2" x 11" over 1500 b/w photographs, drawings, profiles, charts, indexes
672 pages, hard cover
ISBN: 0-7643-0090-3 $75.00

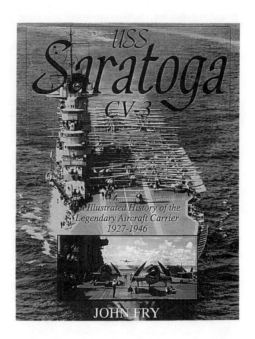

USS SARATOGA (CV-3)
An Illustrated History of the Legendary Aircraft Carrier
1927-1946
John Fry

Originally laid down as one of six giant battle cruisers, the *Saratoga* survived the 1922 Washington Disarmament Treaty's cutting torch through her conversion to a new, and seemingly benign type of vessel – the aircraft carrier. She reported for duty off Long Beach, California in 1927 and for the next twelve years trained the men who would eventually fight World War II. One of only three carriers on duty at the outset of World War II, *Saratoga*, at one point, was the sole American carrier available to Naval Aviation. She suffered two torpedo attacks and a horrifying kamikaze attack, and was reported sunk many times by the Japanese. Refitted as a night-attack carrier, then relegated to the role of training carrier, *Saratoga* survived the war only to be sacrificed in the atomic bomb tests at Bikini Atoll in 1946. No carrier, or ship, played a greater role in developing the men and tactics that became the massive force that is United States Naval Aviation.

Size: 8 1/2" x 11" over 200 b/w photographs
176 pages, hard cover
ISBN: 0-7643-0089-X $39.95

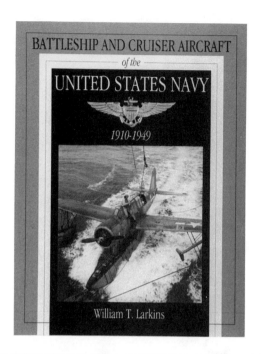

BATTLESHIP AND CRUISER AIRCRAFT
OF THE UNITED STATES NAVY
1910-1949
William T. Larkins

This thorough study of the history, development and service of floatplanes carried on battleships and cruisers documents a long neglected subject for the first time in over 400 photographs. From the 1920s through World War II, aircraft operating from catapults were used for spotting gunfire and scouting ahead of the fleet. Flying these planes was unique and the dramatic launching and recovery operations are covered by both photographs and text. Colors and markings are detailed and special attention has been paid to images showing catapult and ship details for both the ship and aircraft modeler. The assignment of all aircraft by type, totals, squadrons and ships is given annually from 1924 to 1949. In addition to rare photos of all of the experimental aircraft that were tested for this purpose, an additional chapter covers floatplanes used on small ships and submarines. William Larkins is also the author of *The Ford Tri-Motor 1926-1992*, and *U.S. Navy Aircraft 1921-1941.U.S. Marine Corps Aircraft 1914-1959* (both titles are available from Schiffer Publishing Ltd.).

Size: 8 1/2" x 11" over 400 b/w photographs, appendices
272 pages, hard cover
ISBN: 0-7643-0088-1 $49.95

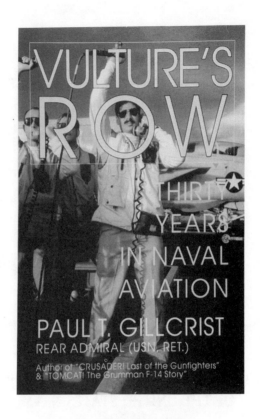

VULTURE'S ROW
Thirty Years in Naval Aviation

Paul T. Gillcrist

Told in anecdotal form, *VULTURE'S ROW* tells a fascinating story about an important period covering nearly one half of the entire history of U.S. naval aviation.
Size: 6" x 9" over 100 color and b/w photographs
256 pages, hard cover
ISBN: 0-7643-0047-4 $29.95

U.S. NAVY AIRCRAFT/U.S. MARINE CORPS AIRCRAFT
Two Classics in One Volume

William T. Larkins

With over 1,000 photos combined, this survey remains the definitive record of the formative years for United States Navy and Marine Corps aviation.
Size: 6" x 9"   608 pages, hard cover
ISBN: 0-88740-742-0 $39.95

The Author

John Harper entered the Naval Service in April 1941 to attend flight training at NAS Pensacola and NAS Miami. Designated Naval Aviator in January 1942, he was immediately ordered back to Miami as a Fighter Gunnery Instructor in Grumman F3Fs and Brewster F2A Buffalos, thence to Landing Signal Officer training and assignment as senior LSO on the light carrier USS *Belleau Wood*.

At war's end, Harper was separated from naval service but soon entered the Organized Naval Air Reserve program to command two fighter squadrons, two carrier air groups, and one attack squadron, winning the coveted Noel Davis trophy twice over a ten year period. In 1962 this freshly frocked captain was ordered to a mobilization billet as Director of Anti-Air Warfare Programs in the Bureau of Naval Weapons. John retired in 1980.

After separation from Naval service, the author began his civilian career by earning an Aeronautical Engineering degree at the University of Michigan. He then served as Aeronautical Research Pilot at the National Advisory Committee for Aeronautics, as an autopilot design engineer and test pilot at Lear, Inc., and as director of missile and space program development at McDonnell Douglas before retiring with wife Peggy in 1985 to manage their California avocado ranch and other real estate holdings. They have four children who have given them ten grandchildren.

Harper has accumulated 3,700 flight hours in 61 different aircraft models and has made 70 carrier landings. He is a Fellow in the Society of Experimental Test Pilots.